JOHN LE NEVE

Fasti Ecclesiae Anglicanae

1300–1541

JOHN LE NEVE

Fasti Ecclesiae Anglicanae
1300–1541

XII
Introduction, Errata and Index

COMPILED BY JOYCE M. HORN

UNIVERSITY OF LONDON
INSTITUTE OF HISTORICAL RESEARCH
THE ATHLONE PRESS
1967

Published by
THE ATHLONE PRESS
UNIVERSITY OF LONDON
at 2 Gower Street, London WC1
Distributed by Constable & Co Ltd
12 Orange Street, London WC2

Canada
Oxford University Press
Toronto

U.S.A.
Oxford University Press Inc
New York

Printed in Great Britain by
WESTERN PRINTING SERVICES LTD
BRISTOL

Preface

WITH the appearance of the twelfth volume containing the introduction, list of errata and the cumulative index the section of the revised edition of John Le Neve's *Fasti Ecclesiae Anglicanae 1300–1541* has now been completed. In the course of the work and particularly in the preparation of the index a number of errors and inconsistencies in the previous volumes have naturally come to light. These have where noticed been included in the list of errata.

Thanks are due from the Institute of Historical Research to many who have made this work possible, particularly the owners of documents and books who have made them accessible to the Editors, also the various scholars who have given much time and trouble to answering questions and reading sections of the work.

F. WORMALD

Contents

Abbreviations

The following abbreviations are given in lower case or in capitals as required

abp. archbishop
A.C. *acta capitularia*, chapter act book
adm. admission, admit, admitted
archdcn. archdeacon
archdcnry archdeaconry
B.A. bachelor of arts
B.C.L. bachelor of civil law
B.Cn.L. bachelor of canon law
B.M. bachelor of medicine
B.Mus. bachelor of music
B.Th. bachelor of theology
bp. bishop
c. *circa*
can. canon
Cant. Canterbury
card. cardinal
cath. cathedral
ch. church
chanc. chancellor
chap. chapel
coll. collation, collated
colleg. collegiate
comp. compiled by
conf. confirmation, confirmed
cons. consecration, consecrated
ct. court
d. death, died
D.C.L. doctor of civil law
dioc. diocese
ed. edition, edited by
el. election, elect, elected
exch. exchange, exchanged
expect. expectation, expectative, provision of a canonry with expectation of a prebend
f. folio
gr. grant, granted

Inc.C.L. inceptor in civil law
instal. installation, installed
judgt. judgment
k. king
Lamb. Lambeth
Lic.C.L. licentiate in civil law
lic.el. licence to elect
Linc. Lincoln
M. *magister*
M.A. master of arts
mand. mandate
mand. adm. mandate to admit
n.d. no date
O.Can.S.A. order of Augustinian canons
O.Carm. order of Carmelites
O.F.M. order of Friars Minor
O.P. order of Preachers
O.S.B. order of St Benedict
occ. occurrence, occurs
P.R.O. Public Record Office
pr. priest
preb. prebendary, prebend
prohibn. prohibition
prov. provision, provided
ratif. ratified
reg. register
res. resignation, resigned
reservn. reservation
s.a. *sub anno*
s.d. same day
Salis. Salisbury
Sch. Th. scholar of theology
temps. temporalities
trans. translation, translated
treas. treasurer
vac. vacancy, vacant, vacated
Worc. Worcester

Introduction

I

JOHN LE NEVE's single volume of *Fasti Ecclesiae Anglicanae* appeared in 1716.[1] Unlike many antiquarians of the leisured eighteenth century, Le Neve was not a wealthy gentleman, nor a clergyman with time on his hands, but his work was the result of stringent financial necessity. His original intention had been to revise and bring up to date Francis Godwin's *De Praesulibus Angliae*, which consisted of lists of the bishops of England and Wales, and was published in 1616.[2] However, the dean of Peterborough, White Kennett, put his valuable collection of manuscripts[3] at Le Neve's disposal, and as he had for years been collecting materials for lists of deans and other principal dignitaries, Le Neve decided to enlarge the scope of his work to include these, together with lists of prebendaries in most of the post-Reformation chapters, the provosts of Eton, deans and prebendaries of Westminster and Windsor, and heads of the colleges of Oxford and Cambridge.

Le Neve was very conscious of his indebtedness to White Kennett, and frequently pays tribute to his 'unparallel'd Generosity', declaring that as to his own part, he aims 'at no higher a character than that of a faithful transcriber'. Browne Willis maintained that 'though Mr John Le Neve has the name and credit of the *Fasti Ecclesiae Anglicanae*, yet the real compiler of that useful work was bishop Kennett'.[4] Thomas Duffus Hardy agreed that on comparing Le Neve's book with White Kennett's collection, it seemed that Le Neve had done little more than publish a different arrangement of those materials. However, Browne Willis's judgment on Le Neve seems a harsh one, since in addition to White Kennett's collection, Le Neve worked through several other collections. He used the library and manuscripts of Sir Robert Cotton (moved from Cotton House to Essex House in the Strand in 1712), and quotes extensively from the manuscripts of Matthew Hutton, who had copied many extracts from the diocesan registers of Lincoln, York, Bath and Wells, and London, with a view to continuing Godwin's *De Praesulibus*. He also used the collections of William Fleetwood, bishop of Ely (on St Asaph), Roger Dodsworth (then in the Bodleian, on York), and John Featley, prebendary of Lincoln. As further evidence of his industry, he cited a formidable list of manuscripts consulted for the diocese of Canterbury, as a sample of the work involved. He received assistance from various people besides White Kennett. One Mr Reynold, registrar of Hereford, provided lists of Hereford deans, Thomas Tanner gave lists of the prebendaries of Ely, John Evans, bishop of Bangor, the Bangor

---

[1] Hereafter cited as Le Neve, *Fasti*.

[2] *De Praesulibus Angliae Commentarius: Omnium Episcoporum, necnon et Cardinalium eiusdem gentis, nomina, tempora, seriem, atque Actiones maxime memorabiles ab ultima antiquitate repetita complexus*, comp. F. Godwin (London, 1616).

[3] Now British Museum, Lansdowne MSS. 935–1041.

[4] J. Le Neve, *Fasti Ecclesiae Anglicanae*, corrected and continued . . . to the present day by T. D. Hardy (3 vols., Oxford, 1854), I xvi (hereafter cited as Le Neve-Hardy, *Fasti*).

deans, and archdeacon Richard Bowchier gave assistance at Chichester.[1] The list of chancellors of Norwich was taken from Sir Thomas Browne's *Posthumous Works* (London, 1712), checked by Thomas Tanner, and the lists of St Paul's dignitaries from Richard Newcourt's *Repertorium Ecclesiasticum Parochiale Londinense* (2 vols., London, 1708).

Le Neve based his work where possible on standard works, such as Godwin, Battely's edition of Somner's *Antiquities*, Isaacson's *Chronology* and Wharton's *De Episcopis et Decanis*.[2] He also consulted the bishops' and archbishops' registers in the various dioceses, and made occasional use of some chapter material. His practice is generally to give full page references to printed works, but hardly ever to give folio references to manuscripts.[3] Moreover, if information were supplied to him by a person of scholastic eminence, that person's authority was thought to outweigh the need for full references.[4] The same applies to information given from memory.[5] In other instances, Le Neve gives tantalisingly vague references, such as 'Cart. Orig.', 'Ex cartis in Baga de Dioc. Cicestr.', 'A Deed in the possession of Peter Le Neve, Esq.', 'In an Old Charter at Chichester', 'in an ancient MS. in the Church of Exeter', or 'MS. in Bibl. Bodl.'.

Le Neve declares in his Preface that he faced 'many Difficulties and Discouragements' in compiling the *Fasti*, even to the extent of suffering a 'maliciously contriv'd Imprisonment, purposely intended to ruin both the author and the design'.[6] He was unable to secure access for work on the prebendaries of Rochester, Worcester, Chester and Durham. There are several indications that he was in a hurry to get the material printed, which affected the order of the lists, and caused some sections to be included in the addenda.[7]

The *Fasti* were not immediately well received, and in consequence Le Neve did not produce the supplement which he had intended. Although 750 copies were printed, there were only forty-five original subscribers. The value of the work was soon apparent

---

[1] Archdeacon Bowchier's notes are now in the Sussex County Record Office (D.R.O. Cap. 1/1/2), and some of Le Neve's information can be traced through these.

[2] William Somner, *The Antiquities of Canterbury; or a Survey of that ancient Citie, with the Suburbs and Cathedral* (London, 1640), 2nd ed. by Nicholas Batteley (London, 1703). Henry Isaacson, *Saturni Ephemerides, sive Tabula Historico-Chronologica, containing a Chronological Series . . . of the foure Monarchyes . . . As also a Succession of the Kings and Rulers over most Kingdomes and Estates of the World . . .*' (London, 1633). Henry Wharton, *Historia de Episcopis et Decanis Londinensibus necnon de Episcopis et Decanis Assavensibus* (London, 1695).

[3] He does give some folio references for the prebendaries of Bristol (Lib. Cap.), deans of Exeter (bishops' registers), Lichfield dignitaries (MS. Ashmole 794), and the bishops of Lincoln (Lambeth registers), but these are the exceptions.

[4] The lists of Ely were provided by Thomas Tanner, 'whose Exactness in Extracts of this Nature is sufficiently known' (Le Neve, *Fasti*, p. 75). Tanner also checked the chancellors of Norwich, 'and being vouched by his Authority, the Truth of it will not be questioned by any Lover of Antiquity' (*ibid.*, p. 214). The lists of prebendaries of Peterborough were provided by White Kennett, 'whose single Authority in any Matters of this Nature, and particularly in what relates to this Cathedral, will (I doubt not) prove of much greater Weight with all Lovers of Antiquity, than all the Books relating thereunto, yet made publick' (*ibid.*, p. 245).

[5] 'I am obliged to the favour of the Lord Bishop' (*ibid.*, p. 43; cf. pp. 30, 37, 41, etc.); 'Ex ore ipsius episcopi' (*ibid.*, p. 23).

[6] Le Neve-Hardy, *Fasti*, I xvii & n.

[7] 'I am very sensible that, according to the Order which I have hitherto observed, the Account of the Church of St David ought to be placed next; but some Materials (which I am promised through the favour of the Right Rev. Father in God, Adam Lord Bishop of this See) not being yet come to Hand, and the Press going forward, I must beg leave to refer the said Account to the latter end of the Book.' (Le Neve, *Fasti*, p. 67). At Llandaff, 'the ancient Books relating to their Entries are to be got at only at the time of their Audit, which is kept every Year at S. Peter's-tide; For which Reason I beg Leave to postpone the said Account' (*ibid.*, p. 120). 'The Succession of the Prebendaries in this Cathedral not being yet come to Hand, I must beg leave to refer them to the Addenda' (*ibid.*, p. 304).

to scholars and antiquarians, and most of the eminent men of the eighteenth century possessed and annotated copies, and several of them made proposals for a second edition.

Probably the most assiduous collector of material for a revision was the antiquarian Browne Willis. He had a copy of Le Neve's *Fasti* interleaved, in order to insert additions and corrections,[1] and when he found he had sufficient for a small volume, offered the material to Le Neve with the request that he should produce a supplement or a new edition. Le Neve, however, had been discouraged by the reception given to his work, and refused to continue it, 'alledging that he could not meet with the least Encouragement'.[2] Browne Willis therefore published his material in a different form, as surveys of the four Welsh cathedrals, and of a considerable number of English ones.[3] Some of the lists were prepared for him by others. That for Durham was given to him by Nathanial Ellison (a prebendary there who died in 1721), and enlarged by John Rymer, head master of the College School (1711–33) and by some of the Durham prebendaries. For York, he used the list of James Torre up to 1693, and continued it to 1722.[4] William Walmisley, dean of Lichfield, extracted information about the dignitaries at that cathedral from the bishops' and chapter registers. In addition to the contributions and suggestions of friends such as bishop Kennett, Dr Tanner and Mr Maker, Browne Willis sought material at the Rolls Chapel, Prerogative and First Fruits Office, Cottonian and Lambeth Libraries, and also made collections from the Bodleian, Ashmolean and private libraries, and examined diocesan and chapter archives for each cathedral in the country, apart from Carlisle.[5] Being a man of considerable private means, Browne Willis had the leisure to pursue his researches without the pressing need that they should yield financial reward, which restricted Le Neve's activity.

As a result, Browne Willis declares that he was able to add to Le Neve's lists for the churches of York, Lichfield and Hereford 'no less than 370 Precentors, Chancellors, Treasurers and Archdeacons . . . besides about 400 Archdeacons and Prebendaries in the Churches of Durham, Chester, Worcester and Gloucester, that he has made no Mention of, not to insist on what I have done in other Cathedrals, or my rectifying numerous Dates of Collations etc.'[6] Unlike Le Neve, Browne Willis attempted lists of prebendaries for such of the cathedrals of the old foundation as he dealt with. He also prepared *Fasti* for several of the cathedrals not covered in his *Surveys*. His notes on these were transcribed by William Cole, and form part of volumes 27–29 of the Cole MSS. in the British Museum.[7]

Other antiquarians left annotated copies of Le Neve with materials for a revision. In the Bodleian Library, in addition to Browne Willis's copy, there is one with additions by John Blackbourne and Samuel Drake,[8] and copies formerly belonging to

[1] Now Bodl. Libr., MS. Willis 50.
[2] Preface to Browne Willis's *Survey* (1742 ed.), I i.
[3] *A Survey of the Cathedral Church of St. Davids* (London, 1717); *A Survey of the Cathedral Church of Llandaff* (London, 1719); *A Survey of the Cathedral Church of St. Asaph* (London, 1720); *A Survey of the Cathedral Church of Bangor* (London, 1721); *A Survey of the Cathedrals of York, Durham, Carlisle, Chester etc.* (London, 1727); *A Survey of the Cathedrals of Lincoln, Ely, Oxford and Peterborough* (London, 1730).
[4] Torre's five folio volumes were presented to the chapter library at York on the death of archbishop Sharp in 1714, and were thus apparently not used by Le Neve.
[5] Preface to Browne Willis's *Survey* (1742 ed.), I iv–viii.
[6] *Ibid.*, p. iii.
[7] British Museum, Add. MSS. 5827–30, 5836, notes on cathedrals of Worcester, Rochester, Salisbury and Gloucester.
[8] Bodl. Libr., MS. Rawl. I 10.

Thomas Tanner,[1] Richard Gough,[2] William Cole,[3] one Brooke, an attorney,[4] John Denne,[5] Richard Rawlinson and Samuel Carte,[6] and Robert Masters.[7] Further copies were at Cambridge[8] and in the British Museum.[9]

It was not until 1854 that a revised edition of Le Neve was eventually produced by Thomas Duffus Hardy. In his introduction, he describes some of the earlier abortive attempts. The Rev. William Richardson of St John's College, Cambridge, issued a Prospectus about 1825 for a new edition in two folio volumes, but lacked sufficient subscribers to defray the expenses. Edward Herbert, 2nd earl of Powis, purchased an interleaved copy of Le Neve filled with annotations and additions by several people, and offered its use to the Roxburghe Club, but the project was not sufficiently popular, and was abandoned. The Rev. John Gutch of Oxford considered producing a revision, and 'was only deterred from the undertaking by its extreme labour, and from the fortunate circumstance of his obtaining the easier and more profitable employment of Registrar to his University'.[10] Later, the Rev. Charles Coates would have brought out a new edition, had the University of Cambridge been willing to publish it. Hardy, likewise, collected materials for many years, but could not find a publisher willing to take the risk of an expensive production unlikely to sell in large numbers. At length the Oxford University Press agreed to undertake the work.

Hardy was at this time working at the Branch Record Office at the Tower of London, and later, in 1861, became Deputy Keeper of the new Public Record Office in Chancery Lane. Le Neve's single volume was now enlarged to three, and his 11,051 entries to 30,000. Hardy continued Le Neve's lists up to his own day, incorporating additional lists of prebendaries for some of the post-Reformation cathedrals, and making occasional corrections and additions from his own researches. He also added a list of the canons of Southwell collegiate church, prepared by the Rev. J. F. Dimock, and appended an Index of Persons, although no attempt was made to identify people of the same or similar names. The principal new sources of information used by him were the patent, charter and close rolls (then at the Tower and Rolls Chapel), the Church Books (in the Home Office), and bishops' certificates (at Carlton Ride and Queen Anne's Bounty Office). He also made use of White Kennett's copy of Le Neve in the library of Sir Thomas Phillipps,[11] and that belonging to Earl Powis. He used such of the diocesan registers as he was able to obtain access to, and consulted local antiquarians, such as the Rev. G. Oliver, whose *Lives of the Bishops of Exeter* was published in 1861.[12] Unlike the first edition, the revision is not based on Godwin and Le Neve's other authorities, but Hardy declared that he had tried to consult the original authorities to whom they referred. He admits that he was not able to see many of these documents, and in these instances he cites the secondary authorities.

If Le Neve is accused of publishing a transcript of White Kennett's material, Hardy may be accused with even more justice of drawing heavily on Browne Willis. The lists

---

[1] Bodl. Libr., Vet. A 4 c 211.
[2] Bodl. Libr., MS. Gough Eccl. Top. 69.
[3] Bodl. Libr., MS. Gough Eccl. Top. 70, 72.
[4] Bodl. Libr., MS. Gough Eccl. Top. 71.
[5] Bodl. Libr., MS. Gough Eccl. Top. 71.
[6] Bodl. Libr., MS. Gough Eccl. Top. 71b.
[7] Bodl. Libr., MS. Gough Eccl. Top. 73.
[8] According to Hardy, Le Neve-Hardy, *Fasti*, I iii n., but so far untraced.
[9] British Museum, 4705 i 7 (formerly belonging to George Fair).
[10] J. Nichols, *Literary Anecdotes of the Eighteenth Century* (9 vols., London, 1812–15), I 127–9. Nichols himself possessed two interleaved copies, one formerly belonging to the Rev. Robert Smyth of Woodstone, Hunts., the other Le Neve's own copy, prepared by himself for a new edition, and including contributions from Browne Willis.
[11] Acquired by the British Museum in 1965, Add. MS. 52926.
[12] Le Neve-Hardy, *Fasti*, I x.

of prebendaries are often copied verbatim from the *Surveys*. Often they are abbreviated, and Browne Willis's valuable references to monumental inscriptions are reduced to an unsupported statement of the date of death. Occasionally some information from the patent rolls is added with references. The bishops' lists are more independent of Browne Willis, though in parts the copying was clearly word for word. Hardy usually abbreviated the biographical material, and added mention of his sources in the chronicles. For the London prebendaries, Hardy reprinted Newcourt's lists, again largely unaltered. The other cathedrals for which Browne Willis did not publish lists (namely, Canterbury, Chichester, Exeter, Norwich, Rochester, Salisbury, Wells and Winchester) are altered only in small details from Le Neve, and otherwise left entirely the same, with the addition of lists of prebendaries, based principally on the bishops' certificates at the Public Record Office. Hardy attempted no pre-Reformation lists of prebendaries, however. For Salisbury, the list of prebendaries begins in 1538, contains not a single reference in thirty-four pages, and gives the prebendaries in chronological order. Hardy clearly did not consult Browne Willis's notes among the Cole MSS. or he could very easily have given reasonably complete lists under their respective prebends. The Wells lists begin about 1537, and although the prebends are listed separately, the only references are to the *Valor Ecclesiasticus* or bishops' certificates. (The list for the prebend of St Decumans goes back to 1295, and a few pre-Reformation prebendaries are also given for Wiveliscombe and Shalford, the latter taken directly from Newcourt's list of patrons presenting to the vicarage of Shalford in Essex.[1]) The Exeter list begins in 1588, and that for Chichester in 1714, again not given according to prebends. One is left with the impression that Hardy's alleged attempt to check Le Neve's secondary authorities by their sources was ineffective. Even his method of giving references is still far from satisfactory. Incomplete references are given for the chronicles, and many other references are of the vaguest.[2] The patent roll references are given more fully and are generally traceable. Occasionally folio references are given for bishops' registers, but this is not the regular practice. There are still very many unsupported statements and dates: whole pages, particularly on Welsh dignitaries, are completely lacking substantiation.

Hardy's revision is thus not an unqualified improvement on Le Neve. Moreover he seems to have accepted somewhat uncritically the information given him by others. Thus his Exeter lists incorporate the mistakes of Oliver, and are less reliable in places than the 1716 edition.[3] In addition, in most cathedrals, he still left untouched chapter act books, account rolls and sundry other records. Small errors and inconsistencies abound, especially before the Reformation. Sometimes references given are wrong, and some names seem purely fictitious.

The need for a revision of Le Neve-Hardy has long been apparent. In several dioceses *Fasti* have been produced which have succeeded in improving considerably upon the 1854 work. Much fuller lists of the prebendaries of St Asaph had already been published in 1801 in *Willis' Survey of St. Asaph, considerably enlarged*, comp. Edward Edwards (2 vols., London, 1801). Only forty copies were printed, and Hardy

[1] Richard Newcourt, *Repertorium Ecclesiasticum Parochiale Londinense* (London, 1708), II 519.
[2] Church Book, Home Office; Letter in Tower of London; London Gazette; Bishops' Certificates.
[3] See, for example, the mistakes in Le Neve-Hardy over precentor John Ryse, chancellors Benedict de Paston, Henry Webber and Owen Lloyd, treasurer Thomas Kirkeby, archdeacons of Cornwall Walter, and Richard Sydnor, archdeacons of Totnes Otto de Northwode and Walter Pennybrooke, and archdeacon of Barnstaple Bartholomew de Sancto Laurentio (Le Neve, *Fasti*, rev. ed., *Exeter*, pp. 8n, 9n, 10n, 11 & n, 15n, 17n, 18n, 19n). In all these instances the 1854 edition has followed Oliver and is less accurate than the 1716 one.

does not seem to have used it. Oliver's *Lives of the Bishops of Exeter* was published in 1861, but as Hardy had consulted Oliver, this adds little to the 1854 *Fasti*. The *Fasti Herefordenses*, compiled by F. T. Havergal (Edinburgh, 1869) likewise adds little to Hardy's work, although it contains fuller biographical detail. Of much greater importance was Edward Yardley's manuscript on St Davids entitled *Menevia Sacra*, which although compiled in 1739–61, had disappeared at the compiler's death in 1770, and was discovered in 1879 in the earl of Cawdor's library at Stackpole Court, Pembrokeshire, and was given by him to the cathedral library at St Davids.[1] Yardley had corresponded with Browne Willis, who urged him to publish his work, saying that the 'series of succession of the Members of each Stall is beyond expectation or imagination compleat, & what no one else would or ever could have so well digested & ranged'.[2] Hardy, therefore, did not see *Menevia Sacra*, and it is a particularly important compilation as four of the bishops' registers cited by Yardley have been lost since his time. In fact, Hardy's lists of dignitaries include some (from patent roll sources) not known to Yardley, but Yardley gives a considerable number of medieval prebendaries, unlike Hardy whose lists begin in 1714. W. H. Jones produced *Fasti Ecclesiae Sarisberiensis* (2 vols., Salisbury and London, 1879–81), a detailed though not entirely accurate work, making use of chapter material, and of Browne Willis's interleaved Le Neve in the Bodleian Library, and his notes in vol. 29 of the Cole MSS. in the British Museum. The latter are copies of the annotations made by Browne Willis in his copy of *The History and Antiquities of the Cathedral-Church of Salisbury and the Abbey-Church of Bath* [comp. Richard Rawlinson] (London, 1719), which contains fairly detailed lists of dignitaries, but exceedingly patchy lists of prebendaries, and is greatly improved by Browne Willis. Jones added references and much biographical material. His lists are more complete, as he used the chapter acts fully, and also consulted the lists of prebendaries with prebends in Dorset drawn up in *The History and Antiquities of the County of Dorset*, comp. J. Hutchins (2nd ed. London, 1796–1814). G. Hennessy in his *Novum repertorium ecclesiasticum parochiale Londinense* (London, 1898) succeeded in improving greatly on Newcourt, and his *Chichester Diocese Clergy Lists* (London, 1900), although no references are given, lists many pre-Reformation prebendaries. Sir Charles Clay has recently produced *York Minster Fasti* (Yorkshire Archaeological Society, Record Series, cxxiii, cxiv, 1958–9) covering the period prior to 1307.

The late Professor A. Hamilton Thompson was particularly concerned about the importance of a revision, and left his annotated copy of Le Neve-Hardy to the Royal Historical Society, with especially full notes of York, Hereford and Lichfield. He indeed planned a new edition for the period up to 1541 with a view to its publication by the Royal Historical Society. At his death, however, the Society felt unable to undertake this, and in 1955 the Institute of Historical Research agreed to assume the responsibility, the period 1300–1541 being chosen as the first portion to be revised.[3]

Since 1854 several new sources of information for this period have become available. The publication of the *Calendar of Papal Letters* and *Calendar of Papal Petitions* has revealed far more claimants to prebends and dignities than were previously known, and has made it possible to fill in the accounts of disputes, or supplement the information

---

[1] *Menevia Sacra*, by Edward Yardley . . . archdeacon of Cardigan 1739–70, ed. F. Green, Cambrian Archaeol. Assoc., supplemental vol. (London, 1927).

[2] Letter of 7 Apr. 1746, *ibid.*, pp. iv–v.

[3] The present volume completes this portion, which consists of 12 volumes: J. Le Neve, *Fasti Ecclesiae Anglicanae*, comp. Joyce M. Horn, B. Jones and H. P. F. King (12 vols., London, 1962–7), hereafter cited as Le Neve, *Fasti*, rev. ed.

when no bishops' registers exist. The Public Record Office *Calendars* of patent, close and fine rolls have likewise produced much more information than Hardy extracted from the public records. The publication of many bishops' registers, especially when these are thoroughly indexed, has made it possible to trace individuals more satisfactorily than in an unpublished register. The massive undertaking of the Rolls Series of mediaeval chronicles, published 1858–96, made access to these sources much simpler, even though in some cases the indexes are not sufficiently detailed. Moreover in many cathedrals records have been classified and catalogued for the first time, as archivists have been appointed.

In the work of preparing the revised edition, all the bishops' registers (printed and manuscript) in each diocese have been thoroughly combed, together with chapter act books and other relevant archive material, in order to draw up fresh lists, which have been checked against earlier ones, but by no means based on them. This has been supplemented by a thorough search of the archbishops' registers at Lambeth Palace Library and the registers of the prior and convent of Christ Church Canterbury. Where dates of death are otherwise unknown, the wills of the Prerogative Court of Canterbury at Somerset House have been consulted. At the Public Record Office, the following classes of records have been consulted fairly thoroughly: Chancery Miscellanea, ecclesiastical (C 47), Ecclesiastical petitions (C 84), Exchequer ecclesiastical documents (E 135), subsidy rolls (E 179) and papal bulls (SC 7), with occasional reference to others such as plea rolls (CP 40) and coram rege rolls (KB 27), though these have been by no means exhaustively searched. The *Valor Ecclesiasticus*, *Calendars* of the patent, close and fine rolls, and of papal letters and petitions, together with the *Letters and Papers of the Reign of Henry VIII*, have also been fully checked, and a large number of printed chronicles consulted. All cardinals have been checked in Eubel's *Hierarchia Catholica Medii Aevi* (Münster, 1913–23).

II

The compilers of the revised edition of the 1300–1541 section of Le Neve have adopted a fairly rigid editorial method in order to give uniformity to the series of volumes. The framework of each volume, however, is not as uniform as it was in the 1854 edition, where the offices for each cathedral were given in the same order. As the order of precedence among the dignitaries in fact varied from place to place, the present edition has followed the order in use in each particular diocese.[1] The sub-dean has been included when he was a member of the chapter. The compilers, being faced with a great variety of forms for the names of the prebends, decided to choose the name used currently in each diocesan handbook, even though it may occasionally differ from that at present written over the appropriate prebendal stall. For some dioceses a table of variant names has been drawn up.[2] In the case of prebends which now no longer exist, the present place-name has been used.[3] This practice has occasionally caused a change in the alphabetical order of the prebends as given by Le Neve-Hardy. In Exeter where the prebends were all of the same value and had no distinguishing name, the topographical arrangement of the prebends could not be followed and a chronological one has been substituted.

[1] cf. *Statutes of Lincoln Cathedral*, ed. H. Bradshaw and C. Wordsworth (Cambridge, 1892–97), I 136–8.
[2] Le Neve, *Fasti*, rev. ed., *Hereford*, p. 53, *St Paul's, London*, p. 72, *Bath and Wells*, p. 85, *Coventry and Lichfield*, p. 72.
[3] e.g. Bedwyn, Blewbury, Charminster and Bere, Ramsbury, in Salisbury.

The account of each man's tenure of office is headed by his name, degree and dates. Where there is more than one claimant, they are grouped together, as it is sometimes difficult to determine which man actually gained possession. Unsuccessful claimants to the bishopric (where it is relatively certain who was successful) are given in square brackets. In general, the name chosen to describe a man is that most commonly found among the variant spellings in the records, for the spelling of names was far from consistent, even within a single diocese. Versions that differ considerably from the principal one are included in the index to each volume, though by no means all the variations found, some of which have only slight differences from each other. If a man was known by alternative names which are completely different (e.g. William Basyng or Kingsmill),[1] these names are given also in the text. Sometimes slightly different names are given to the same man in different dioceses,[2] and in this case, the variant names are brought together in the cumulative index. An attempt has also been made in the cumulative index to distinguish men of the same name, by giving their date of death if known, or the period during which they were known to have been active. Unless there is sufficient evidence for the certain identification of two men with the same name, they are entered separately. As several members of the same family often had the same Christian name it is dangerous to conclude that two men of the same name and period must be one person. Names are normally given in the contemporary form. Thus 'de' has been left in the names (except in the first volume of the series), until it was dropped round about 1390. An exception has been made in the case of a few famous men, such as William of Wykeham, whom it would seem pedantic to refer to otherwise. This method of following contemporary usage has meant that place-names used as surnames have not always been rendered by their modern counterpart. John de Cantebrugg,[3] for example, is not referred to as John de Cambridge. This method ensures uniformity of style with the other surnames, and avoids anachronisms and the numerous pitfalls in identifying a place of origin, especially since this may relate to the man's forebears several generations previously. Where foreigners occur, their Christian names have been Anglicized if possible,[4] and their surnames given in the language which they appear to have spoken. In the volume on the Welsh dioceses, personal names have been rendered in the Welsh form, except when it is impossible to tell whether a man was Welsh or English.[5] Cross-references in the cumulative index bring together Welshmen who may be given in both the Welsh form and an Anglicized form in different volumes.

Dr A. B. Emden's *Biographical Registers* of the Universities of Oxford and Cambridge[6] have been followed for degrees, and the forms LL.D. and S.T.P. which occur on occasion in Le Neve-Hardy have been rejected in favour of D.C.L. and D.Th. etc. (except in the first volume). The *Biographical Register* of Oxford was only partly published when the first volume went to press, and that for Cambridge

[1] Le Neve, *Fasti*, rev. ed., *Monastic Cathedrals*, p. 48.
[2] e.g. Richard Derham (Le Neve, *Fasti*, rev. ed., *Salisbury*, p. 74), Richard Dereham (*Monastic Cathedrals*, p. 29); John Bourgchier (*Lincoln*, p. 16), John Bourchier (*St Paul's, London*, p. 47); Ralph Repyngton (*Salisbury*, p. 9), Ralph Repingdon (*Chichester*, p. 41), Ralph de Repynton (*Coventry and Lichfield*, p. 64); John Jeffreys (*Monastic Cathedrals*, p. 32), John Geffray (*Coventry and Lichfield*, p. 31).
[3] Le Neve, *Fasti*, rev. ed., *St Paul's, London*, p. 10.
[4] e.g. John de Gigliis, Bartholomew de Ferentino, James de Hispania, Christopher Marini, Raymond Pelegrini.
[5] Le Neve, *Fasti*, rev. ed., *The Welsh Dioceses*, p. vi.
[6] *Biographical Register of the University of Oxford to 1500*, comp. A.B. Emden, 3 vols. (Oxford, 1957–9); *Biographical Register of the University of Cambridge to 1500*, comp. A.B. Emden (Cambridge, 1963).

was published midway through the revision of the 1300–1541 section of Le Neve-Hardy. Consequently there are some additional degrees given in the errata and addenda, especially for men occurring in the earlier volumes of the series. Our grateful thanks are due to Dr Emden for supplying many of these. The degrees given are the highest known to have been held at the beginning of a man's tenure of office (or his first occurrence), rather than the highest which he ultimately obtained. Thus there will be differences in any one volume in the degrees given to one man, if he entered various offices at different dates.[1] The description 'M' has been given if it is found sufficiently regularly in the sources. This was supposed to indicate a University graduate, but seems to have been used frequently as a courtesy title.

After the man's name and degree, details are given of any particularly important office held at the time of appointment, such as a bishopric or cardinalate. In view of the varied descriptions of the cardinals' titles, the forms given in Eubel's *Hierarchia Catholica* have been adopted throughout. Next, dates have been given for the man's tenure of the office in question. If both the terminal dates are known with certainty these are given. If one is uncertain, a question mark is substituted in the heading, and in the text the earliest or latest occurrence is given with references. It should be understood that any entry is given to an individual only when he appears explicitly in the relevant documents. The occurrence of an individual as a canon of a given church is always specified as such, as it in no wise guarantees his possession of a prebend. If neither terminal date is known, the date of an occurrence is given in the heading, or if more than one is known, the earliest and latest, separated by a comma. The man may of course be known to occur on other occasions between these two dates. The first date given for bishops is that of their first claim to the office (not licence to elect), rather than their consecration.[2]

The account of a man's tenure of office is not a biography, and not all known material has been included. Essentially it is a description of how and when the man secured and left the office. Thus, for each bishop, an attempt has been made to discover the licence to elect, election, archbishop's confirmation and royal assent (unless the appointment was by papal provision), followed by the consecration or translation, enthronement, and manner of terminating his tenure of the see. In the case of prebendaries, where possible, the appointment of each (whether by bishop's collation, royal grant, or papal provision), his admission and installation, and his death, resignation, relinquishment by exchange or deprivation are recorded. If a man terminated his tenure of office on becoming a bishop, the normal practice in the revised *Fasti* has been to give the first date at which he had a claim to the bishopric, as the terminal date for his tenure of the previous office. If the consecration was delayed for more than a year, this fact has been noted.[3] In some dioceses, where there is a dearth of episcopal and chapter material, lists have been supplied of men occurring as canons, or receiving

[1] e.g. Geoffrey Blythe, M.A. in 1494 and 1495 (Le Neve, *Fasti*, rev. ed., *Salisbury*, pp. 20, 45), D.Th. by 1499 (*ibid.*, pp. 13, 90; cf. xii. 52, 56); Richard Dudley, M.A. in 1507 and 1508 (*Salisbury*, pp. 16, 70), D.Th. by 1517 (*ibid.*, pp. 49, 99); Alexander Sparrow, B.Cn. & C.L. in 1423 and 1426 (*ibid.*, pp. 12, 24, 52), D.Cn. & C.L. by 1432 (*ibid.*, p. 10).
[2] e.g. Richard Beauchamp, provided 4 Dec. 1448, consecrated 9 Feb. 1449 (Le Neve, *Fasti*, rev. ed., *Hereford*, p. 2); Simon de Meopham, elected 11 Dec. 1327, consecrated 5 June 1328 (*Monastic Cathedrals*, p. 3); Stephen de Gravesend, elected 11 Sept. 1318, consecrated 14 Jan. 1319 (*St Paul's, London*, p. 1).
[3] e.g. William de Greenfield, elected archbishop of York 4 Dec. 1304, consecrated 30 Jan. 1306 (Le Neve, *Fasti*, rev. ed., *Northern Province*, p. 3, cf. *ibid.*, p. 64); Simon Sydenham bishop of Chichester by provision 14 Oct. 1429, consecrated 12 Feb. 1431 (*Chichester*, p. 2, cf. *Salisbury*, p. 4).

papal grants of a canonry with expectation of a prebend.[1] These men may or may not have secured actual enjoyment of a prebend. In the dioceses with fairly complete series of records, lists of this kind have been considered unnecessary, as it is unlikely that anyone reaching the position of a dignitary or prebendary would not find a mention. It must also be pointed out that it is not within the range of the introduction to indicate the ways in which this edition offers fresh material for a fuller understanding of the sort of men who were promoted to be dignitaries of the cathedral churches.

In view of the amount of repetitive material, space has been saved by the use of a certain number of abbreviations, and by not repeating the year date already given in the entry. No references are given when a man terminated his tenure by going to another prebend in the same diocese, or by becoming a bishop, as these may be found in detail in the appropriate place, or in Eubel in the case of foreign bishops. Nor are references given if a man entered office by exchange with the previous holder, as details may be found in the account of the latter's tenure. The titles of printed works which are cited three or more times in a volume are given in an abbreviated form, and these abbreviations are listed at the beginning of each volume, together with a full bibliographical description of the work. These lists of works do not by any means include all the works consulted.

Where major differences from Le Neve-Hardy occur, for example the omission through lack of evidence of a name given in the original edition, this fact is noted in a footnote. It is not overlooked that there are divergences between the revised Le Neve and other standard works, such as the *Handbook of British Chronology*, *Dictionary of National Biography*, *Victoria County History* and diocesan histories. These differences, however, are not mentioned, as the revision is primarily concerned with Le Neve-Hardy, and has been made from manuscripts and not from secondary authorities. As references are given for all statements, it is assumed that these can be checked and compared with those given in secondary works.

[1] Le Neve, *Fasti*, rev. ed., *Chichester*, pp. 54–60; *Bath and Wells*, pp. 81–3; *Coventry and Lichfield*, pp. 70–1; *The Welsh Dioceses*, pp. 16–17, 30–4, 46–50, 83–5.

Errata

VOLUMES I–XI

VOL. I. LINCOLN DIOCESE

p. ix   *Add to list of works in print:*
      Desiderata Curiosa.   *Desiderata Curiosa*, comp. F. Peck. London, 1779.
      Emden, Reg. Camb.   *Biographical Register of the University of Cambridge to 1500*, comp. A. B. Emden. Cambridge, 1963.

p. x   *Survey of Cath.*   *Survey of . . . Cathedrals*, comp. Browne Willis. 3 vols. in 2. London, 1742.

p. xi   *Add to list of manuscript references:*
      Somerset House
   PCC: Registers of wills proved in the prerogative court of Canterbury.

p. 1   **John Dalderby**   *For* 1299–1320. *read* 1300–1320.
     John Buckingham   *For* 1363–1398. *read* 1362–1398.

p. 2   **Henry Beaufort**   *Add* Sch.Th.
     Richard Fleming   *For* 1425–1431. *read* 1419–1424.
     John Mackworth   *Delete* M. *and* B.Cn.L.
     William Alnwick   *For* O.S.B., D.C.L. *read* D.C.L.
     Marmaduke Lumley *Add* B.C.L.

p. 3   **Thomas Rotherham** *For* 1471–1480. *read* 1472–1480.
     John Russell   *For* D.C.L. *read* D.Cn.L.
     William Smith   *For* B.C.L. *read* B.Cn. & C.L.
      For from Lichfield *read* from Coventry and Lichfield
     Thomas Wolsey   *For* M.A. *read* D.Th.
     Joceline Kirmington *Add* M.
     Raymond de Got   *For* 1305–1310. *read* 1306–1310.

p. 4   **William Bateman**   *For* D.Cn. & C.L. *read* D.C.L.
     John Stretley
      Add at end of entry D. 1368 or 1369 (*Emden, Reg. Ox.* III 1804).
      Add new entry after **John Stretley** *as follows:*
     M. Robert Stretton D.C.L. 1369.
      Occ. 20 Oct. and 13 Dec. 1369 (*Reg. Stretton* II 85, 86).
     John Sheppey   *For* D.Th. *read* D.C.L.
     John Mackworth   *Delete* M. *and* B.Cn.L.
     George Heneage   *For* B.C.L. *read* B.Cn.L.
     John Taylor   *Add* D.Th.

p. 5   **Hamo Belers**
        Add at end of entry Probably to d., 1 May 1370 (*Survey of Cath.* II 97).
        Robert Aiscough   *For* B.Cn.L., D.C.L., *read* D.Cn.L.
        Robert Wymbyssh   *For* B.C.L. *read* B.Cn.L. *For* 1471–? *read* 1471–1478.
        Add at end of entry D. 30 March 1478 (*Survey of Cath.* II 98).
        Philip Leipyates   *For* B.Cn.L., Lic.C.L. *read* B.Cn.L.

p. 6   **Brian Higdon**
        For Res. by 1 July *read* Exch. this and preb. Clifton with John Talbot for
        preb. Aylesbury 26 June
        John Talbot
        For Coll. 26 June *read* By exch. 26 June
        John Prynne
        For D. by 22 July . . . p. 154). *read* D. 29 Apr. 1558 (*Survey of Cath.* II 98;
        Chapter Acts 1547–1559 p. 154).
        John Stratford   *For* D.Cn. & C.L. *read* D.C.L.
        William Askeby *or* **Scoter**
        For 1 June 1354 *read* 1 June 1352
        William Wykeham   *For* 1363–1367. *read* 1363–1366.
        For Bp. of Winchester 1367. *read* Bp. of Winchester 1366.

p. 7   line 8 **Henry Bowet** *Add* M. *and* (again)
        After vacated it Sept. 1401 *insert* on becoming bp. of Bath and Wells
        William Feriby   *Delete* B.Cn.L.

p. 8   **Walter Wutton**   *For* **Wutton** *read* **Wotton**
        William Wittlesey   *Delete* D.Cn. & C.L.

p. 9   **William Welborne**
        After preb. Empingham *insert* and ch. of Withern, Lincs.
        Eudo la Zouche
        Add at end of entry Probably to d., by 13 March 1414 (A.C. A2/29 f. 60b).
        John Tibbay
        For D. by 26 July 1414 *read* D. 22 July 1414
        John Morton   *For* D.Th. *read* D.C.L.
        John Blithe   *Delete* M. *and* LL.D.

p. 10   **John Buckingham**   *For* 1351–1363. *read* 1351–1362.
        For Bp. of Linc. 1363. *read* Bp. of Linc. 1362.

p. 11   **Henry Wakefield**   *For* 1371–1373. *read* 1371–?
        Delete Bp. of Ely 1373.
        Add new entry after **Henry Wakefield** *as follows:*
        Peter Gomez d'Albornoz Card. pr. of S. Praxedis. 1372.
        Occ. 26 May 1372 (*CPL.* IV 173). D. (in possession?) 2 June or 3 July
        1374 (*Eubel* I 21).

Walter Skirlaw   *For* 1381. *read* 1381–1385.
    Add at end of entry Bp. of Coventry and Lichfield 1385.

John Bremor   *Add* B.C.L.

Robert FitzHugh   *For* D.Th. *read* Sch.Th.

William Gray   *For* D.Th. *read* M.A.

George Neville   *For* 1454–1457. *read* 1454–1456.
    For Res. by . . . f. 316b). *read* Bp. of Exeter 1456.

p. 12   John Bottlesham   *Add* Lic.C.L.

John Elvet   *For* 1392–? *read* 1392–1405.

p. 13   line 4 *For* Occ. 27 May 1421 . . . (see below). *read* D. by 31 March 1405 (Reg. XIV f. 474).

Roger Rotherham   *For* LL.D. *read* D.C.L.

John Morton   *For* D.Th. *read* D.C.L. *For* 1478–1479. *read* 1478.
    For Bp. of Ely 1479. *read* Bp. of Ely in Dec.

    After John Morton *delete* Next archdcn. known is *and add new entry as follows:*

M. William Chauntry 1479.
    Occ. 17 May 1479 (*CPL.* XIII ii 662). Probably to d., by 12 Oct. 1485 (Lichfield, Reg. XII (Hals) f. 69).

Henry Wilcocks
    Add at end of entry Probably to d., by June 1518 (Reg. XXV f. 39).

p. 14   Gilbert Segrave   *For* 1303–1313. *read* 1303–1312.
    For D. by 12 March 1313 (*ibid.* f. 289b). *read* D. by 31 May 1312 (*ibid.* f. 289b; A.C. A2/21 f. 16b).

Thomas Southam   *Add* Lic.C.L. *For* 1356–1404. *read* ?–1404.

John Southam   *Add* Lic.C.L.

Lionel Woodville   *Delete* M. *and* B.Cn.L.

Oliver King   *For* Lic.C.L., D.Cn.L. *read* D.Cn. & C.L. *For* 1482–1493. *read* 1482–1492.
    For Bp. of Exeter 1493. *read* Bp. of Exeter 1492.

George Heneage   *For* B.C.L. *read* B.Cn.L.

p. 15   George de Saluzzo
    For archdcnry 'Transuigenen' *read* archdcnry 'Transuigenen'[1]

Anibaldus Gaetani de Ceccano *Delete* M.

John Skyret   *Add* M. *and* B.C.L.

William Aston   *For* Aston *read* Ashton *Add* D.C.L.
    For William Aston *read* William Ashton

Ralph Selby   *For* LL.D. *read* D.Cn. & C.L.

Walter Cook   *Delete* M.

Thomas Tutbury   *For* ?–1403. *read* ?–1402.
    For D. by 26 Feb. *read* Res. by 26 Feb.

William Milton   *For* Lic.C.L. *read* B.C.L.
>*Add new footnote as follows:*
1. Archdcnry of Outre-Vienne (*Gallia Christiana* XIV 3).

p. 16   **John Bourgchier**   *Delete* D.Cn.L.
      Thomas Neville   *Delete* D.C.L.
      John Daubeny   *Add* D.Cn.L.
      Philip Daubeny
>*For* Exch. 30 Aug. *read* Exch. this archdcnry 30 Aug.
>*For* Clifford-by-Shefford *read* Clifton

p. 17   **William Derby**   *For* 1431–1439. *read* ?–1438.
>*For* D. as archdcn. . . . f. 107b). *read* D. as archdcn. by 2 Oct. 1438 (Reg. XVIII ff. 107b, 108).
      Thomas Salisbury
>*For* D. by 13 Dec. . . . f. 78). *read* D. 15 Nov. 1460 (*ibid.* f. 78; *Survey of Cath.* II 124).
      Joceline Kirmington *Add* M.
      William Langwath   *For* 1301–1303. *read* 1301–1302.
>*For* D. by 22 March 1303 *read* D. by 22 March 1302
      William Ockham (again)   *For* 1303–1328. *read* 1302–1328.
>*For* coll. 22 March 1303 *read* coll. 22 March 1302

p. 18   line 3 *For* (A.C. A2/23 f. 10).[1] *read* (A.C. A2/23 f. 10).
>*Add new entry before* **Walter Stauren** *as follows:*
      Thomas[1] 1326/7.
>Occ. Sept. 1326–Sept. 1327 (Linc. Accounts, cited in *Eng. Sec. Caths.* p. 344).
      Walter Stauren
>*For* Res. *read* Res. this archdcnry
      John Islip
>*For* Easton near Stamford, Lincs. *read* Easton-on-the-Hill, Northants.
      Simon Islip   *Delete* Lic.Cn. & C.L.
      Thomas Chandos
>*For* Exch. *read* Exch. this archdcnry
      Thomas Aston   *Add* B.Cn.L.
      Hugh Hanworth
>*For* D. by 9 March . . . f. 82b). *read* D. 7 March 1419 (*Survey of Cath.* II 128).
>*Footnote*
>*For* No trace . . . Le Neve-Hardy. *read* Possibly this is Thomas Northwode D.Th., who Le Neve-Hardy says had coll. 14 Apr. 1328. No trace has been found of Walter Maidstone, said by Le Neve-Hardy to have had coll. 10 Nov. 1328.

p. 19 Edmund Booth *Delete* B.Cn.L.
   John Blithe *Delete* M. *and* LL.D.
   Robert Frost *Add* B.Cn.L.
   Edward Derby *or* Derley *For* Derby *or* Derley *read* Derby
    For D. by 15 Jan. . . . f. 16). *read* D. 9 Jan. 1543 (*Survey of Cath.* II 129;
   Reg. XXVII f. 16).

p. 20 Peter Dalderby *For* 1340–? *read* 1340–1350.
    Add at end of entry D. by 7 Apr. 1350 (*CPL.* III 318).
   Anthony Goldsborough *For* c. 1357–c. 1366. *read* 1350–?
    For Occ. Sept. . . . , s.a.). *read* Prov. 7 Apr. 1350 (*CPL.* III 318).
    For Thence yearly *read* Occ. yearly
   William Clive *For* Clive *read* Clynt
    Add at end of entry Probably to d., 17 Feb. 1425 (*Survey of Cath.* II 84).
   Marmaduke Lumley *Add* B.C.L.
   Robert Burton *For* M.Th. *read* D.Th.
   Alexander Prowet *For* B.C.L. *read* Lic.Cn.L.
    For D. by 23 Feb. . . . f. 44). *read* D. 6 Feb. 1471 (*Survey of Cath.* II 84).
   William Towne *For* 1471–? *read* 1471–1473.
    Add at end of entry Preb. of Dunham and Newport 1473.

p. 21 Richard Cowland *Add* B.Cn.L.
   Christopher Tamworth *Delete* B.A.
    For D. by 29 May . . . f. 19). *read* D. 13 Jan. 1546 (*Survey of Cath.* II
   86; Reg. XXVII f. 19).
   William Balaeto *For* Balaeto *read* de Balaeto

p. 22 Peter Dalton *or* Ncubold *For* 1384–? *read* 1384–1402.
    For Occ. . . . p. 357). *read* D. by 20 Nov. 1402 (*Calendars of Lincoln Wills*,
   ed. C. W. Foster (Index Libr., 1902–30) I 5; Reg. XIII f. 337b).
   John Haket *Add* B.Cn.L.
   Thomas Skeyman *Add* M.
   John Smeton *Add* M.
   John Cutler *or* Cutter
    For D. by 14 July . . . f. 26). *read* D. 11 June 1508 (*ibid.* f. 26; *Survey of
   Cath.* II 94).

p. 23 George Heneage *For* B.C.L. *read* B.Cn.L.
   John London *For* 1522. *read* 1522–1525.
   William Exeter *Add* D.Th.
    *Delete last sentence on page, and footnote, and add new entry at foot of page
   as follows:*
   M. Thomas Cotte of Sutton D.Th. ?–1384.
    D. as chancellor 13 Apr. 1384 (*Desiderata Curiosa* p. 314).

p. 24   Martin Joynour *or* Jones *or* Bovelyth   *Add* D.Th.
        For D. by 6 Aug. . . . f. 34b). *read* D. 20 July 1485 (*ibid.* f. 34b; *Survey of Cath.* II 90).
        William Atwater
        For Res. . . . f. 28b). *read* Preb. of Liddington 1512.
        Nicholas Bradebridge *For* 1512–1532. *read* 1512–1533.
        For D. 1532 . . . f. 10). *read* D. 14 March 1533 (*Survey of Cath.* II 91; Reg. XXVII f. 10).
        Christopher Massingberd *For* 1532–1543. *read* 1533–1543.
        For Coll. n.d. [1532] *read* Coll. n.d. [1533]

p. 25   Robert Miles   *For* ?–1329. *read* 1327–1329.
        Add at beginning Prov. 14 July 1327 (*CPL.* II 262 – 'Robert FitzMeles').
        For D. as preb. *read* D.
        Simon Islip   *Delete* Lic.Cn. & C.L.
        Philip Beauchamp   *Delete* D.C.L.

p. 26   Thomas Walton
        For Res. . . . f. 496b). *read* Preb. of Leighton Buzzard 1419.
        Robert FitzHugh   *For* D.Th. *read* Sch.Th.
        John Urry   *Add* M.
        Thomas Chichele   *Delete* M. *and* D.Cn.L.
        John Beverley
        For Res. by . . . f. 74). *read* Preb. of Caistor 1458.
        John Marshall   *Delete* D.Th.
        Ralph Scrope
        Add at end of entry Probably to d., 2 March 1517 (memorial brass in Hambleden ch., Bucks.: see Le Neve, *Fasti, 1300–1541*, rev. ed., VI 115n).
        Richard Maudeley
        For Archdcn. of Leicester 1518. *read* Preb. of All Saints in Hungate 1518.
        Brian Higdon
        For D. by 29 Aug. . . . f. 13b). *read* D. 5 June 1539 (*Survey of Cath.* I 69; Reg. XXVII f. 13b).

p. 27   Thomas Bray
        For Res. . . . f. 293). *read* Preb. of Lafford 1311.
        Giles Radener   *For* Radener *read* Redmere *Add* M. *and* D.Th.
        For f. 296).[1] *read* f. 296).
        Add at end of entry Occ. as a can. of Lincoln (probably this preb.) in 1325 (*CPL.* II 244).[1]
        Robert Braybroke   *For* B.A., Lic.C.L. *read* B.C.L.
        Thomas Wardrober
        For Res. by 6 May (*ibid.*). *read* Preb. of Bedford Major in May.
        Footnote   *After* John Winwick *insert* (Wynwyk)

p. 28 John Stone *Add* Sch.Th.
Richard Lichfield *For* D.Cn. & C.L. *read* D.C.L.
William Woodcock *Add* M. *and* Inc.M.
Robert Harom
Add at end of entry Probably to d., 6 Feb./3 March 1516 (PCC 15 Holder).
Richard Maudeley *For* 1518–? *read* 1518–1519.
Add at end of entry Preb. of Thame 1519.
James Mallet
For Preb. vacant . . . f. 153). *read* Preb. of Lafford 1520.

p. 29 Ralph Ingham *Add* M. *and* D.C.L.
John Southam *Add* Lic.C.L.
John Wade
For Res. . . . f. 488b). *read* Preb. of Stow Longa 1413.

p. 30 *Add new entry after* Thomas Russell *as follows:*
M. John Stone Sch.Th. 1429–?
Coll. 12 May 1429 (Reg. XVII f. 32b). Vac. by 24 Oct. 1430, probably to become preb. of All Saints in Hungate (cf. *ibid.* ff. 34, 34b).
Adam Moleyns
Add at end of entry Probably until bp. of Chichester 1445.
John Aleyn
For Res. . . . f. 6b). *read* Abp. of Dublin 1528.
John Bell *For* D.Cn.L. *read* D.C.L.

p. 31 George de Solario of Ivrea *For* 1304–? *read* 1304–1332.
For Occ. . . . p. 13). *read* D. by 16 Aug. 1332 (*CPL.* II 358).
Replace the entries for Paul de Monte Florum *and* Ugolino de Adigheriis *by the following entry:*
M. Paul de Monte Florum 1332–?
Ugolino de Adigheriis 1332–?
Royal gr. to Paul de Monte Florum 12 Apr. 1332 (*CPR. 1330–1334* p. 337). Ugolino de Adigheriis prov. 16 Aug. (*CPL.* II 358), not in possession 14 Oct. 1333 (*ibid.* p. 510). Prohibn. in favour of Paul de Monte Florum 10 Oct. 1334 after judgt. in ct. (*CPR. 1334–1338* p. 29). Last occ. in Accounts Sept. 1336–Sept. 1337 (Linc. Accounts Bj/2/5 f. 159), Ugolino occ. Sept. 1339–Sept. 1340 (*ibid.* f. 183b).
line 22 Ugolino de Adigheriis *Add* (again)
Five lines from foot of page, after Ugolino res. *insert* on becoming bp. of Cremona
Michael Northburgh *Add* D.C.L.
John Stretley *Add* D.C.L.
John de Parma *Add* M.

p. 32   William Pakington   *Delete* M.
         Robert Appleby   *Add* M.
         William Wittlesey   *For* D.Cn. & C.L. *read* B.Cn. & C.L.

p. 34   Thomas Chichele   *Delete* M. *and* D.Cn.L.
         Nicholas Billesden   *Add* D.C.L.
              For D. by 16 June . . . f. 47). *read* D. 31 May 1441 (Salis., Reg. Aiscough
         pt. ii f. 5).
         John Derby   *For* 1445–? *read* 1445–1447.
              Add at end of entry Preb. of North Kelsey 1447.
         Robert Catesby   *Add* B.A.

p. 35   William Askeby *or* Scoter *For* 1349–? *read* 1349–1361.
              Add at end of entry Preb. of Welton Ryval 1361.

p. 36   John Bradeston
              For Res. . . . f. 109). *read* Preb. of Langford Manor 1449.
         Robert Wymbyssh   *Add* M. *and* B.Cn.L. *For* 1449–? *read* 1449–1465.
              Add at end of entry Preb. Centum Solidorum 1465.
         John London
              For Res. by 6 Apr. 1526 (*ibid.*). *read* Preb. Sanctae Crucis in Apr.
         Robert Forth   *Add* M.
              For Res. . . . f. 5). *read* Preb. Decem Librarum in Oct.
         Richard Scrivener
              For Res. . . . f. 13b). *read* Preb. of Welton Ryval 1539.
         John Tayler   *For* Tayler *read* Taylor
         Thomas Northflete   *Add* M.
              Add at beginning Occ. Sept. 1304–Sept. 1305 (Linc. Accounts, cited in
         Eng. Sec. Caths. p. 335).
              For D. as preb. *read* D.

p. 37   Robert Stratton   *For* Stratton *read* Stretton
         John Bourgchier   *Delete* D.Cn.L.
         Edward Croxton   *For* Edward *read* Edmund
              For D. by . . . f. 25b). *read* D. 27 Jan. 1508 (T. G. Jackson, *The Church of
         St. Mary the Virgin, Oxford* (Oxford, 1877) pp. 201–2; Reg. XXIII f. 25b).
         William Smith
              For D. by 16 Jan. . . . f. 26b). *read* D. 15 Sept. 1508 (*Emden, Reg. Ox.* III
         1723; Reg. XXIII f. 26b).

p. 38   George Heneage   *For* B.C.L. *read* B.Cn.L.
         Geoffrey Eyton   *Delete* M.
         Richard Bury (again) *For* 1331–? *read* 1331–1333.
              Add at end of entry Bp. of Durham 1333.

Thomas Bradwardine *For* D.Th. *read* B.Th.
Add at end of entry Probably until abp. of Canterbury 1349 (*Reg. J. de Trillek*, ed. J. H. Parry (Canterbury and York Soc., viii) p. 127).
Stephen Brokesbourne
Add at beginning Possibly by prov. 17 Aug. 1349 (*CPL.* III 315).
William Somerford *Add* D.C.L.

p. 39   **Robert Stonham**   *For* 1401–? *read* 1401–1407.
Add at end of entry Preb. of Liddington 1407.
John Welbourne
After Exch. *insert* this, and preb. Fenton, York,
John Haket   *Add* D.C.L.
Philip *or* **John Tylney** *For* **Philip** *or* **John** *read* **Philip**
For D. by 12 Nov. . . . . f. 317b). *read* D. 30 Oct. 1453 (*Survey of Cath.* II 149; Reg. XX f. 317b).

p. 40   **Henry Nassington**
Add at beginning Occ. Sept. 1304–Sept. 1305 (Linc. Accounts, cited in *Eng. Sec. Caths.* p. 335).
For D. as preb. *read* D.
John Wynwyk
For p. 324), *read* p. 324).
For and Sept. . . . s.a.). *read* D. by 28 June 1360 (Lamb., Reg. Islip f. 161).

p. 41   **Roger Holme** (again)
For Exch. *read* Exch. this preb.
Thomas Neuby
For ch. of Wearmouth *read* ch. of Bishop Wearmouth
Simon Langham   *Add* O.S.B.
John Bottlesham   *Add* Lic.C.L. *For* 1391–1399. *read* 1391–1400.
For Bp. of Rochester 1399. *read* Bp. of Rochester 1400.

p. 42   **John Marshall**   *Add* M.
Thomas Ringstede *Delete* M. *and* B.Cn.L.
For Occ. . . . . 259). *read* Preb. of Caistor by Sept. 1445.
Richard Caudray   *For* ?–1457. *read* ?–1458.
Add at end of entry D. by 11 Sept. 1458 (A.C. A2/35 f. 73).
Thomas Downe   *Delete* D.Cn.L.
John Raynes   *For* D.C.L. *read* D.Cn. & C.L.
For Res. . . . f. 8b). *read* Preb. of Thame 1531.
John Hawkes   *For* B.Th. *read* D.Th.
Walter Wutton   *For* **Wutton** *read* **Wotton**
For Coll. to Wutton *read* Coll. to Wotton

p. 43   **Thomas Fastolf**   *Add* M. *and* D.C.L. *For* 1344–1355. *read* 1344–1352.
For Bp. of St. Davids 1355. *read* Bp. of St. Davids 1352.

Edward Boteler
Add at beginning Reservn. 13 Nov. 1352 (*CPL.* III 470).
Richard Boule   *Add* B.C.L.
William Navesby   *Delete* M.
Robert Trays
For D. by 22 Dec. . . . f. 21). *read* D. 21 Dec. 1426 (*Survey of Cath.* II 155; A.C. A2/31 f. 21).
John Deeping   *For* B.C.L. *read* Lic.C.L.

p. 44   **John Waltham**   *For* D.C.L. *read* B.C.L.
Stephen Ravenser *or* del See   *Add* M.

p. 45   **John Fox**   *For* D.C.L. *read* D.Cn.L. *For* 1476–? *read* 1476–1477.
Add at end of entry Preb. of Caistor 1477.

p. 46   **William Walcote**
For Res. *read* Res. this preb.

p. 47   **Thomas Balding**
Add at end of entry D., probably as preb., 13 Aug. 1433 (*Desiderata Curiosa* p. 303).
Peter Courtenay   *For* 1463–? *read* 1463–1470.
Add at end of entry Preb. of Thame 1470.
Robert Wymbyssh *For* B.C.L. *read* B.Cn.L.
Thomas Alford   *For* 1471–? *read* 1471–1486.
Add at end of entry D. 9 Feb. 1486 (*Desiderata Curiosa* p. 315).
Thomas Hill   *Add* B.Cn. & C.L.
Richard Roiston *or* Smith *For* D.C.L. *read* D.Cn.L.
John Underhill   *Add* B.Cn.L.
Arthur Lowe   *Add* M. *and* B.C.L.

p. 48   **John Stratford**   *For* D.Cn. & C.L. *read* D.C.L.
Tydo de Waresio   *Delete* M.
John Gynewell   *For* 1343–? *read* 1343–1347.
For Occ. . . . p. 121). *read* Bp. of Lincoln 1347.

p. 49   **John Ravenser**   *Add* M.
Roger Walden   *For* 1393–1398. *read* 1393–1397.
For Abp. of Cant. 1398. *read* Abp. of Cant. 1397.
Richard Hethe
For (Reg. XVI f. 15).[1] *read* (Reg. XVI f. 15).
Add at end of entry D., probably as preb., 8 Oct. 1443 (*Survey of Cath.* II 163).[1]
John Chedworth   *Delete* M. *For* 1454–1457. *read* 1454–1458.
For Archdcn. of Northampton 1457. *read* Preb. of Thame 1458.

John Beverley   *Add* D.Th.
    For D. 15–28 June . . . 137). *read* D. 21 June 1473 (A.C. A2/35 ff. 136b–137; *Desiderata Curiosa* p. 312).
John Lillyford
    For D. 4–13 Jan. . . . 91b).² *read* D. 7 Jan. 1477 (*ibid.* ff. 63b, 91b; *Desiderata Curiosa* p. 302).²

p. 50   John Fox   *For* D.C.L., B.Cn.L. *read* D.Cn.L.
    For D. by 6 Feb. . . . f. 275). *read* D. 2 Feb. 1483 (Reg. XXII f. 275; Lichfield, Acta Capitularia II f. 8).
    Add new entry before John Offord *as follows:*
M. James de Hispania 1304, 1306.
    Occ. Sept. 1304–Sept. 1305, and Sept. 1305–Sept. 1306 (Linc. Accounts, cited in *Eng. Sec. Caths.* pp. 335, 337).
James de Hispania 1330–1332. *Add* M. *and* (again)

p. 51   Thomas Aston   *Add* B.Cn.L.
Richard Wetton   *For* 1457–? *read* 1457–1465.
    Add at end of entry D. 1/9 Aug. 1465 (PCC 10 Godyn).
Robert Wymbyssh   *For* B.C.L. *read* B.Cn.L.
    For Res. . . . f. 321b). *read* Preb. of Carlton Paynell 1470.
Robert Belamy   *Add* D.Cn.L.
William Stevyns
    Add at end of entry D. (as preb.?) 2 March 1498 (*Survey of Cath.* II 170).
Richard Roiston *or* Smith   *For* D.C.L. *read* D.Cn.L.
Edward Derby *or* Derley   *For* Derby *or* Derley *read* Derby
    For Res. . . . f. 21). *read* Preb. of Dunham and Newport 1503.

p. 52   Richard Pates
    For Res. . . . f. 4). *read* Preb. of Cropredy 1525.
Roger Lupton
    For Res. . . . p. 97). *read* Preb. of Caistor 1528.
Robert Aldrich
    For Res. . . . p. 117). *read* Preb. Decem Librarum 1529.
Elias Muschamp   *For* 1313–1327. *read* 1313–1326.
    For Occ. . . . f. 95). *read* D. by June 1326 (Reg. IV f. 16b).

p. 53   John Kington   *Add* B.Cn. & C.L.
David Price *or* Ap Rees
    Add at end of entry Occ. as a can. of Lincoln (probably this preb.) in 1423 (*Reg. T. Spofford*, ed. A. T. Bannister (Canterbury and York Soc., xxiii), p. 34).
John Carpenter   *For* B.Th. *read* D.Th.
John Lillyford   *Add* D.C.L. *For* 1465–? *read* 1465–1473.
    For Occ. . . . f. 11). *read* Preb. of Dunham and Newport 1473.
John Docket *or* Dogget   *For* D.Th. *read* D.Th., D.Cn.L.

Charles Booth
  For Res. . . . f. 21b). *read* Preb. of Farndon-cum-Balderton 1504.
Robert Toney
  For Res. . . . f. 77). *read* Preb. of Langford Manor 1505.
John Fothed   *Add* B.Th.
Christopher Massingberd *For* 1512–? *read* 1512.
  Add at end of entry Preb. of Empingham in Dec.
Brian Higdon
  After Exch. *insert* this preb. and subdeanery

p. 54   Nicholas Colshull
  Add at end of entry Had probably res. it by 6 Dec. 1352 (*ibid.* p. 546; cf.
Eubel I 18).
William Thyngull   *Add* D.Cn. & C.L.
Perinus Tomacelli   *For* 1384, 1387. *read* ?–1389.
  For p. 401) *read* p. 401).
  For and Sept. 1386 . . . f. 182b). *read* Pope Boniface IX 1389 (*CPL.* IV
383–4).
John Thorpe   *Add* M.
Simon de Teramo   *Add* D.C.L.

p. 55   Thomas Poole *or* de la Pole
  For Res. . . . 84). *read* D. by 15 July 1433 (Reg. XVII ff. 83b, 84; York,
Reg. Kempe f. 11b).
William Hoper   *For* D.C.L. *read* D.Cn. & C.L.
William Witham
  For Res. . . . f. 59). *read* Preb. of Stoke 1457.
John Morton   *For* B.Cn.L., D.C.L. *read* D.C.L.
John Chamber   *Delete* M. *and* M.D.
Richard Roiston *or* Smith *For* D.C.L. *read* D.Cn.L. *For* 1506–? *read*
1506–1518.
  For Occ. . . . m.6). *read* Preb. of Nassington 1518.
George Heneage   *For* B.C.L. *read* B.Cn.L.

p. 56   John Bottlesham
  For Res. . . . f. 434b). *read* Preb. of Brampton 1391.
John Ixworth   *Add* M. *and* D.C.L.
Walter Ixworth   *Add* M. *and* B.Cn.L.
John Sybeley   *For* 1459–? *read* 1459–1466.
  Add at end of entry D. by May 1466 (Reg. XX f. 143).

p. 57   Simon Stalworth
  For Res. . . . f. 276). *read* Preb. of Kilsby 1483.

p. 58   William Rothwell   *Delete* M.
         Guy de Pestello   *Add* D.Cn.L.

Robert Allerton
> *For* D. by 4 May . . . 554–6). *read* D. 19 Apr. 1437 (*Survey of Cath.* II 175).

Fulk Birmingham   *Delete* M. *and* B.Cn.L.
> *See also* p. 43 *below*

p. 59   **George FitzHugh**   *For* 1486–1506. *read* 1486–1505.
> *For* D. by 20 Nov. *read* D. 20 Nov.

Henry Wilcocks
> *Add at end of entry* Probably to d., by June 1518 (Reg. XXV f. 39).

Richard Roiston *or* Smith   *For* D.C.L. *read* D.Cn.L.
> *For* D. by 25 Sept. . . . p. 64). *read* D. 18/25 Sept. 1525 (*Chapter Acts 1520–1536* p. 64; PCC 37 Bodfelde).

John Fox   *For* B.Cn.L. *read* B.Cn. & C.L.

Thomas Cotte of Sutton   *For* 1360–1383. *read* 1360–1384.
> *For* Occ. . . . 353). *read* D. 13 Apr. 1384 (*Desiderata Curiosa* p. 314).

p. 60   **Geoffrey Gidding**   *Add* B.C.L.

John Barnet   *For* B.C.L. *read* Lic.C.L.

Robert Osanne
> *For* Worth, dioc. Salis. *read* Worth Matravers, Dors.

Walter Schiryngton
> *Add at end of entry* D. (as preb. ?) by 20 Feb. 1449 (Salis., Reg. Aiscough pt. i f. 113b).

John Wygryne   *For* Wygryne *read* Wygrym
> *Add at end of entry* Probably to d., by 20 Oct. 1468 (*Reg. of R. Stillington and R. Fox*, ed. H. C. Maxwell-Lyte (Somerset Record Soc., lii) p. 19).

Nicholas Chedworth
> *For* Res. . . . f. 322). *read* Preb. of Milton Manor 1471.

William Gisborne   *Add* B.C.L.

p. 61   **Thomas de Perariis**
> *Add at beginning* Occ. Sept. 1304–Sept. 1305 (Linc. Accounts, cited in *Eng. Sec. Caths.* p. 334).
> *For* D. as preb. *read* D.

William Colby
> *Add at end of entry* Probably to d., 8/10 Nov. 1336 (York, Reg. Wills I f. 20; York, Reg. Melton f. 116).

Henry Dale   *For* Dale *read* de la Dale   *Add* M.
> *Add at end of entry* Probably to d., by 4 March 1349 (*CPP.* I 155).

William Gynewell   *For* ?–1362. *read* ?–1361.
> *For* Vacated . . . s.a.). *read* Preb. of Leighton Buzzard 1361.

Thomas Banastre *or* Fryskenay of Elteslee
> *For* prebs. in Salisbury and Llandaff *read* preb. Axford, Salisbury and a preb. in Llandaff

Richard Croxton   *Add* M.

p. 62   John Southam   *Add* Lic.C.L.
         John Burdet   *Add* M.
         Thomas Loughborough *Add* M.
         John Lillyford
             Add at end of entry Preb. of Caistor 24 June.
         William Talbot   *Add* D.Cn.L.
         John Constable   *For* D.Cn.L. *read* B.Cn.L.
             For Res. . . . f. 21). *read* Preb. of Caistor 1503.

p. 63   Edward Derby   *For* 1503–? *read* 1503–1506.
             Add at end of entry Preb. of Langford Ecclesia 1506.
         William FitzHerbert *For* D.C.L. *read* D.Cn.L.
             Add at end of entry Preb. of Langford Ecclesia in Dec.
         William Clif'   *For* Clif' *read* Cliff
             For in favour of Clif' *read* in favour of Cliff
             For gr. to Clif' *read* gr. to Cliff

p. 64   Eudo la Zouche
             For Exch. 24 Feb. 1394 *read* Exch. this preb. and ch. of Withern, Lincs.
         24 Feb. 1394
         William Welborne
             For D. by 8 Oct. . . . f. 9b). *read* D. 5 Oct. 1404 (A.C. A2/29 f. 9b; *Desider-
         ata Curiosa* p. 314).
         John Mackworth   *Delete* M. *and* B.Cn.L.
         John Fraunceys   *Add* B.Cn.L.
         John Barnard   *Add* M. *and* Lic.C.L.
         John Langton   *Add* B.Cn.L. *For* 1433–? *read* 1433–1447.
             For Occ. . . . 36). *read* Bp. of St. Davids 1447.
         Thomas Whitfeld   *Add* M.
         George FitzHugh   *Delete* M.

p. 65   Roger Northburgh   *Delete* M.
             Combine the entries for Francis son of Neapoleo Orsini *and* William
         Dalton *as follows*:
         Francis son of Neapoleo Orsini 1328–1348.
         William Dalton 1343–?
             Prov. to Orsini 7 May 1328 (*CPL.* II 270). Occ. 28 Jan. 1332 (*CPR.
         1330–1334* p. 243) and 1 Feb. 1340 (*CPR. 1338–1340* p. 413). Royal gr. to
         Dalton 25 July 1343 and 28 Jan. 1344 (*CPR. 1343–1345* pp. 59, 188). Preb.
         in king's hands 20 June 1348, and Orsini d. by 8 Nov. (*CCR. 1346–1349*
         p. 522; *CPP.* I 141, 145).
         Thomas Baddeby   *For* 1351–1379. *read* 1349–1379.
             For Royal gr. to Thomas Baddeby 11 Aug. 1351 *read* Prov. to Baddeby
         13 Jan. 1349 (*CPP.* I 145); royal gr. 11 Aug. 1351
         Reginald Hulton   *Delete* M.

p. 66   **Thomas Kemp**   *Delete* M. *and* B.Th. *For* 1432, 1443. *read* ?–1450.
     Add at end of entry Bp. of London 1448; cons. 1450.

     Edmund Audley   *Delete* D.Th.

     Thomas Davet   *For* **Davet** *read* **Danet**
     For D. by 18 Sept. . . . f. 276). *read* D. 18 Sept. (Reg. XXII f. 276; *Survey of Cath.* II 185).

     John Walleys   *For* **Walleys** *read* **Walles**

     William Knight   *For* 1516–1542. *read* 1516–1541.
     For Bp. of Bath and Wells 1542. *read* Bp. of Bath and Wells 1541.

     Boniface de Saluzzo *For* 1298–? *read* 1298–1323.
     Add at end of entry D. by 26 Oct. 1323 (*CPL.* II 235, 236).[1]

     Replace the entry for **Robert Holden** *by the following entry :*

     Robert Holden 1324–?

     Philip de Meledun 1324–?
     Royal gr. to Holden 2 Jan. 1324, temps. being in king's hands (*CPR. 1321–1324* p. 357). Prov. to Meledun s.d. (*CPL.* II 236). Res. it, but fresh prov. 18 Feb. 1327, although Holden in possession (*ibid.* p. 261).

     Guy Chaume   *Add* Lic.C.L.

     Add new footnote as follows :
     1. There is no evidence that Albert de Lausanne d. in possession of preb. of Gretton in 1303 as stated by Le Neve-Hardy. This is an error for the preb. of Ketton, cf. p. 70.

p. 67   **Arnold Brocas**
     For D. by 20 Aug. . . . f. 442). *read* D. 14 Aug. 1395 (*Survey of Cath.* II 187; Reg. XI f. 442).

     William Waltham   *Add* B.C.L.

     John Barnard   *Add* M. *and* Lic.C.L.

     Richard Hall   *Add* D.Cn.L.

p. 68   **William Skelton**   *Add* M.
     For f. 67b). *read* f. 67b).[1]

     James Whitstons
     For Res. . . . f. 16b). *read* Res. this preb. 28 June 1498 on becoming preb. of Banbury (Reg. XXIII f. 16b).[1]

     Geoffrey Scrope   *Delete* M. *and* B.C.L.
     For Scrope continued . . . 349–53). *read* Scrope d. 25 Jan./11 Apr. 1383 (*Lincoln Wills*, vol. I, ed. C. W. Foster (Lincoln Record Soc., v) pp. 11–19).

     Add new footnote as follows :
     1. Skelton and Whitstons may have exchanged this preb. for Welton Brinkhall (see p. 124).

p. 69   **Richard Maudeleyn** *Delete* M. *and* B.C.L.

     Hugh Hanworth
     After preb. St. Botolph *insert* and preb. Fenton, York

Alan Kyrketon
Add at end of entry Probably to d., by 21 Aug. 1443 (London, Reg. Gilbert f. 51b).
William Percy   *Delete* M.

p. 70   **Robert Wodehouse**   *For* 1314–1343. *read* 1314–1344.
For Wodehouse d. . . . f. 118). *read* Wodehouse said to be dead by 6 Feb. 1344 (Reg. VI f. 118; cf. *CPL.* III 128), although certainly alive after this date, and d. 3/7 Jan. 1346 (*CPR. 1343–1345* pp. 328, 370; York, Reg. Zouche ff. 309, 67).
Replace the entries for **Thomas Hatfield, Thomas Dalton, William Dalton** *and* **Robert Askeby** *by the following entries:*
Thomas Hatfield 1344–1345.
Bp's mand. adm. 6 Feb. 1344 (Reg. VI f. 118). Bp. of Durham 1345.
Aquilinus Guillelmi de Sparra 1346–1347.
Had prov. with expectation of a Lincoln preb. 26 May 1342 (*CPL.* III 79), and occupied preb. after d. of Raymond des Farges, who d. 5 Oct. 1346; vac. it by 8 July 1347 (*Eubel* I 14; *CPL.* III 257).
M. Robert Askeby 1347–1349.
M. Thomas Dalton 1349.
M. William Dalton 1349.
Prov. to Askeby 8 July 1347 (*CPL.* III 257). Royal gr. to Thomas Dalton 28 May 1349 by reason of late vac.; the like to William Dalton 15 June (*CPR. 1348–1350* pp. 293, 308). But Askeby exch. this preb. Aug. 1349 with Simon Islip for ch. of Pagham, Suss. (*ibid.* p. 377).
Simon Islip
For Dec. *read* Oct.

p. 71   **Hugh Hanworth**
For D. by 9 March . . . f. 82b). *read* D. 7 March 1419 (*Survey of Cath.* II 128; A.C. A2/30 f. 82b).
Thomas Warre   *Delete* Lic.A.
William Smith   *Add* M. *and* B.Cn. & C.L.
John Prynne
For D. by 22 July . . . p. 154). *read* D. 29 Apr. 1558 (*Survey of Cath.* II 98; *Chapter Acts 1547–1559* p. 154).

p. 72   **John Walles**   *For* 1485–? *read* 1485–1493.
Add at end of entry Preb. of Farndon-cum-Balderton 1493.
Edward *or* **Edmund Hanson**   *For* Edward *or* Edmund *read* **Edmund**
For 1501–? *read* 1501–1504.
After f. 198b). *insert* Preb. of Sutton-in-Marisco 1504.
William Exeter   *Add* D.Th. *For* 1337–? *read* 1337–1340.
Add at end of entry Preb. of North Kelsey 1340.
John Ufford   *Add* M.
Thomas Warre   *Delete* M. *and* Lic.A.

p. 73 **Nicholas Clerke** *Delete* M.
> *Add at end of entry* D. (as preb. ?) by 12 Aug. 1441 (York, Acta Capitularia 1427–1504 f. 47b).

Simon Alcock *For* ?–1458. *read* ?–1459.
> *For* II 455) *read* II 455).
> *For* and Sept. 1457 . . . s.a.). *read* D. 10 Aug. 1459 (*Desiderata Curiosa* p. 313).

Thomas Salisbury
> *For* D. by 13 Dec. . . . f. 78). *read* D. 15 Nov. 1460 (*Survey of Cath.* II 124; A.C. A2/34 f. 78).

Thomas Gauge
> *For* Res. *read* Res. this preb.

William Langton
> *For* Res. *read* Res. this preb.

Richard Norton *For* D.Cn. & C.L. *read* D.C.L.

James Mallet *For* 1520–1533. *read* 1520–1532.

John Bourn *Add* M.

p. 74 **Robert Burbache** *Delete* M. *and* D.C.L.

John Lech *or* **Lechole** *Add* D.Cn.L.

John Bryane
> *For* D. by 16 Feb. . . . p. 10). *read* D. 4 Feb. 1389 (*Survey of Cath.* II 196).

Thomas Stanley
> *For* with William Aston *read* with William Ashton

William Aston *For* Aston *read* Ashton *Add* M. *and* D.C.L.

Roger Westwode
> *After* Exch. *insert* this preb., and preb. Sandiacre, Lichfield
> *After* for preb. *insert* Sexaginta Solidorum, preb. Lusk, Dublin and preb.

John Legborne
> *Add at end of entry* Occ. as a can. of Lincoln (probably this preb.) in 1425 (*CPL.* VII 413).

John *or* **William Faukes** *Delete* M. *For* John *or* William *read* John

p. 75 **John** *or* **William Faukes** (again) *Delete* M. *For* John *or* William *read* John

Laurence Cokkys *For* B.C.L., D.Cn.L. *read* D.Cn.L.

John Hobbull
> *Add at end of entry* Probably to d., by 16 Jan. 1505 (Salis., Reg. Audley f. 20).

John *or* **Richard Rawston** *For* John *or* Richard Rawston *read* Richard Rawson *Add* D.Cn. & C.L.

Edward Derby *or* **Derley** *For* Derby *or* Derley *read* Derby
> *Add at end of entry* Preb. of Liddington in Dec.

William FitzHerbert
> *Add at end of entry* Probably to d., by 20 Apr. 1514 (London, Reg. FitzJames f. 51).

Edward Hord   *For* Edward *read* Edmund   *Add* D.Cn.L.

Nicholas Halswell
  For (Reg. XXVII f. 5b) *read* (Reg. XXVII f. 5b).[1]

Richard Sampson
  For (Reg. XXVII f. 5b). *read* (Reg. XXVII f. 5b).[1]

Edward Waller *or* Walley   *For* Edward Waller *or* Walley *read* Edward Whalley

Robert Crowham *or* Peterson
  For Res. . . . f. 12b). *read* Preb. of Milton Ecclesia 1538.
  Add new footnote as follows:
1. Probably error for 1528. Halswell's will is dated 20 Jan. 1528, proved 31 July (PCC 36 Porch).

p. 76   Ralph Fodringhey   *Add* M.
        Eudo la Zouche   *Delete* D.C.L.
        Roger Basset   *Add* M. *and* D.Cn. & C.L.

p. 77   Thomas Colas
          Add at end of entry Probably to d., by Nov. 1439 (*Emden, Reg. Ox.* I 459).
        John Burdet   *Add* M.
          For D. by 1 Feb. *read* D. as preb. by 1 Feb.
        Robert Sherbourne
          For Res. . . . f. 280). *read* Preb. of Milton Manor 1493.

p. 78   John Barnet   *For* B.C.L. *read* Lic.C.L.
        Richard Yonge   *For* B.C.L. *read* Lic.Cn. & C.L. *For* 1391–1399. *read* 1391–1398.
          For Bp. of Bangor 1399. *read* Bp. of Bangor 1398.
        Thomas Barnesley
          For Coll. 1421 *read* Coll. 28 Dec. 1421
        William Bryconel   *For* Bryconel *read* Byconel   *Add* D.C.L.
        John Wardall
          Add at end of entry Probably to d., by 5 May 1472 (London, Reg. T. Kempe pt. i f. 134).
        Roger Rotherham   *For* LL.D. *read* D.C.L.
        John Blakwyn
          Add at end of entry Probably to d., by Aug. 1485 (Lichfield, Reg. XII (Hals) f. 53b).

p. 79   Simon Stalworth
          For with Robert Mome *read* with Robert Monie
        Robert Mome *or* Mone   *For* Mome *or* Mone *read* Monie
        John Cutler *or* Cutter
          For Res. . . . f. 25b). *read* Preb. of Louth 1508.
        Richard *or* John Dudeley *For* Richard *or* John *read* Richard *Delete* DT.h.

Hugh Normanton
Add at end of entry D. by 20 Apr. 1319, probably by 10 Apr. 1317 (*CPL.* II 185; cf. Reg. II f. 295b).

John de Puy Barzac *Delete* M.

William Weston   *Add* D.C.L.

p. 80   line 3 *For* John de Puy *read* John de Puy Barzac

John Pipe   *For* 1343–1360. *read* 1343–1361.
     For D. 10 Aug. . . . 346b). *read* D. 10 Aug. 1361 (Reg. XI f. 346b; Lichfield, Reg. IV (Stretton) f. 9b).

William Pakington *Delete* M.

Henry Bowet   *For* D.C.L. *read* D.Cn. & C.L.

p. 81   **John Holland**   *Add* M. *and* D.Th.

Hugh Oldham   *For* 1497–1505. *read* 1497–1504.
     For Bp. of Exeter 1505. *read* Bp. of Exeter 1504.

Thomas Ruthall   *For* D.Cn. & C.L. *read* D.Cn.L.

p. 82   **Henry Iddesworth**   *Add* M.

Simon Briselee   *For* 1347–1362. *read* 1347–1360.
     For Vacated . . . s.a.). *read* D. by June 1360 (York, Reg. Thoresby f. 45b; Linc. Accounts Bj/2/6 list, s.a.).

Thomas Warre   *Delete* Lic.A.
     After Vacated the preb. 1419 *insert* on becoming preb. of Ketton

William Constable
     For Res. *read* Res. this preb.

John Blithe   *Delete* LL.D.

Thomas *or* **John Fincham**   *For* 1485–1517. *read* 1485–?
     Add at end of entry Probably to d., 22 Jan./15 Feb. 1518 (PCC 5 Ayloffe).

p. 83   **Walter Wermington** *Add* M.

William Edington   *Delete* M.

     Add new entry after **William de Savinhaco** *as follows:*

Peter de St. Martial ?–1357.
     Res. this preb. on becoming bp. of Rieux 1357 (*CPL.* III 625.)

Francis de St. Maximo   *For* St. Maximo *read* Sancto Maximo   *For*
?–1358. *read* 1357–1358.
     Add at beginning Prov. 29 June 1357 (*CPL.* III 625).
     For D. as preb. . . . 591). *read* D. by 21 March 1358 (*ibid.* p. 591).

William Navesby   *For* 1361–1364. *read* 1361–?
     Delete Preb. of Buckden 1364.

p. 84   **Thomas Southam**   *Add* Lic.C.L.

William Waltham   *Add* B.C.L.

John Bremor   *Add* B.C.L.

John Bremor (again)   *Add* B.C.L.

Thomas St. Just
> *For Emden, Reg. Ox.* III 6 *read Emden, Reg. Camb.* p. 503.

p. 85   Thomas Aston   *Add* B.Cn.L.
Robert Wintringham
> *For* D. by 7 July . . . f. 163). *read* D. 5 July 1420 (*Survey of Cath.* II 210; Reg. XVI f. 163).

Richard Burnham
> *For* Res. . . . f. 163b). *read* Preb. of Stoke 1421.

p. 86   John Grantham
> *Add at end of entry* Probably to d., by March 1506 (Reg. XXIII f. 157b).

William Chessege
> *Add at beginning* Occ. Sept. 1306–Sept. 1307 (Linc. Accounts Bj/2/4 f. 29).[1]

William Salman   *Add* M. *and* Sch.C.L.

> *Add new footnote as follows:*
> 1. The holder in Sept. 1304–Sept. 1305 is described as 'thesaurarius regine' (Linc. Accounts, cited in *Eng. Sec. Caths.* p. 336). This is probably an inaccurate description of William Chessege, who held the office until 1300 (T. F. Tout, *Chapters in Administrative History* (Manchester, 1920–33) V 239), though it may mean that his successor as queen's treasurer, John Godley, held the prebend.

p. 87   John Warsopp
> *For* D. by 8 June . . . f. 1). *read* D. 6 Apr. 1386 (A.C. A2/28 f. 1; *Desiderata Curiosa* p. 310).

Alan Humberton   *Delete* M.
John Marshall
> *For* D. by 3 July . . . f. 16b). *read* D. 12 June 1446 (A.C. A2/33 f. 16b; *Desiderata Curiosa* p. 313).

John Collinson   *For* 1455–1481. *read* 1455–1482.
> *For* D. 1481 . . . 134). *read* D. by 24 March 1482 (Reg. XXII f. 275; A.C. A3/1 f. 12).

Thomas Barrow   *For* 1482–? *read* 1482–1499.
> *For* Occ. Sept. 1495 . . . s.a.). *read* D. 23 June/10 July 1499 (PCC 37 Horne).

Richard Cowland   *For* 1499–? *read* 1499–1506.
> *Add at end of entry* D. by 17 July 1506 (A.C. A3/2 f. 115).

John Cutler *or* Cutter
> *For* D. by 14 July . . . f. 26). *read* D. 11 June (Reg. XXIII f. 26; *Survey of Cath.* II 94).

p. 88   Peter Dalderby   *For* 1335–? *read* 1335–1350.
> *For* Occ. . . . p. 275). *read* D. by 7 Apr. 1350 (*CPL.* III 318).

Anthony Goldsborough *For* 1357, 1366. *read* 1350–?
> *For* Occ. Sept. 1357 . . . thence yearly *read* Prov. 7 Apr. 1350 (*CPL.* III 318). Occ. yearly

William Sheffield   *Delete* D.Cn.L.
William Masse   *For* Masse *read* Massey
William Birley
    For Res. . . . f. 276b). *read* Preb. of Stow Longa 1484.

p. 89   Christopher Twynho
    For Reg. Mayew p. 275 *read Reg. Mayew* p. 277
    William Blynckoo *or* Blencow   *For* 1539–1546. *read* 1539–1545.
    For Vacated it . . . f. 19). *read* D. 9 Dec. 1545 (*Survey of Cath.* II 215; Reg. XXVII f. 19).
    Ralph Ivingho
    For Res. *read* Res. this prcb.

    Add new entry after William Everdon *as follows:*
    Thomas[1] 1326/7.
    Occ. Sept. 1326–Sept. 1327 (Linc. Accounts, cited in *Eng. Sec. Caths.* p. 344).
    Richard Stretton   *Add* B.C.L.

    Add new footnote as follows:
    1. Thomas is also archdcn. of Stow, and may therefore be Thomas Northwode (cf. p. 16 above).

p. 90   Henry Rumworth *or* Circeter   *Add* M. a*nd* B.Th.
    John Werkworth   *For* 1438–? *read* 1438–1445.
    For Occ. Sept. 1440 . . . s.a.). *read* Exch. 3 Feb. 1445 with John Auncell for preb. Sandiacre, Lichfield (Lichfield, Reg. IX (Heyworth) f. 93).
    John Auncell   *Add* B.Cn. & C.L. *For* ?–1452. *read* 1445–1452.
    For Occ. Sept. 1445 . . . s.a.). *read* By exch. Feb. 1445.

p. 91   Christopher Tamworth *Delete* B.A.
    Gilbert Segrave   *Add* M. *and* D.Th.
    Gaillard de la Motte
    For Select Pleas K.B. IV 131). *read Select Pleas K.B.* IV 131; *CPL.* II 104, 214).
    John Harewell   *Add* M. *and* B.C.L.
    Add at end of entry Bp. of Bath and Wells Dec. 1366.
    Francis Teobaldeschi
    Add at end of entry D. (as preb.?) 6/7 Sept. 1378 (*Eubel* I 46).
    Walter Skirlaw   *For* ?–1386. *read* ?–1385.
    For Bp. of Coventry and Lichfield 1386. *read* Bp. of Coventry and Lichfield 1385.

p. 92   John Bottlesham   *Add* Lic.C.L.
    Walter Cook   *Delete* M. *For* 1395–1424. *read* 1395–1423.
    For D. by 3 Jan. . . . f. 165b). *read* D. 9 July/4 Aug. 1423 (PCC 1 Luffenam; St. Paul's MS. WD 13 f. 93/90; Reg. XVI f. 165b).

Robert Neville
Add at end of entry ?Until bp. of Salisbury 1427.
Robert Fleming   *Delete* M.
Robert Isham
Add at end of entry Probably to d., by March 1501 (Worc., Reg. S. de Gigliis f. 13b).
Thomas Winter   *Delete* M.
John Ricardi Mathie de Urbe
For Res. *read* Res. this preb.
Richard de Anibaldis de Urbe   *For* 1300–? *read* 1300–1329.
For Occ. . . . f. 81b). *read* D. by 3 Sept. 1329 (*CPL.* II 297, 310).
Anibaldus Gaetani de Ceccano   *Delete* M. *For* 1331. *read* 1329–1331.
Add at beginning Prov. 8 Nov. 1329 (*CPL.* II 310).

p. 93   **Manuel de Fieschi**   *Add* M. *For* 1331–? *read* 1331–1343.
For Occ. 28 Apr. . . . p. 417). *read* Bp. of Vercelli 1343.

Replace the entries for **William Bateman** *and* **Thomas Brembre** *by the following entry:*
M. William Bateman D.C.L. 1343–1344.
  Thomas Brembre 1343–1344.
    Prov. to Bateman 15 July 1343 (*CPL.* III 129). Royal gr. to Brembre 25 July (*CPR. 1343–1345* p. 104). Bateman became bp. of Norwich 1344; further royal gr. to Brembre 15 May (*ibid.* p. 258). Bp's mand. adm. 6 June (Reg. VI f. 120); instal. 4 July (A.C. A2/25 ff. 17, 18b–19).
John Chandeler   *Add* M.
Robert FitzHugh
For Res. by 16 June 1419 *read* Res. this preb. by 16 June 1419 on becoming preb. of Aylesbury
John Stafford   *Add* D.C.L.
Richard Petteworth *or* **Pettelborth**   *For* Petteworth *or* Pettelborth *read* Petteworth
William Danyell   *For* 1459–? *read* 1459–1464.
Add at end of entry D. 13 Oct./ 17 Nov. 1464 (A. W. Gibbons, *Early Lincoln Wills* (Lincoln, 1888) p. 182; A.C. A2/35 f. 164b).

p. 94   **John Higdon**
For Res. . . . f. 9b). *read* D. Feb. 1532 (*L. & P.* VI No. 735; Reg. XXII f. 9b).

p. 95   **Raymond des Farges**
Delete whole entry
Raynald Orsini   *For* 1347. *read* 1343–1347.
For Claimed 26 Feb. . . . 106–7). *read* Prov. 29 Aug. 1343 (*CPL.* III 128). Res. claims by 4 March 1347 (*CPP.* I 107).
Lewis Charlton   *For* D.Th. *read* Lic.Th.

Robert Stretton   *Add* M. *and* D.C.L.

John Sheppey   *For* D.Th. *read* D.C.L.

p. 96   Robert Leke
          For Res. . . . f. 164b). *read* Preb. of Thame 1422.

John Mackworth   *Delete* M. *and* B.Cn.L.

Thomas Manning   *For* D.Cn.L. *read* B.Cn.L.

Richard Lamport   *Add* B.Cn.L.

Henry Hornby
          Add at end of entry Probably to d., by 1 Apr. 1518 (Exeter, Reg. Oldham f. 75b).

Richard Roiston *or* Smith *For* D.C.L. *read* D.Cn.L.
          Add at end of entry Preb. of Cropredy in June.

John Talbot
          For Occ. . . . f. 142). *read* Preb. of Aylesbury 1519.

p. 97   *Replace the entry for* Thomas Northwode *by the following entry :*
M. Thomas Northwode D.Th. 1329–1354.
M. William Askeby *or* Scoter 1352.
          Coll. to Northwode 18 May 1329 (Reg. IV f. 401b). Said to be about to res. 1 June 1352, and papal reservn. of preb. for Askeby (*CPL.* III 462). Apparently ineffective, as Northwode d. as preb. by 24 May 1354 (A.C. A2/26 f. 38b).

Philip Beauchamp   *Delete* M.

Audoen Aubert
          For D. by 24 June 1363 (Reg. X f. 153). *read* D. 10 May 1363 (*Eubel* I 19; Reg. X f. 153).

Thomas Greenwood
          For D. by 4 May . . . f. 16). *read* D. 2 May 1421 (*Survey of Cath.* II 226; A.C. A2/31 f. 16).

Stephen Wilton
          For Exch. *read* Exch. this preb.

p. 98   William Constable   *Add* M. *and* B.Cn.L.

Robert Hawburgh   *Add* M.

Richard Bird   *Add* M. *and* B.Cn.L.

John Baker *or* Elton   *Add* B.Cn. & C.L.

Thomas Neville   *Add* M.

Richard Wynwyk
          For D. by 13 Dec. . . . f. 481b). *read* D. 12 Dec. 1408 (*Survey of Cath.* II 228; Reg. XIV f. 481b).

John Southam   *Add* Lic.C.L.

p. 99   Fulk Birmingham   *Delete* M. *and* B.Cn.L.

John Leke   *For* Leke *read* Leek *Add* Lic.Cn.L.

John *or* Richard Friston
    For with Thomas Caudour *read* with Thomas Candour
Thomas Caudour   *For* Caudour *read* Candour
Thomas Langton   *For* B.Th. *read* D.Th., D.Cn.L.
    For Res. by 9 Sept. 1483 *read* Res. this preb. by 9 Sept. 1483 on becoming
bp. of St. Davids

p. 100 Christopher Bainbridge *For* D.Cn. & C.L. *read* D.C.L.
Peter Roos
    Add at beginning Occ. Sept. 1304–Sept. 1305 (Linc. Accounts, cited in
Eng. Sec. Caths. p. 335).
    For D. as preb. *read* D.
Henry Mansfield   *Add* M. *and* D.Th.

p. 101 William Hunden   *Add* Lic.Cn. & C.L.
John Southam   *Add* Lic.C.L.
John Leek   *For* 1439–? *read* 1439–1462.
    Add at end of entry Preb. of North Kelsey 1462.
John Cokkes
    Add at end of entry Probably to d., by March 1476 (Reg. XXII f. 84).
William Massey   *For* 1476–? *read* 1476–1477.
    Add at end of entry Preb. of Marston St. Lawrence 1477.
Henry Carnebull
    Add at end of entry Preb. of Stow Longa in Oct.
William Bolton   *For* B.Cn. & C.L. *read* B.C.L.

p. 102 John Fynne   *For* B.Cn.L. *read* B.C.L.
Edward Croxton   *For* Edward *read* Edmund *For* 1506–? *read* 1506–
1507.
    Add at end of entry Preb. of Biggleswade 1507.
John Kidwely
    For Vacated preb. *read* Vacated this preb.
John Baker   *For* 1509–? *read* 1509–1513.
    Add at end of entry Preb. of Welton Paynshall 1513.
Richard Pates
    For Res. . . . f. 6). *read* Preb. of Sutton-cum-Buckingham 1528.
Edward Derby *or* Derley *For* Derby *or* Derley *read* Derby
See also p. 43 *below*

p. 103 Robert Hereward   *Delete* Lic.C.L.
Robert Wykford   *For* D.C.L. *read* Sch.Cn.L.
    For list, s.a.).[1] *read* list, s.a.).

    Add new entry after Robert Wykford *as follows:*
John Cheyne ?–1373.
    Exch. this preb. by 27 May 1373 with William Osmundeston for preb.
Chardstock, Salisbury (Salis., Reg. Wyville II ii f. 91b).

William Osmundeston *For* 1374–1387. *read* 1373–1387.
For Occ. . . . f. 7). *read* By exch. May 1373.
John Burbache
Add at end of entry Preb. of Gretton in Aug.
Walter Bullock *For* Lic.C.L. *read* B.C.L.
Nicholas Burton *Add* B.C.L. *For* ?–1435. *read* 1429–1435.
For Occ. . . . f. 85). *read* Coll. 25 Nov. 1429 (Reg. XVI f. 84).
John Haket *Add* D.C.L.
William Percy *Delete* M.
John Arundell *Delete* M.D.
Nicholas Karaunt *Add* Lic.C.L.
Robert Wymbyssh *For* B.C.L. *read* B.Cn.L.
Footnote
Delete whole footnote

p. 104 **John Seymour** *Add* M.
John Alcock *Add* M. *and* D.Cn.L.
For Res. *read* Res. this preb.
John Kirkby *For* ?–1362. *read* 1351–1362.
Nicholas Welton *Add* M. *and* B.C.L.

p. 105 line 2 *After* (*CPP*. 1 228). *insert* Prov. to Kirkby 9 May (*CPL*. III 416).
John Barnard *Add* M. *and* Lic.C.L.
For for preb. . . . 50–1). *read* for preb. of Witton in Auckland colleg. ch.,
co. Durham and ch. of Bletchley, Bucks. (*Reg. Langley* 1 50–1; *CPR. 1405–
1408* p. 433).
Thomas Lyes *For* 1408–? *read* 1408–1437.
For Occ. 1433 . . . (f. 130). *read* Exch. c. 28 Jan. 1437 with Ralph Knolles for
preb. Birtley in Chester-le-Street colleg. ch., co. Durham (*CPR. 1436–1441*
p. 33).
Ralph Knolles *Add* M. *and* D.C.L. *For* ?–1451. *read* 1437–1451.
For Occ. Sept. . . . s.a.). *read* Royal gr. 28 Jan. 1437 on exch. (*CPR. 1436–
1441* p. 33).
William Barre *For* Barre *read* de la Barre
Edmund Lichfield
After Exch. *insert* this preb., and chancellorship of Chichester
Richard Brakenburgh *Add* B.C.L.
Edmund Albon
Add at end of entry D. 23 Sept./22 Nov. (PCC 19 Logge).

p. 106 **Thomas Bedell**
For Res. . . . 7b). *read* Preb. of Milton Ecclesia 1529.
Robert Lacy
For Res. *read* Res. this preb.
Walter Wermington *Add* M.

p. 107   Henry Iddesworth (again)   *For* 1337–1349. *read* 1337–?

William Crawley   *Add* M. *and* Sch.Cn.L. *For* ?–1373. *read* 1371–1373.
Add at beginning Prov. 12 June 1371 (Cambridge Univ. Libr., Add. MS.
7207 (Lloyd Collections, Reg. Avin. 179 f. 203b), cited in *Emden, Reg. Camb.*
p. 166).
For Exch. 15 Nov. *read* Exch. 15 Nov. 1373

John Legborne
After Westminster *insert* , preb. Lusk, Dublin

Thomas Ludham
For Res. by 25 July 1438 *read* Res. this preb. by 25 July 1438 on becoming preb. of North Kelsey

p. 108   John Gygur   *Add* B.Th.

William Smith   *Add* B.Cn.L.
For D. by 14 June . . . f. 23). *read* D. 13 Apr. 1505 (*Survey of Cath.* II
238; Reg. XXIII f. 23).

Roger Northburgh   *Delete* M.
For Bp. of Lichfield *read* Bp. of Coventry and Lichfield

William Cliff
Add at end of entry Preb. of Empingham in Aug.

William Ayremynne *For* 1324–1326. *read* 1324–1325.
For bp. of Norwich 1326. *read* bp. of Norwich 1325.

John Grandison
For Vacated preb. . . . f. 585). *read* Bp. of Exeter 1327.

John Norwode   *For* 1328–? *read* 1327–1349.
Add at beginning Prov. 14 Dec. 1327 (*CPL.* II 265).
For Occ. . . . f. 183b). *read* D. by 4 May 1349 (*CPP.* I 156).

p. 109   Hugh Pelegrini   *For* ?–1375. *read* 1349–1375.
For Occ. . . . p. 12). *read* Prov. 4 May 1349 (*CPP.* I 156).
For Preb. seized *read* Preb. in king's hands 1375

Alan Humberton   *Delete* M.

Richard Burnham   *For* B.Th. *read* Sch.Th.

Robert Walkington
For Stoke, dioc. Coventry and Lichfield *read* Stoke-upon-Trent, Staffs.
After f. 154, 154b *insert* ; *Reg. Stretton* I 115

p. 110   Simon Marcheford
After Exch. *insert* this preb. and preb. Middleton, Chichester

Richard Petteworth *or* Pettelborth *For* Petteworth *or* Pettelborth *read*
Petteworth

John Stafford   *Add* D.C.L. *For* 1424–1425. *read* 1424.
For (*Reg. Chichele* I 335) . . . 1425. *read* (*Reg. Chichele* I 335), but already bp.
of Bath and Wells 18 Dec.

John Alcock   *Add* M.

Thomas Swain   *For* B.Cn.L. *read* B.Th. *For* 1516–? *read* 1516–1517.
       Add at end of entry Preb. of Haydour-cum-Walton 1517.
Edward Hord   *For* Edward *read* Edmund *Add* D.Cn.L.

p. 111   William Thornton
       Add at beginning Occ. Sept. 1304–Sept. 1305 (Linc. Accounts, cited in
Eng. Sec. Caths. p. 334).
       For D. as preb. *read* D.
       Hugh Normanton   *For* 1313–? *read* 1313–1316.
       Add at end of entry Preb. of Thame 1316.
       John Arundell   *Add* M.
       Simon Montacute   *Add* M. *For* ?–1334. *read* ?–1333.
       For Bp. of Worcester 1334. *read* Bp. of Worcester 1333.
       Thomas Yokflete
       Add at end of entry Probably to d., 10 Feb./7 Apr. 1406 (PCC 11 Marche).
       Thomas Polton   *Add* M. and B.Cn. & C.L.

p. 112   Nicholas Dixon
       For Res. . . . f. 130b). *read* Preb. of Sutton-cum-Buckingham 1438.
       John Chedworth   *Add* M.
       For Res. . . . f. 77). *read* Res. this preb. by 4 Sept. 1458 on becoming preb.
of Thame (A.C. A2/35 ff. 77, 78b).
       Vincent Clement
       Add at end of entry Probably to d., March 1475 (*Emden, Reg. Ox.* I 433).
       Roger Rotherham   *For* LL.D. *read* D.C.L.
       William Massey
       For Res. *read* Res. this preb.
       Cuthbert Tunstal   *Add* D.Cn. & C.L.
       Richard Layton   *Delete* LL.D.

p. 113   James Berkeley   *Add* D.Th.
       Add at end of entry (Preb. of Buckden in Oct.)
       Replace the entry for Thomas Brembre *and* Baldrac de Malebayle *by
the following entry:*
       Thomas Brembre 1347–?
       Baldrac de Malebayle 1347–1348.
       M. Robert de Chikewell 1347, 1349.
       Royal gr. to Brembre 20 Feb. 1347 and 22 Feb. by reason of vac. (*CPR.
1345–1348* pp. 256, 528). Royal right to present maintained against claims of
Baldrac de Malebayle c. 20 July, and Chikewell 8 Nov. (*ibid.* pp. 393, 421–2;
CPR. 1348–1350 pp. 153, 452). Baldrac de Malebayle bp. of Asti 1348; prov.
to Brembre 29 Apr. 1349 (*CPP.* I 157; *CPL.* III 274).
       William Wykeham   *For* 1362–? *read* 1362–1366.
       For Occ. . . . 165). *read* Bp. of Winchester 1366.

John Bacon   *For* 1384. *read* ?–1385.
    For Card. re-entered by 1385. *read* D. by 9 Dec. 1385, probably by 31
Oct. (Torre, MS. York Minster p. 773; cf. A.C. A2/27 f. 33).
Perinus Tomacelli (again)
    For Elected pope in 1389. *read* Pope Boniface IX 1389.
Richard Field
    Add at end of entry Preb. of Thame 1390.

p. 114 John Breton
    For D. by 12 Apr. . . . f. 98). *read* D. 6 Apr. 1465 (*Survey of Cath.* II 247;
A.C. A2/35 f. 98).

p. 115 Thomas Hill   *Add* B.Cn. & C.L.
    Edward Powell   *For* 1525–1535. *read* 1525–1534.
    For imprisoned 1535 *read* imprisoned 1534

p. 116 Elie Talleyrand de Périgord   *For* 1335–? *read* 1335–1364.
    For and thence yearly . . . s.a.). *read* and thence yearly till d., 17 Jan.
1364 (*Eubel* I 16).
John Buckingham
    After (*CPR. 1350–1354* p. 68). *insert* Buckingham became preb. of
Gretton by Oct.
Hugh de St. Martial *Add* of Tulle

p. 117 John Wakering   *For* 1406–1416. *read* 1406–1415.
    For Bp. of Norwich 1416. *read* Bp. of Norwich 1415.
    William Gray   *Delete* D.Th.
    George Neville   *For* 1454–1458. *read* 1454–1456/8.
    For Bp. of Exeter 1458. *read* Bp. of Exeter 1456; cons. 1458.
    John Chedworth   *For* 1458–1464. *read* 1458–1465.
    Add at end of entry Preb. of Sutton-cum-Buckingham 1465.
    Peter Courtenay   *For* D.C.L. *read* D.Cn.L.
    Adrian de Bardis   *Add* M. *and* B.C.L.
    For Occ. . . . s.a.). *read* D. by 21 Aug. 1519 (Salis., Reg. Audley f. 78).
    George Heneage   *For* B.C.L. *read* B.Cn.L.

p. 118 Anthony Bek   *Add* M. *and* D.Th.
    John Thoresby   *Add* B.C.L.
    Richard Lyntesford
    For CPL. V 72 *read* CPL. IV 72

p. 119 William Crawley   *Add* B.Cn.L.
    Thomas Loughborough *Add* M.
    John Smeton   *Add* M.

Robert Morton   *Delete* Lic.C.L.
William Banks   *Add* Lic.Cn.L.

p. 120 John Forneby   *For* 1512–? *read* 1512–1513.
          Add at end of entry Preb. Sanctae Crucis 1513.
        Nicholas Whitechurch
          Delete whole entry
        John Winchelsea   *Add* M. *For* 1311–? *read* 1311–1326.
          Add at end of entry Became Franciscan friar at Salisbury 1326 (A. G.
        Little, *Grey Friars in Oxford* (Oxford Hist. Soc., 1892) p. 223).
        Walter Seton
          Add at end of entry Occ. as a can. of Lincoln (probably this preb.) in 1331
        (*CPL.* II 329).
        Simon Islip   *Delete* Lic.Cn. & C.L.

p. 121 Simon Islip (again) *Delete* Lic.Cn. & C.L.
          For Abp. of Canterbury 1349. *read* Preb. of Ketton 1349.
        Henry Brauncewell
          For D. by 23 Feb. . . . f. 443). *read* D. 23 Feb. 1396 (*Survey of Cath.* II
        256; Reg. XI f. 443).
        Richard Hethe
          For Res. . . . f. 491b). *read* Preb. of Caistor 1415.
        John Southam   *Add* Lic.C.L.
        Richard Ingoldesby
          For D. by 31 May . . . f. 109b). *read* D. 26 Apr. 1448 (Reg. XVIII f.
        109b; *Desiderata Curiosa* p. 316).

p. 122 Thomas Spark
          For Res. . . . f. 20b). *read* Preb. of Welton Ryval 1504.
        William Atkins *or* Atkinson *Add* D.Th.
          For D. by 6 Nov. . . . f. 27b). *read* D. 8 Aug. 1509 (*Survey of Cath.* II
        257; Reg. XXIII f. 27b).
        Edward Lee   *Delete* D.Th. *For* 1512–1532. *read* 1512–1531.
          For Abp. of York 1532. *read* Abp. of York 1531.
        Christopher Plummar *Add* B.C.L.
        Robert Bridlington
          Add at end of entry Occ. as a can. of Lincoln (probably this preb.) in 1331
        (*CPL.* II 366).

p. 123 Walter London
          Add at beginning Occ. as a can. and preb. of Lincoln (possibly this preb.)
        6 March 1334 (*CPL.* II 521).
        Roger Nassington   *Add* M.
        John Haket   *Add* D.C.L.
        Nicholas Burton   *Add* B.C.L.

Thomas Colas   *For* B.C.L. *read* D.Cn. & C.L. *For* 1438–1439. *read* 1438.
    For Res. . . . f. 107b). *read* Preb. of Langford Manor in Nov.

p. 124 Richard Graystock
    Add at end of entry Probably to d., by May 1496 (York, Reg. Rotherham I f. 92).
James Whitstons   *Add* M. *and* D.Cn.L. *For* 1496–? *read* 1496–?[1]
William Skelton   *For* B.Th. *read* D.Th. *For* ?–1501. *read* ?–1501.[1]
Roger Rothwell
    For Res. . . . f. 289). *read* Preb. of Welton Ryval 1312.
    Add new footnote as follows:
1. Whitstons and Skelton may have exchanged this preb. for preb. of Gretton, see p. 68.

p. 125 Edmund Stafford   *For* D.C.L. *read* B.C.L.
Thomas Whiston   *Add* D.Cn.L.
Richard *or* Robert Hayman   *For* Richard *or* Robert *read* **Richard**
William Mason *For* 1492–? *read* 1492–1513.
    For Occ. . . . f. 26). *read* Preb. of Welton Ryval 1513.

p. 126 John Pope   *Add* M. *and* B.C.L.
Nicholas Whitchurch *Add* D.C.L. *For* ?–1312. *read* 1297–1312.
    Add at beginning Coll. 9 March 1297 (Reg. I f. 360b).
    For D. as preb. *read* D.
Roger Rothwell
    For Occ. . . . p. 549). *read* Occ. Sept. 1328–Sept. 1329 (Linc. Accounts, cited in *Eng. Sec. Caths.* p. 345).
John Acton   *For* 1329–1351. *read* 1329–1349.
    For D. by 29 March . . . f. 9b). *read* D. by Nov. 1349 (Reg. IX f. 159).
William Askeby *or* Scoter
    Add at end of entry Probably to d., 11 Nov. 1371/5 Jan. 1372 (Reg. XII f. 103b).
Edmund Stafford
    Add at end of entry Preb. of Welton Paynshall 1379–80.
Edward le Strange
    For Harrimere Drain *read* Stretham
Brian Willoughby
    For Res. *read* Res. this preb.

p. 127 William Hoper   *For* D.C.L. *read* D.Cn. & C.L.
Walter Sandwich   *Add* D.Cn. & C.L.
Vincent Clement   *For* 1452–? *read* 1452–1458.
    Add at end of entry Preb. of Stow Longa 1458.
Stephen Clos   *Add* B.Th.

p. 128   William Mason   *For* B.C.L. *read* D.Cn. & C.L.

           Thomas Lark   *Add* M. *and* D.C.L.

           Richard Skryven   *For* Skryven *read* Scrivener

           Robert Langton   *Delete* M. *and* D.C.L.

           William Bourbanks *For* Bourbanks *read* Bourbank *For* D.Cn. & C.L.
              read B.C.L.

p. 58   John Thomas

           Add at end of entry Probably ineffective as already preb. of Ketton

p. 102   Thomasius natus Petri comitis de Catansano   *For* Thomasius natus
           Petri comitis de Catansano *read* Thomas Ruffo, son of Peter count of
           Catansaro

           For Thomasius natus Petri comitis de Catansano *read* Thomas Ruffo

p. x   *Add to list of works in print:*
    Survey of Cath.   *Survey of . . . Cathedrals*, comp. Browne Willis. 3 vols. in 2. London, 1742.

p. 1   **Lewis de Charlton**   *For* D.Th. *read* Lic.Th.

p. 2   **John Gilbert**   *For* O.P., D.Th. *read* O.P., B.Th.
    Thomas Polton   *For* B.C.L. *read* B.Cn. & C.L.
    Reginald Boulers   *For* 1450–1452. *read* 1450–1453.
        For Trans. to Coventry and Lichfield 1452. *read* Trans. to Coventry and Lichfield 1453.
    John Stanbury   *For* D.Th. *read* O.Carm., D.Th.

p. 3   **Charles Booth**
        For Cons. 31 Nov. *read* Cons. 30 Nov.

p. 4   **John Baysham**   *Add* M. *and* B.Cn.L.

p. 5   **John Stanewey**   *Add* M. *and* B.C.L.
    James Goldwell   *Add* D.Cn. & C.L.
    Thomas Chaundeler
        For D. by 2 Nov. . . . . p. 198). *read* D. 2 Nov. 1490 (*ibid.* p. 198; *Survey of Cath.* I 534).
    Oliver King   *For* D.Cn.L. *read* D.Cn. & C.L.
    Gamaliel Clifton   *For* D.C.L. *read* D.Cn.L.
    Richard de Hertford *Add* M.

p. 6   **Richard Martyn**   *For* D.Cn.L. *read* B.Cn.L. *For* 1478, 1482. *read* ?–1483.
        For Bp. of St Davids, 1481, *read* Bp. of St Davids, 1482,
        Add at end of entry D. 1483 (*Emden, Reg. Ox.* II 1236).
    Thomas Morton   *For* B.C.L. *read* B.Cn. & C.L.

p. 7   **William son of Thomas le Mercer of Rosse** *Add* M.

p. 8   **Henry Martyn**
        For D. by 28 Jan. . . . . p. 336). *read* D. 27 Jan. 1524 (*Survey of Cath.* I 555; *Reg. Booth* p. 336).
    John de Swinfield   *Add* M.

Richard de Havering *For* 1311–1342. *read* 1311–1341.
> *For* D. by 14 Nov. 1342 (*CPL.* II 75). *read* D. by 22 July 1341 (*CPL.* II 551).

> *Add new entry after* **Richard de Havering**, etc., *as follows:*

M. Giles de Stamford 1341.
> By coll.; ordered by pope to resign, 22 July 1341 (*CPL.* II 551).

Thomas de Winchester   *Add* M.

p. 9   **Richard Talbot**   *Delete* B.Cn. & C.L.

Thomas Downe   *Add* M.
> *For* D. by 2 Apr. . . . p. 197). *read* D. 26 March 1489 (*ibid.* p. 197; *Survey of Cath.* I 540).

William Porter
> *For* D. by 6 Nov. . . . p. 338). *read* D. 5 Nov. 1524 (*Survey of Cath.* I 540; *Reg. Booth* p. 338).

Richard Benese   *Add* M. *and* B.Cn.L.

p. 10   **John de Ewe**   *Add* M.

Robert Upcote
> *For* Upcote became preb. *read* Upcote became treasurer

Footnote
> *For* Northleach, Glos.? *read* Probably Eastleach Martin, Glos.

p. 11   **Adrian de Bardis**   *Add* M.

Owen Pole   *For* D.Th. *read* D.Cn.L.

p. 12   **Nicholas Walwen**   *Add* M.

Nicholas Hereford   *Delete* D.Th.

p. 13   **John de Nottingham**
line 1 *For* Nottingham exch. . . . p. 538). *read* Nottingham exch. chanc'ship, preb. of Gaia Major in Lichfield and preb. in St George's chap., Windsor, c. 6 Jan. 1389 with Thomas Hanley for ch. of Cottingham, Yorks. (*CPR. 1385–1389* p. 538; Lichfield, Reg. VI (Scrope) f. 34b).

John Dylew   *Add* M. *and* B.Cn. & C.L.

Ralph Heathcott   *For* B.Cn. & C.L. *read* B.Cn.L.

James Bromwich   *Add* B.Cn.L.

p. 14   **Roger Albritrone**   *For* ?–1381. *read* ?–1382.
> *For* 20 Feb. 1381 *read* 20 Feb. 1382
> *For Reg. Gilbert* p. 123 *read Reg. Gilbert* p. 123; *Reg. of T. de Brantyngham*, ed. F. C. Hingeston-Randolph (London, 1901–6) I 76)

William de Borstall *For* 1381–? *read* 1382–1389.
> *For* By exch. Feb. 1381. *read* By exch. Feb. 1382. D. 12 Nov. 1389 (*Survey of Cath.* I 557).

Robert Jordan
> *For* D. by 1 Apr. . . . p. 182). *read* D. 11 Feb. 1466 (*ibid.* p. 182; *Survey of Cath.* 1 557).

William Chapmon *For* Chapmon *read* **Chapman**

p. 15   Robert Tehy
> *Add at end of entry* D. (as. preb.?) by Nov. 1506 (PCC 13 Adeane).

John Wardroper
> *Add at beginning* Occ. as a can. of Hereford (probably this preb.) by 1508 (*Reg. Mayew* p. 276).
> *For* (*Reg. Mayew* pp. 234, 283). *read* (*ibid.* pp. 234, 283).

p. 16   John de Waltham
> *For* Exch. 3 May *read* Exch. 8 May

Richard Judde
> *Add at beginning* Occ. as a can. of Hereford (probably this preb.) by 1491 (*Reg. Stanbury* p. ix).

p. 17   Simon de Northwood
> *For* (*CPL.* II 293) *read* (*CPL.* II 292)

Robert de Chikewell *Add* M.

William de Somerford *Add* D.C.L.

William Corne   *For* **Corne** *read* **Corfe**
> *For* Coll. to Corne *read* Coll. to Corfe

p. 18   William Dorset   *Add* D.C.L.

John de Ewe   *Add* M.

John Cateby   *Add* Lic.C.L.

John Barnet   *Add* M. *and* Lic.C.L.

p. 19   John Cateby (again) *Add* D.Cn.L.

John Bridbroke   *For* D.Cn.L. *read* Lic.Cn.L.

Thomas Mannynge *Add* D.Cn.L.

Edmund Audley   *Delete* M. *and* D.Th.

Richard Bromefeld
> *For* D. by 28 Oct. . . . p. 332). *read* D. 24 Oct. 1518 (*Survey of Cath.* 1 562; *Reg. Booth* p. 332).

Gamaliel Clifton   *For* D.C.L. *read* D.Cn.L.

Roger de Sevenake   *Add* M.

p. 20   John de Middleton   *Add* M. *and* D.Th.

Thomas Busshebury
> *For* D. by 31 March . . . p. 174). *read* D. 29 March 1409 (*Survey of Cath.* 1 563; *Reg. Mascall* p. 174).

Peter Carmelian   *Add* M.
> *For* (*Reg. Mayew* p. 234) *read* (*Reg. Mayew* p. 235)

Peter Vannes   *Add* M. *and* B.Th.
Roger de Sutton   *Add* D.C.L.

p. 21   John Paslewe   *Add* M. *and* B.Cn. & C.L.
Ralph Durward   *Add* M.
Richard Hewes   *Add* M.
Oliver King   *Add* M. *and* D.C.L.
Ralph Hauyes   *Add* M. *and* B.Cn.L.

p. 22   William Chell   *Add* B.Mus.
Nicholas Brydeport
     Add at end of entry Occ. as a can. of Hereford (probably this preb.) in 1399 (*Reg. Trefnant* p. 158).
John Dylew   *Add* M. *and* B.Cn. & C.L.

p. 23   Robert Kent   *Add* D.Th.
William Porter
     For D. by 6 Nov. . . . p. 338). *read* D. 5 Nov. 1524 (*Survey of Cath.* I 540; *Reg. Booth* p. 338).

p. 24   Nicholas Long   *Add* M.
John Elvet
     For (*Reg. Trefnant* p. 178) *read* (*Reg. Trefnant* p. 179)
Richard Jaquessone
     For D. by Dec. . . . 1011). *read* D. 23 Nov. 1497 (*Survey of Cath.* I 568).
William Buckmaster *Add* M. *and* D.Th.
Michael de Bereham *Add* M.

p. 25   John Prat
     For D. by 2 Apr. . . . p. 181). *read* D. 10 March 1416 (*Survey of Cath.* I 572; *Reg. Mascall* p. 181).
Thomas Mannynge   *Add* B.Cn.L.
Robert Keynell
     Add at end of entry Probably to d., by May 1483 (Lincoln, Reg. XXII (Russell) f. 223b).
Thomas Chaundeler
     For D. by 2 Nov. . . . p. 198). *read* D. 2 Nov. 1490 (*ibid.* p. 198; *Survey of Cath.* I 535).

p. 26   John Pole   *For* Pole *read* de la Pole
James de Henley
     Add at beginning Occ. as a can. of Hereford (probably this preb.) by 1317 (*Reg. Orleton* p. 42).
Robert Catesby   *Add* B.A.
Thomas Alcock   *Add* M.

Thomas de Lugore
> *Add at beginning* Occ. as a can. and preb. of Hereford (possibly this preb.)
> July 1306 (*CPL.* II 21).

Stephen de Thaneto
> *Add at end of entry* Occ. as a can. of Hereford (probably this preb.) Jan.
> 1316 (*ibid.* p. 505).

p. 27   **Itherius de Concoreto**   *For* B.C.L. *read* B.Cn. & C.L. *For* 1337. *read*
1331–?
> *Add at beginning* By prov. 20 Feb. 1331 (*CPL.* II 327).
> *Add at end of entry* Had married by 15 June 1343 (*CPP.* I 57).
> *This entry should now precede that of* **Laurence de St. Maur.**

John Rees   *Add* D.Cn.L.

Nicholas Kaerwent
> *For* Occ. 13 Nov. . . . p. 13). *read* Occ. 23 Dec. 1385 (*Reg. Gilbert* p. 87).

David ap Jake
> *Add at beginning* Occ. as a can. of Hereford (probably this preb.) by 1393
> (*Reg. Trefnant* p. 17).
> *For* (*Reg. Trefnant* p. 181) *read* (*ibid.* p. 181)

Reginald Wolstone   *Add* M. *and* B.Cn.L.

Robert Dobbys   *Add* D.Cn.L.

Robert Dobbys (again)   *Add* D.Cn.L.

John Olyver *or* **Smythe**   *For* 1512–1558. *read* 1512–1552.
> *For* D. by 8 Dec. . . . p. 58). *read* D. by 5 July 1552 (Salis., Reg. Capon
> f. 48; *Cant. Inst. Sede Vac.* p. 58).

p. 28   **Gilbert de Segrave**   *Add* M.
> *Add at beginning* Occ. as a can. and preb. of Hereford (probably this preb.)
> in 1306 (*CPL.* II 11).

Nicholas Hethe   *Delete* M.

William de Aston   *For* Aston *read* Ashton

John Walwyn
> *Add at end of entry* Occ. as a can. of Hereford (probably this preb.) in
> 1415 (*ibid.* p. 85).

p. 29   **John Cheyne**   *Delete* M.

p. 30   **John de Lech**   *For* D.Cn. & C.L. *read* D.Cn.L.

p. 31   **Hugh Holbach**   *Delete* M. *and* D.Cn.L.
> *For* and again 17 Dec. *read* and again 19 Dec.

Stephen Surteis   *Add* M. *and* B.Th.

Henry Martyn
> *For* D. by 28 Jan. . . . p. 336). *read* D. 27 Jan. 1524 (*Survey of Cath.* I
> 555; *Reg. Booth* p. 336).

p. 32 John de Olham *or* Eltham *For* John de Olham *or* Eltham *read* John de Elham

Henry de Resteshale of Campeden
  Add at beginning Expect. 9 June 1343 (*CPL.* III 130).
Roger de Sutton   *Add* D.C.L.
Richard Winchcombe *Add* M.

p. 33 Thomas Burton   *For* B.C.L. *read* B.Cn. & C.L.
John Breton
  For D. 28 May . . . Godyn). *read* D. 6 Apr. 1465 (*Survey of Cath.* II 247).
Adrian de Bardis   *Add* M.
Geoffrey Downes   *Add* M. *and* D.Th.
  After (Liber Primus f. 61). *insert* D. (as preb.?) by 20 July 1562 (York, Acta Capitularia 1559–1673 f. 11b).

p. 34 *Replace the first two entries by the following entry:*
Philip de Comite of Milan 1291.
Edward de Monte Martini 1307–?
  Philip de Comite occ. c. 1291 (*T.P.N.* p. 169). Bp's mand. adm. Edward de Monte Martini 5 June 1307, by virtue of prov. (*Reg. Swinfield* p. 440). Philip vac. a preb. of Hereford (possibly this one) 19 Aug. 1311 (*CPL.* II 87).
Thomas de Staunton *Add* B.C.L.
  Add at beginning Occ. as a can. of Hereford (probably this preb.) by 1346 (*Reg. Trillek* p. 373).

p. 36 John Catryk   *For* B.Cn. & C.L. *read* Lic.Cn.L.
Footnote 3
  For Langton by Spilsby, Lincs.? *read* Langton, Leics. (Lincoln, Reg. XVIII (Alnwick) f. 152).

p. 37 John de Orleton
  Add at end of entry Occ. as a can. of Hereford (probably this preb.) in 1340 (*CPL.* II 549).
John Hereford   *Delete* M.
John Home
  Add at end of entry D. (as preb.?) 26 Nov. 1473 (*Survey of Cath.* I 588).

p. 38 Richard de Bello   *Add* M.

p. 39 Simon Alcock
  For D. by 24 Aug. . . . p. 176). *read* D. 10 Aug. 1459 (*Reg. Stanbury* p. 176; *Survey of Cath.* I 590).
Roger de Northburgh *Delete* M.

p. 40 Richard Chester
  For with Elias de Holcote *read* with Elias Holcote
Elias de Holcote   *For* de Holcote *read* Holcote *For* M.A. *read* B.Th.
Ralph Hauyes   *Add* M. *and* B.Cn.L.

p. 41   John Abraham   *Add* M.
        Nicholas Hereford   *For* M.A. *read* D.Th.

p. 43   John de Excestre
            For with Walter Grote *read* with Walter Trote
        Walter Grote   *For* Grote *read* Trote
        Nicholas Hereford   *For* M.A. *read* D.Th.
        Walter Hylle   *Add* Sch.Th.

p. 44   Gamaliel Clifton   *For* D.C.L. *read* D.Cn.L.
        Hugh Charnock   *Add* M.
        William de Winterton *Add* M.
        Edmund Ryall
            For D. by 8 Apr. . . . . p. 354). *read* D. 7 Apr. 1428 (*Survey of Cath.* I
            592; *Reg. Spofford* p. 354).
        Thomas St. Just   *Add* D.Mus.

p. 45   John Yorke   *For* Yorke *read* Gorle
            For (*Reg. Booth* p. 345) *read* (*Reg. Booth* p. 345–'Yorke')
            For Preb. vac. . . . f. 133). *read* D. by 18 May 1552 (Lamb., Reg. Cranmer
        f. 133; *Valor* III 11; *Emden, Reg. Ox.* II 793).
        Michael de Bereham *Add* M.
        Richard de Havering
            Delete whole entry
        William of Edington *For* 1344–1346. *read* 1344–1345.
            For bp. of Winchester 1346 *read* bp. of Winchester 1345

p. 46   Richard de la Barre *Add* M.
        John Godmanston
            Add at end of entry Probably to d., by 18 June 1401 (London, Reg. Bray-
            broke f. 191b).
        Richard Talbot   *Delete* M.
        John Sebrond   *Add* M.
        Footnote
            For (cf. *CPL.* XIII i 446). *read* (cf. *CPL.* XIII i 446; *Reg. Myllyng* p. 192).

p. 47   John de Swinfield   *Add* M.
            Add new entry after John de Swinfield *as follows:*
        M. Richard de Havering ?–1341.
            Expect. 21 Nov. 1310 (*CPL.* II 80). Estate as preb. ratif. 10 Dec. 1330
        (*CPR. 1330–1334* p. 25). D. by 22 July 1341 (*CPL.* II 551).
        Giles de Stamford   *Add* M. *For* ?–1367. *read* 1341–1367.
            For Occ. 18 Nov. . . . p. 40). *read* By coll.; prov. 22 July 1341 (*CPL.* II
        551).

John Trefnant *or* ap Howell *Add* M. *and* B.C.L.

William Drokyll
  Add at end of entry Occ. 14 July 1463 (*Reg. Stanbury* p. 75).

p. 48 John Prat *For* B.Cn.L. *read* B.Cn. & C.L.

Richard de Hertford *Add* M.

Henry de Shorne
  Add at end of entry Occ. as a can. of Hereford (probably this preb.) in
  1332 (*Reg. T. Charlton* p. 91).

John de Offord *Add* D.C.L.

Humphrey de Charlton *Add* M. *For* B.Th. *read* D.Th.

Laurence Allerthorpe
  For D. by 22 July . . . p. 215). *read* D. 21 July 1406 (*Survey of Cath.* 1
  601; *Reg. Mascall* p. 169).

p. 49 William Kynwollmerssh *Delete* M. *and* B.Th.

John Grenewey *Add* B.C.L.

p. 50 John Walwyn
  After CPL. II 316 *insert* ; cf. *Select Cases* . . . *King's Bench*, ed. G. O.
  Sayles (Selden Soc., 1936–58) V 31–2

p. 51 James Goldwell *For* D.C.L. *read* D.Cn. & C.L.

Thomas Downe
  For D. by 2 Apr. . . . p. 197). *read* D. 26 March 1489 (*Reg. Myllyng* p.
  197; *Survey of Cath.* 1 540).

Ralph Hauyes *Add* M. *and* B.Cn.L.

p. 52 Richard de la Barre *Add* M.

John Trefnant *or* ap Howell *Add* M. *and* B.C.L.

John Cole *Add* M.

John Elton *or* Baker *Add* M. *and* B.Cn. & C.L.

p. viii *Add to list of works in print:*
Survey of Cath.   *Survey of . . . Cathedrals*, comp. Browne Willis. 3 vols. in 2. London, 1742.

p. 2 **Thomas Langton**   *For* B.Th. *read* D.Th., D.Cn.L.

p. 3 **John Capon** *or* **Salcote** *For* D.D. *read* D.Th.

p. 4 **Thomas Montacute**
    For occ. 5 Nov. . . . p. 9). *read* occ. 10 March 1383 (*CPR. 1381–1385* p. 237).

p. 5 **Robert de Bluntesdon** *Add* M.

p. 6 **John de Vyse**   *Add* M. *and* B.C.L.

p. 7 **John Robinson**   *Add* M. *and* B.C.L.
    Giles Hackluyt   *Add* M. *and* B.C.L.
    John de Kirkeby   *Add* M.
    Thomas Pays   *Add* M.
    Robert Ragenhull   *Add* Lic.C.L.

p. 8 **John Mackworth**   *For* Tredington, Worcs. *read* Tredington, Glos.

p. 9 **Robert de Ayleston** *For* 1331–? *read* 1331–1334.
    Add at end of entry D. 21 March 1334 (*Emden, Reg. Ox.* 1 83).

p. 11 **Robert Luffenham** *Add* M.

p. 12 **Simon Sydenham**   *For* D.C.L. *read* D.Cn. & C.L.
    William Alnwick   *Add* M. *and* D.C.L.
    Richard Caunton   *For* D.Cn. & C.L. *read* D.C.L.
    William Eure   *For* M.A. *read* B.Th.

p. 13 **Geoffrey Blythe**   *For* B.Th. *read* D.Th.

p. 15 **Boniface de Saluciis** *Add* M.
    Thomas de Staunton *Add* B.C.L.
    Adam Mottrum   *Add* M. *and* Lic.Cn.L.

p. 17 **William de Bosco** *Add* M.

p. 18 John Dogett *For* D.Th. *read* D.Th., D.Cn.L.

p. 19 Gaillard de la Motte *For* 1345. *read* 1345–1356.
Add at end of entry Treas'ship in dean's hands July 1351 (*CPR. 1350–1354* p. 132). Motte d. 20 Dec. 1356 (*Eubel* I 50).

p. 21 Richard Hilley *Add* B.Cn.L.

p. 23 Ralph Selby *For* D.C.L. *read* D.Cn. & C.L.

p. 24 Richard Croxton *Add* M.
Thomas Banaster of Eltisley *For* B.C.L. *read* B.Cn. & C.L.

p. 25 Edmund Bekenham *Add* D.Th.

p. 26 John Pinnock *Add* O.Can.S.A.   Bp. of Sidon.

p. 28 William Toly *Add* M.
Rigaud de Asserio *Add* M. *and* D.C.L.
Bertrand de Asserio *For* 1319–? *read* 1319–1337.
Add at end of entry Bertrand d. by July 1337 (Winchester, Reg. Orleton I f. 100Bb).

p. 29 John Gynewell *For* 1338–1347. *read* 1337–1347.
After (*CPL.* II 398, 532). *insert* Coll. 24 July 1337 (Winchester, Reg. Orleton I f. 100Bb).
Simon de Teramo *Add* D.C.L.

p. 31 John Payne *Add* M.
William Barton *Add* B.Cn.L.

p. 33 Robert Toneys
Add at end of entry D. (as preb.?) by 30 July 1526 (York, Acta Capitularia 1504–1543 f. 141).
Richard de Havering
For Occ. 26 Apr. 1317 *read* Prov. 12 Oct. 1306 of preb. formerly held by Master John de Havering, or claims thereto (*CPL.* II 19; cf. *ibid.* pp. 2, 15). Occ. as preb. 26 Apr. 1317
Robert Ragenhull *Add* Lic.C.L.

p. 34 John Barnby *Add* M.

p. 35 Robert de Ayleston
Add at end of entry Probably to d., 21 March 1334 (*Emden, Reg. Ox.* I 83).
John Godewyke *Add* D.C.L.

p. 36 Roger Harewell *Add* M. *and* B.C.L.
For Res. . . . f. 9b). *read* Preb. of Wilsford and Woodford 1428.
John Dogett *For* D.Th. *read* D.Th., D.Cn.L.

p. 37   John Geraud   *Add* M.
        David Calveley
             Add at end of entry Pardoned 8 Nov. 1384 (*CPR. 1381–1385* p. 481).

p. 39   John Piers   *Add* M. *and* D.C.L. *For* 1336–? *read* 1336–1344.
             Add at end of entry D. by 5 Oct. (*CPR. 1343–1345* p. 411).

p. 40   John Dogett   *For* D.Th. *read* D.Th., D.Cn.L.
        Thomas Mades   *Add* B.Th.

p. 41   John Pinnock   *Add* O.Can.S.A.   Bp. of Sidon.
        Robert Bysse   *For* D.C.L. *read* D.Cn. & C.L.

p. 42   Nicholas Domerham *Add* M.
        William Byde   *Add* M. and D.C.L.

p. 43   Thomas Danet
             For D. 19 Sept. . . . 1 540). *read* D. 18 Sept. 1483 (*Survey of Cath.* 1 445).
        Robert Booth   *Add* M.

p. 45   Peter Carmelian   *Add* M.

p. 47   Nicholas Wardeden
             Add at end of entry Occ. as a can. of Salisbury (probably this preb.) in
        1327 (*CPL.* ii 262).

p. 48   Richard Rawson   *For* D.Cn.L. *read* D.Cn. & C.L.

p. 49   John Pinnock   *Add* O.Can.S.A.   Bp. of Sidon.
        William de Excestre *For* D.Th. *read* D.M., B.Th.
        Henry de la Dale   *Add* M.
        Nicholas Hethe   *Delete* M.

p. 52   William Chauntry   *Add* M.

p. 53   Andrew Ammonius   *Add* M.

p. 54   John Southam
             For D. by 7 March . . . f. 34b). *read* D. 23 Feb. 1441 (Reg. Aiscough pt. i
        f. 34b; *Survey of Cath.* 1 111).

p. 55   John Fotehede   *Add* B.Th.
        John Rayne   *For* D.C.L. *read* D.Cn. & C.L.

p. 56   Matthew de Briselee
        line 2: *For* Briselee d. by 7 Aug. 1350 (*CPL.* iii 361). *read* Briselee d. by 8 Dec.
        1349 (*CPL.* iii 315, 361).

p. 57   Thomas Worston   *Add* M.

p. 58   William Barton   *Add* B.Cn.L.

p. 60   William Hayton   *Add* B.C.L.

p. 62   Christopher Bainbridge *For* 1486–1508. *read* 1486–1507.
            For Abp. of York 1508. *read* Bp. of Durham 1507.

p. 63   Adam Mottrum   *Add* M. *and* Lic.Cn.L.

p. 64   Edward Pole   *For* 1479–? *read* 1479–1485.
            Add at end of entry Res. by Jan. 1485 (Winchester, Reg. Waynflete II f.
            103).
            Adrian de Bardis   *Add* B.C.L.

p. 65   John Dunwich   *Add* M. *and* D.Cn.L.
            John Wardeyn   *Add* M.

p. 66   *Insert between* Ralph de Querendon *and* William de Ayston *the following
            name :*
            M. Nicholas Tyngewick   M.A. (again) 1337.
            After (Reg. Wyville I f. 11). *insert* Tyngewick in possession 8 Aug 1337
            (Salis. Cath. Arch. 4/1/1, cited in *Hemingby's Register*, ed. Helena M. Chew
            (Wiltshire Archaeol. and Nat. Hist. Soc., Records Branch, xviii, 1963) p.
            242); possibly until d., by Feb. 1339 (Reg. Wyville II i f. 62b).

p. 67   Robert Ragenhull   *Add* Lic.C.L.
            Oliver Dyneley   *Add* M.

p. 69   Walter Wyville
            After AC f. 10). *insert* Instal. 22 June 1335 (*ibid.* f. 64b).
            John de Kirkeby   *Add* M.

p. 70   Richard Payne   *Add* M. *and* B.Cn.L.

p. 71   Manuel de Fieschi   *Add* M.
            Add at beginning Occ. as a can. and preb. of Salisbury (possibly this
            preb.) in 1329 (*CPL.* II 314).
            Stephen la Porta   *For* 1346–1351. *read* 1345–1351.
            For La Porta instal. 22 May 1346 *read* Reservn. on behalf of La Porta
            1 Jan. 1345 (*CPL.* III 200); instal. 22 May 1346

p. 72   Thomas Rotherham *For* D.Th. *read* B.Th.

p. 73   Ralph Selby   *For* D.C.L. *read* D.Cn. & C.L.

p. 74   Hugh Dacre   *Add* D.Th., D.C.L.

p. 75   **John Rivers**
    For Ripley, Hants *read* Ripple, Worcs.
  John de Ravenser   *Add* M.
  William Clynt
    For D. by 23 March . . . f. 79). *read* D. 17 Feb. 1425 (*Survey of Cath.* II
84; Reg. Chaundeler pt. i f. 79).

p. 76   **Robert Aiscough**   *For* B.C.L. *read* D.C.L.
  John de Kirkeby   *Add* M.
  Robert Thresk   *Add* M.

p. 78   **William de Grandisson** *For* 1325, 1329. *read* ?–1330.
    Add at end of entry D. 5 June 1330 (*Reg. J. de Grandisson*, ed. F. C.
Hingeston-Randolph (Exeter, 1894–99) III 1277, 1280).
  William de Lardo   *Add* D.C.L.

p. 79   **Adrian de Bardis**   *Add* B.C.L.

p. 81   **John Chaundeler**   *Add* M.
    For Kent *read* Suss.

p. 83   **John Dogett**   *For* D.Th. *read* D.Th., D.Cn.L.
  William Barton   *Add* B.Cn.L.

p. 85   **Roger Lupton**   *For* D.Th. *read* D.Cn.L.

p. 87   **John Dowman**
    Add at end of entry D. (as preb.?) by 11 Nov. 1526 (London, Reg.
Tunstal f. 16).
    Replace the entries for **John Piers** *and* **John de Sarum** *by the following
entry:*
  M. **John de Sarum** *or* **John Pictoris** 1334–1350.
    Prov. at request of chapter 20 Feb. 1334 (Hemingby, AC f. 24; *CPL.* II
399 – 'John Pictoris'). Papal conf. 18 Oct. 1343 (*CPL.* III 112 – 'John Pictoris') and 17 June 1344 (*ibid.* p. 174 – 'John Sarum'). Estate ratif. 20 Oct.
1347 (*CPR. 1345–1348* p. 416). D. by 30 Dec. 1350 (*CPP.* I 205–6).

p. 89   **Bernard de Cucinaco**
    For Cucinaco d. by 27 Aug. *read* Cucinaco res. by 27 Aug.
    After CPL. III 241, 256 *insert* ; cf. *CPP.* I 286
  Thomas de Brembre
    Add at end of entry Brembre occ. as a can. of Salisbury (probably this
preb.) in 1357 (*CPL.* III 625). Probably until d., by Oct. 1361 (*CPR. 1361–
1364* p. 96).
  Roger Harewell   *Add* M. *and* B.C.L.

p. 90   **Geoffrey Blythe**   *For* B.Th. *read* D.Th.
  Robert de Bluntesdon *Add* M.

p. 94   Robert Ragenhull   *Add* Lic.C.L.
         Robert Aiscough   *For* M.A. *read* B.Cn.L.
         William Chauntry   *Add* M.

p. 95   Peter de Inkepen
         Add at end of entry Occ. as a can. of Salisbury (probably this preb.) in
         1347 (*ibid.* f. 6b).

p. 96   Richard Harewell   *For* Richard *read* Roger *Add* M. *and* B.C.L.

p. 98   Adam de Lakenhyth *Add* M. *and* B.Th.
         John Clerevaus   *Add* M. *and* B.Cn.L.
         Walter Easton   *Add* M. *and* B.Cn.L.
         Oliver Dyneley   *Add* M.
         John Moreton   *For* Moreton *read* Morton

p. 99   Leonard Say
         For D. by 29 Apr. . . . f. 47). *read* D. 25 Apr. 1493 (*Survey of Cath.* I 111;
         Reg. Langton pt. i f. 47).

p. 102   Nicholas Lambert
         Add at end of entry Occ. as a can. of Salisbury (probably this preb.) in
         1336 (Hemingby, AC f. 63).
         Richard Pittes   *Add* M.

p. 103   John Haket
         For D. by 14 Nov. . . . f. 52b). *read* D. 6 Oct. 1442 (*Survey of Cath.* II
         94; Reg. Aiscough pt. i f. 52b).

VOL. IV. MONASTIC CATHEDRALS
(*Southern Province*)

p. 3   **Thomas de Cobham** *Add* D.Th.

p. 7   **Hugh de Angoulême** *Add* M.
        Bernard Sistre   *Add* M.

p. 8   **Adam Mottrum**   *Add* M. *and* Lic.Cn.L.
        William Chichele   *Add* M.
        Thomas Chichele   *Delete* M. *and* D.Cn.L.
        Replace the entry for **Thomas Winterbourne** *by the following entry:*
        M. Thomas Winterbourne D.C.L. 1467–1479.
        M. Thomas Rotherham B.Th. 1467.
        Winterbourne occ. 25 Feb. 1467 (*Reg. Bourgchier* p. 288). Rotherham occ.
        June (*Wars of the English in France*, ed. J. Stevenson (R.S. 22) II 787). Bp. of
        Rochester 1468. Winterbourne d. before Feb. 1479 (*Reg. Bourgchier* p. 335).

p. 9   **John Bourgchier**   *Delete* D.Cn.L.
        For D. before 26 Nov. .... f. 159b). *read* D. 6 Nov. 1495 (*Survey of* . . .
        Cathedrals, comp. Browne Willis (London, 1742) II 121; Reg. Morton I
        f. 159b).
        Hugh Peynthwyn   *Add* M. *and* D.C.L.

p. 13   **Ralph de Walpole**   *Add* M. *and* D.Th.

p. 14   **John Buckingham**
        For El. of Buckingham, bp. of Lincoln, *read* El. of Buckingham
        Peter de Ely   *For* 1425. *read* 1426.
        William Alnwyk   *Delete* O.S.B.,

p. 15   **Thomas Bourgchier** *For* D.Th. *read* Sch.Th.

p. 17   **Ralph de Fodringhey** *Add* M.

p. 18   **Edward Burnell**   *Add* M.
        Thomas Dalby   *Add* M.
        Adam Mottrum   *Add* M. *and* Lic.Cn.L.

p. 23   **William de Ayremynne**
        For bp. of Vienne *read* abp. of Vienne
        William Bateman *or* de Norwyco *For* D.Cn. & C.L. *read* D.C.L. *For*
        1343–1355. *read* 1344–1355.

p. 24 William Alnwyk *Delete* O.S.B., *For* 1425–1436. *read* 1426–1436.

p. 26 William Spynke *Add* M. *and* B.Th.
Thomas de Skerning *Add* M.
Roger de Snetisham *Add* M.
William Bateman *or* de Norwyco *For* D.Cn. & C.L. *read* D.C.L.

p. 27 John Berenger *Add* M.
John de Middleton *Add* M.
William Westacre *Add* M. *and* Lic.Cn.L.
John Hals
 For Bp. of Coventry and Lichfield 1495. *read* Bp. of Coventry and Lichfield 1459.

p. 28 Thomas de Kerdeston
 Delete whole entry and insert new entry before R. de S. *as follows:*
M. Thomas de Kerdeston 1315.
 Occ. 8 March and 30 Apr. 1315 (*Select Cases . . . King's Bench*, ed. G. O. Sayles (Selden Soc., 1936–58) IV 64). Will referred to 28 Sept. 1326 (*CCR. 1323–1327* p. 619).

p. 29 John de Middleton *Add* M.
Ralph Selby *For* D.C.L. *read* D.Cn. & C.L.

p. 30 Simon de Creake *Add* M. *and* D.C.L.
Firmin de Lavenham *Add* M.
Gilbert de Marewell *or* Yarewell *Add* M.
Thomas de Winchester *Add* M.
Henry de la Zouche *Add* M.

p. 31 William Graa de Trusthope *For* B.C.L. *read* B.Cn. & C.L.
Thomas Hetersete
 For Gillingham, Wilts. *read* Gillingham, Dors.
Richard Maudeleyn *Add* M.
Eudo de la Zouche *Add* D.C.L.
Clement Denston *Add* M. *and* B.Th.
John Wiggenhall *For* D.C.L. *read* D.Cn.L.

p. 32 Thomas Shenkwyn *For* B.C.L. *read* D.C.L.
John Finneys *For* B.C.L. *read* B.Cn.L.
Richard Woleman *For* D.Th. *read* D.Cn.L.
William de Fieschi *or* de Flisco
 For D. before 28 Feb. 1357 *read* Exch. declared invalid by pope 28 Feb. 1357
Francis de St Maximo *For* St Maximo *read* Sancto Maximo

p. 33   William Graa de Trusthope *For* B.C.L. *read* B.Cn. & C.L.
         John de Ufford   *Add* M.
         John Clervaus   *Add* M. *and* B.Cn.L.
         Thomas de Shirford *Add* M.
         John Thorpe   *Add* M.
         William Pykenham
              For D. 7/19 Apr. *read* D. 6 Apr./8 May

p. 34   Richard Sampson   *For* D.C.L. *read* D.Cn. & C.L.

p. 37   William Wittlesey   *For* B.Cn. & C.L. *read* D.C.L. *For* 1360–1364. *read*
         1361–1364.

p. 38   Thomas Brinton   *For* D.Th. *read* D.Cn.L.
         William de Bottlesham *Add* M. *and* D.Th.
         John de Bottlesham *Add* Lic.Cn. & C.L.

p. 41   William Hunden   *Add* B.Cn. & C.L.

p. 42   Henry Edyall   *Add* M.
         Maurice Griffith   *Add* M. *and* B.Th., B.Cn.L.

p. 45   Henry Woodlock de Merewell *For* 1304–1316. *read* 1305–1316.
         Rigaud de Asserio   *Add* M. *and* D.C.L.

p. 47   Richard Fox   *For* D.Cn.L. *read* D.C.L.
         Henry Woodlock de Merewell *For* 1295–1304. *read* 1295–1305.
              For Bp. of Winchester 1304. *read* Bp. of Winchester 1305.
         Robert de Enford   *For* Robert *read* Richard

p. 48   Thomas de Skerning *Add* M.

p. 49   John Catryk *or* Ketterich *For* B.Cn.L. *read* Lic.Cn.L.

p. 50   Philip de St Austolo *or* Cornewayles *For* St Austolo *read* Sancto Austolo
         Philip Sapiti   *Add* M.

p. 51   John Pakenham   *For* D.Cn. & C.L. *read* B.Cn. & C.L.
         John Frost   *Add* B.Th.

p. 56   Wulstan de Bransford (again) *For* 1338–1349. *read* 1339–1349.
         John de Thoresby   *Add* B.C.L.
         William Wittlesey   *For* B.Cn. & C.L. *read* D.C.L.

p. 60   Walter de Burdon   *Add* M.
              For (Lamb., Reg. Reynolds f. 3b). *read* (Reg. Reynolds f. 3b).

William de Birstone
   For (Lamb., Reg. Reynolds f. 3b). *read* (Reg. Reynolds f. 3b).
Joceus de Kinebauton *Add* M. *and* D.Cn. & C.L.

p. 61   John de Uske   *Add* M.
       Richard de Ledbury *Add* M.
       Thomas de Stratford *Delete* B.C.L.
       William de Thirsford *Add* M.
       Richard Winchcombe *Add* M.
       Nicholas Herbury   *For* 1406–1428. *read* 1404–1428.
          For Coll. 5 Nov. 1406 *read* Coll. 5 Nov. 1404
       Geoffrey Blythe   *Delete* D.Th.

p. 62   Peter Carmelian   *Add* M.
       Nicholas Wooton   *Add* M. *and* D.C.L.
       Henricus filius Imberti Delphini de Vienna *For* Henricus filius Imberti
       Delphini de Vienna *read* Henry Delphinus, son of Imber, of Vienne
       John Blanchard   *Add* M.

p. 63   Robert Inkbarrow   *Add* M.
       Richard Burton   *Add* B.C.L.

VOL. V. ST PAUL'S, LONDON

p. viii   *Add to list of works in print:*
    Survey of Cath.   *Survey of . . . Cathedrals*, comp. Browne Willis. 3 vols.
    in 2. London, 1742.

p. 1   **Stephen de Gravesend**
    Add at beginning Lic. el. 1 Sept. 1318 (A/60/40).
    For El. 11 Sept. 1318 *read* El. 1 Sept.

p. 7   **Richard Sampson**   *For* D.C.L. *read* D.Cn. & C.L.

p. 8   **Thomas Baketon**   *Add* D.C.L.

p. 11   **Richard Rawson**   *For* D.Cn.L. *read* D.Cn. & C.L.

p. 13   **E—**   *For* E— *read* E—[1]
    Richard de Newport
    For (A/66/14).[1] *read* (A/66/14).[2]
    William de Meleford *Add* M.
    Richard de Plessis
    For Occ. . . . 275). *read* Occ. 4 Apr. 1345 (*Cal. Letter Books, City of London,
Book F*, ed. R. R. Sharpe (London, 1904) p. 135).
      Add new footnote as follows:
    1. Possibly Giles (Egidius) Filliol, who occ. as archdcn. 15 May 1298 (WD 1
f. 70).
    Footnote 1
      For 1 *read* 2

p. 14   **John Clerke**   *For* D.Cn. & C.L. *read* D.Cn.L.

p. 15   **John Doneys**   *Add* M.

p. 16   **Thomas Danet**
    For D. by 18 Sept. . . . f. 196). *read* D. 18 Sept. 1483 (*ibid.* f. 196; *Survey
of Cath.* 1 445).

p. 18   **Robert de Clothale**   *For* 1309, 1319. *read* 1308, 1319.
      For 3 July 1309 (A/24/1367) *read* March 1308 (P.R.O., C 85/119/6)
    Thomas de Wilton   *For* B.Th. *read* D.Th.
    Thomas Young   *Add* M. *and* Lic.Cn. & C.L.

p. 19   **John Godmanston**   *Add* M.

p. 20   **William de Borstall**
         Add at end of entry D. (as preb. ?) 12 Nov. 1389 (*Survey of Cath.* I 557)

p. 23   **John Doneys**   *Add* M.

p. 25   **Laurence Allerthorpe**
         For D. by 25 July . . . p. 215).[1] *read* D. 21 July 1406 (*Survey of Cath.* I
         601; *CPR. 1405–1408* p. 215).[1]

p. 27   **William de Waltham** *Add* B.C.L.

p. 28   **Clement Denston**   *For* B.Cn.L. *read* B.Th.
         Richard Layton
             For 18 Oct. *read* 17 Oct.
         Thomas de Northflete *Add* M.
         John Barnet
             After William de Hoo. *insert* Instal. as can. (possibly this preb.) 1340–1
         (A/52/14).

p. 30   **John Isaak**   *Add* M. *and* B.Cn.L.
         William Bryan   *Add* M.
         John Notyngham   *For* 1406–1419. *read* 1406–1418.
             For D. by 20 Feb. . . . 61). *read* D. 20 Dec. 1418 (*Survey of Cath.* I 84;
         WD 13 f. 64A/61).

p. 31   **Robert Newbald**
             Add at end of entry Newbald d., probably as preb., by 15 July 1473 (*Reg.
         of R. Stillington and R. Fox*, ed. H. C. Maxwell-Lyte (Somerset Record Soc.,
         lii) p. 100).
         Richard Sampson   *For* D.C.L. *read* D.Cn. & C.L.

p. 34   **Peter Carmelian**   *Add* M.
         Rigaud de Asserio   *Add* M. *and* D.C.L.

p. 35   **Thomas de Aston**   *Add* B.Cn.L.

p. 37   **John Hill**   *For* B.Cn.L. *read* B.C.L.

p. 38   **Walter de Thorp**   *For* ?–1319/20. *read* ?–1319/21.
             For 8 Jan. 1320 *read* 8 Jan. 1321

p. 44   **Adam Holme**   *Add* B.C.L.

p. 45   **Peter de Dene**
             After Giles Filliol *delete* , who d. 1298 (*Emden, Reg. Ox.* II 684)

p. 47   **John Bourchier**
             For D. by 23 Nov. . . . f. 18). *read* D. 6 Nov. 1495 (*Survey of Cath.* II 121;
         Reg. Hill f. 18).

William de Meleford   *Add* M.
Nicholas de Hethe   *Delete* M.

p. 49   **John de Swinfield**   *Add* M.

p. 50   **Brian Higdon**
     For D. as preb. .... f. 42). *read* D. as preb. 5 June 1539 (*Survey of Cath.*
     I 69; Reg. Stokesley f. 42).

p. 52   **John Young**
     For D. by 29 Apr. .... f. 64). *read* D. 26 Apr. 1516 (*ibid.* f. 64; *Survey of*
     Cath. I 69).

p. 53   **Thomas de Aston**   *Add* B.Cn.L.
     John Bernyngham
     For D. by 27 May ... f. 48b). *read* D. 23 May 1457 (*ibid.* f. 48b; *Survey*
     of Cath. I 85).

p. 54   **Robert de Ross**   *Add* M.

p. 55   **William Bryan**   *Add* M.

p. 56   **Thomas de Segrave** *Add* M. *and* D.C.L.

p. 58   **William de Coloinge** *Add* M.
     Thomas Arderne   *For* B.Th. *read* B.Cn.L.
       For ibid. ff. 128, 130 *read ibid.* ff. 129, 130
     John Hill   *For* B.Cn.L. *read* B.C.L.

p. 60   **Robert Bradegare**   *Add* M.
     John Morgan   *For* D.C.L. *read* B.Cn.L.

p. 64   *Add new entry after* **Bartholomew de Ferentino** *as follows:*
     M. John de Ewe   ?–1328.
       Exch. this preb. 19 July 1328 with Laurence Fastolf for deanery of St
     Chad's colleg. ch., Shrewsbury (Lichfield, Reg. II (Northburgh) f. 206).
     Laurence Fastolf   *For* 1354. *read* 1328–?
       Add at beginning By exch. July 1328.
       Delete Occ. in catalogue ... f. 60b/67b).
       For Occ. as preb. *read* Occ.

p. 65   **Robert Wytton**   *For* D.C.L. *read* D.Cn.L.
     Elias de Holcote   *For* de Holcote *read* Holcote
     William Woodcock   *For* Lic.M. *read* Inc.M.

p. 66   **William de Chaddleshunt** *Add* M. *and* D.C.L.
     Reginald de Sancto Albano *Add* M.

p. 67   **William Alnwick**   *Add* M. *and* D.C.L.

p. 68   **John Hill**   *For* B.Cn.L. *read* B.C.L.

p. 69   **Humphrey de la Pole** *Add* M. *and* D.C.L.

p. 70   **Thomas Baketon**   *Add* D.C.L.

p. 71   **William Worsley**   *For* B.Cn.L. *read* D.C.L.

(*York, Carlisle and Durham*)

p. vii   *Add to list of works in print:*
Emden, *Reg. Camb.*   *Biographical Register of the University of Cambridge to*
1500, comp. A. B. Emden. Cambridge, 1963.

p. viii   *Survey of Cath.*   *Survey of . . . Cathedrals,* comp. Browne Willis. 3 vols.
in 2. London, 1742.

p. 4   **Philip Morgan**   *For* 1423–1424. *read* 1424.

p. 5   **George Neville**   *For* 1464–1476. *read* 1465–1476.

p. 8   **William Felter**
   For D. 6/10 Apr. . . . 115). D. 10 Apr. 1451 (*Survey of Cath.* I 68).
James Harrington   *Add* M.
John Young
   For D. 25 Apr./2 May . . . f. 82). *read* D. 26 Apr. 1516 (*Survey of Cath.*
I 69).

p. 9   **John Rykynghale**   *For* M.Th. *read* D.Th.
John Kexby
   For D. before 30 June . . . f. 77b).[1] *read* D. 30 May 1452 (*Survey of Cath.*
I 79; Reg. Kempe f. 77b).[1]

p. 10   **Thomas de Cobham**   *For* D.Cn.L. *read* D.Th., D.Cn.L.

p. 11   **William Eure**   *Add* B.Th.

p. 12   **John Hert**   *For* B.C.L. *read* B.Cn.L.
   For D. 3/12 Dec. . . . f. 13). *read* D. 8 Dec. 1495 (*Survey of Cath.* I 75).
William Langton
   For D. before 18 Nov. . . . f. 108). *read* D. 10 Nov. (*Survey of Cath.* I 75;
Reg. Rotherham I f. 108).
Martin Colyns   *For* B.Cn.L. *read* D.Cn.L.
Edward Kellet
   For D. before 19 Sept. . . . 228). *read* D. 5 Sept. 1539 (*ibid.* ff. 227b–228;
Survey of Cath. I 76).
Robert de Baldock   *For* D.C.L. *read junior*

p. 13   line 6 *Delete* Probably ineffective . . . patron, 1326.
      Francis son of Neapoleo Orsini
         For Orsini occ. as treasurer . . . pp. 156, 367). *read* Orsini occ. as treasurer
      25 Apr. 1348 (*CPL.* III 269).
      Anibaldus Gaetani de Ceccano *Delete* M.Th.
      John de Clifford   *Add* Lic.C.L.

p. 14   **John de Neweton**   *Add* M. *and* D.C.L.
      Richard Pittes   *Add* M.
      John de Nottingham
         For D. 20/22 Dec. . . . f. 66). *read* D. 20 Dec. 1418 (*Survey of Cath.* I 84;
      Reg. Bowet I f. 66).
      John Berningham
         For D. 30 March/27 May . . . 284). *read* D. 23 May 1457 (*Survey of
      Cath.* I 85).
      Martin Colyns   *For* B.Cn.L. *read* D.Cn.L.
         For D. before 1 Apr. . . . f. 52). *read* D. 4 Feb. 1509 (*Survey of Cath.* I 86;
      Reg. Bainbridge f. 52).

p. 15   **Launcelot Colyns**
         For D. before 9 Apr. . . . f. 70b). *read* D. 8 Apr. 1538 (*Survey of Cath.*
      I 86; Reg. Lee f. 70b).

p. 16   **Ralph de Selby**   *For* D.C.L. *read* D.Cn. & C.L.
      Richard Arnall   *Add* M. *and* B.C.L.

p. 17   **Thomas Pearson**
         For D. before 24 Dec. . . . f. 104). *read* D. 28 Oct. 1490 (*ibid.* I f. 104;
      Survey of Cath. I 89).
      Edward Grisacre
         For D. 18 March/3 Apr. . . . 37). *read* D. 31 March 1504 (*Survey of Cath.*
      I 89).
      James Harrington   *Add* M.

p. 19   **Henry Carnebull**   *Add* M.
      Innocent de Fieschi
         For preb. of Clonmetham *read* preb. of Clonmethan

      See also p. 73.

p. 20   **Richard Pittes**   *Add* M.

p. 21   **William Pelleson**
         For D. 24 Aug./14 Sept. . . . 239). *read* D. 28 Aug. 1434 (*Survey of Cath.*
      I 102).
      William Duffield
         For D. 2 Feb./11 March . . . 28b). *read* D. 7 March 1453 (*Survey of Cath.*
      I 102; Reg. W. Booth f. 27b).

William Brande　　　*Add* M.
Thomas Crossley　　　*Add* M.
John Reynald　　　　*For* B.C.L. *read* B.Th., B.Cn.L.

p. 23　William de Waltham (again) *Add* B.C.L.
　　　Henry Carnebull　　*Add* M.

p. 24　　　*Replace the entries for* Gilbert de Alberwick *and* Manuel de Fieschi *by the following entry:*
　　　M. Gilbert de Alberwick M.A. 1328–?
　　　M. Manuel de Fieschi 1329–1331.
　　　　　Coll. to Alberwick 12 July 1328; adm. 4 Aug. (Reg. Melton ff. 363, 363b). Prov. to Fieschi 20 Dec. 1329; prov. conf. 15 Feb. 1330, with dispensation for plurality (*CPL.* II 314, 317). Mand. adm. 27 March (Reg. Melton f. 369). Exch. archdcnry with Anibaldus Gaetani for preb. of Milton Manor, Lincoln, 10 Sept./23 Nov. 1331 (*CPL.* II 359; Reg. Melton f. 375b).
　　　Anibaldus Gaetani de Ceccano *Delete* M. *and* M.Th.

p. 25　Thomas Crossley　　*Add* M.

p. 26　Thomas Dalby　　　*Add* M.

p. 27　Thomas Dalby
　　　　For D. before 13 Feb. . . . f. 138). *read* D. 26 Jan. 1526 (*ibid.* f. 138b; *Survey of Cath.* I 97).
　　　Manuel de Fieschi　*Add* M.
　　　Henry de la Zouche　*Add* M.

p. 29　Peter Carmelian　　*Add* M.
　　　John Southam
　　　　For D. 18/21 March . . . 253). *read* D. 23 Feb. 1441 (*Survey of Cath.* I 111).

p. 30　William Felter　　　*For* 1442–1451. *read* 1441–1451.
　　　　For Coll. 28 Feb. 1442 *read* Coll. 28 Feb. 1441
　　　John Reynald　　　*For* B.C.L. *read* B.Th., B.Cn.L.
　　　Martin Colyns　　　*For* B.Cn.L. *read* D.Cn.L.

p. 31　*See* p. 73 *below*

p. 32　Richard Arnall　　　*Add* M. *and* B.C.L.
　　　John Sendale　　　*Add* M.
　　　William Brande　　　*Add* M.

p. 33　William de Ferriby
　　　　For Exch. preb. with William de Wodehouse *read* Exch. preb. with Walter de Wodehouse
　　　William de Wodehouse *For* William *read* Walter *Add* M.

p. 34   Elias Holcote   *For* M.A. *read* B.Th.
         Thomas Hope   *For* D.Cn.L. *read* D.C.L.

p. 35   Thomas de Neville[1] *For* Neville[1] *read* Neville
         Simon de Multon   *Add* M. *and* D.C.L.
         Footnote 1
              Delete whole footnote

p. 36   John Booth   *For* B.C.L. *read* Lic.C.L.
         Thomas Chaundeler
              For D. before 18 Nov. . . . f. 104). *read* D. 2 Nov. 1490 (*Survey of Cath.*
         I 534; Reg. Rotherham I f. 104).

p. 37   John de Wodehouse *Add* M.

p. 38   Oliver King   *For* D.Cn. & C.L. *read* Lic.C.L.
         John Hert   *For* B.C.L. *read* B.Cn.L.

p. 40   William Malster   *For* B.Cn.L. *read* Lic.Cn.L.

p. 41   John Gisburn   *For* 1459–1482. *read* 1459–1481.
              For D. before 28 Jan. . . . f. 175b). *read* D. 11 Nov. 1481 (*ibid.* f. 175b;
         Survey of Cath. I 127).
         Martin Colyns   *For* B.Cn.L. *read* D.Cn.L.
         James Harrington   *Add* M.
         John Young
              For D. 25 Apr./2 May . . . f. 82). *read* D. 26 Apr. 1516 (*Survey of Cath.*
         I 69).

p. 42   Nicholas de Hethe   *Delete* M. *For* Hethe *read* Hethe[2]
         Henry de la Zouche *Add* M.
         Nicholas de Hethe (again) *For* Hethe (again) *read* Hethe[2]
              Add new footnote as follows:
         2. There appear to be two men named Nicholas de Hethe. One held various
         prebends from 1343, and occurs as *magister* from 1357. The younger man
         occurs from 1382, is called *magister*, and died in 1390 (*Emden, Reg. Camb.*
         p. 302).

p. 43   William de Waltham *Add* B.C.L.

p. 44   Henry de la Dale   *Add* M.
         Ralph de Selby   *For* D.C.L. *read* D.Cn. & C.L.

p. 45   Richard Ronhale   *Add* M. *and* Lic.C.L.
         William Felter
              For D. 6/10 Apr. . . . 115). *read* D. 10 Apr. (*Survey of Cath.* I 68).

p. 46   John de Neweton   *Add* M. *and* D.C.L.
         William de Waltham *Add* B.C.L.

p. 48   Thomas de Cobham *For* D.Cn.L. *read* D.Th., D.Cn.L.

p. 49   Adam Mottrum   *Add* M. *and* Lic.Cn.L.
         Hugh Hanworth
              For D. before 8 March . . . f. 67). *read* D. 7 March 1419 (*Survey of Cath.*
         II 128; Reg. Bowet I f. 67).
         John Langton   *For* D.C.L. *read* B.Cn.L.
         Robert Ascough   *For* D.Th. *read* B.Th.
         William Malster   *For* B.Cn.L. *read* Lic.Cn.L.

p. 51   Richard Pittes   *Add* M.
         John Rykynghale   *For* M.Th. *read* D.Th.
         John Hert   *For* B.C.L. *read* B.Cn.L.

p. 54   Nicholas de Welton *Add* M.

p. 55   Richard de Wynwyk *Add* M.
         Richard Pittes   *Add* M.

p. 56   Nicholas Chauntrell *Add* M.
         William de Wodehouse *For* William *read* Walter *Add* M.
         John de Ravenser   *Add* M.

p. 57   William Brande   *Add* M.

p. 59   John Alcock   *Add* M. *and* D.Cn.L.
         Thomas de Neville   *Add* M.
         Thomas de Neville[1] (again) *For* Neville[1] *read* Neville *Add* M.
         For 1352–1361. *read* 1352–1363.
              For D. before . . . 374). *read* D. 1363 (*Emden, Reg. Ox.* II 1351).
         Footnote 1
              Delete whole footnote

p. 60   *Replace the entries for* Androynus de la Roche *and* William de Dalton
         by the following entry:
         William de Dalton 1363–1371.
              Adm. 22 Aug. 1363 after prov. (Reg. Thoresby f. 55b). D. before 9 July
         1371 (*ibid.* f. 73b).
         Thomas Greenwood
              For D. before 3 May . . . f. 72). *read* D. 2 May 1421 (*Survey of Cath.* I
         146; Reg. Bowet I f. 72).
         William Alnwyk   *For* O.S.B., D.C.L. *read* D.C.L.

p. 61   Geoffrey Wrenne
              For D. before 22 Apr. . . . f. 144). *read* D. 5 Apr. 1527 (*ibid.* f. 144; *Survey
         of Cath.* I 432).

p. 62 Eudo de la Zouche *Add* D.C.L.

p. 63 Richard Arnall *Add* M. *and* B.C.L.
       Thomas Barrowe *For* D.C.L. *read* Lic.C.L.
       Thomas Mercer
            For D. before 9 Jan. . . . f. 30b). *read* D. 8 Jan. 1547 (*Survey of Cath.* I
       150; A.C. 1543–1558 f. 30b).

p. 67 Robert de Stretton *Add* M. *and* D.C.L.
       John Bernard *Add* M. *and* Lic.C.L.

p. 68 John Blithe *Delete* D.C.L.
       Henry Carnebull *Add* M.

p. 70 Richard Gabriel *For* D. or res. *read* Res.

p. 71 William de Prés *Add* M. *For* de Prés *read* de Prato
       Nicholas de Ros *Add* M.
       Anthony de St Quintin *Add* M.

p. 74 John de Bottlesham *Add* Lic.C.L.
       Edward Fox *Delete* D.Th.

p. 75 Hugh de Angoulême *Add* M.

p. 76 Thomas de la Warre *Add* M.

p. 78 John Berenger of Ypres *Add* M.
       Adam de Holme *Add* M. *and* B.C.L.

p. 79 William de Beverley *Add* M.

p. 80 John Reynald *For* B.C.L. *read* B.Th., B.Cn.L.
       Thomas Dalby
            For D. before 13 Feb. . . . f. 138). *read* D. 26 Jan. 1526 (*ibid.* f. 138;
       Survey of Cath. I 97).

p. 82 William de Wodehouse *For* William *read* Walter *Add* M.

p. 83 Thomas Dalby *Add* M.
       Richard Colhame *Add* M.
       William Pelleson
            For D. 24 Aug./14 Sept. . . . 239). *read* D. 28 Aug. 1434 (*Survey of
       Cath.* I 102).
       Thomas Gange *For* Gange *read* Gawge

p. 84 John Hert *For* B.C.L. *read* B.Cn.L.
       John Curwen *Add* M.
       Nicholas Miles *Add* M.

p. 85   **Lawrence Allerthorp**
        For D. before 24 June . . . p. 205). *read* D. 21 July 1406 (*Survey of Cath.*
I 601).
        Richard Colhame   *Add* M.

p. 86   **Robert Wellington**   *Add* M.

p. 89   **John Sendale**   *Add* M.
        William Brande   *Add* M.

p. 90   **Anibaldus Gaetani de Ceccano** *Delete* M.Th.

p. 92   **Francis son of Neapoleo Orsini**
        Delete Orsini occ. . . . III 252).

p. 93   **John de la Pole**
        For D. before 11 Feb. . . . f. 55). *read* D. 4 Feb. 1416 (*Survey of Cath.* I
179; Reg. Bowet 1 f. 55).
        William Duffield
        For D. 2 Feb./11 March . . . 28b). *read* D. 7 March 1453 (*Survey of Cath.*
I 102; Reg. W. Booth f. 28b).

p. 94   **Gamalial Clifton**   *For* B.Cn.L. *read* B.C.L.
        Walter de Burton   *For* M.A. *read* D.Th.

p. 97   **John de Horncastle**   *For* 1352. *read* 1353.

p. 98   **William Strickland**   *For* 1395. *read* 1396.

p. 99   **John Kite**   *Add* B.Cn.L.

p. 100   **Thomas Hathwaite**
        For Cumberland County Record Office, Mounsey-Hayford Collection
read Cumb. and Westmld. County Record Office, Mounsey-Heysham
Collection
        Thomas Gudybour
        Add at end of entry 'Thomas' prior of Carlisle occ. 20 Sept. 1487 (Cumb.
and Westmld. County Record Office, Ca/2/70).

p. 102   **Stephen Close**   *Add* M. *and* B.Th. *For* ?–1470. *read* 1452, 1480/1.
        For D. 1470 . . . 115)[3]. *read* Occ. 1480/1 (Cumb. and Westmld. County
Record Office, DRC 2/14, bps' accounts 1480/1).
        Cuthbert Conyers   *Add* M. *and* D.Cn.L. *For* 1510. *read* 1510, 1511.
        Rewrite whole entry as follows:
        Instituted to ch. of Great Salkeld[3] 1509/10 (Cumb. and Westmld. County
Record Office, DRC 2/23, bps' accounts 1509/10). Occ. as archdcn. 6 May
1511 (*ibid.*, Musgrave Deed, unnumbered).

William Bourbank   *For* William Bourbank[5] *read* William Burbank[4]
Add D.Cn.L.

Footnote 3	*Footnote 4*	*Footnote 5*
Delete whole footnote	*For 4 read 3*	*For 5 read 4*

p. 111 John Aukland   *Add* M. *For* O.S.B. *read* O.S.B., D.Th.
Thomas Castell   *Add* M. *For* O.S.B. *read* O.S.B., D.Th.
Thomas de Goldesburgh *Add* M.

p. 112 Thomas de Neville   *Add* M. *For* 1334–1361. *read* 1334–?
        Delete D. before 11 Aug. . . . f. 129).
James Orsini
        For (*Eubel* I 22)[2]. *read* (*Eubel* I 22).
        Add new entry after James Orsini *as follows:*
M. William *or* Mundy de Basingstoke 1379.
        Coll. 17 Aug. 1379 (Reg. Hatfield f. 160A).
Alan de Newark   *Add* B.C.L.
Footnote 2
Delete whole footnote

p. 113 Thomas Rotherham *For* D.Th. *read* B.Th.

p. 114 William de Beverley *Add* M.
John de Dalton   *Add* M.
John Rykynghale   *For* M.Th. *read* D.Th.
John Akum   *Add* Lic.Th.
John Rykynghale (again) *For* M.Th. *read* D.Th.

p. 115 Robert Burton   *For* M.Th. *read* D.Th.

p. 19   Thomas Winter
        For D. before 26 June *read* Res. before 26 June

p. 31   William de Boudon
        For CPR. *1321–1324* p. 321 *read* CPR. *1321–1324* p. 331

p. 6   John Goldiff   *For* 1512. *read* ?–1513.
        For Preb. of Highleigh . . . 1518. *read* Exch. 31 Aug. 1513 with Thomas
        Gronowe for ch. of Broughton Gifford, Wilts. (Salis., Reg. Audley f. 62).
        Thomas Gronowe   *Add* B.C.L. *For* ?–1532. *read* 1513–1532.
        For Occ. . . . f. 101). *read* By exch. Aug. 1513.

p. 8   John de Lacy
        Add at end of entry Probably to d., 23 Dec. 1301 (*Reg. of S. Gandavo*, ed.
        C. T. Flower and M. C. B. Dawes (Canterbury and York Soc., xl, xli) II 609)

p. 9   Richard Brakenburgh *Add* B.C.L.

p. 13   Robert Chapell   *Add* D.Th.

p. 14   Anthony Wayte   *Add* M.

p. 15   Robert de Tresk   *Add* M.
        Thomas de Wormenhale *Add* M. *For* B.Cn.L. *read* B.Cn.L., Lic.C.L.

p. 18   William Welles   *Add* M.

p. 19   William Toly   *Add* M.

p. 20   Adrian de Bardis   *Add* B.C.L.

p. 21   William Talbot   *Add* D.Cn.L.

p. 22   Robert Chapell   *Add* D.Th.

p. 26   Thomas Mercer
        For D. by 19 March . . . f. 41b). *read* D. 8 Jan. 1547 (Reg. Day f. 41b;
        Survey of . . . Cathedrals, comp. Browne Willis (London, 1742) I 150).

p. 27   Richard Darrell   *Add* B.C.L.

p. 28   John Godmanston   *Add* M.

p. 29   Thomas Danet
        For D. (as preb. ?) . . . f. 196). *read* D. (as preb. ?) 18 Sept. 1483 (*Survey
        of . . . Cathedrals*, comp. Browne Willis (London, 1742) I 445).

William Underhill *For* William *read* John
   For (Reg. FitzJames f. 37). *read* (Reg. FitzJames f. 37 – 'William Under-
hill').
   Delete – 'John Underhill'

p. 31 William de Wittlesey *For* ?–1360. *read* ?–1361.
   For Bp. of Rochester 1360. *read* Bp. of Rochester 1361.

p. 41 John Doneys   *Add* M.

p. 49 John Kyte   *Add* B.Cn.L.

p. 51 Richard Shirley   *Add* M.

p. 52 Edmund Lichfield   *Add* B.Th.
       Edward Wylsford   *For* Edward *read* Edmund
       Richard Rawson   *For* D.Cn.L. *read* D.Cn. & C.L.
       Footnote
          After to that date. *insert* He probably d. by Feb. 1423 (*Emden, Reg. Cantab.*
       pp. 329–30).

p. 54 Andrew Swynowe   *Add* M. *and* B.Th.

p. 56 William de Bosco   *Add* M. *and* D.Th.
       Walter de Buxton   *Add* M.

p. 57 Nicholas de Hethe   *Delete* M.

VOL. VIII. BATH AND WELLS DIOCESE

p. ix   *Add to list of works in print :*
     Collinson   J. Collinson, *History . . . of Somerset*. 3 vols. Bath, 1791.

p. x   *Survey of Cath.*   *Survey of . . . Cathedrals*, comp. Browne Willis. 3 vols. in 2. London, 1742.

p. 1   **William de Marcia**   *For* 1292–1302. *read* 1293–1302.
     Walter de Haselschawe *Add* M.

p. 3   **John Clerke**   *For* D.C.L. *read* D.Cn.L.
     Walter de Haselschawe *Add* M.
     Wibert de Lutleton   *Delete* B.C.L.

p. 6   **Thomas Winter**   *Delete* M.

p. 7   **Thomas Overary**   *For* **Overary** *read* **Overay**
     Thomas Cornish
         For D. 31 March . . . Fetiplace). *read* D. 3 July 1513 (*Collinson* III 400)
     Robert de Haselscawe *Delete* 1306.
         For Occ. 17 Jan. 1306 *read* Referred to 17 Jan. 1306 as being chancellor about a year previously

p. 8   *See* p. 82 *below*

p. 9   **Thomas Overary**   *For* **Overary** *read* **Overay**

p. 11   **John Auger**   *For* **Auger** *read* **Aunger**

p. 12   **Thomas Byngham**   *For* M.Th. *read* D.Th.
     John Spekyngton   *For* 1451–1463. *read* 1451–1462.
         For D. before . . . p. 380). *read* D. 30 Dec. 1462 (*Collinson* III 400); *Reg. Bekynton* I 380).
     John Hans   *For* **Hans** *read* **Nans** *Add* M. *and* D.Cn. & C.L. *For* 1505–1509. *read* 1505–1508.
         For D. before 8 Feb. 1509 (*ibid.* p. 211). *read* D. before 15 Nov. 1508 (*ibid.* p. 211; PCC 9 Bennett).
     William Boureman   *For* 1536, 1546. *read* 1535, 1546.
         For Occ. 4 Aug. . . . p. 30). *read* Occ. 15 Nov. 1535 (*L. & P.* IX No. 823).

p. 13   **Wibert de Lutleton**   *Delete* B.C.L.

p. 15   **Robert Shorton**   *For* 1535. *read* 1529, 1535.
         For Occ. 1535 (*Valor* I 133). *read* Occ. 1529 (*L. & P.* IV iii No. 6047 p. 2698). *For* D. 17 Oct. *read* D. 17 Oct. 1535

p. 16   **William Thingull**   *For* 1364, 1366. *read* 1364, 1370.
    For Occ. 18 Sept. . . . p. 49). *read* Still litigating about it 28 May 1370
(*CPR. 1367–1370* p. 417).

p. 17   **Richard Langport**   *Add* M. *For* B.C.L. *read* B.Cn.L.
    Richard Sampson   *For* D.C.L. *read* D.Cn. & C.L. *For* 1535. *read* 1535–
1536.
    Add at end of entry Bp. of Chichester 1536.

p. 18   **John Roland**   *For* 1417–1426. *read* 1417–?
    Delete D. before . . . I 40).
    John Hillier   *For* Hillier *read* Hiller
    John Sperkhauke   *For* Sperkhauke *read* Sperwhauke
    Robert Bisse
    For Occ. 1535 *read* Occ. as a can. of Wells (probably this preb.) in 1529
(Somerset Record Office, D/D/C A2 p. 122). Occ. as preb. 1535

p. 19   *Replace the entry for* **Robert de Baldock** *and* **Peter de Nantolio** *by the
following entry:*
    M. **Robert de Baldock** *senior* D.C.L. 1323–1324.
      Robert de Baldock *junior* 1324–1353.
      Peter de Nantolio 1326.
      Coll. to Baldock *senior* 31 March 1323 (Reg. Drokensford f. 193). Preb. of
Yatton 1324, and apparently succeeded by Baldock *junior*. Baldock exch.
May 1326 with Nantolio for preb. of Monkton in Ripon colleg. ch., Yorks.
(*ibid.* ff. 241, 244); but Nantolio res. 31 Aug. and Baldock re-adm. (*ibid.* f.
245). D. before 21 Jan. 1353 (*Reg. R. de Salopia* II 707–8).
    William Colvyle   *Add* M. *For* 1372. *read* ?–1397.
    For Occ. 27 Feb. 1372 *read* Occ. 18 Oct. 1385
    For I 488). *read* I 488–9).
    Add at end of entry D. 1397 (*ibid.* II 32).

p. 20   **William Boureman**   *For* 1523, 1535. *read* 1523.
    Delete Occ. 15 Nov. . . . No. 823).

p. 23   **John Wygrome**   *For* 1449–1468/70. *read* 1449–1468.
    For D. 1468/1470 *read* D. by 20 Oct. 1468
    For II 92). *read* II 92; *Reg. Stillington* p. 19).

p. 24   **John Argentyne**   *For* D.Th., D.M. *read* D.M.
    William de Pencriz
    Add at end of entry ? Held preb. until d., before 15 Dec. 1340 (*Reg. J. de
Grandisson*, ed. F. C. Hingeston-Randolph (Exeter, 1894–99) III 1329).

p. 25   **Michael Cleve**   *Add* M.

p. 26   **Robert de Stonore**   *Add* M. *and* M.A.
    Adam Holme   *Add* B.C.L.

p. 27   **William Toby**
         Delete whole entry

p. 28   **William Toly**   *For* ?–1460. *read* 1424–1460.
         Add at beginning Coll. 13 Oct. 1424 (*Reg. Bubwith* II 459 – 'William Toby';
         cf. *CPL.* VIII 84).
         For D. as preb. *read* D.
         Henry Penwortham   *Add* M.
         William Bernham   *Add* M. *and* B.Cn.L. *For* ?–1445/6. *read* ?–1445.
         For D. as preb. .... II 74). *read* D. as preb. by 15 Jan. 1445 (*Reg. Bekynton*
         I 22).
             Add new entry after **William Bernham** *as follows:*
         M. Vincent Clement D.Th. 1445–1475.
             Coll. 15 Jan. 1445 (*Reg. Bekynton* I 22). D. by March 1475 (*Reg. Stilling-*
         ton p. 106).
         Footnote
             For 1445/6 *read* 1445

p. 31   **Nicholas Burton**   *Add* B.C.L.

p. 32   **Stephen Martin of Hull**
             Add at end of entry Occ. as a can. of Wells 30 Apr. 1357 (Somerset Record
         Office, Church Commissioners' deposit, 110,025, 26/44).
         John de Ware   *Add* M. *and* B.C.L.
         John Blancherd   *Add* M.
         William Bernham   *Add* M. *and* B.Cn.L.

p. 33   **Thomas Cowton**   *Add* M. *and* B.C.L.

p. 35   **Thomas Barowe**   *For* D.C.L. *read* Lic.C.L.
         John Barough   *For* Barough *read* Barough[2]
         John Becham   *Add* M. *and* B.Cn.L.
             Add new footnote as follows:
         2. Probably an error for Thomas Barowe.

p. 38   **William de Weston**
             For Nicholas de Ilford *read* Nicholas de Iforde
         Nicholas de Ilford *For* Ilford *read* Iforde
             Add at end of entry Occ. as a can. of Wells (possibly this preb.) 18 Nov.
         1366 (*Reg. Langham* p. 65).
         Robert Wytton   *For* D.C.L. *read* D.Cn.L.
         Henry Edyall   *Add* M.

p. 39   **Richard Pittes**   *Add* M.

p. 40   **John Bourgchier**
        Add at end of entry ? Held preb. until d. 6 Nov. 1495 (*Survey of Cath.*
        II 121).

        Peter Carmelian   *Add* M.
        Edward Fox   *Delete* D.Th.
        Alan de Hothom   *Add* M.

p. 41   **Thomas Overary**   *For* Overary *read* Overay
        Thomas Cornish
        For D. 31 March . . . Fetiplace). *read* D. 3 July 1513 (*Collinson* III 400).
        Andrew Ammonius   *Add* M.

p. 42   **James Gilbert**
        For Occ. 1535 *read* Occ. as a can. of Wells (probably this preb.) in 1529
        (Somerset Record Office, D/D/C A2 p. 122). Occ. as preb. 1535

p. 43   **William Excestre**   *For* William *read* John de
        Delete Probably res. . . . since
        Footnote
        For Overary *read* Overay

p. 44   **John Roland**   *For* 1419–? *read* 1419–1427.
        For ? Held preb. . . . I 40). *read* D. 2 Dec. 1427 (*Collinson* III 401).
        Peter Stukeley   *Delete* B.C.L.

p. 45   **Henry de Harewedon** *Add* D.Cn. & C.L.

p. 46   **William Hoper**   *For* D.C.L. *read* D.Cn. & C.L.

p. 47   **John Spekyngton**   *For* 1455–1463. *read* 1455–1462.
        For D. before . . . p. 380). *read* D. 30 Dec. 1462 (*Collinson* III 400; *Reg.*
        Bekynton I 380).

p. 51   **Richard Rawson**   *Add* D.Cn. & C.L.

p. 52   **John Argentyne**   *For* D.Th., D.M. *read* D.M.
        John Hans   *For* Hans *read* Nans *Add* M. *and* D.Cn. & C.L.
        For 1505–1509. *read* 1505–1508.
        For D. before 8 Feb. 1509 *read* D. before 15 Nov. 1508
        For p. 211). *read* p. 211; PCC 9 Bennett).

p. 53   **Thomas Pipe**   *Add* M. *For* O.S.B. *read* O.S.B., Lic.Th.

p. 56   **Thomas Winter**   *Delete* M.
        Footnote
        Add at end of footnote Harewell occ. as preb. of Litton by 5 Aug. 1380 and
        probably by 29 May 1374 (*Cal. MSS. D. & C. Wells* I 280, 486).

p. 58   John Auger   *For* Auger *read* **Aunger**
            John Algar   *For* 1535. *read* ?–1536/7.
            Add at end of entry D. 7 Nov. 1536/16 Jan. 1537 (PCC 1 Dyngeley).

p. 61   *Replace the entry for* **Benjamin Bernard, Bernard Brocas** *and* **Reginald**
            de Bugwell *by the following entry :*
            Benjamin Bernard 1349.
            M. Bernard Brocas 1349–1366.
            M. Robert de Askeby 1349–1351.
            M. Reginald de Bugwell B.Cn. & C.L. 1349.
            Estate of Brocas ratif. 7 Oct. 1349 (*CPR. 1348–1350* p. 395). Bernard said
to have held preb. 1349 before Brocas coll. (*Reg. R. de Salopia* II 642). Prov.
to Askeby 17 Oct. (*CPL.* III 342). Bugwell accepted prov. to preb. 9 Nov.
(*CPP.* I 185). Royal prohibn., 10 Feb. 1350, against all ecclesiastical persons
taking proceedings in derogation of k's right to collate to preb. (*CPR. 1348–
1350* p. 526). Royal gr. to Brocas 26 Feb. (*ibid.* p. 475), second gr. 17 March
(*Reg. R. de Salopia* II 631). Estate ratif. 3 July (*CPR. 1348–1350* p. 542).
Askeby still litigating at curia over claims 6 Sept. 1351 (*Cal. MSS. D. & C.
Wells* I 550–1), but Brocas occ. as preb. 11 July 1352 (*Reg. R. de Salopia* II
702). Exch. preb. with Arnald Brocas for chap. of Whipstrode St James,
Fareham, Hants, 18 Oct. 1366 (*Cal. MSS. D. & C. Wells* I 269).
            Arnald Brocas
            For d. before 20 Aug. . . . f. 442). *read* d. 14 Aug. 1395 (*Survey of Cath.*
II 187).

p. 62   John Hillier   *For* Hillier *read* **Hiller**
            Thomas Langton
            For Bp. of St Davids 1483. *read* Bp. of St Davids 1483.[1]
            Henry Edyall   *Add* M.
            Add new footnote as follows :
1. No evidence has been found for Richard Fox, said by Le Neve-Hardy to
occur in 1485. He became bp. of Exeter in 1487, and this would fit well with
the adm. of Henry Edyall to the preb. in that year. The compiler of the list
of prebs. of St Decumans in Le Neve-Hardy seems to have used the bishops'
registers and the Liber Ruber as his sources, and it is possible that this mention of Richard Fox occurs in the first five folios of Liber Ruber part 2, which
are now missing (*Cal. MSS. D. & C. Wells* II 101n).

p. 63   William de Melbourne
            For Occ. 16 Oct. 1366 *read* Claimed preb. 16 Oct. 1366, though not in
possession
            John Walrond
            For Epping Upland *read* Epping

p. 64   Richard Clarkson   *Add* M. *and* B.Th.
            John de Kynardeseye *Add* M.

p. 66   Hugh Holbache   *Delete* M. *and* D.Cn.L.

p. 67   James Villiers   *For* Villiers *read* Villers
       William Villiers   *For* Villiers *read* Villers

p. 68   Thomas Lane   *Add* M. *and* B.Cn.L.

p. 70   Robert de Sambourne
       Delete whole entry
       Roger Wyte
       Add at beginning Occ. 28 Sept. 1366 (*Reg. Langham* p. 20).
       For D. as preb. *read* D.
       Ralph Berners   *Add* M. *and* D.C.L.

p. 71   Robert de Sambourne
       For Occ. 12 Feb. . . . 282). *read* Occ. 18 Nov. 1366 (*Reg. Langham* p. 69).
       John Cole   *Add* M.

p. 73   William Burton   *Add* M. *and* B.Cn. & C.L.

p. 74   Robert de Luffenham   *Add* M.

p. 75   John Fitzjames   *Add* M.
       Footnote
       For Chaundeler d. . . . p. 198). *read* Chaundeler d. 2 Nov. 1490 (*Survey of Cath.* 1 534).

p. 76   Wibert de Lutleton   *Delete* B.C.L.
       Thomas Byngham   *For* M.Th. *read* D.Th.

p. 77   Robert de Haselscawe
       For (*Reg. Drokensford* p. 200). *read* (*Reg. Drokensford* p. 201).

p. 79   Edward Rogers   *Add* M.

p. 81   John de Cadomo   *Add* M.
       Add new entry after Thomas Madefrey *as follows:*
       M. William Courtenay Lic.C.L. 1366.
       Occ. as preb. of Wells 16 Oct. 1366 (*Reg. Langham* p. 58).

p. 82   Thomas Frome   *For* 1386. *read* 1384, 1386.
       Add at beginning Occ. as preb. of Wells 24 Sept. 1384 (Lamb., Reg. Courtenay f. 307).
       For Occ. as can. and preb. of Wells *read* Occ. as can. and preb.
       Add three new entries after John de Tyssebury *as follows:*
       John Storthwayt 1407/8.
       Instal. as preb. of Wells Sept. 1407–Sept. 1408 (*Cal. MSS. D. & C. Wells* II 40).

Roger Wodehale 1407/8.
   Instal. as preb. of Wells Sept. 1407–Sept. 1408 (*Cal. MSS. D. & C. Wells* II 40).

M. James Huyte 1529.
   Occ. as a residentiary can. of Wells 13 July 1529 (Somerset Record Office, D/D/C A2 p. 122).

p. 83   *Add two new entries after* **Elias de Walwayn** *as follows:*

M. John Piers D.C.L. 1342.
   Prov. 22 July 1342 (*CPP.* I 2).

M. Henry de la Dale B.C.L., B.M. 1345.
   Prov. 25 Jan. 1345 (*CPL.* III 148).

Add new entry after **John de Horsington** *as follows:*

M. William Bildeston B.C.L. 1406.
   Royal pardon 1 Dec. 1406 for accepting prov. of a canonry and preb. of Wells (*CPR. 1405–1408* p. 277).

p. 8   **Thomas de Luggore**
   Delete whole entry

p. 6   William Sumaster   *Delete* B.Th.

p. 7   Nicholas Weston   *Add* M.

p. 10   William Leveson   *Add* M. *and* B.Cn. & C.L.

p. 11   Richard Tischo   *Add* M. *and* B.Cn.L.

p. 13   *Footnote* 1
        For Coronait *read* Coronati

p. 23   Robert de Haselschawe *Delete* M.

p. 26   Wibert de Littelton *Add* M.

p. 28   William Legilden
        Delete whole entry
        John de Buckingham *Add* M.
        William de Gulden
        After Northwode's possession *insert* , claiming it by virtue of expect. gr.
        15 Nov. 1330 (*CPL.* II 338).

p. 33   William de Wittlesey *Add* B.Cn. & C.L.

p. 37   Hugh de Bridham
        For Occ. . . . Ex. 2796). *read* Occ. Aug. 1363 (*CPP.* I 455).
        Whole entry should now come between Nicholas Bagthorpe *and* Thomas
        Madefray.

p. 39   Richard Tischo   *Add* M. *and* B.Cn.L.

p. 50   John Stanway   *For* B.Cn.L. *read* B.C.L.

p. 53   John Floure   *Add* B.Cn. & C.L.

p. 54   John Kirkeby   *Add* M.

p. 55   Thomas Rotherham *For* D.Th. *read* B.Th.

p. 57   Thomas Danet
        For D. (as preb. ?) . . . f. 196). *read* D. (as preb. ?) 18 Sept. 1483 (*Survey
        of . . . Cathedrals*, comp. Browne Willis (London, 1742) I 445).

p. 58   William Sumaster   *Delete* B.Th.

VOL. X. COVENTRY AND LICHFIELD DIOCESE

p. vi   *Add to list of works in print:*
    Emden Reg. Camb.   *Biographical Register of the University of Cambridge to 1500,* comp. A. B. Emden, Cambridge, 1963.
    Survey of Cath.   *Survey of . . . Cathedrals,* comp. Browne Willis. 3 vols. in 2. London, 1742

p. 1   **Robert de Stretton**   *For* 1358–1385. *read* 1359–1385.

p. 2   **John Catryk**   *For* 1414–1419. *read* 1415–1419.
         Reginald Boulers   *For* 1452–1459. *read* 1453–1459.

p. 8   **Thomas Heritage**   *Add* M.

p. 9   **John Maureward**   *Add* M. *and* B.C.L.

p. 10   **John Godyng**   *For* 1421–1435. *read* 1421–1438.
         For 17 May 1435 *read* 17 May 1438
         John Lane   *For* 1435–1447. *read* 1438–1447.
         For 17 May 1435 *read* 17 May 1438
         For 23 July 1438 *read* 23 July
         John Doket   *For* D.Cn.L., B.Th. *read* D.Th., D.Cn.L.

p. 13   **Henry de Halsall**   *Add* M.

p. 15   **Thomas Mills**   *Add* M.

p. 18   **Thomas Lye**   *Add* M.

p. 25   **William Faucon**
         For 28 Feb. 1345 *read* 28 Feb. 1344
         John de Charnele
         After p. 552). *insert* Papal conf. 20 May 1351 (*CPL.* III 429).
         Footnote
         For 1345 *read* 1344

p. 26   **Stephen Scrope**   *Delete* M. *and* D.C.L.

p. 29   **Geoffrey Wrenne**
         For D. 4 March . . . f. 38). *read* D. 5 Apr. 1527 (*Survey of Cath.* I 432; A.C. IV f. 38).

p. 30   **William Norton**   *Delete* M. *and* B.Cn. & C.L.
        Henry de Halsall   *Add* M.

p. 31   **Thomas Mills**   *Add* M.

p. 41   **Thomas Danet**
        For D. before 30 Oct. . . . f. 52b). *read* D. 18 Sept. 1483 (*ibid.* f. 52b; *Survey of Cath.* I 445).

p. 45   **John Gerard**   *Add* M.
        For by virtue of prov. (*ibid.* f. 160). *read* by virtue of prov., the prebend having been 'unlawfully conferred by king Edward' (*ibid.* f. 160; *CPL.* II 129).

p. 47   **Stephen Scrope**   *Delete* M. *and* D.C.L.

p. 48   **Peter Greves**   *Add* M.

p. 51   **Thomas de Goldesburgh** *Add* M.

p. 54   **John Auncell**   *Add* B.Cn. & C.L. *For* 1431–? *read* 1431–1445.
        For (A.C. I f. 139).[2] *read* (A.C. I f. 139).
        Add at end of entry Exch. preb. with John Werkworth for preb. of St Martin's in Dernestall, Lincoln, 3 Feb. 1445 (Reg. IX (Heyworth) f. 93).
        John Werkworth   *For* ?–1450. *read* 1445–1450.
        Add at beginning By exch. Feb. 1445.
        For (Reg. X (Booth) f. 22).[2] *read* (Reg. X (Booth) f. 22).
        Robert Mome   *For* Mome *read* Monie
        Footnote 2
        Delete whole footnote

p. 56   **William Orell**   *Add* M.

p. 58   **Simon Bache**
        For D. before 20 May . . . p. 187). *read* D. 19 May 1414 (*Survey of Cath.* II 231; *CPR. 1413–1416* p. 187).

p. 59   **William Worsley**   *Delete* M.

p. 60   **Nicholas de Hethe**   *For* 1361–1390. *read* 1361–?
        For Hethe d. before Aug. *read* Hethe d. before Aug.[1]
        Ralph Birom
        For Res. preb. of Offley in Dec.[1] *read* Res. preb. of Offley in Dec.[2]
        Add new footnote as follows:
1. This is a mistake for the d. of Nicholas de Hethe *junior*. According to Dr Emden, there are two men of the same name (*Emden, Reg. Camb.* p. 302). The d. of Nicholas de Hethe *senior* is unknown, and it seems possible that some of the references to him above may in fact concern the younger man.
        Footnote 1
        For 1 *read* 2

p. 61   **Richard de Tysho**   *Add* M.
          For (*Reg. Langham* p. 73). *read* (*Reg. Langham* p. 34).

p. 65   **Hugh de Wymondeswold** *For* 1353–1379. *read* 1350–1379.
          Add at beginning Prov. to Wymondeswold 13 Nov. 1350 (*CPL.* III 361).
          For Mand. adm. Wymondeswold *read* Mand. adm.

p. 66   **Thomas Mills**   *Add* M.

p. 67   **Tydo de Waresio**   *Delete* M.
        John de Bryane
          For D. before 22 Feb. . . . 18). *read* D. 4 Feb. 1389 (*Survey of Cath.* II
          196; A.C. I ff. 17b–18).
        John Cole   *Add* M.

p. 69   **John Maureward**   *Add* M. *and* B.C.L.

p. 70   **Edmund Willisford** *For* 1500–1517. *read* 1500–1516.
          For D. before . . . f. 121b). *read* D. 3 Oct. 1516 (*Emden, Reg. Ox.* III
          2116; A.C. III f. 121b).
        Joachim Bretunne   *For* 1517–1520. *read* 1516–1520.
          For 10 Oct. 1517 *read* 10 Oct. 1516
        Thomas de Clone
          For (*CPL.* II 319) *read* (*CPL.* II 318)

p. 71   **Richard de Cornubia** *For* 1331–? *read* 1330–?
          Add at beginning Prov. 30 March 1330 (*CPL.* II 324).

VOL. XI. THE WELSH DIOCESES
(*Bangor, Llandaff, St Asaph, St Davids*)

p. 6   **Philip Clyffeld**   *For* 1396–? *read* 1396–1397.

Add at end of entry Exch. with William Clyve for ch. of Woolaston, Glos., 24 May 1397 (*Reg. Trefnant* p. 190).

Add new entry after **Philip Clyffeld** *as follows:*

William Clyve (again) 1397–?

By exch. May 1397.

Footnote 2

Add at end of footnote An agreement of 1445 in which John Martin occurs as dean is referred to in a letter of 1657, but is not now extant (Nat. Libr. Wales, B/Misc./200, ex. inform. Professor M. L. Clarke).

p. 8   **John Parsons**   *For* 1460, 1468. *read* 1453, 1468.

For Occ. 15 Oct. 1460 *read* Occ. 17 Apr. 1453

For p. 57 *read* p. 6

Footnote 4

For 'affeiriad' *read* 'offeiriad'

p. 11   **Richard Bromfield**

Add at end of entry ? Held archdcnry until d., 24 Oct. 1518 (*Survey of . . . Cathedrals*, comp. Browne Willis (London, 1742) I 562).

William de Melton *For* 1308. *read* ?–1309.

Add at end of entry Res. before 17 July 1309 (*CPR. 1307–1313* p. 176). Succeeded by Ralph de Melton (see below).

Add new entry after **Thomas de Cauntebreg** *as follows:*

M. Ralph de Melton 1309–?

Royal gr. 17 July 1309 of preb. vac. by William de Melton (*CPR. 1307–1313* p. 176; see above).

Adam de Murimuth *For* M. Adam de Murimuth D.C.L. *read* M. **Alphalipnus**

p. 12   **Robert de Tresk**   *Add* M.

Add new entry after **Edmund Trefor** *as follows:*

Peter de Gildesburgh ?–1352.

Occ. 28 May 1349 (*CPL.* III 314). Exch. preb. with Peter de Wotton for preb. of Bonehill, Tamworth colleg. ch., Staffs., 3 Feb. 1352 (*CPR. 1350–1354* p. 212; see below).

Add two new entries after **Hugh de Monyngton** *as follows:*

Peter de Wotton 1352–?
By exch. with Peter de Gildesburgh for preb. of Bonehill, Tamworth colleg. ch., Staffs., 3 Feb. 1352 (*CPR. 1350–1354* p. 212; see above).

Peter de Gildesburgh (again) 1357.
Occ. 16 Feb. 1357 (*CPP.* I 293–4).

Thomas de Lynton
For Allington, Lincs. *read* Ellington, Hunts.

John de Carleton
For Allington, Lincs. *read* Ellington, Hunts.

p. 13   **William de Humblestane** *For* 1380–1408. *read* 1380–1409.
For D. before 19 Oct. 1408 *read* D. before 19 Oct. 1409

Add new entry after **William de Humblestane** *as follows:*

John Benteley ?–1387.
Exch. preb. with William Seman for ch. of Newton (in Kesteven), Lincs., 25 July 1387 (*CPR. 1385–1389* p. 353; see below).

William Seman   *For* ?–1395. *read* 1387–1395.
For Occ. 25 July 1387 *read* By exch. with John Benteley for ch. of Newton (in Kesteven), Lincs., 25 July 1387

p. 14   **William**   *For* 1408–? *read* 1409–?
For Coll. 19 Oct. 1408 *read* Coll. 19 Oct. 1409

p. 16   **Dafydd Llwyd**
For Valor IV 418). *read Valor* IV 418).[2]

Dafydd ap Madog
For Reg. Cranmer f. 273). *read* Reg. Cranmer f. 273)[2].

Add new footnote as follows:
2. It is possible that Dafydd Llwyd and Dafydd ap Madog are the same person, since Dafydd Llwyd ap Mad' resigned the preb. of Penmynydd 9 Sept. 1554 (Nat. Libr. Wales, B/BR/2 f. 14b).

p. 29   **Richard Bermyngham** *Add* M.

See also p. 90.

p. 30   **Richard de Croxton** *Add* M.

p. 39   **Fouke Salisbury**
For L. & P. VIII No. 1014 *read L. & P.* VIII No. 1015

p. 40   **Hywel ap Madog ap Cyffin** *Add* M.

p. 42   **Robert de Stretton**
Add at end of entry ? Until bp. of Coventry and Lichfield 1359.
John Trefnant *or* ap Hywel *Add* B.C.L.

p. 45   Huw Bochenhull
       For ibid. p. 190 *read* ibid. p. 198

p. 46   *Replace the entries for* William Villiers *and* Thomas Vele *by the following entries:*
       Thomas Vele ?–1494.
         Exch. this preb. with William Villers for ch. of Kirtling, Cambs., 7/15 March 1494 (*CPR. 1494–1509* p. 13; Norwich, Reg. Goldwell f. 184).
       M. William Villers D.C.L. 1494–?
         By exch. March 1494. Probably to d., before Dec. 1498 (*Emden, Reg. Camb.* p. 608).

p. 50   Hywel Cyffin *junior Add* M. *For* Hywel Cyffin *junior read* Hywel ap Madog ap Cyffin
       Add two new entries after John Lassy *as follows:*
       M. Lewis Sutton 1488.
         Occ. 24 Apr. 1488 (*Collectanea Anglo-Premonstratensia*, ed. F. A. Gasquet (Camden 3rd Ser., vi, 1904) p. 88).
       M. John Staveley 1488.
         Occ. 24 Apr. 1488 (*Collectanea Anglo-Premonstratensia*, ed. F. A. Gasquet (Camden 3rd Ser., vi, 1904) p. 88).

       See also p. 90.

p. 56   William Barlow
       After f. 206). *insert* Temps. Apr. (P.R.O., E 368/310).
       For (ibid. ff. 205–205b) *read* (Lamb., Reg. Cranmer ff. 205–205b).
       For (ibid. f. 205). *read* (ibid. f. 205)[1].

       David Lee   *For* 1350–?[1] *read* 1350–?[2]

       Add new footnote as follows:
       1. The date of Barlow's cons. is unknown. 11, 18, and 26 June have been suggested, as his precedence is fixed between Norwich (cons. 11 June) and St Asaph (cons. 2 July (*R.S.A.*)). He is still called bp.-elect 12 June (Bodl. Libr., MS. Ashmole 857 f. 48).
       Footnote
       For 1 *read* 2

p. 66   **John Godmeston**   *Add* M.

p. 71   **John Godmeston**   *Add* M.

p. 75   Robert Broun
       For Reg. St Davids II *read* Reg. St Davids I
       John Grandon
       For Reg. St Davids II *read* Reg. St Davids I (*bis*)

p. 76   Robert Broun
       For Reg. St Davids II *read* Reg. St Davids I

p. 80 **Walter Alexander**
After of Rosemarket *insert* and Robert Burbach
Rhys ap Hywel   *Add* M.

p. 81   *Replace the entries for* **David Martin of Rosemarket** *and* **Robert Burbach** *by the following entry:*
M. David Martin of Rosemarket B.C.L. 1349–1361.
    Robert Burbach 1353–?
    Martin prov. 14 June 1349 to preb. vac. by Walter Alexander (*CPP.* I 169; see above p. 80). Royal gr. to Burbach 28 May 1353 (*CPR. 1350–1354* p. 445). Martin vac. preb. before 16 July 1361 (*CPR. 1361–1364* p. 40). Succeeded by John de Saxton (see below).
Walter de Elisaundre
    Delete whole entry
Robert Burbach
    Delete whole entry (*now combined with that for* **David Martin of Rosemarket**)

p. 29 *Add new entry after* **Nicholas de Newton** *as follows:*
M. Henry Ware
    Occ. 17 Dec. 1401 (Lamb., Reg. Arundell I f. 329).

p. 50 *Add new entry before* **Hywel Cyffin** *junior as follows:*
M. David de Engelfeld 1356.
    Occ. 18 Feb. 1356 (Lamb., Reg. Islip f. 342b).
Add two new entries after **Lewis Trefor** *as follows:*
M. Walter Kode 1405.
    Occ. 19 Dec. 1405 (Lamb., Reg. Arundell I f. 335).
M. Morgan Fitzwilliam 1412.
    Occ. 28 May 1412 (Lamb., Reg. Arundell II f. 100b).

Cumulative Index

LIST OF VOLUMES

INDEX OF PERSONS

Abberbury (Eadberbury), John, i. 109
Abberbury, Thomas de, *see* Eaderbury
Abbot, Thomas, xi. 75, 83
Abbotsbury, John de, iii. 93
Abel, Richard, viii. 82; x. 21
Abendon, Henry, viii. 33, 72, 73
Abendon, *see also* Abingdon, Abyndon
Aber, Lewis, xi. 4, 13, 47, 59
Aberford, Henry de, vi. 38
Abingdon (Abendon), John de, iii. 24, 63
Abingdon (Abendon, Abyndon), Richard de, iii. 60, 68; viii. 79; x. 65
Abingdon, *see also* Abendon, Abyndon
Abraham, John, ii. 41; ix. 42(*bis*); xi. 73; xii. 50
Abyndon, Henry, viii. 52
Abyndon, Richard de, *see* Abingdon
Abyndon, *see also* Abendon, Abingdon
Acciajoli (Acciaioli, Acciaiuoli), Angelo, i. 81; iii. 4, 37; iv. 8; v. 30; vi. 7; viii. 78; ix. 14
Ace, Philip, ii. 15
Acome, John de, vi. 64, 87
Acome, *see also* Akum, Hakun
Acton, John, i. 126; xii. 42
Adam (c. 1279–1303), xi. 61
Adam (c. 1302), iv. 17
Adam (c. 1328), xi. 6
Adam, William, i. 36
Adams, John, v. 41, 49
Adams, Maurice, xi. 69
Adams, Walter, i. 30
Adda, Tudur ab, *see* Tudur ab Adda
Adderbury, *see* Eaderbury
Addished, Peter, vii. 36
Adigheriis, Ugolino de, i. 31(*bis*); xii. 19(*bis*)
Adished, Thomas, vii. 25(*bis*), 32, 33, 37, 46
Admondeston, Thomas, x. 21
Admondeston, William de, x. 19, 30, 42
Adria, *see* Turre de Adria
Affeiriad (Effeiriat), Iorwerth, xi. 8 & n
Agard, Philip, x. 34, 51
Aghton, William, i. 17
Aigrefeuille (Agrifolio), William d' (d. 1369), vi. 67

Aigrefeuille (Agrifolio), William d' (d. 1401), i. 54; iii. 9, 41, 59; viii. 16
Ainian, *see* Einion
Airemynne, *see* Ayremynne
Aiscough, Robert (c. 1439–48), viii. 73
Aiscough (Ascough, Ayscogh), Robert (d. 1449), iii. 8, 43, 44, 50, 54, 72; v. 14, 67; vi. 49; xii. 70
Aiscough (Ayscogh), Robert (d. 1471), i. 5; iii. 23, 34, 94; xii. 14, 57
Aiscough (Ayscogh), Robert (d. 1482), iii. 43, 76; ix. 14, 55; xii. 56
Aiscough (Ascough, Ayscogh), William (d. 1450), i. 114; iii. 2; vii. 49
Aiscough (Ayscogh), William (d. 1486), iii. 8; ix. 55
Aislaghbie, William, vi. 35
Aislaghbie, *see also* Aslaby
Akum, Adam, viii. 51
Akum, John, vi. 114; x. 70
Akum, *see also* Acome, Hakun
Alatri, *see* Giudice
Albert (Aubert), Stephen, vi. 17, 93; viii. 13
Albert, *see also* Aubert
Alberwick, Gilbert de, vi. 24; xii. 68
Alberwick, *see also* Alburwyk
Albini, *see* Jargolio
Albon (Albone), Edmund, i. 105; iii. 22; v. 54; xii. 37
Albornoz, *see* Gomez
Albret, d', *see* Breto
Albryghton (Albritrone), Roger, ii. 14; v. 15, 37; vii. 47; xii. 45
Alburwyk, William de, vi. 9, 10, 33, 37n
Alburwyk, *see also* Alberwick
Albusaco (Aubussac), William de, vii. 43
Alcobasso, Peter de, iii. 10; v. 42
Alcock, Hugh, xi. 6, 17 & n
Alcock, John (d. 1500), iii. 23; iv. 15, 39, 58; v. 22; viii. 40
Alcock, John (d. 1507), i. 104, 110; vi. 59; xii. 37, 38, 70
Alcock, Simon, i. 73; ii. 39; xii. 29, 49
Alcock, Thomas (c. 1394), x. 69

Alcock, Thomas (d. 1523), ii. 26; xii. 47
Alcock, Thomas (d. 1527), iv. 19, 63
Aldeburgh, Humphrey de, iii. 96
Alderbury, Walter de, v. 5 & n, 40, 56 & n; vii. 11; viii. 37, 51
Alderford, see Dalderby
Aldreford, William, vii. 6n
Aldrich (Aldridge), Robert, i. 52, 61; v. 14; vi. 99; xii. 23
Aldryngton (Allerton), Richard, viii. 48, 63; ix. 20, 45
Aldyngton, see Oldington
Alen (Aleyn), John, i. 30; v. 59; ix. 64; xii. 19
Alen, see also Aleyn(e)
Alençon, Philip d', iv. 33; vi. 67; ix. 13
Aleston, see Ayleston
Alexander (Elisaundre), Walter (de), xi. 80, 81; xii. 90(bis)
Aleyn (Aleyne, Alyn), John (d. 1373), iv. 33; v. 47; ix. 38
Aleyn, John (d. 1534), see Alen
Aleyn, Samson (Sampson), ii. 13; x. 34
Aleyne, John (d. 1373), see Aleyn
Aleyne (Alyn, Carver, Kerver, Kervour), John (d. 1516), i. 100; v. 13, 50, 57; vi. 19, 82, 89
Aleyn(e), see also Alen
Alford, Thomas, i. 47, 56; xii. 22
Algar, John, viii. 58; x. 71; xii. 80
Alifia, see Renzio
Alkerton (Alkeryngton), Richard, vii. 48
Allerthorpe (Allerthorp), Laurence (Lawrence), ii. 48; v. 25; vi. 85; xii. 51, 63, 72
Allerton, Richard, see Aldryngton
Allerton, Robert (c. 1419–21, ? R.A. d. 1437), ix. 48
Allerton, Robert (d. 1437, ? R.A. c. 1419–1421), i. 58; vii. 16; xii. 25
Almaly, Walter (de), ii. 43; vii. 42; xi. 66
Almoner, see Bluntesdon, Henry de; Henry
Alnwick (Alnwyk, Annewyk), William (d. 1449), i. 2; iii. 12; iv. 14, 24; v. 67; vi. 60; xii. 13, 52, 58, 59, 65, 70
Alnwick, William (d. 1461), i. 44
Alphalipnus, xii. 87
Alston, Thomas (de), viii. 20; xi. 24, 27, 31
Altham, Alexander, v. 34
Alyn, John (d. 1373), see Aleyn
Alyn, John (d. 1516), see Aleyne
Amberle, William de, vii. 19
Ambresbury, see Amesbury
Ambrose, Eliseus, v. 45
Amelio (Amelia), John de, x. 67
Ameny (Jakes), Walter, ii. 32

Amesbury (Ambresbury), John de, ii. 12; v. 38
Amie, Alexander, x. 70
Ammoigner, le, see Bluntesdon, Henry de
Ammonius, Andrew, iii. 53; viii. 41; xii. 54, 79
Ampleford, Robert, iii. 32, 34, 81
Andiliers (Audilliers), John de, vii. 58
Andrew (Andrewe), Richard, i. 16; iii. 12, 50, 56, 89; vi. 8, 70, 87; vii. 60; xi. 78
Angerville, Thomas d', vii. 57
Angerville, see also Aungerville
Anglesey, see Madog ap Meurig
Angoulême, see Engolisma
Anian, see Einion
Anibaldis, Hildebrand de, v. 9
Anibaldis, John de, i. 57
Anibaldis, Richard de, see Riccardi
Annewyk, see Alnwick
Antilla, see Nerii, Philip
Apelderham, Richard, of Tangmere, vii. 17
Apeldreham, William de, vii. 55
Apeltre, William de, x. 19, 32, 50, 58
Appilton, see Appleton
Appleby, John de (c. 1364–79), vi. 102
Appleby, John (de) (d. 1389), i. 78, 105; v. 6, 29(bis); vi. 69
Appleby (Appulby), Robert (d. 1458), i. 32; xi. 17; xii. 19
Appleby, Robert de (c. 1315), vi. 15
Appleby, Thomas de, vi. 97
Appleton (Appilton, Appulton), Robert (de), i. 42; vi. 33; viii. 30
Appleton, Thomas de, vi. 77
Appulby, see Appleby
Appulton, see Appleton
Aptis (Atti), Francis de, iii. 19
Aquablanca, John de, ii. 3, 15
Arblaster, Thomas de, x. 69
Arche, Richard, iii. 50, 64, 78
Archedeakne, see Lercedekne
Archllechwedd (Arthlethwed), Matthew de, xi. 12
Arderne, Hugh de, vii. 59
Arderne, Thomas, v. 58; xii. 64
Arenna, Blasius de, iii. 73
Argentein, Edmund, see Shireff
Argentyne (Argentein), John, viii. 24, 52; x. 24, 34, 51; xii. 77, 79
Arnald, John, viii. 29, 31
Arnall, Richard, vi. 16, 32, 63; xii. 67, 68, 71
Arscott, Alnetheus (Alnott), ix. 63 & n
Arthlethwed, see Archllechwedd
Arthuret, Richard de, vi. 101n
Arum, see Erghum, John; Harom

Arundel, Edmund (de), vi. 58; vii. 10

Arundel (Arundell), John (d. 1477), i. 103; ii. 19; iii. 25; v. 46; vi. 26, 30, 87, 91, 108; vii. 3; ix. 52; x. 33; xii. 37

Arundel (Arundell), John (d. 1504), ii. 11, 13, 20; iii. 33, 48; vi. 36; viii. 36; ix. 3, 5, 57; x. 3 & n

Arundel (Arundell), John (de) (d. 1331), i. 111; vi. 68–9; vii. 23; x. 53; xii. 39

Arundel, Richard de, vii. 48

Arundel (Arundell), Thomas (de), ii. 15; iv. 4(bis), 14; vi. 4; vii. 59; viii. 16; xi. 38n

Arundell, John (c. 1419–53), viii. 64

Aschele, Thomas de, xi. 83

Ascough, see Aiscough

Ashbourne, see Hervey

Ashby, Nicholas, xi. 22

Ashby, see also Asheby, Assheby

Ashcombe (Asshcombe), Robert, ii. 29; vii. 33; viii. 28

Ashden, see Ashton, Assheden

Asheby, John de, x. 16

Asheby, see also Ashby, Assheby

Ashridge, William, iii. 27

Ashton (Ashden, Asseden, Asshton, Aston), Hugh, iii. 66; iv. 51; vi. 19, 82; ix. 17, 61

Ashton, John de (c. 1330, ? J. de Aston), ii. 8

Ashton (Assheton), Matthew, i. 53; vi. 62, 69

Ashton (Aston), William (de), i. 15, 29, 70, 74, 80; ii. 28; iii. 42, 96; x. 28, 35(bis), 47; xii. 15, 29, 48

Ashton, see also Assheton, Aston, Ayston

Ashwell, John, v. 36

Ashwell, see also Asshewell

Askeby, Robert de (c. 1316), vii. 32 & n

Askeby, Robert (de) (c. 1345–51), i. 70; iii. 51; vii. 39; xii. 28, 80

Askeby, William (de) (William Scoter), i. 6, 10, 35, 126; v. 18, 61; xii. 14, 20, 35, 42

Aslaby, John, vii. 22, 49

Aslaby, see also Aislaghbie

Aslokby, William (William Kelsey de Aslokby), i. 125

Aspall, Geoffrey, v. 20

Asplion, John, i. 41

Aspynhalgh, Richard, vii. 8

Asseden, see Ashton

Asserio, Bertrand de, iii. 28; xii. 53

Asserio, Rigaud de, iii. 28; iv. 45; v. 34; xii. 53, 60, 63

Asshcombe, see Ashcombe

Assheby, John, ii. 11, 13, 20, 36

Assheby, see also Ashby, Asheby

Assheden (Asshedale), Thomas, viii. 71

Assheford, Thomas, x. 35

Assheton, Matthew, see Ashton

Assheton, William, vi. 39

Assheton, see also Ashton, Aston, Ayston

Asshewell, John, ii. 13

Asshewell, see also Ashwell

Asshton, see Ashton

Astariaco, Amaneuus de, viii. 10

Astel, Thomas (d. 1439), viii. 65

Astell, Hugh, of Higham Ferrers, i. 60

Astel(l), see also Austell

Astley (Asteleye, Astleye), Thomas de (d. 1349), ii. 23; iii. 80; v. 11, 15, 37, 43 & n; ix. 23, 27; x. 55

Aston, Hugh, see Ashton

Aston, John de (c. 1336, ? J. de Ashton), ix. 6

Aston, Nicholas de, vii. 4

Aston, Richard de (c. 1321–4), v. 8, 18

Aston, Richard de (c. 1358–66), v. 37

Aston (Aysshton), Thomas (de), i. 18, 51, 85; v. 35, 53; viii. 42; xii. 16, 23, 32, 63, 64

Aston, William (de), see Ashton

Aston, see also Ashton, Assheton, Ayston

Atgerius, Bertrand, iii. 59

Athequa, George, xi. 23

Atkins (Atkinson), William, i. 122; xii. 41

atte Chirche, see Chirche

atte Halle, see Halle

atte Herne, see Heron

atte Hill, see Hill

Attehurne, see Heron

atte See, see See

Attewater, John, xi. 28 & n

Attewater, see also Atwater

atte Wode, see Wode, Patrick atte; William atte

Atti, see Aptis

Attingham, William, iii. 88

Atwater, Richard, vii. 31n

Atwater, William, i. 3, 10, 24, 86; iii. 5, 83; vii. 14; xi. 69; xii. 18

Atwater, see also Attewater

Aubert, Audoen, i. 6, 97; vi. 66; xii. 35

Aubert, Hugh, i. 6

Aubert, Stephen, see Albert

Aubussac, see Albusaco

Audele, Audeley, see Audley

Audenard, Giles de, vii. 51

Audilliers, see Andiliers

Audley, Alexander, iii. 95

Audley (Audele, Audeley, Awdeley, Awdley), Edmund, i. 66; ii. 3, 19; iii. 3, 77; iv. 39; v. 10, 48; vi. 23, 53; viii. 42; x. 43; xii. 27, 46

Audley, Robert, iii. 11, 79
Auger, see Aunger
Augustinis, Augustine de, vi. 70
Aukland, John, vi. 111; xii. 73
Aulton, William, iv. 48
Aulton, see also Elton, Olton
Aumenet, William, x. 46
Auncell, John, i. 90; x. 54 & n; xii. 33, 85
Aunger, John, viii. 11, 58 ('Auger'); xii. 76, 80
Aungerville, Richard d', see Bury
Aungerville, see also Angerville
Austell, John, viii. 58, 59
Austell, Thomas, iii. 91; viii. 79; ix. 12, 58
Austell, see also Astel(l)
Austeyne, see Gumby
Avenbury, Giles de, ii. 3
Averburi, Peter de, viii. 16
Averel, see Haverel
Avignon, see Possewyk
Awdeby, see Oudeby, Outheby
Awdeley, Awdley, see Audley
Ayala, Peter de, v. 9, 24
Ayermin, see Ayremynne
Ayleston, John (c. 1412–34), i. 90
Ayleston (Aleston), John de (c. 1336–60), x. 48
Ayleston, Robert (de), i. 48, 82; iii. 9, 13, 35, 66; vi. 80; xii. 52, 53
Ayleward, Thomas, iii. 67; vii. 19; xi. 75
Aylington, Thomas de, viii. 32
Aylmer, John (d. 1392), ix. 41
Aylmer, John (d. 1419), see Eylmer
Aylmer, William, iii. 84
Aylmere, see Eylmer
Aynesworth, Henry, i. 69
Ayra, Henry, viii. 64
Ayremynne, Adam de, iv. 28
Ayremynne (Eyremynne), Richard (de), i. 46; iii. 17; vi. 41; vii. 25; x. 64
Ayremynne (Airemynne, Ayermin, Ermyne, Eyremynne), William (de), i. 42, 79, 108; ii. 50; iii. 76; iv. 23; v. 26, 52; vi. 22, 50, 64, 66, 97; vii. 25 & n; viii. 32; x. 65; xii. 38, 58
Ayscogh, see Aiscough
Aysshton, see Aston
Ayston, William de, iii. 5, 66; xii. 55
Ayston, see also Ashton, Assheton, Aston

Baben, John, vi. 58
Babington, Henry, iii. 66
Babthorpe, Thomas, vi. 53
Babyngle, John, x. 25

Bache, Alexander, xi. 38
Bache, Simon, i. 101, 116; v. 25; x. 58; xii. 85
Bache, see also Beche
Bachiler, William, i. 56
Bacon, Adam, xi. 26
Bacon, John, i. 113; vi. 26, 44, 58, 93; xii. 40
Bacon, Roger de, vi. 16, 28
Baconthorpe (Bakonthorpe), William, iv. 26
Bacton, see Baketon
Badby, John de, iii. 45
Baddeby, Thomas (c. 1362), x. 65
Baddeby, Thomas (de) (c. 1339–79), i. 65; vii. 58; x. 7; xii. 26
Badgeworth, see Beggeworth
Bagart, William, ii. 39
Baggeston, Osbert de, iii. 93
Baghe (Bawthe, Williams), Thomas, iv. 49; v. 19
Bagthorpe, Nicholas, ix. 37
Bagworth, Henry de, vii. 59
Bailly, John, v. 65
Bailly, William, ii. 43
Bailly, see also Bayli
Baily (Bayly), John, ii. 9, 22, 24, 49
Baily, see also Bayli
Bainbridge (Baynbridge, Baynbrigg), Christopher, i. 100; iii. 40, 56, 62; iv. 49 & n; v. 16; vi. 5, 8, 82, 109; ix. 60; xii. 36, 55
Bainbridge, see also Baynbridge
Baker, Edward, see Elton
Baker, Hugh, v. 34
Baker, John (d. 1488), i. 28; viii. 73
Baker, John (c. 1509–13), i. 102, 125; xii. 36
Baker, John (d. 1547), see Elton
Baketon (Bacton, Bakton), Thomas, i. 105; v. 8, 70; xii. 62, 65
Baketon, Walter de, vii. 39
Bakonthorpe, see Baconthorpe
Bakton, see Baketon
Balaeto, William (de), i. 21, 96; xii. 17
Balderston, Christopher, vi. 56
Balding, Thomas, i. 47; ii. 33; xii. 22
Baldock, Ralph de, v. 1, 4, 43 & n, 51
Baldock, Richard de, vi. 88
Baldock (Baldok), Robert (de) (d. 1327), i. 6, 25, 91; iii. 13; iv. 23, 45; v. 11, 36; viii. 19, 80; x. 1, 34, 37; xii. 77
Baldock, Robert de (d. 1353), iii. 27; vi. 12; viii. 19; xii. 66, 77
Baldwin, William, xi. 64
Baldwin, see also Bawdewyn
Ballard, Robert, v. 16, 28
Ballshaw, William, x. 47
Balton, John, viii. 73

Bamburgh, John de, vi. 114
Bampton, John, vii. 14, 35 & n
Bampton, Walter de, ix. 38
Bampton (Baunton), William, ix. 43
Banastre, John, vii. 43
Banastre, Richard, viii. 43
Banastre, Thomas (c. 1369, ? T.B. of Eltisley, d. 1399), viii. 30
Banastre, Thomas (d. 1440), xi. 8(bis), 48
Banastre (Banaster, Fryskenay), Thomas, of Eltisley (d. 1399, ? T.B. c. 1369), i. 61; iii. 24; ix. 41; xi. 24, 30; xii. 25, 53
Banastre, William, viii. 30(bis), 46
Banbury, John (John Hode de Bannebury), i. 27
Bandinellis, Bindus de, vii. 50
Bangor, Richard, xi. 7
Banks, William, i. 119; xii. 41
Bannebury, see Banbury
Banqueto (Benqueto), William Reymund de, iii. 32
Barbar, Lawrence, i. 128
Barbo, Peter (de), i. 114; iii. 12; vi. 55
Barbour, Anthony, viii. 39
Barbour, Henry, see Duke
Barbour, John, ii. 24; ix. 53
Barde, Frederick de, vi. 48
Bardelby, Robert de, vi. 46; vii. 28
Bardis, Adrian de (Adrian Florentinus), i. 117; ii. 11, 33; iii. 64, 79; vii. 20; xii. 40, 45, 49, 55, 56, 74
Bardolf, Edmund, i. 32
Baret (Barret), Andrew, i. 92(bis); v. 40; viii. 13, 63, 79; xi. 22
Baret, see also Barett, Barret
Bareth, Adam, xi. 61n
Barett (Barret), Ivo, vii. 29, 50
Barett, see also Baret, Barret
Barforth, Robert, ix. 11, 21, 56
Barforth(e), see also Bereford, Berford
Barker, Anthony, i. 50
Barker, John, vii. 6
Barker, Thomas, vii. 47, 49
Barking, see Berking
Bar-le-Duc (Barra, Barres), Theobald de, i. 31; vi. 12, 66
Barlow, John, xi. 79
Barlow, Thomas, xi. 71
Barlow, William, xi. 39, 56; xii. 89(bis)
Barnaby, Thomas, vi. 100 & n
Barnaby, see also Barnby, Barneby, Barnolby
Barnard (Bernard), John, i. 64, 67, 105; vi. 67; xii. 26, 27, 37, 71
Barnard, see also Bernard

Barnard Castle, see Bernard Castle
Barnardiston, William, vi. 56
Barnby, John, iii. 34; xii. 53
Barnby, Thomas, see Talour
Barnby, see also Barnaby, Barneby, Barnolby
Barne, John, iii. 14, 65
Barneby, William, xi. 25
Barneby, see also Barnaby, Barnby, Barnolby
Barnesley, Thomas, i. 13, 78; xii. 30
Barnet, John (d. 1373), ii. 1; iv. 14, 56; v. 5n, 8, 28; viii. 1; x. 68; xii. 63
Barnet, John (d. 1407), i. 60, 78; ii. 18; iv. 38; v. 10, 51; vi. 53; xii. 25, 30, 46
Barnolby, Thomas, ix. 9, 40
Barnolby, see also Barnaby, Barnby, Barneby
Barns, Robert, iii. 74
Baron, John, i. 39
Barons, William, v. 4; viii. 26
Barough, John (d. 1499, ? Thomas Barrow), viii. 35; xii. 78
Barough, see also Barrow, Barwe
Barowe (Berewe), John (d. 1462), ii. 5, 6, 52
Barowe, Thomas, see Barrow
Barow(e), see also Barrow, Barwe
Barra, Robert, vi. 74
Barra, Theobald de, see Bar-le-Duc
Barre, Laurence (Lawrence) de la, ii. 50; viii. 70
Barre, Richard de la, ii. 46, 52; xi. 68; xii. 50, 51
Barre, William de la, i. 105 ('William Barre'); xii. 37
Barres, see Bar-le-Duc
Barret, Andrew, see Baret
Barret, David, xi. 56 & n, 57, 58
Barret, Ivo, see Barett
Barret, John, xi. 72
Barret, Thomas (c. 1466–7), vi. 65
Barret, Thomas (d. 1544), i. 76; v. 49; vii. 17
Barret, see also Baret(t), Bareth
Barrow (Barough, Barow, Barowe, Barrowe), Thomas (d. 1499, ? John Barough), i. 87; v. 14; vi. 63; viii. 35; x. 28; xii. 32, 71, 78(bis)
Barrow (Barrowe), William, i. 39; v. 56; vi. 98; xi. 4
Barrow, see also Barough, Barow(e), Barwe
Barry, John, xi. 69n
Barry, Ralph, i. 23, 98
Barry, Thomas, xi. 56
Barton, Henry (de), i. 123; vi. 11, 13, 73; x. 50
Barton, John (c. 1457–66), vi. 30
Barton, John de (c. 1333), ii. 6

Barton, John de (c. 1384–5), ix. 41; xi. 30

Barton, Peter de, iii. 86; viii. 48

Barton, Philip (de), i. 83; iv. 48; v. 33; x. 49

Barton, Ralph, *see* Bartone

Barton, Robert de (13th cent.), v. 70

Barton, Robert de (c. 1348–9), vi. 31

Barton, Thomas (d. 1416), ix. 42

Barton, Thomas (d. 1434), x. 8, 12, 19, 30, 69

Barton, William (d. 1421), i. 101; v. 25, 56; ix. 18

Barton, William (d. 1518), iii. 31, 58, 83; xii. 53, 55, 56

Barton, William de (c. 1343), vii. 58

Barton, *see also* Berton

Bartone, Ralph, ii. 42

Barville, John, v. 55

Barwe, Walter de, xi. 83

Barwe, *see also* Barough, Barow(e), Barrow

Barzac, *see* Podio Barzaco

Basing, Richard, iii. 53

Basing, *see also* Basyng

Basingstoke, William (Mundy) de, vi. 112n; xii. 73

Baskerville, John de, xi. 83

Baskervyle (Baskervilde), Edward, ii. 49

Basleiden, *see* Busleiden

Basset, John, vi. 85; vii. 22

Basset, Reginald, vii. 45

Basset, Roger, i. 76; iii. 75; xi. 59, 83 & n; xii. 30

Basset, William, viii. 42

Basyng, Hugh, iv. 47

Basyng (Kingsmill), William, iv. 48

Basyng, *see also* Basing

Bate, John, vi. 17, 47; viii. 76; ix. 51

Bate, Simon, i. 58

Bate, Walter, v. 54; vi. 47; ix. 57

Bateman (de Vienna), John, ii. 45; iii. 24

Bateman, Thomas, xi. 77

Bateman (de Norwyco), William, i. 4, 93; iv. 23, 26; xii. 13, 34, 58, 59

Bath, *see* Bathonia

Bathe (Bawthe), John (d. 1438), i. 97; iii. 27, 39; v. 34; viii. 78

Bathe, John (d. 1542), Robert, William, *see* Booth

Bathonia, Edmund de, v. 30

Baunton, *see* Bampton, William

Bawdewyn, Richard, ii. 42

Bawdewyn, *see also* Baldwin

Bawthe, John, *see* Bathe

Bawthe, Thomas, *see* Baghe

Baxter, William, i. 110

Bayli, John, i. 60; ii. 27

Bayli, *see also* Bailly, Baily

Bayliff (Bayly), Walter, iii. 88

Bayly, *see* Bailly, Baily, Bayli

Baynbridge, Christopher, *see* Bainbridge

Baynbridge, Reginald, viii. 37

Baynbrigg, *see* Bainbridge

Bays, Robert, viii. 25

Baysham, John, i. 74; ii. 4, 33(*bis*), 51, 52; ix. 50; xii. 44

Beake, *see* Bek, Anthony (d. 1343)

Beamounde, *see* Beaumont, Robert

Béarn, *see* Tylyo

Beauchamp (Bello Campo), Philip (de), i. 25, 97; vi. 35; viii. 1; ix. 13(*bis*), 35; xii. 18, 35

Beauchamp, Richard, ii. 2; iii. 2; iv. 33

Beauchamp, Thomas, iii. 62

Beauchamp, *see also* Becham

Beauford, Thomas de, viii. 59

Beauford, *see also* Beaufort

Beauforest (Bewforest), Robert, x. 28

Beaufort (Bewforth), Henry, i. 2, 113, 116; iii. 62; iv. 46; vi. 76; viii. 4; xii. 13

Beaufort, James (de), iii. 84, 89; iv. 18; v. 8; ix. 10; x. 69

Beaufort (Bewforth), Ralph, vi. 28

Beaufort, *see also* Beauford

Beaumont (Bello Monte), Amaury de, vi. 111 & n

Beaumont (Bello Monte), Louis de, iii. 19; vi. 29, 107; viii. 45

Beaumont (Beamounde), Robert, i. 123; iii. 32, 67, 91

Beaumont (Bello Monte), Thomas, viii. 14, 15, 35, 49, 66

Beautre, John de, ix. 31

Beauveyr, John, i. 5(*bis*), 38(*bis*)

Becham, John, viii. 35; xii. 78

Becham, *see also* Beauchamp

Beche (Beeche), Edmund de la, iii. 9, 78; v. 52; vii. 34

Beche, *see also* Bache

Beck, John, vi. 33

Beck, *see also* Beeke, Bek

Beckingham, *see* Bekenham, Bekingham

Beckington, *see* Bekyngton

Bedale, John, i. 69; iii. 86; vii. 44

Bedall, William, vii. 42

Bedell, *see* Bedyll

Bedewardine, Bedewardyn, *see* Bedwardine

Bedwynd (Bedewynde), Walter de, vi. 12, 13n, 73, 92; viii. 82

Bedewynd, *see also* Bedwynd

Bedford, John de, v. 7 & n, 45

Bedwardine (Bedewardine, Bedewardyn, Smythes), John de, ii. 6, 15, 16

Bedwynd, Thomas, i. 118

Bedwynd, see also Bedewynd

Bedyll (Bedell), Thomas, i. 92, 106; v. 9, 47; vi. 21, 68; vii. 26; viii. 56; ix. 17; xii. 37

Beeche, see Beche

Beeke, Thomas, ix. 59

Beeke, see also Beche, Beck, Bek

Beer, John, viii. 13

Beere, Richard, viii. 61

Beer(e), see also Delabere

Beford (Blower, Byford), William, ii. 41

Beford, see also Bifort, Byford

Beggeworth (Badgeworth, Boggeworth), Walter de, viii. 51; ix. 31

Bek (Beake), Anthony (d. 1343), i. 1, 3, 23, 98, 118; iv. 23; xii. 40

Bek, Anthony (Antony) (de) (d. 1311), v. 62; vi. 107

Bek, Thomas (de), i. 1, 52; iii. 82

Bek, see also Beche, Beck, Beeke

Bekenham, Edmund, iii. 25; xii. 53

Bekenham, see also Bekingham

Bekensall, Adam, xi. 48

Bekensaw, Robert, i. 22, 29

Bekingham, John, i. 18

Bekingham, Simon de, vi. 9, 10 & n

Bekingham (Bekyngham), Thomas, i. 7, 11, 41, 85; iii. 89

Bekingham, see also Bekenham

Bekyngton (Beckington, Bekynton), Thomas, i. 16, 77; iii. 29, 83; v. 40; vi. 34, 79, 87; vii. 29; viii. 2, 44, 79; x. 46

Belamy, Robert, i. 51; xii. 23

Belassis, Anthony, ix. 66

Bele, Richard, see Wraxall

Bele, Thomas, v. 42

Belers, Hamo (de), i. 5; iv. 27; vii. 57; xii. 14

Bell, John (d. 1491/2), xi. 69

Bell, John (d. 1556), i. 30; iv. 58, 62; v. 59; x. 34; xii. 19

Bell, Richard, vi. 99, 111

Belles, see Gyddyng

Bellingham, John, x. 34, 59

Bello (Haldingham), Richard de, ii. 38; iii. 9, 45, 58; xii. 49

Bello Campo, see Beauchamp

Bello Monte, see Beaumont

Belton, Simon, i. 47; viii. 26

Belton, Thomas, see Woodford

Beltryng, Richard, de Pecham, vii. 59

Benedict (c. 1345), xi. 40

Benedict, see also Benet

Benelard (de Bono Villario), John, ii. 51

Benese, Richard, ii. 9; xii. 45

Benestede (Benstede), John (de), iii. 90; x. 53

Benestede, see also Benstede

Benet, see Benedict

Benet ab Iorwerth, see Montealto

Benet, Nicholas, see Nicholls, Benedict

Benet, Thomas, x. 67

Benet, William, iii. 92

Benet, see also Bennet

Beneyt, John, viii. 25 & n, 35

Beneyt, Michael, viii. 82

Beneyt, see also Bennet

Benlloyde (Benloyde), Roger, ii. 22

Bennet, Thomas, iii. 16, 26, 45; v. 16, 36, 60; viii. 27

Bennet, William (c. 1512, ? W.B. d. 1533), vii. 22

Bennet, William (d. 1533, ? W.B. c. 1512), iii. 8; v. 34; viii. 56

Bennet, see also Benet, Beneyt

Bennington, Robert, of Walworth, vi. 110

Benniworth, Henry, i. 4

Benqueto, see Banqueto

Benson, Richard, ii. 30

Benstan, see Bestane

Benstede (Bensted), Andrew, i. 119, 122; vii. 29, 44; viii. 71

Benstede, John, see Benestede

Benteley, John, xii. 88

Benteworth, see Bentworth

Bentham, Thomas, ix. 41

Bentworth (Benteworth, Bynteworth), Richard (de), i. 106; iii. 29; iv. 17; v. 2, 27, 47; viii. 63

Benyngworth, see Benniworth

Bere, see Delabere

Bereford, Edmund (de), i. 25, 120; iii. 84

Bereford, see also Barforth, Berford

Bereham (Boreham), Michael de, ii. 24, 45; v. 38; vii. 56; xii. 47, 50

Berenger, John, of Ypres, iv. 27; vi. 78; xii. 59, 71

Beresford, James, x. 49

Berewe, see Barowe

Bereworth (Berworth), Stephen, i. 37; iii. 10, 11, 60 (bis)

Berewyk, John de (d. 1312), iii. 36; v. 31; vi. 48; viii. 48; ix. 23, 24; x. 55

Berewyk, John de (d. 1377), viii. 21 & n

Berford (Barforthe), William, i. 88; x. 22

Berford, see also Barforth, Bereford

Berges, William de, iii. 9, 55

Bergeveney (Bergevenny), William de, vii. 48; viii. 77; xi. 27

Bergevenny, Vincent de, xi. 32

Bergeveny, John Fliwe of, see Fliwe

Berkeley, Eudo de, viii. 46

Berkeley, Ivo de, viii. 49

Berkeley, James (de), i. 8, 10n, 43, 79, 113; ii. 42; vii. 46; viii. 46, 68; ix. 1, 23; xi. 80; xii. 39

Berkeley, Peter (de), i. 38; iii. 61; viii. 34, 46; xi. 84

Berkeley, Thomas, ii. 28

Berkham, Thomas de, vii. 58

Berking, John de, v. 64

Bermyngham (Bermyngeham, Birmingham), Fulk, i. 14, 58, 99; iii. 29, 52, 74, 91, 92; v. 24, 29; vi. 59; vii. 31; viii. 40; x. 66; xii. 25, 35

Bermyngham (Birmingham), Richard (de), x. 15, 19, 49; xi. 29; xii. 88

Bermyngham (Birmingham, Byrmyncham), William (de), ii. 4, 21, 32; ix. 36

Bermyngham, see also Bernyngham, Brynnyngham

Bernard, Benjamin, viii. 61; xii. 80

Bernard, John (c. 1397–1432), see Barnard

Bernard, John (d. 1460), viii. 7, 11, 52, 79

Bernard, Richard de, x. 17

Bernard, William, vii. 60

Bernard Castle, Richard de, vi. 114

Bernardi, William, de Ranato, v. 27

Bernardini (Bernardyn), Philip, iii. 100

Berners, Ralph, viii. 70; xii. 81

Bernham, William, viii. 28 & n, 32 & n; xii. 78(bis)

Bernham, see also Burnham

Bernyngham (Berningham), John, iii. 85; v. 26, 46, 53; vi. 8, 14, 90 & n; xii. 64, 67

Bernyngham, see also Bermyngham, Brynnyngham

Bernyngton, Henry de, ii. 8

Berowne, William, ii. 38

Berton, Thomas de, vi. 10

Berton, see also Barton

Berworth, see Bereworth

Bessia, Nicholas de, vii. 43

Bestane (Benstan, Bestan), John de, ii. 29; iii. 31

Betts, William, iii. 26

Betty, Richard, v. 58; viii. 48; ix. 49

Beverlay, Peter, see Irford

Beverlay, Richard (de), see Beverley

Beverley, John, i. 26, 49; xii. 18, 23

Beverley (Beverlay), Richard (de), i. 51, 85; iii. 46, 77; x. 11

Beverley, Simon, ii. 38

Beverley, William (c. 1493, ? W.B. d. 1494), ix. 59

Beverley, William (d. 1494, ? W.B. c. 1493), vi. 12, 45

Beverley, William de (c. 1361–71), v. 59; vi. 79, 114; xii. 71, 73

Bewforest, see Beauforest

Bewforth, see Beaufort

Bifort, Llywellyn, xi. 4

Bifort, see also Beford, Byford

Bigge, see Bygge

Bigges, John, iii. 70, 99

Biggleswade (Bikeleswade), Geoffrey (de), i. 104; xi. 83

Bigod, Richard, v. 62

Bikeleswade, see Biggleswade

Bildeston, Nicholas, see Billesden

Bildeston, William, xii. 82

Billesden (Bildeston, Billeston), Nicholas, i. 34; iii. 4, 29; iv. 51 & n; v. 61; vi. 87; viii. 47; xii. 20

Billyngsford, James de, viii. 65

Bilton, Adam de, vi. 39

Bingham, see Byngham

Birchold, Thomas, iii. 93

Birckinshawe, see Brekynshall

Bird (Britt), Ralph, vi. 51, 83

Bird, Richard, i. 98; xii. 35

Bird, Thomas, xi. 38

Birde, John, xi. 5

Bird(e), see also Byrd(e)

Birkenhead, John (c. 1490), x. 14n

Birkenhead, see also Brikenhead

Birkhead (Brigett), Edmund, xi. 39

Birkhed (Birkhede, Bryhed), John (d. 1468), vii. 24; viii. 67

Birkhed, see also Birkenhead, Brikenhead

Birland, Thomas, i. 44

Birley, William (d. 1510), i. 88, 112; vi. 76; xii. 33

Birley, William (c. 1510–25), vii. 9, 17, 23, 31, 40, 45(bis), 47

Birley, see also Burley

Birmingham, see Bermyngham

Birom, Ralph, x. 48 & n, 60 & n; xii. 85

Birom (Byrom), Thomas, vi. 24; x. 28, 46, 56

Birstall, William de, vi. 38

Birstall, see also Borstall, Burstall

Birston (Birstone), William (de), i. 48; iv. 60; xii. 61

Bis, see Bysse

Bishopston (Bishopstone, Bisshopeston), John (de) (d. 1384), ii. 34; iii. 71; vi. 24, 40; vii. 8 & n, 10, 35 & n, 41

Bishopstone, John de (c. 1303), vii. 8n

Bismano, William de, ix. 10, 21

Bisse, see Bysse

Bitton, Thomas de, ix. 1

Blacket, Walter, vii. 26; x. 41

Blake, John, i. 88

Blakeborne (Blakeborn, Blakebourn), Henry (de), i. 27, 74; iii. 77; ix. 40

Blakedon, James, xi. 5

Blakmoor, Henry, viii. 40

Blakwyn, John, i. 78; iii. 34; xii. 30

Blanchard (Blancherd), John, iv. 62; viii. 32; xii. 61, 78

Blandiaco (Blanzac), John de, iii. 19

Blankney, William, i. 100

Blanzac, see Blandiaco

Blasgrove, Robert, viii. 74

Blaston (Glaston), Geoffrey de, x. 16, 20 & n, 59 & n

Blebury, see Blewbury

Bleddyn ab Einion, xi. 40

Bleddyn, Dafydd ap, see Dafydd ap Bleddyn

Bleddyn, Evan ap, see Evan ap Bleddyn

Blencow, see Blynckoo

Blewbury (Blebury), John de, iii. 75; v. 63; viii. 56 & n, 68

Blewe, John, ix. 45

Bleynorhasset, Thomas, x. 8

Bliburgo (Bliburgh, Blibury), William de, vi. 54, 71; viii. 54; x. 43 & n

Blida, Walter, i. 48

Blida, see also Blyda, Blyth(e)

Blithe, see Blythe

Blodwell (Blodwel), David (Dafydd), ii. 49; xi. 41

Blodwell (Blodewell, Blodwel), John, ii. 49; viii. 29; x. 28; xi. 41, 50, 72

Blounham, John, vii. 7, 10, 26

Blount, Walter, iii. 22, 66, 70

Blower, see Beford

Bloxham, John, iv. 50

Bloyou, Henry, ix. 27

Bloyou, John, ix. 25, 26

Bloyou, William, ix. 24

Bluet, Thomas, xi. 82

Bluntesdon, Henry de (Henry le Ammoigner, ? Henry the king's almoner), iii. 7, 44; v. 26n; vii. 55; x. 40

Bluntesdon, Robert de, iii. 5, 90; xii. 52, 56

Blyda, Adam de, vi. 33

Blyda, see also Blida, Blyth(e)

Blynckoo (Blencow), William, i. 89; xii. 33

Blyth, William de, vi. 15

Blythe, Edward, vii. 21n

Blythe (Blithe), Geoffrey (d. 1530/1), iii. 13, 20, 45, 90; iv. 61; v. 62; vi. 8, 21, 82; x. 3; xii. 52, 56, 61

Blythe (Blithe), Geoffrey (d. 1541), x. 8n, 12, 20 & n, 49, 61

Blythe (Blithe), John (d. 1499), i. 9, 19, 82; iii. 3; vi. 26, 68; xii. 14, 17, 31, 71

Blythe (Blithe), John (d. 1547), x. 10, 16 & n, 44, 46, 59, 61, 65

Blythe (Blithe), John (d. 1558), ii. 45, 51; vii. 21 & n

Blythe (Blithe), John (d. 1561), x. 16n, 20 & n, 40, 65

Blythe, Robert, v. 62

Blythe (Blithe), Thomas, x. 27

Blythe (Blithe), William de, iv. 28; vii. 36

Blythe, see also Blida, Blyda

Bochell, John, viii. 73

Bockenhull (Bochenhull, Bukunhull), Huw (Hugh) (de), vii. 59; xi. 45 & n; xii. 89

Bockyng (Bokyng), Thomas de, viii. 54 & n

Bocland, see Bokland

Bocton, Thomas de, iii. 5, 68, 93

Bocton, see also Bucton, Buketon, Bukton

Bodeln, John (c. 1390, ? John Bodilly), xi. 82

Bodenham, Richard de, viii. 67

Bodilly, John (c. 1389, ? John Bodeln), xi. 71

Bodley, Helesius, viii. 31

Bodrigan, Thomas de, vii. 33

Bodrigan, William de, ix. 15

Bodringham, John de, xi. 83

Boerio, Bernard, iii. 79; viii. 81

Boerio, Jerome, viii. 80

Boerius, John (Boerius Genensis), vi. 113n

Boeti, Oliver, i. 48

Boggeworth, see Beggeworth

Bohun, Ralph de, v. 70

Bokbridge, Bokebrugg, see Burghbridge

Bokelly, Richard, viii. 51

Bokelyn, see Robelyn

Bokemar, see Sabello, James de

Boket, William, viii. 12, 64, 76

Bokingham (Buckingham), John de (d. 1387), vi. 64

Bokingham, John (de) (d. 1399), see Buckingham

Bokland (Bocland, Bubland), William de, viii. 6

Bokulton, Richard, xi. 73

Bokyng, see Bockyng

Bokyngham, see Bokingham, Buckingham

Bolde, John (d. 1443), vii. 37; x. 38
Bolde, John (d. 1451), iii. 94
Bole, Richard, iv. 19; v. 58
Bole, *see also* Boule, Boyle
Boleie (Boley), Thomas de, ii. 10
Boleyn, Henry, i. 20; vii. 12
Boleyn (Bolen), John, viii. 52
Boleyn, Robert, xi. 26
Boleyn (Bolen, Boleyne), Thomas, ii. 37; iii. 25; v. 57 & n; viii. 7, 12, 44
Boleyn (Bolen), William, iv. 51; v. 25; vi. 82
Boloigne, Pascasius de, v. 64
Bolter, Roger, ix. 5, 7, 11, 14, 46
Bolton, William (d. 1489), i. 101; iii. 68; v. 32; viii. 48; xii. 36
Bolton, William (d. 1532), ii. 16; xi. 39
Bonaura, John de, vii. 51
Bonawnter, Richard, vii. 35
Bondeby, Andrew, vi. 16
Bondeby, Nigel, xi. 6
Bondeby, Ralph de, viii. 83
Bone, Robert, iii. 66
Bonewell, James, iv. 26
Boniface, Peter, iii. 59
Bonifant (Bonyfaunt, Twynge), Thomas, i. 117; iii. 72; v. 20; ix. 55
Bonner, Edmund, i. 13; ii. 3; v. 4, 31
Bono Villario, John de, *see* Benelard
Bonovillario, William de, i. 54
Bontempi, Andreas (Andrew), ii. 12; iii. 9
Bonyfaunt, *see* Bonifant
Bonyngton, John, viii. 72
Boor, John, iii. 42, 96; vi. 67; vii. 24
Boord (Boorde), Edmund le, ii. 21
Booth (Bothe, Bowthe), Charles, i. 16, 53, 66; ii. 3; v. 59; x. 12 & n; xii. 24, 44
Booth (Bothe), Edmund, i. 19; v. 30; xii. 17
Booth (Bothe), Hamo, ix. 56 (*bis*)
Booth (Bothe), John (d. 1478), v. 46; vi. 14, 26, 36, 81, 94; ix. 2; xii. 69
Booth (Bothe), John (d. 1496), vi. 76; x. 12
Booth (Bathe, Bothe, Bowthe), John (d. 1542), ii. 6, 31; iii. 24
Booth (Bothe), Lawrence (Laurence), i. 19; v. 6, 46, 53, 63, 67; vi. 5, 26, 91, 93, 108; x. 41, 48(*bis*) & n, 60 & n
Booth (Bothe), Ralph, vi. 19, 113
Booth (Bathe, Bothe, Bowthe), Robert, iii. 43; vi. 8, 28, 91; xii. 54
Booth (Bothe), Thomas (d. 1501), vi. 29
Booth (Bothe), Thomas (c. 1533–40), ii. 49
Booth (Bathe, Bothe, Bowthe), William, i. 62, 74; iii. 40; v. 12, 19n, 29, 32; vi. 4; x. 2
Boreham, *see* Bereham

Borough, *see* Burgh
Boroughbridge, *see* Ponteburgh
Borsano, Simon de, iii. 57, 102
Borstall (Borstal, Borstalle), William (de), i. 33; ii. 7, 9, 14; v. 20; viii. 23; ix. 40; xii. 45, 63
Borstall, *see also* Birstall, Burstall
Borstan, William de (c. 1341, ? W. de Worston, W. de Plumstock), v. 17
Bosco, John de, vii. 57
Bosco, William de (d. 1313), iii. 17, 75; xii. 52
Bosco, William de (d. 1328), vii. 56; x. 9; xii. 75
Bosco, *see also* Boys
Bosham, John, ii. 40
Bosoun, Robert, ix. 9, 40
Bostock, John, iii. 48, 70; ix. 60
Boston, William, vii. 34
Boteler, Edward, i. 43; xii. 22
Boteler, John, i. 14, 26, 99, 122
Boteler(e), *see also* Botiler, Botler, Butiller, Butler
Boter, John, ii. 10, 41
Bothe, *see* Booth
Botheby, William, vi. 81
Botiler, Simon de, iv. 59
Botiler, Botiller, *see also* Boteler, Botler, Butiller, Butler
Botler, Thomas, viii. 50
Botler, *see also* Boteler, Botiler, Butiller, Butler
Botriaux, Walter de, ix. 29
Bottal, Roger de, xi. 59, 63, 78
Bottisham, *see* Buck!sham
Bottlesham, John (de), i. 12, 41, 56, 92; iv. 38; vi. 74; xii. 15, 21, 24, 33, 60, 71
Bottlesham, Thomas de, iv. 41n
Bottlesham, William de, iv. 38; xi. 21, 22n; xii. 60
Boucer, Boucher, *see* Bourgchier
Boudon, William de (? W. de London), v. 38; vi. 31; xii. 73
Boudon, *see also* Bowdon
Bouhs, *see* Bush, John
Bouker, Robert, i. 98
Bouland (Bowland), John de, x. 37; xi. 60 & n, 66(*bis*) & nn
Boule, Richard (de), i. 43; viii. 20; x. 15, 21, 43; xi. 24; xii. 22
Boule, William, x. 37
Boule, *see also* Bole, Boyle
Bouler, Edmund, viii. 8
Boulers, Reginald, ii. 2; x. 2; xi. 22; xii. 44, 84
Boulers, William, ii. 35

Bourbank, Thomas, vi. 102n
Bourbank (Burbank), William (c. 1512–31), i. 128 ('Bourbanks'); iii. 55; vi. 49, 102; xii. 43
Bourbank (Burbank, Smithson, Smythson), William (d. 1532), i. 128; vi. 49, 84; xii. 73
Bourchier, see Bourgchier
Boureman (Bowreman), William, viii. 12, 20, 66; xii. 76, 77
Bourgchier (Boucer, Boucher, Bourchier, Bourghchier, Bowser), John, i. 16, 37; iv. 9; v. 47; viii. 40; xii. 16, 20, 58, 63, 79
Bourgchier (Boucer, Boucher, Bourchier, Bourghchire), Thomas, i. 55; iii. 85; iv. 5, 15(bis), 57; vi. 94; viii. 36; x. 26; xii. 58
Bourghill, see Burghill
Bourle, see Burley
Bourn (Bourne), Bartholomew (de), i. 56, 65, 76; iii. 65; vi. 13, 92
Bourn, John (d. 1349), i. 32
Bourn, John (c. 1329–51), i. 73; xii. 29
Bourne (Burne), Thomas, iv. 40
Bourne, see also Burne
Bourser, see Bouser
Bourton, see Burton
Bouser (Bourser, Burghchier), John de, v. 10
Bovelyth, see Joynour
Bovisville, Gaspard de, vi. 35
Bovy, see Morton, John (d. 1459)
Bowdon, Thomas, i. 40
Bowdon, see also Boudon
Bowen, Dafydd, see Dafydd ab Owain
Bowen, Huw, see Huw ab Owain
Bowen, Lewis, see Owain, Lewis, ab Owain
Bowet, Henry (d. 1423), i. 7(bis), 11, 58, 80; iii. 19, 42; v. 23; vi. 4, 60; vii. 59; viii. 2; xii. 14, 31
Bowet, Henry (c. 1410–47), ii. 36; vi. 23, 26, 43, 65, 67, 81
Bowet, Robert, vi. 24, 28
Bowland, see Bouland
Bowreman, see Boureman
Bowser, see Bourgchier, John
Bowthe, see Booth
Boxley, Walter, iv. 41
Boyden, William, x. 54
Boyle, Nicholas, x. 27
Boyle, see also Bole, Boule
Boys, John de, xi. 83
Boys, see also Bosco
Bozoun, Simon, iv. 25
Bozoun, Thomas, iv. 26

Brabazon, John de, vi. 12; vii. 55; viii. 26n, 42
Brackerne, David, xi. 47
Braclesham (Brakelesham), Walter de, vii. 16
Braclesham, see also Brakelesham
Bracy, John, viii. 53
Bradden, Bartholomew de, iii. 19, 24, 93
Bradebridge, Nicholas, i. 24, 86, 128; vii. 30; xii. 18
Bradegare (Bragar), Robert, v. 60; vii. 27; xii. 64
Bradeley, see Bradley
Bradeneye, Anthony de, viii. 46
Bradenham, Henry de, iv. 30
Bradeston, see Bradston
Bradley (Bradeley), William de, v. 42; vii. 27; x. 27
Bradston (Bradeston), John, i. 36, 77; vi. 49; viii. 62; xii. 20
Bradwardine, Thomas (de), i. 4, 38; iv. 3 (bis), 27; v. 18, 25; xii. 21
Bragar, see Bradegare
Braie, John (c. 1501, ? J. Bray), vi. 52
Brakelesham, Walter de, see Braclesham
Brakelesham, William, vii. 9n
Brakenburgh, Richard, i. 105; vii. 9; xii. 37, 74
Brambre, see Brembre
Brampton (Brankton), John (d. 1402/3), viii. 28
Brampton, John (c. 1410), xi. 14
Brancatiis (Brancacio), Raynald de, i. 54; vi. 18, 81; viii. 10, 79
Branche (Branke), Henry, see Saracenis
Branche (Branor), Nicholas, de Urbe, iii. 76
Branche, Robert, see Braunche
Branche, William, iii. 7
Brande, William, vi. 21, 32, 57, 89; xii. 67 (bis), 70, 72
Brandisby, see Bransby
Brandon (Braundon), Reginald (de), i. 34; v. 60
Brandon, Thomas (de), i. 51, 56, 123; vi. 16, 35, 40, 60; x. 56
Brandoun, Walter, xi. 50
Branke, see Saracenis
Brankescombe (Braynscomb), Richard de, iii. 49
Branketre, John de, v. 63n, 68; vi. 13
Brankton, see Brampton, John (d. 1402/3)
Branor, see Branche, Nicholas
Bransby (Brandisby), John, i. 52; vi. 61, 75
Bransford, Wulstan de, iv. 56(bis), 59 & n; xii. 60

Brantingham (Brantyngham), Thomas (de), i. 80; ii. 1, 24; v. 50; viii. 10, 33; ix. 2 & n, 37

Braose, Hugh de, ii. 22

Braose (Brewosa), Thomas de, v. 70

Brauncewell, Henry, i. 35, 51, 88, 121; xii. 41

Braunche (Branche), Robert, viii. 64

Braunche, *see also* Branche

Braundeston, Thomas de, xi. 25, 26

Braundeston, *see also* Braunston, Brenston

Braundon, *see* Brandon, Reginald (de)

Braunston, William, i. 107

Braunston, *see also* Braundeston, Brenston

Brawby, John de, vi. 77

Brawode, Stephen de, viii. 81

Bray, Edward, iii. 101; viii. 56

Bray, Henry de, viii. 81

Bray, John (c. 1503, ? J. Braie), viii. 56

Bray (Brey), Paul, ix. 31

Bray, Richard, iii. 101

Bray, Thomas (c. 1306–23), i. 27, 72, 111; xii. 18

Bray, Thomas (d. 1383), viii. 19, 26

Bray, William de, v. 54

Braybroke, Nicholas (de), v. 50 & n; viii. 23; ix. 16, 36

Braybroke (Braybrok, Braybrooke), Reginald, i. 27; ii. 14; iii. 30, 81; v. 22, 37

Braybroke, Robert (de), i. 27; iii. 4; v. 2; vi. 48, 50; vii. 59; viii. 23; ix. 16, 40; x. 25; xii. 18

Braybroke, William, iii. 30

Brayleigh, Richard de, ix. 4, 6, 25

Brayne, Roger, ii. 12, 42, 49

Braynscomb, *see* Brankescombe

Braynton (Breynton), Roger de, ii. 28, 38, 50; iv. 61

Braynton, *see also* Breynton

Breakspear, *see* Saunders, Hugh

Brech, John, v. 24

Brechonia (Brecon), Llywelyn de, xi. 84

Bredon, John de, iii. 19

Bredon, Simon de, vii. 11, 12n, 48

Bredon, Thomas de, iii. 19, 71; v. 46n; vii. 59

Breerton, John, v. 42

Breerton, *see also* Breneton

Breinton, *see* Breynton

Brekesbourne, *see* Brokesbourne

Brekles, *see* Brykles

Brekynshall (Birckinshawe, Byrchynshawe), Maurice, viii. 47; xi. 42

Brembre (Brambre), Thomas (de), i. 93, 113; iii. 89; v. 61; vii. 45; xii. 34, 39, 56

Bremesgrove, *see* Bromsgrove

Bremore (Bremor), John, i. 11, 84(*bis*); v. 35; vii. 26, 41; ix. 16; xii. 15, 31(*bis*)

Brencheslee, *see* Brinchesle

Brenston, William, x. 44

Brenston, *see also* Braundeston, Braunston

Brent, Thomas, v. 41

Brereton, William, viii. 45

Brereton, *see also* Breerton

Brerewood, Thomas, v. 62; ix. 5, 21, 63, 64

Brescia, Peter de, *see* Carmelian

Brescia, William de, i. 42

Bresley, *see* Briselee

Breto, Arnald de le, i. 8, 40; viii. 10

Breto, Bernard Ezius de le, iv. 7; vi. 90

Breto, Guicard (Guichard) de le, i. 8, 40; iv. 7

Breton, John, i. 114, 125; ii. 33; vii. 22; xii. 40, 49

Breton, *see also* Bretten, Bretunne

Bretoun, Alan le, x. 11

Bretoun, *see also* Bretten, Bretunne

Brett, William, viii. 72

Bretten, William, i. 86

Bretten, *see also* Breton, Bretoun, Bretunne

Brettevill, John, v. 60

Bretunne, Joachim, x. 18, 31, 65, 70; xii. 86

Bretunne, *see also* Breton, Bretoun, Bretten

Breus, John, vii. 19

Brewer, Gilbert de, *see* Bruera

Brewer, Richard, v. 6n

Brewosa, *see* Braose

Brewster, John, x. 44, 52

Brewster, William, i. 84; v. 50; vii. 16; ix. 51

Brey, *see* Bray

Breynton (Breinton), John de, viii. 60

Breynton, Roger de, *see* Braynton

Brian (Bryane, Bryenne), John (de), i. 74, 98; iii. 56, 92; ix. 32 & n; x. 67; xi. 81; xii. 29, 86

Brian (Bryenne), Philip de, xi. 82

Brian (Bryan, Bryenne), Reginald (de), iii. 73, 80; iv. 14, 56; vi. 66; ix. 32n; xi. 53, 81

Brian (Bryan), Walter de, iii. 33

Brian, William de, *see* Bryan

Brichill (Bricchull, Brykehul), William de, x. 32, 40; xi. 46

Bridbroke, John, ii. 9, 19; xii. 46

Bridd, John (c. 1380), vi. 82

Bride (Bryde), John (d. 1478), x. 16, 43, 68

Bridekirk, John de, vi. 77

Bridelington, *see* Bridlington

Bridham, Hugh (de), vii. 19; ix. 18, 37; xi. 84; xii. 83

Bridlington, John de, vi. 73

Bridlington (Bridelington), Robert, i. 122; vi. 71; xii. 41

Bridlington, Thomas, viii. 14

Bridport, *see* Brydeport

Brigencourt, Peter de, viii. 81

Brigencourt, *see also* Briguencourt

Brigett, *see* Birkhead

Brigge, John, viii. 57

Brigge, *see also* Brugge

Briggeford, William, v. 44, 51

Brightwell, Thomas, i. 78; v. 40

Briguencourt, John de, viii. 82

Briguencourt, *see also* Brigencourt

Brikenhead (Brikhed), Ralph, xi. 48

Brikenhead, *see also* Birkenhead, Birkhead, Birkhed

Brimpton, William de, iii. 84

Brinchesle (Brencheslee), Richard (de), i. 8, 46; v. 20, 31

Brinkele (Brynkeleye), John de, v. 15, 53, 63; vi. 24

Brinklowe (Brynkelowe), William, x. 28

Brinknell, Thomas, i. 89

Brinton (Brunton), Thomas, iv. 38; xii. 60

Brinton (Brytone), Walter de, viii. 46

Briscia, *see* Carmelian

Briseban, William de, vi. 101

Briselee (Bryslay), Matthew (de), i. 86; iii. 55; x. 55; xii. 54

Briselee (Bresley, Brisele, Brislay, Bryslay), Simon (de), i. 4, 82; vi. 73; x. 6; xii. 31

Bristol, Simon de, viii. 8

Brita, *see* Bryte

Britt, *see* Bird, Ralph

Brocas, Arnold (Arnald), i. 67; viii. 61; xii. 27, 80

Brocas (de Brocariis, de Broquas), Bernard, vii. 32; viii. 61; ix. 37; xii. 7

Brockholes (Brokhole), John, vi. 36; viii. 29

Brode, Roger, x. 34

Broke, Ralph de, vi. 35

Broke, Robert, ix. 11, 39

Broke, Thomas, viii. 54

Brokeburn, William, xi. 25

Brokesbourne (Brekesbourne), Stephen (de), i. 38; viii. 54; xii. 21

Brokhole, *see* Brockholes

Brokland, Henry, ix. 41

Brom, Roger de, vi. 44

Brome, Adam, i. 17

Brome, Robert, *see* Broun

Bromefeld (Bromfield, Bromfyld, Bromfylde), Richard, ii. 19; xi. 11; xii. 46, 87

Bromefeld, *see also* Bromfield

Bromehale, Thomas, viii. 38, 76

Bromfield, Edmund, xi. 22 & n

Bromfield, Llywelyn de, *see* Llywelyn ab Ynyr

Bromfield, Richard, *see* Bromefeld

Bromford, *see* Brunforte

Bromfyld(e), *see* Bromefeld

Bromsgrove (Bremesgrove, Brommesgrave, Brymesgrave, Brymmesgrave, Dypphull, Dyppull), John, i. 97; iii. 32; vii. 42; viii. 69

Bromwich (Bromwiche, Bromwyche), James, ii. 13, 18; iii. 13, 26, 46, 50, 58, 64; xii. 45

Bromyerd (Bromyard), William de, x. 27

Bronde, *see* Catton, Robert

Brook, Henry, iv. 48

Brook(e), *see also* Broke

Broquas, *see* Brocas

Broun, Richard (d. 1414), ix. 45

Broun, Richard (d. 1452), *see* Cordon

Broun (Brome, Browne), Robert, iii. 46, 79; iv. 50; xi. 75, 76; xii. 89(*bis*)

Broun (Broune), Walter, viii. 11; ix. 15n

Broun (Windsor), William, i. 49

Brouns, Richard, *see* Cordon

Brouns, Thomas, i. 5, 18, 39, 76; iii. 4, 10, 81; iv. 24, 39, 57; vii. 2, 60; x. 38

Brouward, John, i. 109

Brouweon, Thomas de, vii. 13

Brown, *see* Cordon

Browne, Gregory, x. 28

Browne, Robert, *see* Broun

Browne, William, x. 56

Browning, John, viii. 66

Brownyng, William, ix. 50

Brucy, John de, iv. 62

Bruera (Brewer, Bruer), Gilbert de, iv. 17; v. 5, 59; vi. 46; vii. 28; viii. 39, 48; x. 52, 68

Bruera, *see also* Brewer

Brugge, Andrew de, vii. 55

Brugge, Edmund, vii. 37

Brugge, John (c. 1404, ? J.B. d. 1407), vii. 60

Brugge, John (d. 1407, ? J.B. c. 1404), ii. 32

Brugge (Brigge), Walter (d. 1395), ii. 48; vi. 48

Brugge, Walter (de) (c. 1389–96), xi. 69, 74 (*bis*) & n

Brugge, *see also* Brigge

Brughill, *see* Burghill

Brunel(l), *see* Burnel

Brunforte (Bromford), John, son of Octavian de, x. 18, 42, 50

Brunton, *see* Brinton, Thomas

Bruton, John (c. 1323, ? de B. d. 1339, or J. de B. c. 1319–39), iv. 7

Bruton, John de (d. 1339, ? J.B. c. 1323, or J. de B. c. 1319–39), ix. 4, 8, 23

Bruton, John de (c. 1319–39, ? J.B.c. 1323, or J. de B. d. 1339), viii. 10, 48

Bruton, John de (d. 1432), viii. 53

Bruton (Frere), Richard, v. 12, 44, 60; viii. 9, 18

Bryan (Brian, Bryenne), William (de), v. 30, 55; vi. 87; xii. 63, 64

Bryan(e), *see also* Brian

Bryconel, *see* Byconyll

Bryde, *see* Bride

Brydeport, Nicholas, ii. 22; xii. 47

Bryenne, *see* Brian, Bryan

Brygon, William, iii. 48, 70, 83, 90

Bryhed, *see* Birkhed

Brykehul, *see* Brichill

Brykles (Brekles), John, vii. 41

Brymesgrave, Brymmesgrave, *see* Bromsgrove

Brynk (Dobeler), John, xi. 77

Brynkeleye, *see* Brinkele

Brynkelowe, *see* Brinklowe

Brynnyngham, John de, vii. 41

Brynnyngham, *see also* Bermyngham, Bernyngham

Bryslay, *see* Briselee

Bryte (Brita), Reynold, viii. 23

Brython, John ap Hywel ap, *see* John ap Hywel ap Brython

Brytone, *see* Brinton, Walter de

Bubbewyth, *see* Bubwith

Bubland, *see* Bokland

Bubwith (Bubbewyth), Nicholas, i. 116; iii. 2, 8, 42; v. 2, 23, 35; vi. 26, 35, 45; vii. 60; viii. 2, 55; ix. 13, 44; x. 47, 52, 69; xi. 29

Bubwith (Bubbewyth), Thomas, iii. 36, 96; v. 69; viii. 9, 14, 20, 62; x. 47

Buckenham, Robert, vii. 14n

Buckingham, John de (c. 1332), ix. 28; xii. 83

Buckingham, John de (d. 1387), *see* Bokingham

Buckingham (Bokingham, Bokyngham), John (de) (d. 1399), i. 1, 10, 46, 67, 116; iii. 77, 89; iv. 14; v. 46; vi. 24; x. 2, 6, 21; xi. 70; xii. 13, 14, 40, 58

Buckingham, John of (d. 1367), *see* Skyret

Buckingham (Bokyngham), Thomas de, ix. 9, 31

Buckingham (Bokyngham), William, v. 53

Buckingham, *see also* Bokingham, Buckenham, Bukingham

Buckmaster, William, ii. 24; v. 41; xii. 47

Bucksham (Bottisham), Nicholas de, x. 40

Buckton, *see* Buketon

Buckworth, *see* Capell

Bucton, Thomas de (d. by 1368, ? T. de Bukton), vi. 88

Bucton, *see also* Bocton, Buketon, Bukton

Budocio, Bertrand de, iii. 89

Bugwell, Reginald de, viii. 51, 61; ix. 4, 34; xii. 80

Buk, Walter, viii. 65 & n, 80n

Bukbrigg, *see* Burghbrigg

Buketon (Buckton), John de, iv. 16

Buketon, *see also* Bocton, Bucton, Bukton

Bukingham, Gilbert de, x. 71

Bukingham, *see also* Bokingham, Buckenham, Buckingham

Bukton, Thomas de (d. 1366, ? T. de Bucton), viii. 19, 51, 63

Bukton, *see also* Bocton, Bucton, Buketon

Bukunhull, *see* Bockenhull

Bulcano, Marius, vi. 112

Bulcote, William, i. 49

Bulgyn, John, v. 41

Bulkeley, Arthur, xi. 5, 16, 48

Bulkeley, Richard, xi. 10, 11

Bullock (Bullok), Walter, i. 103; ix. 45; x. 9, 16, 33 & n, 36 & n, 46, 58; xii. 37

Bulmere, John de, v. 25

Bulneye, Hugh, viii. 45

Bulneys, John, i. 15

Bumsted, Richard de, vii. 57

Burbache, John, i. 67, 103; xii. 37

Burbache (Burbach), Robert (de), i. 74; ix. 35; xi. 81; xii. 29, 90(*bis*)

Burbank, *see* Bourbank

Burdet (Burdett), John (d. 1448/9, ? J. Burdett c. 1410), i. 62, 77; ii. 31; iii. 38; iv. 63; v. 22; viii. 28 & n, 32 & n; ix. 50; x. 13, 43; xi. 78; xii. 26, 30

Burdett, John (c. 1410, ? J. Burdet d. 1448/9), vi. 102

Burdon, Geoffrey de, vi. 110

Burdon, Walter (de), iii. 21, 60; iv. 60; xii. 60

Burell, John (c. 1410–24, ? J. Burrell), vi. 11; vii. 35

Burges, John, i. 22, 28, 55, 68(*bis*), 75

Burges, Robert (c. 1402, ? R. Burgeys), i. 45

Burgeys (Burgoys), Robert (c. 1408, ? R. Burges), xi. 76

Burgh (Borough), Benedict, i. 64; v. 14, 34

Burgh, Thomas de (c. 1326–30, ? T. de Burgo), v. 66
Burgh, William (d. 1525), vi. 30
Burgh, William de (c. 1353), vi. 20 (line 1)
Burghash, Robert de, v. 49
Burghashe, Burghasshe, *see* Burghersh
Burghbridge (Bokbridge, Bokebrugg, Bukbrigg, Burghbrigg), William (de), ii. 17; iii. 75; viii. 69; xi. 82
Burghchier, *see* Bourgchier, Bouser
Burghersh (Burghashe, Burghasshe, Burghershe), Henry (de), i. 1; iv. 45; vi. 75
Burgherssh, Thomas de, xi. 24
Burghill (Bourghill, Brughill), John de, x. 2; xi. 22
Burghill (Burghille, Burghylle), William, ii. 12, 15, 40
Burghstede, Richard de, ix. 28
Burght, John, vi. 55
Burgo, Thomas de (d. 1361, ? T. de Burgh), ix. 36
Burgoys, *see* Burgeys
Burley, Adam de, viii. 68
Burley (Bourle), Thomas, iii. 95
Burley (Bourle), Walter de, iii. 71; vii. 46; viii. 63; ix. 27
Burley, *see also* Birley
Burline, John, ii. 26
Burnby, John, vi. 111
Burnby, *see also* Burneby
Burne, John, vi. 51
Burne, Thomas, *see* Bourne
Burne, William de, viii. 82
Burne, *see also* Bourne
Burneby, John, ix. 11, 18, 52, 53
Burneby, *see also* Burnby
Burnel (Brunel, Brunell), William, iii. 60; vi. 27; viii. 34; ix. 22; x. 36; xi. 79
Burnell, Edward, iii. 42; iv. 18; xii. 58
Burnell, Peter, x. 24
Burnett, — (d. c. 1498), vii. 38
Burnett, John (d. 1409), viii. 33
Burnham, Richard, i. 85, 109; xii. 32, 38
Burnham, Robert de, iv. 25
Burnham, *see also* Bernham
Burrell, Gerard, vii. 13, 15
Burrell, John (c. 1418–36, ? J. Burell), ii. 39
Burrell, Ninian, vii. 26, 40
Burstall, Thomas de, vi. 33
Burstall, *see also* Birstall, Borstall
Burton (Bourton), John (d. 1431), iii. 62
Burton, John (d. 1498/9), iv. 63

Burton, John (d. 1505), ix. 56
Burton, John (de) (d. 1394), i. 74; v. 37; vi. 87; viii. 65; xi. 13
Burton, Nicholas, i. 103, 123; viii. 31; xii. 37, 41, 78
Burton, Richard (d. 1495), iv. 63; xii. 61
Burton, Richard (d. 1504), ii. 39
Burton, Richard (d. 1506), x. 57, 59
Burton, Robert (d. 1449), i. 20; vi. 115; xii. 17, 73
Burton (Bourton), Robert de (d. 1361), iii. 75, 84; iv. 50; vii. 57
Burton, Roger, i. 89
Burton (Bourton), Thomas, ii. 33; iii. 92; xii. 49
Burton, Walter de, vi. 15 & n, 94; viii. 11, 66; xii. 72
Burton, William (d. 1423), i. 20, 101; v. 32
Burton, William (d. 1511), viii. 73; xii. 81
Burwell, Thomas, vii. 9, 31
Bury, John, vii. 37, 38
Bury, Ralph, viii. 23
Bury (Aungerville, Sancto Edmundo), Richard de (d. 1345), i. 10, 38(*bis*); iii. 11, 32, 61; v. 68; vi. 69, 107; vii. 14, 43; viii. 3; ix. 28; x. 29; xii. 20
Bury, Richard de (c. 1354), v. 53
Bush (Bouhs, Busshe), John, v. 26n, 27; vi. 78; xi. 84
Bush, Paul, iii. 35
Bush, Robert (d. 1416), iii. 98
Bush, Robert (d. 1546), *see* Bysse
Busleiden (Basleiden), Francis de, v. 11; viii. 14
Busshe, *see* Bush
Busshebury, Lewis, i. 66
Busshebury (Bysshebury), Thomas, ii. 20, 36; xii. 46
Bustard, William, x. 64
Butiller (Botelere, Botiller, Butler), Thomas, i. 11, 58(*bis*), 80; ii. 31; iii. 11, 27; iv. 8; vii. 17–18, 41, 48
Butiller, *see also* Boteler, Botiler, Botler, Butler
Butler, James, i. 52
Butler, Thomas, *see* Butiller
Butler, *see also* Boteler, Botiler, Botler, Butiller
Buttele, John de, viii. 69
Buttrie, John, vi. 38
Buxton, Walter de, vii. 56; xii. 75
Buyton, Henry, ii. 28
Buytone (de Huyton), Hugh, ii. 21

Byconyll (Byconel, Bykonill), William, i. 78 ('Bryconel'); iii. 48, 72; v. 36; vii. 21, 47; viii. 44, 59; ix. 52; xii. 30

Byde, William, iii. 42, 94; ix. 42; xii. 54

Byford, Lewis, xi. 24

Byford, William, *see* Beford

Byford, *see also* Beford, Bifort

Bygge (Bigge), Robert, ii. 41

Bygge, *see also* Bigges

Bykonill, *see* Byconyll

Byngham, Thomas, viii. 12, 76; xii. 76, 81

Bynteworth, *see* Bentworth

Byrceam, William de, ix. 24

Byrchynshawe, *see* Brekynshall

Byrd, Ralph, v. 45, 55

Byrde, William, viii. 22

Byrd(e), *see also* Bird(e)

Byrecombe, Walter de, viii. 20

Byres, Rauland, i. 62

Byrmyncham, *see* Bermyngham

Byrom, *see* Birom

Bysse (Bis, Bisse, Bush), Robert, iii. 41; viii. 18; xii. 54, 77

Bysshebury, *see* Busshebury

Bysshope, William, iv. 40

Bywell, William, vi. 77

Cabasolle, Philip de, i. 12, 95; vi. 17

Caen (Cadomo), John de (of), i. 83; vi. 44; viii. 81; xii. 81

Cahors, *see* Eause

Caldebeck, Thomas de, vi. 101

Caldwell, Robert de, vi. 52

Calf, William, viii. 59

Calton, Nicholas, iii. 71

Calvacante (Covocaunte), Guy de, iii. 51

Calveley (Calvyley, Canyle), David (de) (c. 1380–1, ? – Calverlegh), iii. 37; xi. 40; xii. 54

Calverlegh, – (c. 1379, ? David Calveley), ix. 40

Calvis, Anthony de, iii. 42; ix. 14

Calvyley, *see* Calveley

Camamille, *see* Canville

Camel, Richard, i. 63

Camel, *see also* Cammel

Camera, Hugh de, i. 6, 63

Camera, John de, *see* Chaumbre

Camera, *see also* Chamber, Chaumbre

Camilla, *see* Canville

Camille, Antony de, v. 26

Cammel, William de, viii. 4, 6, 11, 27, 73 & n, 79

Cammel, *see also* Camel

Campden, Walter de, vi. 37

Campeden, Henry de, *see* Resteshale

Campeden (Campden), John, iv. 49

Campeggio, Laurence, iii. 3

Campo Arnulphi, *see* Chambernoun

Campo Veteri, Peter de, i. 104

Camswell, *see* Carnswell

Candour, Thomas, i. 99 ('Caudour'); xii. 36

Canley, Robert de, iii. 55

Canner, Thomas, i. 36, 91

Canning, William, iii. 26, 70, 88

Canon, Ralph (c. 1387, ? R.C. d. 1422), vii. 23

Canon, Ralph (d. 1422, ? R.C. c. 1387), viii. 45; x. 67

Canon, William, xi. 63

Cantebrugg, John de, v. 10

Cantebrugg, *see also* Cauntebreg

Cantelaus, Gerald de, v. 20n, 21 & n

Canterbury, Benedict, ix. 44

Canterbury (Cantuaria), Robert de, v. 10, 46; viii. 26

Canterbury, Roger de, ii. 6, 10, 26, 44, 50

Cantilupo, *see* Frangerius

Cantlow, John, viii. 22

Cantrell, Nicholas, *see* Chauntrell

Cantrell (Chauntrel), Ralph, x. 31, 59

Cantuaria, *see* Canterbury

Canville (Camamille, Camilla), Gabriel de, iii. 57

Canyle, *see* Calveley

Capell, John, de Buckworth (John Buckworth), vii. 37

Capell, *see also* Chapel(l)

Caple, William de, ii. 35

Caple, *see also* Chapel(l)

Capoci, Nicholas, i. 46

Capon (Salcote), John, iii. 3; xi. 5; xii. 52

Capon, William, iii. 93; viii. 24; xi. 10n, 16

Capron, Nicholas, x. 58

Caraccioli (Carraciolus, Misquinus), Nicholas, i. 116. *See also* Naples, cardinal of

Caraunt (Caraunte, Carent, Karaunt), Nicholas, i. 103; ii. 24; iii. 58, 83; viii. 5, 38; xii. 37

Carbonel, Henry, i. 30

Carboni, Francis, vi. 18, 81

Cardon, *see* Clyve, John

Carent, *see* Caraunt

Carew, George, ix. 19, 65

Caris, Bernard de, ix. 10n

Cariter, John, iii. 88; v. 69

Carleton, Adam de, ix. 15, 24

Carleton, Henry de, viii. 23

Carleton (Carlton), John (c. 1385–98, ? J. de C. c. 1375–80), i. 33; v. 13, 20

Carleton, John (John Pycard de Carleton) (d. 1405, ? J. de C. c. 1375–80), i. 5(bis), 38

Carleton, John (d. 1436), vi. 34, 76

Carleton, John de (d. 1340), vi. 114

Carleton (Carlton), John (de) (d. 1361), i. 56; v. 62; viii. 4, 8, 39, 48

Carleton (Carlton), John (de) (d. 1366), i. 118; iv. 33; viii. 66

Carleton, John de (c. 1375–80, ? J.C. c. 1385–98, or J.C. d. 1405), xi. 12; xii. 88

Carleton (Carlton), Nicholas, viii. 16, 39

Carleton, Richard de (d. 1381), viii. 6, 41

Carleton, Richard (de) (d. 1393), v. 40; vi. 87

Carleton, William de, viii. 19

Carlisle (Karliolo), Henry de, vi. 101

Carlton, see Carleton, Charlton

Carman, John, xi. 85

Carmelian (de Brescia, de Briscia, de Carmeliano), Peter, ii. 20; iii. 45; iv. 62 & n; v. 34; vi. 29; viii. 40; xii. 46, 54, 61, 63, 68, 79

Carne (Karne), Edward, iii. 18

Carnebull, Henry, i. 84, 101, 112; iii. 99; vi. 19, 21, 23, 51, 68, 91; xii. 36, 67, 68, 71

Carnswell (Camswell), Thomas, x. 5

Carnyka (Karneka, Karnyka), Thomas, i. 111; vi. 81; viii. 5

Carnyka, see also Kernyk

Carnyn, John de, xi. 8

Carozolis (Carolis, Corozulo, Karolis), Matthew de (d. 1305), iii. 95

Carozolis, Matthew de (c. 1305–12), iii. 95

Carp, John, iii. 77; v. 63; vi. 33, 62, 74; x. 11; xi. 41, 45n

Carpenter, John (c. 1398–1424), see Hereford

Carpenter, John (c. 1426), xi. 77 & n

Carpenter, John (c. 1459), x. 33

Carpenter, John (d. 1476), i. 53; iv. 58; xi. 70, 71n, 76, 77 & n; xii. 23

Carpenter, William, i. 112

Carraciolus, see Caraccioli

Carreu, John de, iii. 54

Carrewe, William de, xi. 53, 84

Carru, Richard, xi. 81

Carselegh, see Carslegh, Peter

Carsidony, Anthony, iii. 74

Carslegh, James, ix. 14, 50

Carslegh (Carselegh), Peter, viii. 64; ix. 60

Carswell (Craswell), Richard, xi. 66

Carswell (Craswell), Robert, viii. 77

Carver, see Aleyne, John (d. 1516)

Cary, Thomas, ix. 41

Cassy, Richard, vi. 74

Castell, John (d. 1430), ii. 13, 22

Castell, John (d. 1457), i. 24, 45; iii. 10, 43, 91, 101; vi. 11, 91

Castell, Thomas, vi. 111; xii. 73

Castelle, Geoffrey, ii. 44

Castellensis, Polydore, see Vergil

Castellensis, Robert, ii. 51

Castello, Adrian (Hadrian) de, ii. 3; v. 34; viii. 3

Castleton, William, iv. 26

Castro, Gervase de, xi. 3

Castro, Richard de, see Gent

Castrogodrici (Goodrich Castle), Thomas de, xi. 32

Catansano, see Ruffo

Cateby (Catesby), John, ii. 18, 19; xii. 46(bis)

Catesby, Robert, i. 34; ii. 26; xii. 20, 47

Catesby, Walter, ix. 59

Catryk (Catrik, Catterick, Ketterich, Ketterick), John, i. 22, 41, 58; ii. 36; iii. 59; iv. 49; vi. 65, 74; ix. 2; x. 2; xi. 54; xii. 49, 60, 84

Catryk (Catterick, Ketterick), Robert, x. 64

Catton, Nicholas de, vi. 31

Catton (Bronde), Robert, iv. 26

Catton, William de, vi. 20

Caudour, see Candour

Caudray (Cawdray), Richard, i. 7, 17, 26, 33, 42, 55; iii. 39, 44, 54; iv. 27; v. 37; vi. 57; viii. 20; ix. 50; xii. 21

Caudray, see also Cordray

Caulason, Bernard de, iv. 17

Cauntebreg, Thomas de, xi. 11

Cauntebreg, see also Cantebrugg

Caunton, Geoffrey, xi. 65n

Caunton, Gruffudd, xi. 63, 64 & n

Caunton, Philip de (c. 1335), xi. 59

Caunton, Philip de (c. 1368), xi. 63

Caunton (Cawnton), Richard (d. 1465), iii. 12, 72; vi. 55; xi. 58 & n, 60, 63, 78, 85 & n; xii. 52

Caunton, Richard de (d. 1401), xi. 63, 82

Caurden, Richard, vii. 5

Causton, Michael, vii. 48

Cave, Nicholas de, vi. 11

Cave, William, ii. 11, 46

Caversham, Peter, i. 30

Cavomonte, Bego de, v. 7, 45

Cawdray, see Caudray

Cawnton, see Caunton

Cawode, William, vi. 37, 58, 83

Cawse, Thomas, i. 52

Caynes, see Keynes

Ceccano, Anibaldus de, see Gaetani
Ceccano, Thomas de, vi. 75
Cecill, Nicholas, iii. 22, 94
Cergeaux (Sergeaux, Sergoys), Michael, iii. 8; vii. 39; viii. 43; ix. 44
Cestre, John de, vi. 22
Cestre, Richard de, see Chester
Chace, Thomas, v. 19
Chaddesden, Henry (de), i. 12, 18, 89; v. 70; x. 53
Chaddesden, Nicholas (de), i. 6, 7, 70; ii. 36; x. 52
Chaddesley (Chaddeslegh, Chadeslegh), Richard de, ii. 32; iii. 51; v. 40
Chaddleshunt (Chadleshunt, Chadshunt), William de, iii. 13, 21, 39; v. 59, 66; x. 22; xii. 64
Chaderton (Chaterton), Edmund, i. 96, 127; iii. 12, 90; v. 26; vii. 21; ix. 19; x. 14 & n; xi. 43
Chadeslegh, see Chaddesley
Chadleshunt, Chadshunt, see Chaddleshunt
Chadword, Chadworth, see Chedworth
Chaloner, Thomas (c. 1400, ? T. Crocer), v. 42 & n
Chamber, John (d. 1503), vii. 51
Chamber, John (d. 1549), i. 17, 55, 81; iii. 47, 88; vi. 91; viii. 11, 78; ix. 8, 64; xii. 24
Chamber, John de (d. by 1365), see Chaumbre
Chamber, William (d. 1412), v. 56
Chamber, William (d. 1539), i. 34
Chamber, see also Camera, Chambre, Chaumbre
Chamberlain, John (c. 1388–99), i. 35, 88
Chamberlain, John (c. 1450–51), i. 62
Chamberlain, William, iii. 84
Chambernoun (Campo Arnulphi), Reginald de, ix. 26
Chambre, John de la, see Chaumbre
Chambre, see also Camera, Chamber, Chaumbre
Champion, John, vii. 6, 22, 46, 47(bis), 54
Chanceler (Chaunceler), Richard, i. 72; vii. 20
Chandeler, see Chaundeler
Chandos, see Chaundos
Chapcliff, Richard de, x. 37n
Chapell (Chapel), Robert, vii. 13, 22; xi. 71; xii. 74(bis)
Chapel(l), see also Capell, Caple
Chapman, Thomas, i. 125; vi. 65
Chapman, William, ii. 14 ('Chapmon'); xii. 46

Charlton (Charleton, Cherleton), Griffin de, ii. 15, 40
Charlton (Charleton, Cherelton, Cherleton), Humphrey de, ii. 48; vi. 25, 75; ix. 33; x. 65; xii. 51
Charlton (Charleton, Cherelton, Cherleton), Lewis (de), i. 95; ii. 1, 50; xi. 45; xii. 34, 44
Charlton (Cherleton), Roger de, ix. 17, 23
Charlton (Cherleton), Thomas de (c. 1296–1330, ? T. de C. c. 1302–26), ix. 17, 22
Charlton, Thomas de (c. 1302–26, ? T. de C. c. 1296–1330), viii. 13, 81
Charlton (Charleton, Cherelton, Cherleton), Thomas de (d. 1344), ii. 1, 17; iii. 37; v. 43 & n; vi. 78, 107, 113; x. 55
Charlton (Cherleton), William de (c. 1322), viii. 26n
Charlton (Charleton, Cherelton, Cherleton), William de (c. 1342–79), ii. 14 & n; iii. 27; xi. 45
Charlton, see also Carleton, Chorlton
Charnele, John de, ii. 12; vi. 62, 64; x. 25; xii. 84
Charnock, Hugh, ii. 44; xii. 50
Chaterton, see Chaderton
Chaumbre, John de (d. 1349), vi. 15
Chaumbre (Chamber, Chambre), John de la (John de Camera) (d. by 1365), ii. 10, 30; iii. 15, 69; xi. 80
Chaumbre, Richard de la, x. 25
Chaumbre, William, viii. 18
Chaumbre, see also Camera, Chamber
Chaume, Guy, i. 66, 67; xii. 27
Chaumpeneys, Adam le, de Sandwico, iv. 62
Chaunceler, see Chanceler
Chaundeler (Chandeler), John (d. 1426), i. 93; iii. 2(bis), 4, 20, 73; v. 16; xii. 34
Chaundeler, John (d. 1431/2), iii. 81; xii. 56
Chaundeler, Thomas, ii. 5, 25, 42; v. 24, 68; vi. 9, 36; viii. 9, 32, 52, 75 & n.; xii. 44, 47, 69, 81
Chaundos, John, ix. 36
Chaundos (Chandos), Richard de, ii. 37
Chaundos (Chandos), Thomas de (c. 1317–1330), ii. 5, 14, 20; iii. 41
Chaundos (Chandos), Thomas (de) (d. 1406), i. 18, 109; ii. 19, 47; xii. 16
Chauntre, see Chauntry
Chauntrel, see Cantrell
Chauntrell (Cantrell), Nicholas, vi. 56; xii. 70
Chauntry (Chauntre), William, iii. 52, 94; x. 17; xii. 15, 54, 57
Chayne, see Cheyne

Chedworth (Chadword), John (bp., d. 1471), i. 3; iii. 14, 64, 76, 88, 98

Chedworth (Chadworth), John (d. 1471), i. 7, 11, 49, 112, 114, 117; iii. 28, 96; v. 51, 69; vi. 63; viii. 55; xii. 22, 39, 40

Chedworth, Nicholas, i. 60, 93; xii. 25

Chedworth, William, i. 93

Chelcheheth, Geoffrey de, viii. 32

Chelenden, see Chillenden

Chell, William, ii. 22; xii. 47

Chelmsford, John de, x. 40

Cheney, see Cheyne

Cherberg, Robert, xi. 62

Cherde, John, viii. 53

Cherdestock (Cherdestok), Edward, i. 46; v. 33

Cherelton, see Charlton

Cheriton, Thomas, xi. 4

Cherleton, see Charlton

Chessege, William, i. 86; xii. 32(bis)

Chesshyre, Roger, xi. 43

Chester, Richard (d. by 1464), ii. 40; v. 65; xii. 49

Chester (Cestre), Richard de (d. 1346), vi. 52

Chester, see also Cestre

Chesterfield (Chestrefeld), John de, iii. 47; vi. 54

Chesterfield, Richard (de), i. 97; v. 66

Chesterfield, Thomas, see Worshop

Chesterfield, see also Chestrefeld

Chesterton, William de, vii. 59

Chestrefeld, John de, see Chesterfield

Chestrefeld, Roger de, vi. 54; viii. 10

Chestrefeld, Thomas, see Worshop

Chestrefeld, see also Chesterfield

Cheyne (Chayne, Cheney, Cheyney), Edward, iii. 4, 32; vi. 38, 91; vii. 37

Cheyne, John (c. 1387, ? J.C. d. 1406), ii. 29; xii. 48

Cheyne (Chayne, Cheyney), John (d. 1406, ? J.C. c. 1387), i. 48, 49, 103n; iii. 29, 39; ix. 13, 37; xii. 36

Cheyne, John (d. 1408), x. 25, 54

Chichele, Henry, iii. 8, 11, 17, 27, 51, 52, 80, 100, 102; iv. 4; x. 66; xi. 54

Chichele, John, viii. 69

Chichele, Thomas, i. 26, 34, 37; iv. 8; v. 26; vi. 51; vii. 33, 47; xii. 18, 20, 58

Chichele, William, iii. 17; iv. 8; xi. 62, 64, 70; xii. 58

Chikewell (Chickwell, Chykewell), Robert (de), ii. 17; iii. 64; v. 58; vii. 28; viii. 63; xii. 39, 46

Child, Lawrence, xi. 38

Chillenden (Chelenden, Chylynden), Thomas, iv. 6, 38

Chilterne, Walter de, x. 30

Chinnock, John, viii. 60

Chipnam, see Chippenham

Chippenham, Richard de, viii. 76

Chippenham (Chypnam), Thomas (d. 1478), iii. 52; vi. 19, 91; ix. 19, 54

Chippenham (Chipnam), Thomas (c. 1512–1516), ii. 39

Chirbury, David, xi. 62

Chirche, Benedict atte, viii. 36

Chirche, see also Churche

Chirchehull, see Churchill

Chishull, John de, v. 13, 47

Chisilden, see Chuseldon

Chitterne, John, ii. 17; iii. 12, 14, 44, 63; v. 70; vii. 31

Chobham, see Cobham

Chock (Chokke), William, iii. 28, 83; viii. 74n, 83

Chomley, Reginald, vi. 56

Chorlton, Robert, vii. 34

Chorlton, see also Charlton

Chosey, William, i. 21

Churche, Roger, viii. 27

Churchill (Chirchehull), William de, vii. 4n, 45

Chuseldon (Chisilden, Chuselden, Chyselden), William (de), v. 40; x. 58

Chychestre, see Gardyner

Chykewell, see Chikewell

Chylynden, see Chillenden

Chymew (Chymow, Chynnow), John, iii. 22; ix. 61

Chypnam, see Chippenham

Chyselden, see Chuseldon

Circester (Circestre, Cyrcetur), Thomas, iii. 65; viii. 26

Circeter, Henry, see Rumworth

Cisterna, Robert de, ix. 24

Clare, Bogo de, x. 24

Clare, Richard de (c. 1317–28, ? R. de C. d. 1338), vi. 59

Clare, Richard de (d. 1338, ? R. de C. c. 1317–28), ix. 26

Clare, William de, iv. 16

Clarel, John, x. 19, 48

Clark, see Clerk(e)

Clarkson, Richard, viii. 64; xii. 80

Clavile, William, vii. 7; x. 7, 67

Clavile, see also Clovil

Claxton, John de, vii. 45

Claxton, William, iv. 25

Clayborough, Claybrooke, Clayburgh, *see* Cleybrooke
Claydon (Cleydon), John de, v. 46; x. 71
Claymonde, John, viii. 75
Clayton, William (c. 1471), i. 127
Clayton, William (d. 1532), vi. 57; x. 57
Cleanger (Cleangre), Richard, ix. 32; xi. 59, 81
Clederowe, *see* Cliderow
Clemens, John, i. 128
Clemens, Simon (c. 1488), iv. 61n
Clement, Simon (c. 1366–71), iv. 62
Clement, Vincent, i. 9, 112, 127; ii. 46; iii. 14; iv. 27, 51; ix. 53; x. 10, 12, 60; xii. 39, 42, 78
Clerc, John (c. 1410–18), *see* Clere
Clerc, John (d. 1440), *see* Lyndefeld
Clerc (Smyth), Nicholas (c. 1427, ? N. Clerke), xi. 50
Clerc, *see also* Clerk(e)
Clere (Clerc, Smith, Smyth), John (c. 1410–1418), ii. 21; iii. 6
Clere, John (c. 1442), vii. 6
Clerevaus (Clervaus), John, iii. 98; iv. 33; xii. 57, 60
Clerk, John (c. 1458), xi. 48
Clerk, Robert, v. 27, 37
Clerk, William, xi. 31
Clerke, Anthony, vii. 30
Clerke, John (d. 1541), v. 14; viii. 3; xii. 62, 76
Clerke (Clark), Nicholas (d. 1441, ? N. Clerc), i. 73; vi. 16; xii. 29
Clerke (Clark), Thomas, x. 70
Clerk(e), *see also* Clerc
Clermont, Anselm of, ii. 3
Clervaus, *see* Clerevaus
Cleve, Michael, viii. 25; xii. 77
Cleve, William, v. 31; vii. 50
Cleve, *see also* Clif, Clyff, Clyve
Cleybrooke (Clayborough, Claybrooke, Clayburgh, Cleyburgh), William, i. 83, 91; iv. 63; vii. 17; xi. 16
Cleydon, *see* Claydon
Cliderow (Clederowe, Clitherowe, Eliot), John, vii. 19; ix. 49; xi. 4
Clif (Cliffe, Cliffs, Clyff, Clyffe), Henry de, iii. 37; vi. 29; vii. 10, 46; viii. 63
Cliff, William, i. 63 ('Clif'), 108; xii. 26, 38
Cliff, *see also* Cleve, Clyff, Clyve
Cliffe, Henry de, *see* Clif
Cliffe, William, *see* Clyff
Clifford, John de, vi. 13; xii. 67
Clifford, Richard (d. 1421), i. 80; iii. 37; iv.

8, 18, 57; v. 3, 23, 30; vi. 7, 48(*bis*), 76; viii. 2, 50, 78; xi. 47
Clifford, Richard (d. 1422), iii. 101; v. 12, 23, 30, 31, 44, 55, 65; vii. 18; viii. 64
Clifford, Richard de (c. 1343), xi. 32
Clifford, Thomas (d. 1321), i. 34, 59 & n
Clifford, Thomas (d. 1419), ix. 47
Clifford, Thomas (d. 1509), viii. 75
Cliffs, *see* Clif, Henry de
Clifton (Clyfton), Gamaliel (Gamalial), ii. 5, 19, 44; vi. 94; xii. 44, 50, 72
Clifton, John, ix. 59
Clifton, Nicholas, xi. 63
Clifton, Robert (d. 1467), vi. 23
Clifton, Robert (c. 1479–1500), vi. 94
Clifton, Thomas, vi. 101
Clifton, William, vi. 17
Clinton, *see* Glynton
Clippling, Simon, vii. 14n
Clipston, John de, x. 29
Clipston, Richard de (c. 1316, ? Robert de C.), viii. 20
Clipston, Robert de (c. 1305–56, ? Richard de C.), viii. 20; x. 21, 36, 43, 55, 70
Clipston, Thomas de, iii. 27
Clipston, Walter de, viii. 20; x. 59 & n
Clitherowe, *see* Cliderow
Clive, *see* Clynt
Clone (Cloyn), John, ii. 27, 41; x. 31, 66
Clone, Roger de, *see* Cloune
Clone, Simon, *see* Cloune
Clone (Cloyn), Thomas (c. 1387), ii. 48
Clone, Thomas de (c. 1330), x. 70; xii. 86
Clone, *see also* Cloune
Cloos, John (d. 1496), vii. 51
Cloos, John (d. 1501), vii. 5, 16
Cloos, Nicholas; Stephen, *see* Close
Clopcote, Robert de, viii. 21
Clopcote, William de, viii. 31
Clopton, Simon de, x. 50, 65
Clopton, Thomas de, x. 21, 37
Clopton, Walter de, ix. 28
Clopton, William de, viii. 10
Close (Cloos), Nicholas, v. 14; vi. 98, 102; viii. 73; x. 2
Close (Cloos, Clos), Stephen, i. 127; vi. 102 & n; xii. 42, 72
Close, *see also* Cloos
Clothale, Robert de, v. 18, 57; xii. 62
Cloune (Clone, Clunne), Roger de, iii. 11, 49, 57
Cloune (Clone, Clunne), Simon, iii. 65
Cloune, *see also* Clone
Clovill, Aumfred de, vii. 55

Clovill, see also Clavile
Cloyn, see Clone
Clunne, see Cloune
Clyewe, John, xi. 64
Clyff, Henry de, see Clif
Clyff (Cliffe), William, v. 9, 65; vi. 12, 15, 21, 50
Clyff, see also Cleve, Clif, Clyve
Clyffe, see Clif, Henry de
Clyffeld, Philip, xi. 6, 13; xii. 87
Clyfton, see Clifton
Clynt, William, i. 20 ('Clive'); iii. 75; xii. 17, 55
Clyst, Robert, viii. 32
Clyve (Cardon), John, iv. 40
Clyve, William, xi. 6, 13; xii. 87
Clyve, see also Cleve, Clif, Clyff
Coale, see Cole
Coates, John, of Tealby, i. 119
Cobeham, James de, viii. 81
Cobeham, see also Cobham
Cobethorn, John, ix. 5, 48
Cobham, Reginald de, iii. 51; vii. 59
Cobham (Chobham), Thomas de, ii. 39; iv. 3, 55; v. 34; vi. 10, 48; vii. 13; viii. 70; xii. 58, 66, 70
Cobham, see also Cobeham
Cockerell, Edmund, iii. 6, 24
Cockes, John, iii. 99
Cockes (Cocks, Cokkes, Cokkys), William (d. 1512, ? W. Cokkys), vi. 32; vii. 27; viii. 28
Cockes, see also Cokkes, Cokkys, Cox
Cockham, William, viii. 72
Cockham, see also Cookham
Cocks, see Cockes
Coddington, see Codyngton
Codeford, John, see Silvestre
Codeford, Philip, iii. 15
Codeford, Ralph de, iii. 77
Codeford, see also Cottysford, Godeford
Codelowe, Thomas de, vii. 13
Codeworth, John de, viii. 53
Codyngton (Coddington), John (de), vii. 28; viii. 44
Codyngton, see also Cudington
Coggeshall, Ralph de, ii. 8
Cok, Alexander, vi. 102
Cok, John, v. 15, 37; viii. 37; xi. 80, 84
Cok, see also Coke, Cook(e)
Cokain, Henry (c. 1343, ? H. de Cookham), vii. 58
Cokayn, see Cokeyn
Coke, John, see Cooke

Coke, Thomas, i. 34
Coke, Walter, see Cook
Coke, see also Cok, Cook(e)
Cokefeld, Thomas, i. 45
Cokenache, John, v. 29
Cokeyn (Cokayn), Thomas, vii. 40
Cokkes, John (d. 1476), i. 101; xii. 36
Cokkes, William, see Cockes
Cokkes, see also Cockes, Cox
Cokkys, John (c. 1472), x. 51
Cokkys, Lawrence, i. 75; iii. 48, 58, 72; x. 63; xii. 29
Cokkys, William (c. 1487, ? W. Cockes), ix. 58
Cokkys, see also Cockes, Cokkes, Cox
Cokworthy, John, ii. 17, 49; ix. 49
Coland, see Cowland
Colas, Thomas, i. 77, 123; vii. 36; xii. 42
Colby, John, i. 124
Colby, William (de), i. 61; vi. 6, 59; xii. 25
Colchester, John de, v. 49
Coldseye, John, viii. 39
Cole, Henry, iii. 103; v. 41, 62
Cole, James, v. 29, 39
Cole, John (c. 1397-1403, ? J.C. d. 1433/4), v. 23
Cole, John (d. 1418), see Colman
Cole, John (d. 1433, ? J.C. c. 1397-1403), viii. 71; x. 67; xii. 81, 86
Cole (Coale), John (d. 1536), ii. 52; viii. 30; xii. 51
Cole, Robert, xi. 24
Coleman, James, de Havante, iii. 32
Coleman, see also Colman
Coleshull (Colshull), Nicholas (de), i. 54; viii. 82; xii. 24
Coleshull, William, iii. 75, 79
Colet, John, iii. 48; v. 7 & n, 49; vi. 38; vii. 11 & n
Colet, Richard, x. 42, 61
Coleton, Richard de, ix. 4, 7, 12, 25
Coleton, see also Colton
Colhame, Richard, vi. 83, 85; xii. 71, 72
Colingham, Hugh de, v. 68 & n
Colle, see Colman
Colles, John, see Colman
Colles, Walter, iii. 98; ix. 7, 49
Collingwood (Colyngwood), Ralph, vii. 21, 25; x. 7, 15, 31
Collinson, John, i. 12, 17, 19, 87; xii. 32
Collins, see Colyns
Colman (Cole, Colle, Colles), John, iii. 65; viii. 55; xi. 57, 63, 69n, 76
Colman, see also Coleman

Colnet, Nicholas, i. 95; ii. 9; v. 61; vii. 50

Coloinge (Colonia), William de, v. 58; xii. 64

Colonna, Agapitus de, vi. 112

Colonna, John de, vi. 66

Colonna, Odo de, x. 7

Colonna, Peter de, x. 7

Colonna, Prosper de, iv. 8; vi. 61, 65(bis) & n

Colshull, see Coleshull

Colson, Thomas (c. 1493–1501, ? T. Colston), viii. 41

Colston, Thomas (c. 1497–1500, ? T. Colson), vi. 113

Colton, John de, vi. 40

Colton, see also Coleton

Columbi, William, son of Raymond, vi. 92

Columpton, Walter, ix. 39

Colville, John, v. 31; viii. 59

Colville, Robert, iv. 17

Colvyle, William, viii. 19; xii. 77

Colwich, John de, x. 24

Colyngtree, John, viii. 70

Colyngwood, see Collingwood

Colyns, Arnulph, ix. 58

Colyns, John, vii. 36, 53

Colyns, Launcelot, vi. 15, 89; xii. 67

Colyns, Martin, vi. 12, 14, 30, 41; xii. 66, 67, 68, 69

Combe, Benedict, xi. 50

Combe, John (c. 1331), i. 23

Combe, John (d. 1499), ix. 8, 11, 56

Combe, see also Cumbe

Comite, Anthony de, ii. 34

Comite, Nicholas de, i. 45

Comite, Paul de, x. 25

Comite, Peter de, x. 24, 66

Comite, Philip de, of Milan, ii. 34; xii. 49

Comminges, John Raymond de, i. 10, 78; vi. 25

Comyn, Alvered, vi. 39

Concoreto, Itherius de, ii. 27; iii. 49, 93; v. 8, 33; xii. 48

Condulmier, Francis, i. 117

Condulmier, Gabriel, vi. 113

Conelee, Robert de, x. 21

Conesburgh, see Coningsburgh

Conestable, Hubert le, iii. 37

Conestable, see also Constable

Conge, John, iii. 86, 88; vii. 35; viii. 42; x. 47

Congham (Coungham), Robert de, x. 53; xi. 65

Coningsburgh (Conesburgh, Cosneburg, Cosneburgh), Alan (de), iii. 82; viii. 34, 80; x. 52

Coningston (Conyngston), Richard, i. 46; vi. 18, 31, 35, 65, 89; x. 43, 69

Constable, John, i. 4, 10, 22, 50, 62; xii. 26

Constable, William (d. 1485), i. 82, 98; vi. 17, 21; xii. 31, 35

Constable, William (c. 1531–54), vi. 89

Constable, see also Conestable

Contarenus, Gaspar, iii. 3

Convenis (Convenys), Roger de, x. 5

Convenis, Simon, iv. 7

Conway, Peter, xi. 44

Conwey, William, xi. 17

Conyers, Cuthbert, vi. 102; xii. 72

Conyngston, see Coningston

Cook (Coke, Cooke), Walter, i. 15, 92; iii., 9 49, 50, 73; v. 15, 19, 23n, 25n, 39n, 40 (bis); vi. 87; vii. 41; viii. 25; ix. 14, 44; xii. 15, 33

Cooke (Coke), John, i. 8; iii. 48; vii. 12

Cooke, Robert, see Thurgarton

Cook(e), see also Cok(e)

Cookham, Henry de (c. 1344–65, ? H. Cokain), vii. 8

Cookham, see also Cockham

Cooper, William, i. 75

Cooper, see also Cowper

Copaunford, Nicholas de, iv. 16

Copendale, Adam, iii. 90, 103

Corbet, Fulk, x. 39

Corbridge (Malton), Thomas (c. 1318–29), i. 118

Corbridge, Thomas de (d. 1304), vi. 3

Cordon (Broun, Brouns, Brown), Richard, iii. 29; iv. 42; vi. 40 & n; viii. 25

Cordray (Curdray), John, vii. 13

Cordray, see also Caudray

Coren, Hugh, ii. 29

Coren, Oliver, i. 40, 44, 100, 104

Coren, Richard, i. 14, 59, 120, 125; iii. 31; v. 14

Corf, John (de), iii. 75, 82; viii. 23

Corfe, William, ii. 17 ('Corne'); xii. 46

Corff, Richard, viii. 79

Corffe, Robert of, see Remston

Coringham (Coryngham), Roger, i. 90; iii. 56; vi. 18, 47, 81

Cornasano, Geoffrey de, xi. 32

Corne, see Corfe

Corner, William de la, x. 24

Cornewallis, Thomas, iv. 28

Cornewayleys, see Sancto Austolo

Cornish, Thomas, viii. 7 & n, 9, 41, 42; xii. 76, 79

Cornubia, Henry de (Henry Toyt), ix. 25; x. 57

Cornubia, Philip de, x. 17

Cornubia (Cornwall), Richard de (c. 1310–1331), vi. 50, 68; x. 71; xii. 86

Cornwaile, Richard (c. 1479), ii. 42

Cornwall, see Cornubia

Corozulo, see Carozolis

Correr, Anthony, i. 7

Cors, John, xi. 33

Corsini, Peter, vi. 18, 81

Cortenay, see Courtenay

Coryndon, Roger, viii. 59

Coryngdon, John, iii. 23; ix. 57(bis)

Coryngham, see Coringham

Cosneburg, Cosneburgh, see Coningsburgh

Cossall, William de, x. 53

Costone, John de, ii. 50

Cosyn (Cousin), Malcolm, iii. 74; v. 24

Cosyn, Thomas, viii. 26

Cosyn (Cousyn), William, i. 17, 36; iii. 68; viii. 5, 15, 55; ix. 59

Cotingham, Robert de, vi. 50

Cotingham, see also Cottenham, Cotyngham

Coton, Nicholas, x. 51

Coton, Roger de, x. 4

Coton, see also Couton, Cowton

Cotte, Thomas, of Sutton, i. 23n, 59; xii. 17, 25

Cottenham, John, iv. 17

Cottysford, John, i. 29

Cottysford, see also Codeford, Godeford

Cotyngham, Hugh (de), v. 22; vii. 39; xi. 40

Cotyngham, William de, x. 52; xi. 70

Cotyngham, see also Cotingham

Coungham, see Congham

Cour, see Matthew, Simon

Court, William de, viii. 13

Courtenay, Peter, i. 47, 117; iii. 14, 43, 76; iv. 46; viii. 31; ix. 3 & n, 5, 14, 55; xii. 22, 40

Courtenay, Philip de, vii. 33

Courtenay (Cortenay), Richard, i. 11, 32, 116; iv. 24; v. 61; vi. 70; vii. 7; viii. 5, 75; ix. 44; xi. 41

Courtenay, Thomas de, ix. 31

Courtenay (Cortenay), William (de), ii. 1; iv. 4; v. 2; vi. 27; ix. 37; xi. 46; xii. 81

Cousin, Cousyn, see Cosyn

Couton, William de, vi. 110

Couton, see also Coton, Cowton

Cova, William de la, ii. 25

Coventry, John de, xi. 21, 24, 25 & n, 26, 30

Coventry, Richard, x. 5

Covocaunte, see Calvacante

Cowland (Coland), Richard, i. 21, 87; x. 22; xi. 6n, 7; xii. 17, 32

Cowper, John, x. 20n

Cowper, see also Cooper

Cowton, Thomas, viii. 33; xii. 78

Cowton, see also Coton, Couton

Cox, Richard, iv. 19

Cox, see also Cockes, Cokkes, Cokkys

Coychurch, Lewis, vii. 14, 29

Craddock, Philip, xi. 83

Cradock, Roger, xi. 21

Cradock, William, vii. 14 & n, 40

Cragge, John, ii. 25, 42

Crakall, Henry, vii. 26

Crakell, John, vii. 45

Crall (Sudbury), John, v. 10, 41; vi. 65

Cranborne (Wager), Henry de, xi. 23

Cranborne, John, iii. 46, 64, 81

Crane, John, vii. 60

Cranley, Thomas, iii. 58

Cranmer, Edmund, iv. 9

Cranmer, Thomas, iv. 5; viii. 17

Craswell, see Carswell

Craucombe (Crowcombe), John de, vi. 22, 54

Crauden (Crawden), John de, iv. 13, 16

Crauthorn', see Crouthorne

Craven, John de (d. 1295), x. 43n

Craven, John de (c. 1350–2), x. 32

Crawden, see Crauden

Crawley (Craweley, Crawle), William (de), i. 107, 119; x. 23; xii. 38, 40

Crayford, John, v. 39; vii. 20; xi. 44

Creake, Simon de, iv. 30; xii. 59

Crecy, see Crees

Credonio, Peter de, iii. 97; vi. 78

Crees (Crecy), John, x. 34

Crekynge, William, viii. 26

Cremona, see Maldesbertis

Crenale, Thomas, vi. 60

Crepping, Alan de, ii. 41n

Cresset, John, ii. 31

Cretyng (Creting, Creton), William, iii. 46; ix. 60

Cretynge, Walter, viii. 15, 72

Crickhowell, John de, xi. 58

Crickhowell, Philip de, xi. 58

Cricklade (Crykkelade), John de, ii. 10; viii. 56 & n, 69n

Crienciis, Dionysius de, v. 56

Crischirch, John, iv. 18

Crist, Thomas, viii. 21

Crocer, Thomas (c. 1411, ? T. Chaloner), v. 42 & n

Crocket, Robert, viii. 44
Croft, George, vii. 9, 32, 37, 46, 53
Crofte, Robert, see Frost
Croham, see Crowham
Croiser, William, iii. 71
Croke, Roger, xi. 33
Crome, Edmund, iii. 97
Crome, Edward, iii. 55
Crome, see also Croume
Crompe (Crumpe), Simon, iv. 59
Cromwell, Thomas, iii. 38; viii. 6
Cromwell, see also Crumwell
Cros, Peter du, v. 8
Crosby, John, i. 22, 56, 119
Crosby, Nicholas, x. 62
Crosby, Richard, x. 4
Cross, Thomas, see Crosse
Cross (Cruce), William (d. 1354), x. 15, 45
Crosse (Cross), Thomas, i. 104; vi. 90
Crosse, William (c. 1411–16), i. 47
Crossley, Thomas, vi. 21, 25; xii. 68(bis)
Crosson, see Grocyn
Croucher, see Crucher
Croucheston (Cruston), Robert, iii. 87
Croucheston (Cruston), William, iii. 92; xi. 31
Croume, John, iii. 82
Croume, see also Crome
Crouthorne (Crauthorn'), William de, iii. 86; ix. 30(bis)
Crowcombe, see Craucombe
Crowham (Croham, Peterson), Robert, i. 75, 92; v. 21; vi. 68; vii. 11, 17; xii. 30
Crowton, William, iii. 101; viii. 68
Croxton, Edmund, i. 37, 102 ('Edward'); xii. 20, 36
Croxton, Richard (de), i. 61; iii. 24; xi. 30 & n; xii. 25, 53, 88
Cruce, see Cross
Cruce Roys (Royston), William de, vii. 28
Cruce Roys, see also Roiston, Royston
Crucher (Croucher), John, vii. 5, 48
Crudge, Roger, ix. 65
Crukadan, Geoffrey, iii. 36; vii. 60
Crukerne, William, viii. 53
Crull, Robert (de), iii. 54; vi. 51; ix. 38
Crump, Matthew, v. 12n
Crumpe, see Crompe
Crumwell, Richard de, vi. 92
Crumwell, see also Cromwell
Cruse, John, v. 54
Cruston, see Croucheston
Crykkelade, see Cricklade
Cryshale, Thomas, viii. 37

Cryspyn, Richard, ix. 66
Cucinaco (Cucinato, Cucinta, Cutinaco, Cuturiaco), Bernard de, iii. 89; xii. 56
Cudington, John, i. 76
Cudington, see also Codyngton
Cumbe, Robert de, ix. 22
Cumbe, see also Combe
Cumpton, Thomas, i. 16
Curdray, see Cordray
Cureton, William, x. 29
Curteys, John, iii. 31
Curwen, John, vi. 84; xii. 71
Cusancia, Renaud de, i. 54
Cusantia, Gerard de, vii. 56
Cusantia (Cusancia), William de, i. 72; v. 68; ix. 15, 33, 34n
Cusornio, Arnoloto de, see Custornio
Cusornio, Aymeric de, i. 66, 67
Cusornio, Gasbert de, iii. 80
Custornio (Cusornio), Arnoloto de, iii. 95
Cutinaco, see Cucinaco
Cutler (Cutter), John, i. 22, 79, 87, 115; xii. 17, 30, 32
Cuturiaco, see Cucinaco
Cuylling, William, ix. 42
Cyrcetur, see Circester
Cyffin, Hywel, see Hywel ap Madog ap Cyffin
Cyffin (Kyffin), Richard, xi. 6
Cynwrig (Kynwic) ap Ros, xi. 49
Cynwrig, Ithel ap, see Ithel ap Cynwrig
Cyrcetur, see Circester

Dabrygcourt, Robert, i. 33
Dacre, Hugh, iii. 74; vi. 102; xii. 55
Dacus, see Denys
Dafydd ab Ieuan ab Iorwerth, xi. 39
Dafydd ab Owain, xi. 39
Dafydd ap Bleddyn, xi. 37, 49
Dafydd ap Gruffudd, xi. 15, 16
Dafydd ap Hywel (Powell) (c. 1398), xi. 32
Dafydd ap Hywel (Powell) (c. 1535–41), xi. 48, 79
Dafydd ap Madog, xi. 16; xii. 88(bis)
Dafydd ap Rhys (David ap Rees, David ap Rhys, David Price, David Pryce), i. 53; v. 40; viii. 18, 62(bis); x. 13 & n, 38; xi. 57, 71 & n, 76; xii. 23
Dafydd, Tudur ap, see Tudur ap Dafydd
Dafydd, see also David
Dagworth, John, i. 118
Dakyn, John, viii. 17
Dalby, Alexander, xi. 3
Dalby, Thomas (d. 1400), i. 121; iv. 18; vi. 26, 83; xii. 58, 68, 71

Dalby, Thomas (d. 1526), vi. 27, 72, 80; xii. 68, 71

Dalby, Walter de, x. 45

Dalderby (Alderford), John, i. 1, 23; xii. 13

Dalderby (Alderford), Peter, i. 20, 56, 72, 88; xii. 17, 32

Dalderby (Alderford), William, i. 88, 100

Dale (Vale), Henry (de la), i. 61; iii. 49; vi. 44; xii. 25, 54, 69, 82

Dale, William de, vii. 55

Dalileye, John de, xi. 79

Dalison, Thomas, i. 28

Dalston, William de, vi. 100

Dalton, John (d. 1432), i. 98, 112, 121; xi. 15

Dalton, John (c. 1483–1503), i. 50

Dalton, John (de) (d. 1411), i. 24; vi. 114; xii. 73

Dalton (Neubald, Neubold), Peter (de), i. 22, 61, 66, 70, 88, 125, 126; vii. 23; x. 63; xii. 17

Dalton, Ralph de, vii. 39

Dalton, Robert (c. 1480–2), vii. 43

Dalton, Robert (de) (c. 1379–1401), i. 51, 121; vi. 82

Dalton, Thomas, i. 70; xii. 28

Dalton, William (de), i. 44, 65, 70(bis); ii. 15; vi. 60; x. 63; xii. 26, 28, 70

Damet, Thomas (c. 1418–36), v. 60

Damport, see Davenport

Danby, John (de), v. 65; vi. 35; x. 56

Danet, Thomas (d. 1483), i. 66 ('Davet'); iii. 43; v. 16; vii. 29; ix. 57; x. 41; xii. 27, 54, 62, 74, 83, 85

Daneys, William, i. 66, 67

Daneys, see also Deneys

Daniel, Nicholas, iii. 62; iv. 50; vi. 7; viii. 8

Daniell, John, vii. 30n

Danvers, John, vi. 36

Danyell, William, i. 93; xii. 34

Dardani, James, iv. 29

Darington, Nicholas, x. 38, 57, 70

Dario, Silvester, i. 29, 36

Daron, David, xi. 6

Darrell, Ivo, vii. 42

Darrell, Richard, vii. 27; xii. 74

Darrell, Stephen, vii. 27

Daubeny, John, i. 16; xii. 16

Daubeny, Philip, i. 16; xii. 16

Daumario (Guardia), Gerard de, iii. 15

Dauntesey, Edward, ix. 16

Davell, Robert, vi. 57, 115; x. 31(bis) & n

Davenport (Damport), Adam, i. 50; v. 23; viii. 42

Daventre, Philip de, viii. 82

Daventry, John (d. 1439), viii. 75

Daventry, John de (c. 1380–1), vi. 44, 93

Daventry, Ralph (de), i. 123, 126; v. 54

Davet, see Danet

David (c. 1334), xi. 8n

David (c. 1504), xi. 79

David, see also Dafydd

David ap Jake, ii. 27; xii. 48

David ap Rhys, see Dafydd ap Rhys

David, John, xi. 57, 64, 75

David, Matthew, xi. 33

David, Maurice ap, see Maurice ap David

David, Philip, xi. 85

David, Thomas (d. 1361), iii. 86; vii. 33; ix. 15, 32; xi. 65

David, Thomas (c. 1518), xi. 7

David, William, ii. 48

David, see also Davyd

Davis, John, v. 55

Davy, John (c. 1423–5), xi. 33

Davy, John (c. 1530), x. 31n

Davy, Philip, xi. 68n, 75n

Davy, Thomas, iii. 38

Davy, William, xi. 33

Davyd, Henry, x. 19, 23

Davyd, see also Dafydd, David

Davyson, John, iii. 4, 34; v. 22, 24; vi. 47

Dawne (Downe), George, iii. 83; vii. 44; x. 38, 39

Dawnes, see Downes

Day, Robert, iii. 25, 55, 81

Ddu, Gruffudd, see Gruffudd Ddu

Ddu, Madog, xi. 17

Deacon, see Diacre

Deanc (Dene), Henry, iii. 3; iv. 5; xi. 5

Deane, Peter de, see Dene

Debire, Robert de, x. 23n

Deeping, John, i. 43; xii. 22

Deeping, see also Depyng

Deerham, William de, vii. 57

Deerham, see also Deram, Derham

Defford, see Desford; Shelton

Deghere (Dynghere), William, v. 40

Dekelan (Dikelan), Richard, x. 23

de la Barre, see Barre

Delabere (Bere, Delaberd, de Labere, de la Bere, Laberd), John, ii. 46; iii. 63; iv. 49; vi. 32; viii. 5, 70; ix. 51; xi. 55 & n, 67

Delabere (de Labere), William, ii. 21, 40, 42

Delabere, see also Beer(e)

de la Hay, see Hay

de la Mare, see Mare

de la Mere, see Mere

de la Pole, *see* Pole
Dele, Adam, viii. 45
Dele, John, viii. 79
Delfau, Bernard, vii. 40
Delphinus, Henry, son of Imber, of Vienne,
    iv. 62; xii. 61
Delves, Richard, x. 24, 51, 57
Delves, Thomas, xi. 12
Denby, John (c. 1490–6, ? J.D. d. 1508),
    xi. 58, 60
Denby, John (d. 1508, ? J.D. c. 1490–6),
    iii. 70
Dene, Henry, *see* Deane
Dene (Deane), Peter de, v. 7, 45; vi. 52, 54;
    viii. 41; xii. 63
Dene, William de le, iv. 41 & n
Deneys, William, iii. 85
Deneys, *see also* Daneys, Denys
Denford, Roger de, iv. 41
Denham, John, i. 34, 108
Denham, Oliver, *see* Dinham
Denis, *see* Denys, William
Denston, Clement, iv. 31; v. 28; xii. 59, 63
Dente, John, iii. 55
Denton, James, *see* Deynton
Denton, John de, ii. 34
Denys (Dacus, Deny, Dionis), Anthony,
    iii. 97
Denys (Dacus, Denis, Dionis, Dionys),
    William, iii. 23; vi. 45
Denys, *see also* Daneys, Deneys
Depedale, Richard, xi. 75
Depeden (Dippeden, Dyppenden), John,
    iii. 92; vii. 50; viii. 72, 73
Depyng, John de, vii. 27; x. 9, 27, 32, 42; xi.
    80
Depyng, Roger de, x. 19, 32
Depyng, *see also* Deeping
Deram, Thomas, x. 5
Deram, *see also* Deerham, Derham
Derby (Derley), Edward, i. 19, 51, 63, 71, 75,
    86, 102; xii. 17, 23, 26, 29, 36
Derby, John (d. 1474), i. 34, 99; v. 42; xii. 20
Derby, John de (d. 1319), iii. 24; x. 5
Derby, John de (c. 1346–58), viii. 33, 77;
    ix. 20
Derby, John de (c. 1370–81), vi. 44, 114
Derby, Richard de, vi. 24
Derby, Robert de (d. by 1342), vii. 8
Derby, Robert de (d. by 1366), iii. 71
Derby, Robert de (Robert Shardelowe de
    Derby) (d. 1383, ? R. de Shardelowe),
    vii. 7
Derby, William, i. 17, 110; viii. 32; xii. 16

Dereham, *see* Derham
Derfeld, Thomas (c. 1403), x. 61
Derfeld, Thomas de (d. 1372), *see* Driffield
Derham (Dereham), Richard, iii. 74, 77; iv.
    29(*bis*); vii. 38
Derham, *see also* Deerham, Deram
Derleigh, *see* Darleigh
Derley, *see* Derby, Edward
Derlyngton (Derlington), John, iv. 27
Derlyngton, Thomas, *see* Dylyngton
Dernford, Nicholas de, vi. 44
Desbunton, Richard, ix. 18
Desford, John (d. 1419, ? J. Dysseford), ii.
    47
Despenser, Henry, iv. 23; xi. 24, 30
Desword, *see* Iddesworth
Deucio (Eux), Bertrand de, iii. 7, 96
Deuza, Gaucelin, *see* Eause
Devenesche (de Veneys, Devenyssh), John,
    iv. 46
Devenolde (Devenold), Philip, viii. 31; ix.
    57
Devenyssh, *see* Devenesche
Dewsbury, John de, vi. 38
Deynton (Denton), James, i. 86; iii. 60; vi.
    21; x. 7, 57
Deynton, *see also* Denton
Diacre (Deacon), Michael, xi. 39
Diaz, Roderic, viii. 33
Dighton, William, iii. 90; v. 59, 63
Dikelan, *see* Dekelan
Dinham (Denham, Dynham), Oliver, i. 71;
    iii. 85; iv. 29, 49; viii. 21, 56, 71; x. 26,
    61, 70
Dionis, Dionys, *see* Denys
Dippeden, *see* Depeden
Ditton, John de, v. 61
Ditton, *see also* Dutton
Dixon (Dixtone), Nicholas, i. 64, 67, 110,
    112, 114; ii. 33; iii. 43; v. 31; vi. 91;
    vii. 50; viii. 37; xii. 39
Dobbys (Dobbes), Robert, ii. 27(*bis*); vi. 11,
    72; xii. 48(*bis*)
Dobeler, *see* Brynk
Dock, *see* Duck
Docket, *see* Doket
Docwra (Docora), John (d. 1511), iii. 38
Docwra (Docora), John (d. 1535), iii. 38
Dodeley, *see* Dudley
Dodyne, Benedict, ii. 40
Dodyngton, John, ix. 11, 43
Dogett, Dogget, *see* Doket
Dogyon (Dudgeon), George, viii. 7
Doket (Docket), Andrew, x. 10, 52

Doket (Docket, Dogett, Dogget), John, i. 53; iii. 18, 36, 40, 83; vii. 11, 12, 14; x. 10; xii. 23, 53(*bis*), 54, 56, 84
Doket, *see also* Ducket
Dolbeare (Dolbeara), Walter, ix. 42; x. 52
Dolbera (Dulbeare), William, viii. 47
Domerham, Nicholas, iii. 42; xii. 54
Donati, Louis, xi. 70
Donclent, *see* Dunclent
Done, John, ix. 66
Done, *see also* Donne, Doune, Downe, Dunne
Donestaple, *see* Dunstaple
Donewych (Dunwich), John, iii. 65; v. 53; xii. 55
Doneys, John, v. 15, 23; vii. 41; xii. 62, 63, 75
Donford, Thomas de, viii. 29
Donne, John de, vii. 57
Donne, *see also* Done, Doune, Downe, Dunne
Donnsbrugg (Dounebrugg), Robert de, v. 21, 35
Donyngton, John de, x. 27
Donyngton, Reginald (de), i. 68; vi. 31; viii. 77
Donyngton, Thomas, vi. 53
Dorking (Dorkyng), Roger de, vii. 30–1; x. 19, 27
Dorset, William, ii. 18; xii. 46
Dortorier, Ralph le, vii. 33
Doune, Matthew, ix. 48
Doune, William (de), i. 12, 63; ix. 33
Doune, *see also* Done, Donne, Downe, Dunne
Dounebrugg, Robert de, *see* Donnsbrugg
Dounebrygge (Dowbrigge), William, ix. 40
Dounton, *see* Upton, Nicholas
Douse, *see* Dowce
Dowbrigge, *see* Dounebrygge
Dowce (Douse), Stephen, viii. 58
Dowcke, *see* Duck
Dowman, John, iii. 87; iv. 34; v. 57, 65; x. 48; xii. 56
Downe, George, *see* Dawne
Downe, Thomas (d. 1392), x. 28, 33
Downe, Thomas (d. 1489), i. 19, 42; ii. 9, 22, 51; viii. 74; xii. 21, 45, 51
Downe, *see also* Done, Donne, Doune, Dunne
Downes (Dawnes), Geoffrey, ii. 33; vi. 10, 57; xii. 49
Downton, John de, iii. 30; vii. 20
Draicote, Anthony, i. 34
Draicote, *see also* Draycott

Draiton, Nicholas de, ii. 16
Draiton, *see also* Drayton
Draper, Christopher, vi. 36
Draper, Richard, v. 65
Draper, Thomas, ix. 6
Drax, Richard de, vii. 17; ix. 18
Drax, Thomas, x. 41, 57
Draycott, William, vi. 72
Draycott, *see also* Draicote
Drayton, Henry, x. 50
Drayton, Richard (de), viii. 31, 76; x. 67
Drayton, Robert de, v. 14, 64
Drayton, *see also* Draiton
Dreff, Ralph (c. 1446, ? R. Drew), xi. 85
Drew, Ralph (d. 1456, ? R. Dreff), iii. 65, 98
Drewery (Drury, Salisbury), John, v. 17, 50; ix. 52
Driffield (Derfeld), Thomas de, vi. 38
Driffield (Dryffelde), William de, iii. 80; x. 15, 60
Drokensford, Andrew de, viii. 79–80
Drokensford (Droxford), John (de), i. 94; iii. 47; vi. 66; vii. 34; viii. 1 & n; x. 31, 67 & n; xi. 80
Drokensford, Michael de, viii. 44
Drokensford, Richard de (d. 1316), viii. 8, 18
Drokensford, Richard de (c. 1326–8), viii. 6, 80
Drokensford, Roger de, vi. 92
Drokensford, Thomas de, viii. 40, 54
Drokyll, William, ii. 47; xii. 51
Droxford, *see* Drokensford
Druell, John (d. 1453), ix. 14, 52
Druell, John (d. 1469), iii. 21, 38, 72, 74, 79; v. 16, 54
Drury, Henry, i. 27(*bis*)
Drury, John, *see* Drewery
Dryffelde, *see* Driffield
Duck (Dock, Dowcke, Duke), Richard, iii. 13, 82; vi. 47; viii. 21; ix. 64
Duck, *see also* Duke
Ducket, William, x. 22
Ducket, *see also* Doket
Dudgeon, *see* Dogyon
Dudley (Sutton), Arthur, x. 27, 46, 51
Dudley (Dodeley), George, vi. 43; vii. 24
Dudley, John, viii. 43
Dudley (Dodeley, Dudeley), Richard, i. 79 ('Richard *or* John'); iii. 16, 49, 70, 99; v. 33; vi. 68; vii. 24; xii. 30
Dudley (Dodeley), William, iii. 103; v. 12, 22, 26, 52; vi. 30, 80, 109; vii. 21
Duffield, Thomas (c. 1369), vi. 114
Duffield, Thomas (d. 1423), i. 24

Duffield, William (d. 1453), v. 13; vi. 21, 93; xii. 67, 72

Duffield, William (c. 1497), x. 20 & n

Dufford, see Offord

Duke (Barbour), Henry, iii. 6

Duke, Richard, see Duck

Dulbeare, see Dolbera

Dulting, Thomas, v. 55

Duncan, Thomas, i. 119

Dunclent (Donclent), Thomas (de), vii. 41; xi. 68n, 73, 75n

Dunmow (Dunmaw, Dunmawe, Dunmoe), John, iv. 61 & n; vi. 32; ix. 57

Dunne, Gabriel, v. 47

Dunne, see also Done, Donne, Doune, Downe

Dunre, Richard de, ii. 37

Dunstable, William de, x. 4

Dunstaple (Donestaple), John de, vii. 33

Dunstavylle, John, ii. 47

Dunster, John (d. 1412), viii. 22

Dunster, John (d. 1496), viii. 22

Dunwich, see Donewych

Durant, Thomas, v. 11, 18, 38

Durfort (Reissaco), Gaillard de, vi. 90

Durward, Ralph, ii. 21; xii. 47

Dutton, Edmund, iii. 56, 92

Dutton, see also Ditton

Dyer, Martin, ix. 54

Dyer, Richard, ii. 26

Dyffrynclwyt, John de, xi. 17

Dyker, Robert, viii. 9, 60

Dylew, John, ii. 13, 22; xii. 45, 47

Dylyngton (Derlyngton), Thomas de, viii. 6

Dyne, John, xi. 45

Dyneley (Dyngeley), Oliver, iii. 67, 98; ix. 50; xii. 55, 57

Dynghere, see Deghere

Dyngle, Roger, vii. 49

Dynham, see Dinham

Dyppenden, see Depeden

Dypphull, Dyppull, see Bromsgrove

Dyrewyne, see Exonia, John de

Dysseford, John (c. 1400–12, ? J. Desford), v. 33

E— (c. 1299, ? Giles (Egidius) Filliol), v. 13; xii. 62(bis)

Eadberbury, see Abberbury

Eaderbury (Abberbury, Adderbury, Eadbury), Thomas de, vi. 90; x. 7, 66

Earle, Thomas, vii. 36

Earle, see also Erle, Herle

Easton (Eston), Adam, i. 25; iii. 8, 102; vi. 7

Easton (Eston), Walter, iii. 98; xii. 57

Easton, see also Eston

Eastry, Henry, iv. 5

Eause, Gaucelin d' (Gaucelin Johannis Deuza of Cahors), i. 10, 86; vi. 44; x. 11

Ebchester (Ewchestre), Robert, vi. 111

Ebchester (Ewchestre), William, vi. 110

Eboraco, see York

Ecclesey, Richard, x. 42

Eccleshale, John de, iii. 63, 98; v. 35; vii. 56

Edderston, John, i. 43, 85

Eden (Edon), Richard, iii. 90; v. 13

Edenhall, Robert de, vi. 100

Edenham, Geoffrey, i. 50, 106, 107

Edenham (Ednam), John, iv. 28; v. 16, 21; viii. 17

Edenham, Matthew, i. 35

Edenham, Richard, xi. 5 & n

Edenham, see also Ethenham

Edenstowe, Henry, i. 44, 118

Edgar, John, iii. 88

Edgeworth (Eggeworth, Egworth), Roger, iii. 87; viii. 70

Ediall, see Edyall

Edington (Edyndon, Edyngdon, Edynton), John (de), i. 78; iii. 49; iv. 49; v. 29; vii. 23

Edington (Edyngdon), Thomas (de), iii. 44; vii. 58; viii. 74

Edington (Edyndon, Edyngdon, Edynton), William (de) (of), i. 83; ii. 45; iii. 71; iv. 4, 46; xii. 31, 50

Edmonds, Thomas, x. 22

Edmondys, John (d. 1520), viii. 71

Edmund, William, xi. 33

Edmunds, John (c. 1505–30), v. 19, 21; vii. 25, 49

Edmunds, John (d. 1544), iii. 19

Ednam, see Edenham

Edon, see Eden

Edward ap John (Joyns), xi. 65

Edward, John, iii. 54

Edwards, Thomas, vii. 38

Edwards (Edwardis), William, ii. 29, 44

Edyall (Ediall), Henry, iv. 42; vii. 18, 45(bis); viii. 38, 62; x. 43, 51n; xii. 60, 78, 80

Edyndon, Edyngdon, Edynton, see Edington

Effeiriat, see Affeiriad

Egerley, Robert, xi. 13

Egerton, Richard, x. 31, 65, 68

Eggecombe, John, ix. 54

Eggecombe, Thomas, xi. 48

Eggeworth, see Edgeworth

Eglescliffe, John de, xi. 21

Egworth, *see* Edgeworth

Einion (Ainian, Anian, Eynion) (d. 1307), xi. 3

Einion (Ainian, Anian, Eynion) (c. 1301–14), xi. 40 & n

Einion (Ainian, Anian, Eynion) (c. 1317), xi. 9

Einion ab Iorwerth, xi. 49

Einion ap Meurig, xi. 17

Einion ap Tegwareth, xi. 12

Einion, Bleddyn ab, *see* Bleddyn ab Einion

Einion, Gregory ab, *see* Gregory ab Einion

Einion, Morgan ab, *see* Morgan ab Einion

Ekerdon, William, ix. 45

Ekys, *see* Hekys

Elam, John de, *see* Elham

Elham, John (d. 1449), iv. 6

Elham (Elam, Eltham, Olham), John de (d. 1331), ii. 32; v. 9, 58; xii. 49

Elias (c. 1306), xi. 49

Elias (c. 1345), xi. 8

Elias ap Kenric, xi. 6n

Eliot, John, *see* Cliderow

Eliot, William, *see* Elliott

Elis, Huw, xi. 7

Elis, Llywelyn ap Madog ab, *see* Llywelyn ap Madog ab Elis

Elis, Nicholas ab, *see* Nicholas ab Elys

Elis, *see also* Ellis, Elys

Elisaundre, *see* Alexander

Elleford, William, viii. 16

Ellerker, John, vi. 19, 37 & n

Elliott (Eliot, Elyot), William, i. 104; iii. 18, 35; ix. 21, 60; xi. 68n, 72, 79(*bis*)

Ellis (Elys), Geoffrey, iii. 46

Ellis, *see also* Elis, Elys

Elmer, *see* Eylmer

Elsfield, Richard de, iii. 84; v. 34

Elteslee, Robert de, xi. 32

Eltham, *see* Elham

Eltisley, *see* Banastre

Elton (Baker), Edward, iii. 31

Elton (Baker, Eltone, Olton), John, i. 98; ii. 52; iii. 55, 57, 58; xii. 35, 51

Elton, *see also* Aulton, Olton

Elveden (Elvedon), Walter, ii. 8; iv. 30

Elvet, John, i. 12, 13, 69, 81; ii. 24; iii. 56; v. 32; vi. 62, 72; xii. 15, 47

Elvet, Richard, i. 13

Ely, Alan de, iv. 30, 32

Ely, Luke de, x. 9

Ely, Peter de, iv. 14, 16; xii. 58

Ely, Simon de, iv. 32

Ely, *see also* Eyli

Elye, Thomas, vi. 100n

Elyot, *see* Elliott

Elys, Geoffrey, *see* Ellis

Elys, John, viii. 70

Elys, Nicholas ab, *see* Nicholas ab Elys

Elys, *see also* Elis, Ellis

Emson, John, i. 68

Emson, Richard, i. 68

Emwell, John, iii. 16, 46, 72

Ende, Thomas atte, viii. 41

Enford (Endeford), Richard de, iv. 47 ('Robert'); xii. 60

Engelfeld, David de, xii. 90

Englefeld, Matthew de, xi. 3, 9n, 17

Engolisma (Ingolisma), Gerald de, v. 43 & n

Engolisma (Angoulême, Ingolisma), Hugh de, iv. 7; v. 27; vi. 75; xii. 58, 71

Enham, Thomas, xi. 32

Enkeston, Thomas, iii. 54

Eppe, John, vii. 31

Erdeleye, John, i. 6

Erghum (Arum), John, viii. 51

Erghum, Peter de, iii. 102

Erghum, Ralph (d. 1400), iii. 1; viii. 2

Erghum, Ralph (d. 1410), iii. 7; viii. 7, 16, 61

Ergum, Ralph (d. 1360), i. 59

Ergym, Henry, viii. 25

Eritage, *see* Heritage

Erle, Guy de, xi. 82

Erle, John, vi. 58

Erle, *see also* Earle, Herle

Ermestede, William, v. 50

Ermyne, William (d. 1401), *see* Eyremynne

Ermyne, William de (d. 1336), *see* Ayremynne

Ermyte, *see* Heremyte

Erpingham, *see* Howe

Eryngton, Richard, viii. 20

Eryom, Richard de, vi. 84

Esbache, Robert, x. 30

Esedene, *see* Estdene

Eseger, *see* Osger

Eslake, Thomas, vii. 31 & n, 33n

Esple, Robert, x. 8, 15

Estaing, William d', i. 6, 54

Estbroke, Thomas, ix. 6

Estcourt, John, vi. 9; xi. 11

Estcourt, William, iii. 68, 79

Estdene, William de (c. 1313), viii. 24

Estdene (Esedene), William de (c. 1313–33), vii. 13, 55; viii. 24

Estington (Estyngton), Thomas, i. 90; iii. 23, 103

Estmond, John, iii. 26, 46, 70, 82

Eston, Adam, see Easton
Eston, John, vii. 35
Eston, Michael de, viii. 82
Eston, Thomas, vii. 40
Eston, Walter (d. 1399), see Easton
Eston (Estone), Walter (d. 1455/6), ii. 29; vii. 21, 47
Eston, see also Easton
Estyngton, see Estington
Ethenham, John, v. 17, 48
Ethenham, see also Edenham
Eton, Henry, vi. 114
Eton, John, xi. 33
Eton, see also Eyton
Etton, John de, x. 30
Eure, Thomas de, v. 6, 48
Eure, William, iii. 12; vi. 11; xii. 52, 66
Eux, see Eause, Deucio
Evan ap Bleddyn, xi. 9
Evans, Robert, xi. 7 & n
Evelyn, John, ix. 56
Everard, Nicholas, vi. 12, 32, 53
Everdon, John (d. 1420), i. 62; iii. 23
Everdon (Everdone), John (d. 1461), ix. 49; x. 23
Everdon, John de (d. 1335), iii. 91; v. 5, 51; viii. 24; ix. 8; x. 22
Everdon, Philip de, x. 65
Everdon, William (de), i. 89; v. 32
Everdoun, Thomas de, xi. 14
Everingham, Adam de, vi. 54
Everino, see Vernhio
Evesham, John de, iv. 56, 59
Evesham, Richard de, vii. 58
Evesham, Thomas de, ii. 38
Evot, John, i. 15, 80; vi. 16
Ewchestre, see Ebchester
Ewe (Oo), John de (d. 1354, ? J. de Ho), ii. 10, 18; xii. 45, 46, 64
Ewell, William de, v. 36
Ewen, Richard, i. 7, 13, 32, 112; iii. 10; v. 45 & n, 46
Ewyas, Philip, xi. 25
Ewyn, William, ix. 65
Excestre (Excetre), John (de), ii. 43; viii. 43 ('William'); ix. 43; xi. 41; xii. 50, 79
Excestre, William (c. 1389), see Pregeet
Excestre, William (c. 1390-2), see Excestre, John (de)
Excestre, William (c. 1392, ? W. de Exeter, W. Pregeet), viii. 25;
Excestre, William de (William Exeter) (d. 1359), i. 20, 23, 72, 98; iii. 49 & n; vi. 15, 75; ix. 29; xii. 17, 28, 54

Exeter, William de (d. 1419, ? W. Excestre, W. Pregeet), x. 56
Exon, Henry de, xi. 33
Exon, John de (d. 1320), see Strange
Exonia, John de (John Dyrewyne) (d. 1314), ix. 22
Exton, see Eyton, Geoffrey de
Eya, Philip de, v. 47
Eye, John (c. 1535-41, ? J. Eyer), viii. 24
Eyer, John (c. 1539-48, ? J. Eye), i. 77; vi. 32
Eyer, see also Eyr
Eyli, John de, iii. 98
Eyli, see also Ely(e)
Eylmer (Aylmer, Aylmere, Elmer), John, vii. 19, 27; x. 42
Eylmer, see also Aylmer
Eyncourt, Oliver, i. 89
Eynion, see Einion
Eyr, John, viii. 29
Eyr, see also Eyer
Eyremynne, Richard (de), see Ayremynne
Eyremynne (Ermyne), William (d. 1401), v. 53; vi. 69; ix. 43
Eyremynne, William de (d. 1336), see Ayremynne
Eysi, John de, ix. 29
Eyton (Exton), Geoffrey (de), i. 38; v. 21, 35, 52; vii. 56; viii. 54 ('Geoffrey or Gilbert'); x. 29, 64; xii. 20
Eyton (Knockyn), Thomas de, x. 11, 25
Eyton, see also Eton
Eyvill, Gilbert, of Navenby, i. 21, 44, 106
Ezius, see Breto, Bernard de le

Facete, Adam, vii. 16, 24, 25, 42
Fairfax, Brian, vi. 11, 63
Faldingworth, William, i. 49, 115
Fallan, William, v. 9; xi. 78
Falle, Nicholas, i. 35
Fallecis, Saladin de, iii. 63; vii. 50
Farewell, John, xi. 31
Farewelle, William, iii. 61
Fargis, Bernard de (Bernard des Farges), i. 70
Fargis, Bertrand de, iii. 3; vi. 22, 61, 73
Fargis, Raymond de (Raymond des Farges), i. 12, 70, 95; iii. 3, 11; xii. 34
Farington, Hugh, iii. 19
Farington (Faringdon, Faryngton), Robert (de), i. 33, 46; vi. 65, 85
Farington (Farrington), William (de), iii. 17; vii. 35; xi. 62
Farington, see also Farrington
Farinier, William, of (de) Gourdon, vii. 7; ix. 13n, 36n

Farley, William, iii. 61
Farlyngton, John, vii. 15, 44
Farnelawe, Thomas de, vi. 9, 35
Farrington, Edmund, x. 26
Farrington, William, *see* Farington
Farrow, *see* Ferrer, Thomas
Faryngton, *see* Farington
Fastolf, Laurence, v. 64; vii. 56; xii. 64
Fastolf (Fastole), Thomas, i. 43; iv. 26; viii. 4, 13; xi. 12, 53 & n; xii. 21
Faucon, William, x. 25 & n; xii. 84
Faukes, John (d. 1349), xi. 59
Faukes (Faux, Fawkes), John (d. 1471), i. 74, 75 ('John *or* William'); vii. 9, 60; x. 50; xii. 29(*bis*)
Faukys (Faukes), Thomas, iii. 15; xi. 15, 83
Fauntleroy (Fawnderay), William, i. 57
Faux, *see* Faukes
Faversham, Simon (de), ii. 26; iv. 7
Fawell, William, ix. 65
Fawkes, *see* Faukes
Fawnderay, *see* Fauntleroy
Federston, *see* Fetherstone
Felde (Fowe), John de la, ii. 19
Felde (Field), Richard, i. 113, 116; iii. 39, 59, 65; vii. 51; xii. 40
Felde (Field), Thomas, i. 81; ii. 4, 34, 49, 52; xi. 42
Felde, Walter, viii. 9, 67; ix. 59
Felde, *see also* Field
Fell, William, vi. 25
Felter, William, vi. 8, 18, 30, 45; viii. 70, 76; xii. 66, 68, 69
Feltewell, *see* Feltwell
Felton, Robert, i. 58; ii. 9, 25; v. 24; vii. 16; x. 66
Felton, Thomas, vi. 102
Feltwell (Feltewell), John, vii. 35; x. 9, 69
Fenrother, Richard, v. 57
Fenton (Fentune), John de, iv. 32
Fenwick, Thomas de, vi. 76
Ferdinand (Ferdinandus), Gonsalvo (Gundisalve, Gundissalvus), iii. 53; v. 18, 19, 63; viii. 21; x. 40; xi. 24n
Ferentino (Florentino), Bartholomew de, v. 64
Feriby, Benedict, i. 56
Feriby (Ferriby), John de, iii. 46; vi. 33
Feriby, Nicholas, vi. 79
Feriby, Richard de, v. 54
Feriby (Ferriby, Feryby), Thomas, iii. 91; iv. 18; v. 42; vi. 29; viii. 43
Feriby (Feryby), William (d. 1415), i. 7; vi. 22; xii. 14

Feriby (Fereby, Ferriby), William de (d. 1379), ii. 4; iii. 71, 82; vi. 20, 33, 46, 56; xii. 68
Feriby (Ferriby), William de (d. 1392), viii. 48; ix. 38
Feringes, Richard, i. 42
Fermer, John, x. 49, 69
Ferrariis, Hugh de, ix. 35
Ferrer, Robert, vi. 39
Ferrer (Farrow), Thomas, vi. 77
Ferriby, *see* Feriby
Ferrono, Arnald de, vii. 30–1
Feryby, *see* Feriby
Fetherstone (Federston, Fetherstonhalgh), Richard, xi. 61n, 62 & n
Fetishugh, *see* FitzHugh
Fewlar, Simon, vii. 36(*bis*)
Fewlar, *see also* Fouler
Field, Richard, *see* Felde
Field, Robert, i. 106
Field, Thomas, *see* Felde
Field, *see also* Felde
Fieschi (Flisco), Adrian de, vi. 19
Fieschi (Flisco), Albert, of Lavagna, vi. 46
Fieschi (Flisco), Anthony, son of Charles de, x. 71
Fieschi (Flisco), Innocent de, iii. 57, 70; vi. 19; xii. 67
Fieschi (Flisco), John de, iii. 90; vi. 50
Fieschi (Flisco), Louis de, vi. 45, 48, 114
Fieschi (Flisco), Luchinus de, i. 72
Fieschi (Flisco), Luke de, x. 45
Fieschi (Flisco), Manuel de, i. 93; iii. 71; vi. 24, 27; xii. 34, 55, 68(*bis*)
Fieschi (Flisco), William de, iv. 32; v. 59; vi. 46, 80; xii. 59
Figeac, *see* Lagier
Fighino, Nicholas de, iii. 87
Fileby, Adam de, ii. 3
Filliol, Giles (c. 1298–9, ? E—), v. 45; xii. 62, 63
Finch, Edward, iii. 14, 35, 40, 43, 50, 53, 58, 91, 97, 99; vii. 52(*bis*)
Finch, *see also* Fynch
Fincham, Thomas, i. 82 ('Thomas *or* John'); xii. 31
Finneys, John, iv. 32; xii. 59
Fisher, Christopher, vi. 59
Fisher, John (d. 1494), i. 125
Fisher, John (d. 1511), v. 55
Fisher (Fyssher), John (d. 1535), iv. 39
Fisscher, William, vii. 60
Fitton, *see* Fyton
Fitz-David, Gervase, xi. 8n

FitzGildae, Robert, ix. 17n
Fitzherbert, Thomas, x. 8, 65
FitzHerbert (Fitzherbert), William, i. 63, 75; ii. 37; v. 65; viii. 20; x. 10; xii. 26, 29
FitzHugh (Fetishugh, Fitzhugh), George, i. 4, 59, 64; iii. 78; vi. 89; xii. 25, 26
FitzHugh (Fitzhugh), Robert, i. 11, 26, 93; iv. 15; v. 3; vi. 55; x. 44; xii. 15, 18, 34
FitzJames (Fitzjames), James, v. 38; viii. 9, 12n, 42, 77, 79
Fitzjames, John, viii. 75; xii. 81
FitzJames (Fitzjames), Richard, iv. 39; v. 4, 16, 57; vii. 3; viii. 66
Fitzjames (Fitzwilliams), William, viii. 6
Fitz Meles, see Miles, Robert
FitzPeter de Marnay, Amadeus, ii. 51
FitzPiers, Walter, iii. 11
FitzRalph (Fitzralph), Richard, i. 23; ix. 28; x. 6, 12n
FitzRogo, William, ix. 12, 19, 25
Fitzthomas, John, vi. 20
FitzUrse, see Orsini, James
FitzWaryn, Peter, iii. 98
Fitzwilliam, Humphrey, vi. 53
Fitzwilliam, Morgan, xii. 90
Fitzwilliams, William, see Fitzjames
Flambard, Simon, v. 58
Flamsted, John de, v. 63
Flandari, Peter, vi. 60
Flanders, see Malo Leone
Fleming, John (d. 1301), i. 79
Fleming, Richard, i. 2(bis), 58; vi. 4, 63, 72; xii. 13
Fleming, Robert (d. 1483), i. 4, 66, 81, 84, 92; xii. 34
Fleming, Robert (d. 1526), i. 100
Fleming, Thomas, xi. 84
Flemmyng, John (d. 1467/8), viii. 29
Fleshmonger (Foster), William, i. 45; iii. 93; vii. 5, 31, 34, 52
Flete, John de, vii. 56
Flisco, see Fieschi
Fliwe, John, of Bergeveny, i. 25
Flore, John (c. 1427, ? J. Floure), xi. 77, 85n
Florence, Balsamus of, see Talami
Florence, Edward of, see Sapiti
Florence, John de Manettis de Portinariis of, see Portinariis
Florence, Pigellus de Manettis of, see Manettis
Florence, Rayner de, see Vichio
Florence, Simon of, see Sapiti
Florence, Thomas of, see Nerii
Florens, William, vi. 101

Florentia, see Sinabaldi
Florentino, Bartholomew de, see Ferentino
Florentinus, see Bardis
Floure (Flour), John (d. 1463, ? J. Flore), ix. 53 & n; xi. 85 & n; xii. 83
Flyghe, Thomas, ix. 53
Flynt, Gregory, xi. 43
Foche, John, vii. 45n
Foderingeye, Walter, i. 87, 94
Foderingeye, William (de), i. 27, 106, 120; iii. 79
Foderinghey (Fodringhey), Ralph (de), i. 76; iv. 17; xii. 30, 58
Fodringhey, Robert de, iv. 17
Folbery, George, vi. 70
Foliot, William, iv. 17
Foljambe, Edward, iv. 48n
Foljambe, Robert, x. 23
Folke, John, ix. 44
Folvyle, Henry, vii. 12
Fonteneye, John de, iii. 61, 70
Foolde, Walter, viii. 24
Forcer, see Fossour
Ford, Nicholas, viii. 75
Ford, Robert de, vi. 73
Forde, Richard de, viii. 10, 81
Forde, William de (d. c. 1408), vi. 37
Forde, William de la, de Yatton (d. 1324), viii. 11, 37
Forden, William, vii. 27
Fordham, John (de) (d. 1425), i. 109; iv. 8, 14; vi. 42, 69, 108; vii. 28; viii. 4; xi. 70
Fordham, John de (d. 1438), iv. 59
Forest (Forrest), John, i. 32, 39, 107; iii. 23; iv. 49; vi. 33, 47; viii. 5 & n, 37; x. 49
Forest, Richard, viii. 28; xi. 48
Forêt, Peter de la, v. 12, 15
Forey, Walter, vii. 13
Forneby, John, i. 102, 120; xii. 41
Forneys, Thomas, ii. 48, 52
Forrest, see Forest
Forrester, Thomas, vi. 28
Forrester, William, iv. 50
Forster, John (d. 1440), i. 26, 37, 39(bis), 60, 76; vi. 51
Forster (Foster), John (d. 1512), i. 10; ii. 35; iii. 52, 57; v. 9, 42, 49; vi. 70
Forster, John (d. 1529), x. 22
Forth, Robert, i. 36, 61; xii. 20
Fossour (Forcer), John, vi. 110
Foster, John, see Forster, John (d. 1512)
Foster, William, see Fleshmonger
Fothed (Fotehede), John, i. 53; iii. 55; xii. 24, 54

Fotherby, *see* Green, Simon

Fotheringhey, *see* Foderingeye, Foderinghey, Fodringhey

Fouler, John, i. 90

Fouler, *see also* Fewlar

Fouleshurst, Henry, xi. 25

Foulmere (Fulemere, Fulmer), Robert, iv. 33

Fowe, *see* Felde, John de la

Fownhope (Fowehop, Fowehope), William de, ii. 42

Fox, Edward, i. 13; ii. 3; iii. 8, 68; vi. 74; viii. 40; xii. 71, 79

Fox, John (d. 1483), i. 45, 50; x. 18, 28, 31, 39, 49; xii. 22, 23

Fox, John (d. 1530), i. 59; iii. 84; iv. 49, 51; vii. 36; viii. 50; xii. 25

Fox, Richard, ii. 38; iii. 34, 56; iv. 47; v. 22; vi. 109; viii. 3; ix. 3; xii. 60, 80

Foxall, William, xi. 79

Foxford, Richard, v. 70

Foxley, John, x. 56

Franceys, David, xi. 57, 59

Franceys, John (c. 1335–45), xi. 57, 59

Franceys, *see also* Fraunceys

Frangerius, Arnald, de Cantilupo, v. 4

Frank (Franks, Fraunks), John, iii. 30, 44, 52, 80; iv. 33; vii. 29; viii. 68(*bis*); x. 39

Franklin, William, i. 69; vi. 80, 113

Franks, *see* Frank

Fraunceys, John (d. 1314), vi. 75

Fraunceys, John (d. 1413), i. 64; iii. 10, 42, 46; vi. 67, 79; vii. 60; viii. 30; xii. 26

Fraunceys, Thomas, ix. 58, 59

Fraunceys, *see also* Franceys

Fraunks, *see* Frank

Fre, *see* Northburgh, Michael de (d. 1383)

Frechvill, John de, xi. 83

Free (Phreas), John, viii. 2

Frelandi, Walter, viii. 35

Frend, Robert, iii. 81

Frende, William, vii. 30, 54

Freningham, Ralph de, v. 57

Frere, *see* Bruton, Richard

Fresapanis, William de, iii. 37, 51

Frescobaldis, John de, iii. 58

Fresingfeld, John de, iv. 16

Fressel (Frysell), William, iv. 41

Freston (Fryston), Richard (d. 1477, ? John or R. Friston), i. 39; v. 26

Freston (Fryston), William, i. 39; v. 68

Freton, John de, iii. 44; iv. 28; v. 33

Freton, Roger de, iii. 30; v. 10; vi. 28; vii. 4

Frisby, John, x. 44

Frisby, *see also* Frysby

Friston, John (Richard) (c. 1466–7, ? R. Freston), i. 99; xii. 36

Frocetur, *see* Froucetur

Frome, Nicholas, viii. 60

Frome, Thomas, viii. 27, 71, 72, 82; xii. 81

Fromond, Geoffrey de, viii. 60

Fromond, Godfrey, ix. 33

Frost, John, iv. 51; xii. 60

Frost (Crofte, Froste), Robert, i. 19; iv. 51; v. 59; vi. 36; viii. 36 & n; x. 41, 49; xii. 17

Froucetur (Frocetur, Frowcester, Frowscetur), Edmund, ii. 5, 11, 19, 39, 46

Fry, John, vii. 37

Fryer, Robert, viii. 55

Frysby, Richard, i. 93

Frysby, *see also* Frisby

Frysell, *see* Fressel

Fryskenay, *see* Banastre, Thomas, of Eltisley

Fryston, *see* Freston

Fulemere, *see* Foulmere

Fulford, John (c. 1423–5), xi. 22

Fulford, John (d. 1518/19), ix. 15, 17, 19, 60

Fulford, William, viii. 42, 59; ix. 20, 52

Fullborne, William, iii. 33; v. 37

Fuller, John, vii. 34

Fulmer, *see* Foulmere

Fulneby, William, i. 63

Furno, Vitalis de, v. 34

Fychan (Vaghan, Vaughan), Dafydd (c. 1361–6), xi. 58, 65

Fychan (Vaghan, Vaughan), Dafydd, ap Dafydd (c. 1385–6), xi. 40, 43n

Fychan (Vaghan, Vaughan), Edward, v. 16, 21, 39, 58; vii. 14; xi. 55

Fychan, Hywel ap Dafydd, *see* Hywel ap Dafydd Fychan

Fychan, Ieuan ap Dafydd, *see* Ieuan ap Dafydd Fychan

Fychan (Vaghan, Vaughan), John, xi. 61, 68

Fychan (Vaghan, Vaughan), Philip, xi. 62 & n

Fychan (Vaghan, Vaughan, Walchan), Richard (c. 1344–52), iv. 48; v. 15, 41; xi. 81

Fychan (Vaghan, Vaughan), Richard (c. 1504–9), xi. 17

Fychan (Vaghan, Vaughan), William (c. 1404–5), xi. 10, 17

Fychan (Vaghan, Vaughan), William (c. 1517–39), xi. 67, 71

Fychan, *see also* Vaghan

Fydyan, William, iii. 45, 65

Fyfhide, John, i. 35

Fylham, William, ix. 9, 16, 48

Fynch, John, iv. 6

Fynch, *see also* Finch

Fyndon, Simon de, vii. 22

Fynne, John, i. 102; xii. 36

Fynyngleye, Henry de, xi. 28

Fyssher, *see* Fisher, Fisscher

Fysshewyke, Thomas, xi. 31

Fyton (Fitton), John, iii. 18, 56, 60, 83; vi. 34; x. 19(*bis*)

Gabriell (Gabriel), Richard, vi. 70; viii. 69; ix. 47; xii. 71

Gaddesden, John de, v. 66; vii. 57

Gaetani, Anibaldus, de Ceccano, i. 15, 54, 92; vi. 13, 24, 90; vii. 23; viii. 49; ix. 15; x. 7; xii. 15, 34, 67, 68, 72

Gaetani, Francis (d. 1317), vi. 6, 25, 59

Gaetani, Francis (c. 1300–30), i. 73; iii. 73; vi. 12, 13n, 78, 92 & n

Gaetani, John, de Orsini, de Urbe, vi. 64, 75; x. 14

Gainsborough (Geynsborough), William de, iv. 55

Gainsborough, *see also* Gaynesburgh

Galaciano, *see* Galicia

Galeys, Philip, vii. 7n, 10, 26

Galicia (Galaciano), Peter de, iii. 51; vii. 32

Gamull, *see* Ganvill

Gandavo (Ghent), Iswin de, iii. 13, 15, 45, 66

Gandavo (Ghent), Simon de, iii. 1

Gange, *see* Gawge

Ganvill (Gamull, Ganville), John, ii. 21; viii. 70; x. 13

Gararo, Garcia de, vi. 59

Gardiner, Henry (c. 1407, ? H.G. d. 1419), xi. 63

Gardiner, Henry (d. 1419, ? H.G. c. 1407), viii. 65

Gardiner (Gardener), Richard (d. 1518), iii. 88, 93; viii. 33

Gardiner, Stephen, i. 13; iii. 91; iv. 30, 47, 63; viii. 17

Gardyner (Chychestre), Richard (d. 1399), vii. 38

Gare (Gaye), William de la, ii. 10, 37

Garland, Henry de, vii. 4, 8, 45

Garland, Richard, xi. 67

Garnesey, John, viii. 35

Garnet, William, iii. 97

Garrett, Thomas, vii. 53, 54

Garsie, Raymond, de St Sauveur, i. 94

Garssia (Gasci), John, x. 6

Garton, John, x. 33(*bis*), 50, 70

Garton, Thomas de, iii. 47; viii. 49, 74; x. 53

Gasci, *see* Garssia, Gascy

Gascoigne, Francis, i. 113

Gascoigne, Thomas, vi. 9 & n; viii. 32

Gascy, Isuard, viii. 77

Gascy, *see also* Garsie, Garssia

Gatagie, John, iii. 80

Gaudeby, Hugh, iv. 31

Gauge, *see* Gawge

Gaunstede (Gounsted), Simon (de), i. 56; iii. 14; vi. 24, 35; vii. 40; viii. 76

Gavarreto (Gavaretto), Arnald de, i. 12, 95; vi. 15

Gawge (Gauge), Thomas, i. 73; v. 55; vi. 83 ('Gange'); xii. 29, 71

Gaye, *see* Gare

Gaynesburgh, Robert, vii. 24, 25, 40

Gaynesburgh, *see also* Gainsborough

Gebaven, vi. 112n

Gedele, *see* Godeley

Geffray (Geoffray, Jeffrey, Jeffreys), John, iv. 32; x. 31, 53 & n

Geffray (Jeffray), Leyson, iii. 40

Geffrey (Geoffrey, Jeffrey), Richard, xi. 72

Geffrey (Jeffrey), Robert, ii. 6, 7, 11, 13, 31, 44

Gele, Dafydd, xi. 47

Gele, Richard, xi. 11

Genensis, *see* Boerius

Genetta, *see* Jenetto

Geneva, Robert of (de), iii. 7; vi. 13n, 16

Genevefe (Gonvena), Laurence, ix. 39

Geneville, *see* Genvyle, Gynewell

Genoa, Johanninus de Silvaticus of, *see* Silvaticus

Genoa, Natavus de Nigro of, *see* Nigro

Gent, Richard, de Castro, x. 71

Gentilibus, *see* Rodolphucci

Genvyle (Geneville), Nicholas de, ii. 51

Genvyle, *see also* Gynewell

Geoffray, *see* Geffray, John

Geoffrey (c. 1320), vii. 11n

Geoffrey (c. 1334), vi. 100

Geoffrey, Richard, *see* Geffrey

George, John, viii. 57

Geors, *see* Jorz

Gerard (Geraud), John (John Gerard de Stratford), iii. 37; x. 45; xii. 54, 85

Gerdeston, *see* Kerdeston

Gerdone (Geydon), John de, ii. 18

Gerlethorp, Thomas, vii. 59

Gerlthorpe, Robert, x. 37

Germeyn, John, ix. 9, 54

Germeyn, Ralph, ix. 7, 19, 23

Gervase ap Madog, *see* Iorwerth ap Madog

Gerveys, Thomas, vii. 42

Gest, Walter, vii. 10, 41
Gest, see also Gyste
Gethyn, Thomas, xi. 33
Getingdon (Getyngton), Richard, v. 39
Getingdon, see also Geytyngton
Geydon, see Gerdone
Geyell, Nicholas, iv. 61
Geynsborough, see Gainsborough
Geytyngton, John, vii. 13
Ghent, see Gandavo
Ghinucchi, Jerome de, iv. 58
Gibbons, John, ix. 10, 63
Gidding, Geoffrey, i. 60; xii. 25
Gidding, see also Gyddyng
Giffard, Godfrey, iv. 55
Giffard, John (d. 1349), see Gifford
Giffard, John (c. 1349), ix. 31
Giffard, Walter, ix. 8, 19, 25
Giffard, William, see Gifford
Gifford (Giffard), John, iii. 102; vi. 54; viii. 61
Gifford, William (d. 1357), x. 64
Gifford (Giffard, Gyfford), William (d. 1491), ii. 37; vii. 34
Gigliis (Gyglis, Gylys), John de (d. 1498, ? J. Gylis), i. 88; iii. 53, 68; iv. 58, 61 & n; v. 9, 42, 49, 57; vi. 34 & n; viii. 38; x. 22 & n
Gigliis (Gylys), Silvester de, iii. 45; iv. 58
Gigliis, see also Gilio, Gylis
Gilbard, see Gilbert, Robert (d. 1448)
Gilberd, Richard (c. 1500, ? R. Gilbert), viii. 66
Gilberd, William, viii. 66 & n
Gilbert, James, viii. 42; xii. 79
Gilbert, John, ii. 2; xi. 3, 54; xii. 44
Gilbert, Richard (d. 1524, ? R. Gilberd), ix. 62
Gilbert, Robert (d. 1404), vii. 44
Gilbert (Gilbard), Robert (d. 1448), i. 20, 101, 110, 114; iii. 16, 43; v. 3 & n; vi. 8, 14, 74, 113
Gilbert, Thomas, i. 28; viii. 50; ix. 59
Gildeford (Guldford), Henry de, vii. 55
Gildeford, see also Gyldesford
Gildesbourgh, see Goldsborough, Anthony
Gildesburgh (Goldsborough), Peter (de), i. 36; ii. 23; iii. 30, 80; ix. 17–18, 32; x. 59–60; xi. 26, 30; xii. 87, 88
Gildesburgh, Thomas de, see Hill, Thomas atte
Giles, see Gyles
Gilio, Andrew de, vii. 57
Gilio, see also Gigliis, Gylis

Gillowe, Henry, vi. 17, 51, 83
Gillyngham, Richard, iv. 6
Gisborne, William, i. 57, 60; vi. 85; xii. 25
Gisburn, John, vi. 11, 41; xii. 69
Gisburne, William de, vi. 110
Giudice, Gregory, de Alatri, x. 14
Glaston, Geoffrey de, see Blaston
Glaston, John de, iii. 63
Gloucester (Gloucestre), Robert de, ii. 12, 28, 29; viii. 61
Gloucester, William, i. 118
Glym, William, iii. 20, 39; viii. 64
Glynn, John, xi. 7
Glynn, William, xi. 7, 10 & n, 11
Glynne, Maurice, xi. 9
Glynton (Clinton), Ivo de, v. 21
Glynton, William de, iii. 6
Goberd (Gobard, Gobert), William, ii. 8, 12, 33, 40
Goch (Gogh, Gouch), Huw, xi. 16
Goch, John (d. 1361), see Gogh
Goch (Gogh, Gouch), John (c. 1535, ? J. Gough), xi. 33
Goch, John ap Goronwy, see John ap Goronwy Goch
Goch (Gogh, Gouch), Madog, xi. 49
Godde, William, viii. 69
Godebarne, Henry de, vi. 46
Godeford, John, viii. 36
Godeford, see also Codeford, Cottysford
Godeley (Godelee), Hamelin de, vii. 13; viii. 18
Godeley (Gedele, Godele, Godeleye, Godley), John (de), vi. 78; vii. 13, 55; viii. 3, 81; ix. 1, 23; xii. 32
Godewyke, John, ii. 34; iii. 35; xii. 53
Godfrey (Godfrith), Nicholas, iii. 6
Godhyve, Geoffrey, i. 68
Godmanston (Godmastone, Godmeston), John, ii. 36, 38, 46, 52; v. 19; vii. 28; xi. 66, 71; xii. 50, 62, 74, 89(bis)
Godwin, Nicholas, iii. 69
Godwin, Simon, vii. 20
Godyng, John, x. 10; xii. 84
Gogh, Huw, see Goch
Gogh (Goch, Gough), John (d. 1361), i. 86; iii. 39, 77; ix. 35; xi. 60, 65, 85
Gogh, John (c. 1535), see Goch
Gogh, Madog, see Goch
Goldesburgh, Thomas (c. 1293, ? T. Goldsborough), xi. 53
Goldesburgh, Thomas (de) (d. 1331), see Goldsborough
Goldeston, William, x. 23

Goldeston, *see also* Goldston
Goldiff, John, vii. 6, 30; xii. 74
Goldsborough (Gildesbourgh), Anthony, i. 20, 88; xii. 17, 32
Goldsborough, Peter, *see* Gildesburgh
Goldsborough (Goldesburgh), Thomas (de) (d. 1331, ? T. Goldesburgh), i. 104; vi. 111 & n; x. 51; xii. 73, 85
Goldston, Thomas (d. 1468), iv. 6
Goldston, Thomas (d. 1517), iv. 6
Goldston, *see also* Goldeston
Goldwege, Thomas, viii. 42
Goldwell, James, ii. 5, 51; iii. 4, 88; iv. 24; v. 10, 45, 61, 67; vii. 21; xii. 44, 51
Goldwell, Nicholas, i. 71; iii. 85; iv. 28, 32, 34; vi. 72; viii. 21
Goldwell, Thomas, iv. 6
Gome, John, xi. 57
Gomecii (Gomes, Portyngale), Laurence, iii. 101
Gomez, Peter (d. 1348), i. 8; x. 13
Gomez, Peter, de Albornoz (d. 1374), vi. 18; xii. 14
Gonvena, *see* Genevefe
Goodrich (Goodrick), Thomas, iv. 15
Goodrich Castle, *see* Castrogodrici
Gorce, Ranulf de, de Monterac, viii. 15
Gorewell, John (d. 1420), ix. 43
Gorewell (Gorewelle, Gorwell), John (d. 1439), ii. 43
Gorges, Thomas de, viii. 6
Gorle, John, ii. 45 ('Yorke'); xii. 50
Gorle, *see also* Gourll
Gormondchester (Gurmonchestre, Gurmuncestre), John de, iii. 23; vii. 16; x. 60
Goronwy, Hywel ap, *see* Hywel ap Goronwy
Goronwy Goch, John ap, *see* John ap Goronwy Goch
Gorwell, *see* Gorewell, John (d. 1439)
Gosewell, John, vii. 60
Gosse, Nicholas, vi. 57, 61; ix. 10, 54
Got, *see* Goth
Goteham, John de, x. 56
Goteham, William de, x. 56
Goth (Got, Gotha), Raymond de, i. 3, 94; v. 4n; vi. 6, 17n, 90; vii. 4; x. 7; xii. 13
Gothurst, Richard de, viii. 57
Gouch, Huw, *see* Goch
Gouch, John (d. 1361), *see* Gogh
Gouch, John (c. 1535), *see* Goch
Gouch, Madog, *see* Goch
Goudybour, *see* Gudybour
Gough, John (d. 1361), *see* Gogh
Gough, John (d. 1544, ? J. Goch), iii. 82

Gounsted, *see* Gaunstede
Gourdon, *see* Farinier
Gourll, John (c. 1468–9, ? J.G. c. 1451–82), i. 123
Gourll (Gourell), John (c. 1451–82, ? J.G. c. 1468–9), vii. 18, 25n
Gourll, *see also* Gorle
Gournay, Edmund, viii. 6, 27, 78
Gowe, Robert, x. 10; xi. 42
Gower (Gowerheria), Henry de, xi. 53, 59, 84
Graa, William, de (of) Trusthope, iv. 31, 33; viii. 66; xii. 59, 60
Grafton, Adam, x. 18, 20, 66
Grandison, John, *see* Grandisson
Grandison (Grandson), Thomas, i. 10, 24, 68
Grandisson, Gerard de, vi. 29
Grandisson (Grandison, Grandson), John (de), i. 68, 108; vi. 23, 66; viii. 74; ix. 1 & n; x. 58; xii. 38
Grandisson (Grandison, Grandson), Thomas, i. 10, 24, 68
Grandisson, William de, iii. 78; viii. 74; ix. 13, 28; xii. 56
Grandon, Benedict, vii. 19
Grandon, John (c. 1406, ? J. Grendon), xi. 75; xii. 89
Grandson, *see* Grandison, Grandisson
Granger, Thomas, i. 28
Grantham, John, i. 86; xii. 32
Graunt, Thomas, v. 17, 48, 63, 69
Grave, John de la, iii. 66
Grave, Roger de la, vii. 54
Graveley, John, i. 30
Gravesend, Richard de (d. 1303), v. 1
Gravesend (Grene), Richard de (d. 1330), v. 7, 14, 30
Gravesend, Stephen de, v. 1, 28, 68; xii. 62
Gray, Richard, ii. 31
Gray, Roger, iii. 71
Gray, William (c. 1431), viii. 21 & n
Gray (Grey), William (d. 1436), i. 2; v. 3; vi. 7, 37, 85 & n
Gray (Grey), William (d. 1478), i. 2, 11, 117; iii. 96; iv. 15; v. 28; vi. 26, 32, 45; viii. 21n; x. 46; xii. 15, 40
Gray (Grey), William (c. 1511, ? W.G. d. 1522), i. 92
Gray, William (d. 1522, ? W.G. c. 1511), ii. 33; iii. 11, 50, 57, 62, 91
Gray, *see also* Greye
Graynevyll, *see* Grenevyle
Graystanes, Robert de, vi. 107
Graystock, Richard, i. 124; xii. 42
Graystock, *see also* Greystok

Graystok (Greystoke), John, xi. 15
Graystok, *see also* Greystok
Gredon, Simon de, vii. 12n
Green (Grene), Henry, i. 88; vii. 41; x. 38
Green (Grene), John, iv. 57, 59
Green (Fotherby), Simon, i. 21, 36, 37, 65, 122
Green, William (d. 1483), i. 30
Green, William (d. 1507), vii. 11, 16, 24(*bis*), 26
Green (Greene), William (d. 1540), v. 41; vii. 38
Green, *see also* Grene
Greenfield, William de, v. 39; vi. 3, 64; vii. 4
Greenstreet (Grenestrete), John de, iv. 40
Greenwood, Thomas, i. 97; vi. 55, 60, 83; xii. 35, 70
Gregger (Grygger), John, xi. 7
Gregory ab Einion, xi. 17
Grelino, Talayrand (Talleyrand) de, i. 80; vii. 57
Grenburgh, William de, x. 19
Grenburgh, *see also* Greneburgh
Grendon, John (c. 1400–31, ? J.G. d. 1441, or J. Grandon), iii. 37
Grendon, John (d. 1441, ? J.G. c. 1400–31, or J. Grandon), vii. 38
Grene, Henry, *see* Green
Grene, Hugh, ii. 40, 42
Grene, John (d. 1395), *see* Green
Grene, John (d. 1410), viii. 51, 58
Grene (Holder), John (d. 1472), ii. 16, 25, 26
Grene, John (d. 1515, ? Richard G. c. 1499), vii. 34 & n
Grene, Richard (d. 1330), *see* Gravesend
Grene, Richard (c. 1499, ? John G. d. 1515), vii. 34 & n
Grene, Stephen, xi. 66
Grene, Thomas (c. 1385, ? T.G. d. 1387), iv. 31
Grene, Thomas (d. 1387, ? T.G. c. 1385), iii. 89
Grene, *see also* Green
Greneburgh, William de, x. 4
Greneburgh, *see also* Grenburgh
Grenestrete, *see* Greenstreet
Grenevyle (Graynevyll), Richard, ix. 48
Grenewey, John, ii. 41, 49; xii. 51
Gresham, Thomas, vii. 52; x. 10
Grete, Thomas, ii. 49
Gretheued, Richard, vi. 52
Grettewell, William, i. 38, 45, 51, 67, 89
Greve, John, vi. 74
Greves, Peter, v. 57; x. 48; xii. 85

Greville, Thomas, iii. 7
Grey, *see* Gray
Greyby, John de, x. 39
Greye, Edward, viii. 27
Greye, *see also* Gray
Greylly, Simon, vii. 54
Greystok, Henry de, ix. 34
Greystok(e), *see also* Graystock, Graystok
Grice, John, vi. 34
Griffin, Hywel, xi. 50
Griffin (Griffyn), Thomas, of Withrington, ii. 23
Griffith (Gryffyth), Maurice, iv. 42; xii. 60
Griffith, Roger, ii. 43
Griffith, *see also* Gruffudd
Grimoaldi (Grimaud), Anglicus (Angelicus), i. 113; vi. 7
Grimsby (Grymesby), Edmund de, ii. 23; v. 27
Grimsby, John (d. 1349), i. 123
Grimsby, John of (d. 1415), *see* Lincoln
Grimstone, Robert de, ix. 37
Grisacre, Edward, vi. 17, 47; xii. 67
Grocyn (Crosson), William, i. 105
Gromville, Peter de, iii. 26
Gronowe, Thomas, vii. 6; xii. 74
Gros, John, ii. 52
Grote, *see* Trote
Gruffudd (c. 1293–1306), xi. 43
Gruffudd ab Ieuan Grath, xi. 42 & n
Gruffudd ab Iorwerth, xi. 3
Gruffudd ap Rhys (Price), xi. 61
Gruffudd, Dafydd ap, *see* Dafydd ap Gruffudd
Gruffudd, Hywel ap, *see* Hywel ap Gruffudd
Gruffudd, John (d. 1523), xi. 59, 73
Gruffudd, John (d. 1547), xi. 48
Gruffudd, John ap (c. 1328), *see* John ap Gruffudd
Gruffudd, Roger, xi. 30
Gruffudd, *see also* Griffith
Gruffudd Ddu (Guiffundun), John, xi. 16, 46
Gryffyth, *see* Griffith
Grygg, Richard, xi. 15
Grygger, *see* Gregger
Grym, John, xi. 28
Grymesby, *see* Grimsby
Guardia, *see* Daumario
Gudman, John, viii. 60
Gudybour (Goudybour), Thomas, vi. 100; xii. 72
Guellt, Dafydd de, xi. 12
Guiffundun, *see* Gruffudd Ddu
Guillelmi, *see* Sparra

Guldefeld (Guldesfeld, Gyllefeld), Thomas, ii. 18, 20; xi. 74
Gulden, William de (William Legilden), ix. 28(*bis*), 30; xii. 83(*bis*)
Guldesfeld, *see* Guldefeld, Gyldesford
Guldford, *see* Gildeford
Gumby (Austeyne), Robert, viii. 44
Gunthorpe, John, i. 32; iii. 23, 36; v. 10, 42, 69; vi. 10, 65; viii. 5
Gunthorpe, William de, iii. 54; vi. 88; vii. 51
Gurmonchestre, Gurmuncestre, *see* Gormondchester
Guyon, William, iii. 93
Gwent (Went), Richard, i. 83; v. 9; x. 46, 51; xi. 27, 62, 68, 69 & n
Gwyn, Dafydd, xi. 83
Gwyn, Lewis, xi. 72
Gwyn, Maurice, xi. 67
Gwynllwg (Wenllong), Thomas, xi. 33
Gwynn, William, x. 57(*bis*)
Gybbes, Walter, ix. 44
Gyddyng (Belles), William de, ii. 36
Gyddyng, *see also* Gidding
Gyfford, *see* Gifford
Gyglis, *see* Gigliis
Gygur, John, i. 108; xii. 38
Gyldesford, Richard, xi. 61
Gyldesford, *see also* Gildeford
Gyles, John (d. 1428), xi. 76
Gylis, John (c. 1483, ? J. de Gigliis), vii. 26
Gylis, *see also* Gigliis, Gilio
Gyllefeld, *see* Guldefeld
Gylys, *see* Gigliis
Gynewell (Gynwell, de Kynewellis), John (de), i. 1, 48; iii. 29; vi. 25, 52; xii. 22, 53
Gynewell, William, i. 15, 40, 61, 80; xii. 25
Gynewell, *see also* Genvyle
Gyste, Robert, vii. 40
Gyste, *see also* Gest

Haburgh, John, i. 103
Haburgh, *see also* Hawberk, Hawburgh
Hache, Robert de, viii. 57
Hackluyt, Giles, iii. 7; xii. 52
Hacluit (Hakelut, Hakeluyt), Thomas (de), ii. 12, 26; viii. 76
Haddon, John, i. 121
Hadham, Nicholas de, xi. 28
Haget, Hagett, Hagget, *see* Haket
Hakelut, Hakeluyt, *see* Hackluyt, Hacluit
Hakeney, John, iii. 47, 51
Haket (Haget, Hagett, Hagget), John, i. 22, 39, 103, 123; iii. 39, 67, 103; ix. 11, 44, 46; xii. 17, 21, 37, 41, 57

Hakun, Geoffrey, vi. 41
Hakun, *see also* Acome, Akum
Haldesworth, Robert, vi. 48
Haldingham, *see* Bello
Hale, John de, xi. 25
Hale, Richard de, iii. 69; x. 25
Hale, William de, iii. 27
Hales, Roger de, v. 11, 35 & n
Hales, *see also* Hayles
Haliburton (Holyburton), Patrick, ix. 58
Haliday (Halyday, Unert), Robert, ii. 52
Hall, James, x. 68
Hall, John (c. 1481), iii. 6
Hall, John (c. 1503–6), iii. 90
Hall, Richard, i. 67; xii. 27
Hall, Robert, iii. 68, 79
Hall, Thomas (c. 1458, ? T.H. d. 1479), i. 82
Hall, Thomas (d. 1479, ? T.H. c. 1458), v. 57
Hallam, *see* Hallum
Halle, Hugh atte, xi. 67
Halle, John, xi. 41
Halle (Hulls), Thomas, iv. 41
Halleswell, *see* Halswell
Hallum, Gilbert, iii. 60, 74, 75
Hallum (Hallam), Robert, iii. 2, 36; iv. 8 & n; vi. 4, 74; vii. 36; ix. 45
Hals (Halse), Edmund, x. 17 & n, 18, 26, 36, 48, 64, 68
Hals (Halse), John, iv. 27, 29; v. 41; vi. 85; ix. 2, 5, 51; x. 3; xii. 59
Hals, Richard (d. 1417), ix. 9n, 11, 45
Halsall (Halsale), Henry de, x. 13, 30; xii. 84, 85
Halse, Richard (c. 1537–60), ix. 65
Halse, *see also* Hals, Hulse
Halswell (Halleswell), Nicholas, i. 73, 75; vi. 63; viii. 26, 72; ix. 62; xii. 30
Halton, Gilbert de, vi. 101
Halton, John de, vi. 97
Halton, Richard de, xi. 24, 26
Halyday, *see* Haliday
Halywell, John, i. 49; viii. 43
Halywell, *see also* Helewell, Holwell, Holwyll
Hambald, William, ii. 18
Hambleton, John, iv. 31
Hambleton, William de, vi. 6, 17, 86
Hamelyn, James, ix. 55
Hamelyn, *see also* Hamlyn
Hamenasch, Richard de, ii. 23
Hamertone, Henry, i. 42, 69; ii. 24
Hamlyn, Robert, viii. 58
Hamlyn, *see also* Hamelyn
Hammes, John, vi. 34n
Hamslape, Henry, *see* Hanslap

Hamslape, John de, xi. 49

Hanemere, Matthew de, xi. 47, 74

Haningfelde, Richard de, xi. 83

Hank, Nicholas, x. 11

Hanley, Thomas, ii. 13(*bis*); x. 41; xii. 45

Hanley, *see also* Henley(e)

Hanlo, William de, viii. 40, 54

Hanney, John de (c. 1375, ? J. Hanneye), v. 69

Hanneye, John (c. 1366, ? J. de Hanney), iii. 89

Hans, *see* Nans

Hanslap (Hamslape), Henry, i. 35, 112

Hanslap, *see also* Hamslape

Hanson, Edmund (Edward), i. 21, 65, 72, 115, 127; vi. 49; xii. 28

Hanwell, Thomas, vii. 14, 52

Hanworth, Hugh (de), i. 18, 39, 41, 43, 69, 71; vi. 49; viii. 43; xii. 16, 27, 28, 70

Hanybal, Thomas, vi. 53

Hanys, *see* Hauyes

Harald, John (c. 1355–61, ? J. Harold), xi. 46

Harborgh, *see* Harburgh, Haverbergh

Harborough, Henry, *see* Harburgh

Harborough, Thomas, xi. 9

Harborough, *see also* Haverbergh

Harburgh (Harborgh, Harborough), Henry, iii. 16, 20, 23, 30, 43, 73, 86; viii. 41

Harburgh, *see also* Haverbergh

Harbury, *see* Herbury

Harcourt, Simon (George), iii. 78

Harden, John, i. 124(*bis*)

Hardgill, George, iii. 22

Harding, Thomas, x. 33

Hardwick (Herdewyk), Thomas (de), i. 119; x. 23

Harewedon (Haroudon), Henry de, viii. 45; x. 29; xii. 79

Harewedon, *see also* Harwedon, Harwardyn

Harewell, John (de), i. 91; iii. 9; iv. 28, 62; viii. 2; ix. 15, 33; xii. 33

Harewell, Richard, viii. 56; xii. 79

Harewell, Roger, iii. 36, 89, 96 ('Richard'); viii. 15, 40; xii. 53, 56, 57

Harewode, John de, x. 25, 42

Harkeley (Horkeley), Henry de, iii. 80

Harleston, Henry de, *see* Spicer

Harleston, John de, *see* Herlaston

Harlyng, Thomas, vii. 12, 21, 23; xi. 47

Harmer, *see* Hermer

Harmon, *see* Veysey

Harnham, John, iii. 81

Harold, John (d. 1393, ? J. Harald), ii. 4, 16, 32, 38

Harom, Robert, i. 28; xii. 19

Haroudon, *see* Harewedon, Henry de

Harper, Hugh, ii. 22

Harper, Thomas, vii. 37

Harrington, James, vi. 8, 17, 41, 59; xii. 66, 67, 69

Harrington, John, i. 27, 44, 100, 106

Harris, Thomas (d. 1511, ? T. Harrys), viii. 11, 46, 50

Harrison, Richard, xi. 48

Harry, John ap, *see* John ap Harry

Harrys, Thomas (d. 1511/12, ? T. Harris), ix. 8, 17, 59

Hartlepool (Hertilpole), John, ii. 24

Harwardyn, Humphrey, x. 36, 41, 61, 68

Harwedon, Robert de, x. 32, 36

Harwedon, *see also* Harewedon

Haryndon (Haryngton), William, v. 45; viii. 74

Haseley, John, vii. 5, 52

Haselschawe (Haselscawe), Robert de, viii. 7, 34, 77; ix. 23; xii. 76, 81, 83

Haselschawe, Thomas de (c. 1305), viii. 31

Haselschawe, Thomas de (c. 1343), viii. 78

Haselschawe, Walter de, viii. 1, 3; xii. 76(*bis*)

Haspys, *see* Hospys

Hastanges, Humphrey (de), i. 94; v. 44; vi. 80; x. 14, 45

Hastynges, John de, vi. 40

Hatfield, Thomas (de), i. 43, 70, 85; iii. 41; v. 52; vi. 50, 108; viii. 78; xii. 28

Hathbrande, Robert, iv. 6

Hathering, *see* Havering

Hathfield, William, iv. 16

Hathwaite (Huthwayte), Thomas, vi. 100 & n; xii. 72

Hatton, John (d. 1516), vi. 25, 53, 86

Hatton, John de (c. 1345–58), vii. 20

Hatton, Ralph, *see* Stratford

Hatton, Ranulph, viii. 63

Hatton, Richard, viii. 74

Haukesworth (Hawkesworth), William, viii. 37; xi. 66

Haukyn, Laurence, vii. 42, 45; ix. 7, 44, 47

Haukyn, Nicholas, ii. 50

Haukyn, *see also* Hawkins

Hautewysil, Simon de, vi. 100

Hautewysil, William de, vi. 99

Hauyes (Hanys), Ralph, ii. 21, 40, 51; xii. 47, 49, 51

Havante, *see* Coleman

Haverbergh (Harborgh, Haverberge), John, iii. 69; x. 30

Haverbergh, *see also* Harborough, Harburgh

Haverel (Averel), Denis, vi. 22

Havering (Hathering), Richard (de), i. 24, 25; ii. 8, 45; iii. 33; vi. 61, 88; vii. 20; x. 12 & n; xii. 45, 50(bis), 53

Haversham, John, i. 28, 39, 121(ter)

Haversham (Haverisham), Richard de, iii. 87; xi. 26, 32

Haward, Edmund (c. 1340–4, ? E. Howard), vi. 114

Hawarde, see Hayward, Richard

Hawberk (Hawbergh), John, i. 84

Hawberk, see also Haburgh

Hawburgh, Robert, i. 90, 98; xii. 35

Hawburgh, see also Haburgh

Hawe, Nicholas, see Welton

Hawe, William, i. 90; x. 62

Hawkes, John, i. 42, 125; xii. 21

Hawkesworth, see Haukesworth

Hawkins, Nicholas, iv. 15, 19

Hawkins, Thomas, iii. 16, 64, 70; iv. 63(bis); vii. 25 & n, 37; x. 20, 31

Hawkins, see also Haukyn

Hawte, Henry, iii. 82

Hawtrey, Edmund, iii. 78

Hawtrey, Edward, iii. 78

Haxby, John, vi. 14n

Haxey, Thomas, i. 66, 103; iii. 32; vi. 14, 31; x. 60

Haxton, Richard, iii. 86

Hay, Robert de la, vi. 53

Hay, Thomas, viii. 47 & n

Haydok, Gilbert, vii. 49; xi. 48

Haydour, John, viii. 42

Hayles, William, i. 28

Hayles, see also Hales

Hayman (Heyman), Richard, i. 9, 125 ('Richard or Robert'); iii. 22, 25, 34; v. 67(bis), 69; vi. 85; viii. 56, 74; xii. 42

Haynes, John, i. 104

Haynes, Simon, ix. 5, 65

Haynes, William, vii. 53

Haynes, see also Heynes

Haynton, Michael, xi. 73

Hays, Richard, i. 102

Hayton, William, iii. 60, 96; xii. 55

Hayward, John (c. 1395, ? J. Haywood), ii. 24

Hayward (Hawarde, Heyward), Richard, iii. 25, 65, 68

Haywardine, Henry, viii. 47

Haywood, John (d. 1412, ? J. Hayward), xi. 70, 72, 75

Haywood, see also Heywood

Hayworth, see Heyworth

Heath (Hethe), Nicholas, iv. 40; x. 20

Heath, see also Hethe

Heathcott (Heicote, Heithcote, Hethcote, Heycote), Ralph, ii. 13; iii. 36, 40, 50, 64, 79; vii. 22; ix. 19; x. 24, 48, 62; xi. 15; xii. 45

Hebbeng, William, i. 107

Hebden, William, x. 28, 33

Hede, Thomas, v. 16, 49

Hedersete, see Hetersete

Hedwich, Madog, xi. 9

Heicote, Heithcote, see Heathcott

Hekys (Ekys), John, x. 34

Helewell, John, vi. 31

Helewell, see also Halywell, Holwell, Holwyll

Helleston, Michael de, iv. 50

Helpeston, Robert de (c. 1308–21), vi. 100

Helpistone, Robert de (c. 1334), vii. 46

Helyer, Richard, ix. 16, 20, 52

Helyer, see also Hiller

Hemenhale (Henmale), Thomas, iv. 23, 56

Hemingborough, John de, vi. 110

Hemingby, Alexander de, iii. 55, 63, 85

Hende, William, iii. 22, 25; iv. 63

Hende, see also Hynde

Hendeman, Thomas, vii. 18; ix. 9, 14, 46

Heneage (Henneage), George, i. 4, 14, 23, 38, 55, 68, 83, 117; iii. 44; vi. 29, 48; viii. 17; xii. 13, 15, 17, 20, 24, 40

Hengham, see Hingham

Henley, James de, ii. 26; xii. 47

Henleye, Robert de, ii. 20

Henley(e), see also Hanley

Henmale, see Hemenhale

Henneage, see Heneage

Henore, Henry, xi. 6

Henry, the king's almoner (? H. de Bluntesdon), v. 26 & n

Henry ap Hywel (Powell), xi. 65

Henry ap John, i. 21, 57, 72, 75

Henshaw, Nicholas, ix. 63

Henton, Adam de, see Houghton

Henton, John de, viii. 53

Henton, Thomas de, ix. 10, 24(bis)

Herbard, see Sparrow

Herbert, Richard, i. 52

Herbury (Harbury), Nicholas, iv. 61; v. 27, 37; xii. 61

Herdeby, Geoffrey, xi. 4

Herdewyk, see Hardwick

Hereford (Carpenter), John, ii. 6, 7, 37; xi. 27; xii. 49

Hereford, Nicholas, ii. 11, 12, 13, 41, 43; v. 19; xi. 71; xii. 45, 50(bis)

Heremyte (Ermyte), Hugh, ii. 8
Hereward, Robert, i. 103; ii. 14; viii. 16; ix. 25; xii. 36
Hereward, Thomas (de), i. 68; viii. 66; ix. 12, 25
Herewynton (Herwynton), Adam de, ii. 34
Herewynton (Herwynton), William de, ii. 32, 51
Heriad, Alexander, iv. 47
Hering, Richard, xi. 46
Heritage (Eritage), Thomas, x. 8 & n; xii. 84
Herlaston (Harleston), John de, vii. 39; x. 13
Herlaston, Roger de, ii. 52
Herlaston, William (de), i. 34; ii. 27, 28; iii. 47, 59; iv. 28; vii. 56; x. 40, 42n; xi. 30
Herle, Alexander, vi. 20; ix. 43
Herle, Hugh, vi. 112; viii. 15
Herle, see also Earle, Erle
Hermer (Harmer), William, iii. 83; xi. 78
Hermesthorp, John de, vi. 22
Hermesthorp, William, v. 23
Heron (Herne, Hurne), Roger (atte) (Roger Attehurne), iii. 81; vii. 33; ix. 50; x. 58n; xi. 76
Herpeswell, William, i. 118
Herring, John, ii. 41
Hert, John (d. 1495), vi. 12, 38, 51, 84; xii. 66, 69, 70, 71
Hert, Walter (d. 1484), v. 36
Hert, Walter Le (d. 1472), see Lyhart
Herte, John (d. 1527), viii. 58
Hertelbury, John, iv. 59
Hertford, Richard de, ii. 5, 48; xii. 44, 51
Hertford, Thomas, vii. 41
Hertilpole, see Hartlepool
Hertington (Hertyndon), Adam de, iii. 71, 73; v. 8, 70; viii. 48; ix. 37
Hertlepe, John de, iv. 38, 40
Hertyndon, see Hertington
Hervey, John, of Ashbourne (d. 1361), i. 15
Hervey, John (d. 1500/1), ii. 5, 9, 47; x. 62
Hervey, Richard, vi. 102
Hervy, Thomas, i. 43; ii. 32
Hervy, Walter (c. 1304–26), iii. 31, 32, 90, 93
Hervy, Walter (archdcn. of Salisbury, c. 1309–28), iii. 11
Herwynton, see Herewynton
Hesil, Gerard, v. 29, 69
Heske, John de; Philip, see Uske
Hetersete (Hedersete), Thomas, iii. 80; iv. 31(bis); xii. 59
Hethcote, see Heathcott
Hethe, Hamo de, iv. 37, 40

Hethe (Heth), John, iii. 34
Hethe, Nicholas (c. 1398), xi. 75
Hethe, Nicholas (d. 1578), see Heath
Hethe (Heth), Nicholas (de) (c. 1343–63), ii. 28; iii. 49; v. 47; vi. 42 (line 21); vii. 57; x. 49, 60; xii. 48, 54, 64, 69(bis), 75, 85(bis)
Hethe, Nicholas (de) (d. 1390), ii. 16; vi. 42 (line 37); xii. 69(bis), 85
Hethe, Richard, i. 5, 9, 49, 121; xii. 22, 41
Hethe, see also Heath
Hetherington, Richard, i. 24
Heugate (Hougate, Hugate, Hungate), Nicholas (de), i. 29; ii. 39; iii. 97; iv. 60; vi. 31
Heverlond, John, iv. 25
Hewes, Richard, ii. 21; xii. 47
Hewes, see also Hewish, Hewys, Hughes, Huws
Hewet (Stock), Thomas, i. 90
Hewish (Huish), John (d. 1399), viii. 57
Hewish, Hews, see also Hewes, Hewys, Hughes, Huws
Hewys (Huys), John (d. 1530), x. 8n, 12
Hewys, John (c. 1534), see Huws
Hewys, John (magister, c. 1534), see Huws
Hewys, see also Hewes, Hewish, Hughes, Huws
Hexham, John de, vi. 77
Heycote, see Heathcott
Heygate (Higate, Higgate), John, x. 33, 56; xi. 8
Heyman, see Hayman
Heynes, John, ii. 23
Heynes, see also Haynes
Heytesbury, William de, vii. 48
Heyward, see Hayward, Richard
Heywood, Thomas, x. 6, 30 & n, 43, 44, 52 & n
Heywood, see also Haywood
Heyworth, John, i. 126; x. 12, 15, 33 & n, 36 & n
Heyworth, William, x. 2
Hichman, William, viii. 39
Hickelyng (Hyckelyng), Hugh (de), viii. 23; ix. 7, 40
Hickman, —, xi. 26
Higate, see Heygate
Higdon (Higden, Hugdon, Hyckden), Brian, i. 6, 26, 53, 128; v. 50; vi. 8, 19, 86; xii. 14, 18, 24, 64
Higdon, John, i. 94; vi. 89, 91; xii. 34
Higdon, Robert, v. 36
Higgate, see Heygate

Higgins (Higgens), Edward, i. 47; iii. 26, 40, 46, 74; vii. 20

Higham, Robert de, xi. 8

Higham, William, iii. 48

Higham Ferrers, *see* Astell

Highwey, William, viii. 28

Hildesley (Ildesleigh, Ildesley), John de, vii. 55; viii. 54; ix. 29

Hildyard, John, v. 65

Hill, John (d. 1494), viii. 19, 75 & n

Hill, John (c. 1493–5), v. 37, 47, 58, 68; xii. 63, 64, 65

Hill (Hylle), John (d. 1500), xi. 61

Hill (Hylle), Richard, iii. 33; v. 3; vii. 14; xi. 72, 79

Hill, Thomas, i. 47, 115; xii. 22, 40

Hill, Thomas atte (Thomas de Gildesburgh), x. 32

Hill (Hyll), William, x. 65, 70

Hill, *see also* Hull(e), Hylle

Hiller, John, viii. 18, 62 ('Hillier'); xii. 77, 80

Hilles, Robert, i. 75

Hilley, Richard, iii. 21; xii. 53

Hillier, John, *see* Hiller

Hillier, Richard, *see* Helyer

Hillum, Robert de, viii. 77

Hilsey, John, iv. 39

Hilton, Adam de, vii. 30–1, 46; viii. 34; ix. 36

Hilton, Thomas (de), i. 46; vi. 31, 89; x. 28, 56

Hingham (Hengham), Ralph de, ii. 31; iv. 62; v. 23

Hinton, *see* Hunton, Hynton

Hiot, John (d. 1420, ? J. Hyot), xi. 56, 60 & n, 66 & n, 73, 85n

Hirst, Richard, vi. 39

Hispania (Ispania, Ispannia), James de, i. 50; iii. 64; v. 62; viii. 63, 76; x. 68; xii. 23

Ho (Oo), John de, of Oxford (c. 1330, ? J. de Ewe), ii. 8

Ho, *see also* Hoo

Hoard, *see* Hord, Edmund

Hobbes, *see* Hobbys

Hobbull, John, i. 75; iii. 40; xii. 29

Hobbys (Hobbes), Thomas (d. 1509), v. 54; vi. 82; ix. 5, 61 & n

Hobbys, Thomas (c. 1541), viii. 49

Hochynson (Richardson), William (John), vii. 26

Hode, *see* Banbury

Hodenet, William, xi. 72

Hody, Alexander (c. 1418–20), viii. 71 & n, 72 & n

Hody, Alexander (d. 1519), viii. 9, 49

Hody, John, iii. 8, 94; vi. 37; viii. 7, 9, 27, 40; ix. 47, 51

Hoel, *see* Trefnant

Hoesee (Huse), John, iii. 84

Hoesee, *see also* Huse(e), Husy

Hogekyn, John, viii. 76

Hogeson, Thomas, xi. 72

Hogeson, William, vi. 56

Hogham, Robert, i. 33

Holand, John (d. 1419), iii. 12; ix. 48

Holand, John de (d. 1369), ix. 36

Holand, *see also* Holland

Holbach (Holbache), Hugh, ii. 31; iii. 96; viii. 66; x. 62; xi. 41, 44; xii. 48, 80

Holbach, *see also* Holebech

Holbeche (Rands), Henry, iv. 60 & n

Holbeche, *see also* Holebech

Holcombe, John de, ix. 31

Holcote, Elias (de), ii. 40; v. 65; vi. 34; xii. 49, 64, 69

Holden, Bernard, iii. 35; vii. 36(*bis*)

Holden, Robert, i. 66; xii. 27

Holder, *see* Grene, John (d. 1472)

Hole, John, vi. 21, 23, 76

Holebech, Ralph de, x. 51, 68

Holebech, *see also* Holbach, Holbeche

Holes (Holles, Huls, Hulse), Andrew, ii. 29; iii. 18; vi. 18, 55, 74, 79; viii. 14 & n, 17, 46; x. 38; xi. 10, 48, 69, 71

Holes, Thomas, iii. 36, 82

Holgate, Robert, xi. 23 & n

Holgil, William, vi. 12, 44, 52, 103

Holland, John, i. 81; xii. 31

Holland, Richard, i. 12, 25

Holland, *see also* Holand

Holles, *see* Holes

Holloway, William, viii. 22

Holme, Adam (de), v. 43n, 44; vi. 78; viii. 26; xii. 63, 71, 77

Holme, Richard, iii. 33, 94; vi. 56

Holme, Roger (de), i. 40, 41; iii. 44; v. 11, 19, 27; vi. 78; vii. 23; viii. 34; xii. 21

Holt, John, vii. 30

Holwell, Thomas de, vi. 19

Holwell, *see also* Halywell, Helewell

Holwyll, John, ix. 64

Holwyll, *see also* Halywell, Helewell

Holyburton, *see* Haliburton

Holym, William de, vi. 16

Home (Homme, Honne), John, ii. 37; xi. 44; xii. 49

Homme, Richard, ii. 39

Hone, John (c. 1519), iii. 24

Hone, *see also* Hoone

Honiwood, *see* Honywood

Honne, *see* Home

Hontman, John, i. 24

Honyngg, *see* Willelmi

Honywood (Honiwood, Honywode), Robert, iv. 28; viii. 17; x. 29

Hoo, Nicholas de, iv. 25

Hoo, Richard de, xi. 83

Hoo, William de, v. 28; vi. 58; vii. 56

Hoo, *see also* Ho

Hoone, William, vii. 30

Hoone, *see also* Hone

Hoore (Hore), Richard, ii. 35; vi. 37; viii. 29, 35; xi. 72

Hoore, *see also* Hore

Hope, John, viii. 51; ix. 42

Hope, Thomas, vi. 34; viii. 28; ix. 56; xii. 69

Hoper, William, i. 35, 55, 127; viii. 46; xi. 43; xii. 24, 42, 79

Hopewas, Hugh de, x. 27, 32

Hopper, Alexander, i. 106

Hopton, David, ii. 19, 38; iii. 31, 36; ix. 14, 57, 58

Horblynge, Thomas, ix. 49

Hord (Hoard), Edmund, i. 75, 110 ('Edward'); xii. 30, 39

Hord, Roger, i. 30

Hore, John, ii. 7

Hore, Richard, *see* Hoore

Hore, Roger, ii. 40, 49

Hore, *see also* Hoore

Horewyk, William de, vii. 29

Horkeley, *see* Harkeley

Horn, Thomas, viii. 66

Hornby, Henry, i. 96; ix. 61; xii. 35

Horncastle, John de, vi. 97, 100; xii. 72

Hornington, Richard de, vii. 33

Hornle, John, vii. 18

Hornyngton, Nigel, vii. 23

Horsey, William, i. 104; v. 9, 18, 38, 64; vii. 8, 40; viii. 73; ix. 62

Horsington, John de, viii. 8, 39, 48, 83

Horston, *see* Shapewyke

Horton, James de, x. 4

Horton, John, v. 69

Horton, Thomas de, v. 17, 48, 69

Horton, *see also* Orton

Hospys, Reginald, x. 51

Hotham (Hothom), Alan de, v. 61; viii. 40, 42; xii. 79

Hothom, John de, iv. 13; vi. 78

Hotoft (Houtot), Thomas de, iii. 7

Hoton, Henry, *see* Howton

Hoton, Richard de, vi. 109

Hoton, Thomas de, vi. 100 & n

Hoton, *see also* Houghton, Howton, Hutton

Houden, John, xi. 27

Hougate, *see* Heugate

Houghton (Henton, Houton), Adam de, vii. 11; xi. 53, 56, 70, 81

Houghton (Houton), Philip de, xi. 70

Houghton, Thomas, vi. 50

Houghton, *see also* Hoton, Howton, Hutton

Houlot, William, i. 63, 76

Houton, *see* Hoton, Houghton, Howton, Hutton

Houtot, *see* Hotoft

Hovyngham, John, vi. 112

Hovyngham, *see also* Ovingham

Howard, Edmund (c. 1338, ? E. Haward), v. 8

Howbell, John, x. 17

Howe, Thomas, of Erpingham, xi. 17

Howe, William, vii. 49, 53

Howel, Rhys ap, *see* Rhys ap Hywel

Howell, Geoffrey, *see* Hywel

Howell, John (c. 1478), viii. 69

Howell, John (c. 1492–1504), *see* Hywel

Howell, John ap (c. 1399–1404), *see* Trefnant

Howell, Thomas; William, *see* Hywel

Howeren, John, viii. 38

Howes, Adam, viii. 30

Howton (Hoton, Hutton), Henry, iii. 86; vii. 8

Howton, *see also* Hoton, Houghton, Hutton

Hoxton, *see* Oxton

Huchyns, Simon, iii. 83

Huddersfield, Robert de, vi. 39

Hugate, Nicholas, *see* Heugate

Hugate, William, i. 44, 46, 70

Hugdon, *see* Higdon, Brian

Hugeford, John, x. 62

Hugh (c. 1344), viii. 13

Hughes, John, vii. 49

Hughes, Hughs, *see also* Hewes, Hewish, Hewys, Huws

Huish, *see* Hewish

Hull, John, i. 52

Hull, Richard, viii. 27

Hull, Stephen of, *see* Martin

Hull, *see also* Hill, Hylle

Hulle, Walter (d. 1494), *see* Hylle

Hulle, Walter de (d. 1353), viii. 11, 15, 24; xi. 84

Hulle, William, ii. 14, 47

Hulle, *see also* Hill, Hylle

Hulling, John, iii. 6

Hulls, *see* Halle, Thomas
Hulse (Huls), Andrew, *see* Holes
Hulse, Thomas, v. 22
Hulse, *see also* Hals(e)
Hulton, Reginald (de), i. 65; vi. 46; vii. 28; xi. 41, 45; xii. 26
Humberston, William de (c. 1372–5), ii. 24, 36
Humberston (Humblestane), William de (d. 1409), xi. 13; xii. 88
Humberton, Alan, i. 87, 109; viii. 68; xii. 32, 38
Humblestane, *see* Humberston
Humphrey (Umfrey), Hugh, x. 38
Humphrey (Umfray), Thomas, viii. 74
Hunden, John, xi. 23 & n, 60 & n, 78 & n
Hunden, William, i. 101; iv. 41; ix. 18, 46; xii. 36, 60
Hundey, William, iv. 41n
Hungarten, Roger, xi. 11
Hungate, *see* Heugate
Hunt (Hurst), Robert, viii. 38
Hunt, Thomas, i. 106
Hunt, Walter, ii. 33
Hunte, Edward, vii. 38
Huntelowe (Huntley), William de, ii. 29, 30, 35
Hunton (Hinton), Thomas, iv. 48
Hurlegh, John, iii. 79
Hurne, *see* Heron
Hursewik, *see* Urswick
Hurst, Robert, *see* Hunt
Hurst, *see also* Hirst
Husbond, David, ii. 37; vii. 20 & n, 29
Huse (Husee), Henry, viii. 3, 7; ix. 21
Huse, John, *see* Hoesee
Huse, Peter, *see* Husy
Husee, Henry, *see* Huse
Husee, Matthew, viii. 24
Huse(e), Husey, *see also* Hoesee, Husy
Hussee, Robert, iii. 65
Hustweyt (Husthwaite, Hustweyte), John de, vi. 58; x. 37
Husy (Huse, Husey), Peter, i. 12, 110, 122; vii. 12, 25 & n, 37; viii. 71
Husy, *see also* Hoesee, Huse(e)
Huthwayte, *see* Hathwaite
Hutton, Henry, *see* Howton
Hutton, Thomas, i. 8, 9, 17, 42, 77; vi. 57
Hutton, *see also* Hoton, Houghton, Hutton
Huw ab Owain (Bowen), xi. 56
Huw ap Robert (Probert), xi. 16
Huws (Hews, Hewys, Hughs), John (c. 1534), xi. 7, 16

Huws (Hews, Hewys, Hughs), John (John ap Hywel) (*magister*, c. 1534), xi. 16
Huws, *see also* Hewes, Hewish, Hewys
Huys, *see* Hewys, John (d. 1530)
Huyte, James, xii. 82
Huyton, *see* Buytone
Hwfa, Llywelyn ap, *see* Llywelyn ap Hwfa
Hyckden, *see* Higdon, Brian
Hyckelyng, *see* Hickelyng
Hyde, Richard, ii. 39
Hyll, *see* Hill, William
Hylle, John (d. 1500); Richard, *see* Hill
Hylle, Robert, viii. 57
Hylle (Hulle), Walter, ii. 43; xii. 50
Hylle, *see also* Hill, Hull(e)
Hynde, Thomas, v. 26
Hynde, *see also* Hende
Hyndelee, William de, v. 44
Hyne, *see* Wendlyngburgh, Robert de
Hynewyk, Peter, v. 13, 35
Hynton, Thomas, viii. 66
Hyot, John (c. 1420, ? J. Hiot), xi. 85 & n
Hywel ap Dafydd, *see* Trefnant, Hywel
Hywel ap Dafydd Fychan, xi. 64
Hywel ap Goronwy (d. 1368), xi. 9
Hywel ap Goronwy (d. 1372), xi. 3, 6
Hywel ap Gruffudd, xi. 63n
Hywel ap Madog (c. 1390–1), xi. 17
Hywel ap Madog ap Cyffin (Hywel Cyffin, Kyffin) (d. c. 1402), xi. 40, 50; xii. 88, 89
Hywel, Dafydd ap, *see* Dafydd ap Hywel
Hywel (Howell), Geoffrey, xi. 69
Hywel, Henry ap, *see* Henry ap Hywel
Hywel (Howell), John, xi. 57
Hywel, John ap, *see* John ap Hywel
Hywel, Philip ap, *see* Philip ap Hywel
Hywel, Rhys ap, *see* Rhys ap Hywel
Hywel (Howell), Thomas (c. 1410–19), xi. 9, 10, 14
Hywel (Howell), Thomas (c. 1535), xi. 33
Hywel, Thomas ap (c. 1487–1512), *see* Thomas ap Hywel
Hywel (Howell), William, xi. 31
Hywel, *see also* Howell

Ibstoke, Laurence de, x. 6
Icklesham, Robert de, ii. 28
Icklington, John de (c. 1392–1401, ? J. Ikelyngton), iii. 102; vi. 33, 60, 62
Iddesworth (Desword, Idesworth), Henry (de), i. 34, 50(*bis*), 82, 104, 106, 107; v. 11, 27, 40; vii. 58; viii. 54; xii. 31, 38
Ieuan ap Dafydd Fychan, xi. 13
Ieuan, John ab, *see* John ab Ieuan

Ieuan Grath, Gruffudd ab, *see* Gruffudd ab Ieuan Grath

Iforde, John de, viii. 21

Iforde, Nicholas de, viii. 38 ('Ilford'); xii. 78

Ikelyngton, John (d. 1419, ? J. de Icklington), viii. 14

Ildesleigh, Ildesley, *see* Hildesley

Ile, Robert de, viii. 57

Ile, *see also* Insula, Lisle

Ilford, *see* Iforde

Ilger (Illiger), Philip, ii. 29

Impingham, John, x. 5

Ince, Henry, x. 14, 70

Incent, John, v. 7, 68

Ine, Thomas, viii. 54

Inge, Hugh, *see* Ynge

Inge, Richard, iii. 22

Inge (Ynge), William, iv. 48

Inge, *see also* Yonge

Ingham, Ralph, i. 29; xii. 19

Ingleby, Henry (de), i. 48, 118; vi. 27, 42, 69; viii. 45

Ingleby, John, xi. 23

Inglesent, Nicholas, iii. 26, 49

Ingoldesby, Richard, i. 28, 121; xii. 41

Ingoldesthorp, Thomas de, v. 51

Ingolisma, *see* Engolisma

Ingram, William, i. 26, 64; ii. 33; iii. 60, 92

Inkbarrow, Robert, iv. 63; xii. 61

Inkepen, Peter de, iii. 33, 95; ix. 31; xii. 57

Insula (Lisle), John de, vi. 38

Insula (Lisle), Peter de (d. 1303), viii. 12; ix. 22; x. 14

Insula (Lisle), Peter de (d. 1311), vi. 15, 34, 101

Insula, Thomas de, *see* Lisle

Insula, *see also* Ile

Interampni, Andrew de, vii. 39

Iorwerth ap Madog (Gervase ap Madog), xi. 8(*bis*) & n

Iorwerth ap Rhys (Price), xi. 43n

Iorwerth, Dafydd ab Ieuan ab, *see* Dafydd ab Ieuan ab Iorwerth

Iorwerth, Einion ab, *see* Einion ab Iorwerth

Iorwerth, Gruffudd ab, *see* Gruffudd ab Iorwerth

Ippart ap Robert, *see* Ithel ap Robert

Ireland, Thomas, vi. 73; vii. 40(*bis*); xi. 7, 15

Irford, John de, vi. 82

Irford, Peter (c. 1439, ? P.I. d. 1452), vii. 22

Irford (Beverlay, Yrford), Peter (d. 1452, ? P.I. c. 1439), i. 19, 112; vi. 49

Irreys, Henry de, x. 4n

Irreys, William, x. 4

Irtlingburgh, John, i. 16, 84

Irton, William de, vii. 9

Isaac, Madog ab, *see* Madog ab Isaac

Isaak, John, v. 30; xii. 63

Isambardi, *see* Longavilla

Isarmy, *see* Ysarni

Isham, *see* Yesham

Islip, John, i. 18; xii. 16

Islip (Islep), Simon, i. 18, 25, 70, 120, 121; iv. 4, 7; v. 47; x. 53, 60; xii. 16, 18, 28, 48(*bis*)

Islip, William, i. 33

Ispania, Ispannia, *see* Hispania

Iterii (Itier, de Périgueux), Peter, i. 54; vii. 7; viii. 10; ix. 13n, 36n

Ithel ap Bleddyn ap Madog, xi. 47

Ithel ap Cynwrig, xi. 8

Ithel (Ippart) ap Robert (Probert), xi. 3, 12, 43, 49

Itier, *see* Iterii

Ive (Ivy, Yve), William, iii. 18

Ives, *see* Yve

Ivingho, Ralph (de), i. 89; v. 18, 25; xii. 33

Ivrea, *see* Solario

Iwardeby, Robert, i. 71, 85, 127

Ixworth, John (d. 1431/2), i. 37, 56; iii. 31, 59; iv. 63; v. 35, 55, 58; vi. 35; vii. 21, 52 & n; ix. 45; xii. 24, 75

Ixworth, John (d. 1447), v. 55; vii. 52n

Ixworth, Walter, i. 56; xii. 24

Jackessone, Jacuessone, *see* Jaquessone

Jake, David ap, *see* David ap Jake

Jakes, Walter, *see* Ameny

Jakes, William, viii. 28

Jane, Thomas, iii. 53; iv. 24; v. 11, 22, 58, 60; viii. 14n, 36

Janetto, Janitus, *see* Jenetto

Janini, Nicholas de, de Ramberticuria, vii. 28

Jankyns, John, xi. 33

Jaquessone (Jackessone, Jacuessone), Richard, ii. 24, 29; xii. 47

Jargolio, John de (John Albini), ix. 24

Jay, Edward, vi. 78 & n

Jay, *see also* Jey

Jeffray, *see* Geffray, Leyson

Jeffrey, John, *see* Geffray

Jeffrey, Robert, *see* Geffrey

Jeffreys, *see* Geffray, John

Jenetto (Genetta, Janetto, Janitus), Guy de, iii. 60

Jevans, John, xi. 34

Jey, William, i. 30

Jey, *see also* Jay

Jodico, Brunus de, i. 40
John (c. 1296–1307), xi. 59
John (c. 1345), xi. 9
John (d. 1361), i. 83
John, Henry ap, *see* Henry ap John
John ab Ieuan, xi. 27
John ap Goronwy Goch, xi. 14
John ap Gruffudd, xi. 12
John ap Harry (Parry), xi. 79
John ap Howell, *see* Trefnant
John ap Hywel (Powell) (d. 1404), *see* Trefnant
John ap Hywel (Powell) (d. 1487), xi. 58
John ap Hywel (Powell) (c. 1534), *see* Huws, John, *magister*
John ap Hywel (Powell) ap Brython (d. 1538), xi. 42
John ap Rhys (Price) (c. 1395–8), xi. 9
John ap Rhys (Price) (c. 1432–9), xi. 63
John ap Rhys (Price) ap Roppert (Probert) (d. 1404), xi. 10, 42
John ap Richard, ii. 5, 11, 52
John, Lewis ap, *see* Lewis ap John
John, William ap, *see* William ap John
Johns, William, xi. 31
Johns, *see also* Jones, Jonys
Jolyff, John, x. 31
Jones, Martin, *see* Joynour
Jones, Robert, ii. 10
Jones, *see also* Johns, Jonys
Jonys, William (c. 1501, ? W.J. d. 1511), xi. 79
Jonys, William (d. 1511, ? W.J. c. 1501), x. 63
Jonys, *see also* Johns, Jones
Jordan (13th cent.), v. 59
Jordan, John, vi. 87
Jordan, Robert, ii. 14, 44; xii. 46
Jorz (Geors), Robert de, iii. 90
Jorz (Geors), Thomas, iii. 53
Jovenzano, Aymo de, vi. 92; vii. 56
Joynour (Bovelyth, Jones), Martin, i. 24; xii. 18
Joyns, *see* Edward ap John
Judde, Richard, ii. 11, 16; xii. 46
Judicis, John de, i. 73
Jugee, William de la, iv. 7
Jugie, Raymond de la, i. 82
Julian, Nicholas, xi. 14

Kaerwent, Nicholas, ii. 27; xii. 48
Kantia, John de, viii. 60
Kantia, *see also* Kent
Karaunt, *see* Caraunt

Karlel (Karlelle), Thomas (de), vi. 102; xi. 84
Karles, Walter, ii. 28
Karliolo, *see* Carlisle
Karne, *see* Carne
Karneka, Karnyka, *see* Carnyka, Kernyk
Karolis, *see* Carozolis
Kay, *see* Key
Kays (Keyes), Henry, iv. 27
Kays, *see also* Keyes
Keale, John, v. 34
Kebow, *see* Kybow
Keir, *see* Keyr
Kele, John, i. 56, 123
Keler, Thomas, xi. 43
Kellawe, Richard de, vi. 107
Kellet, Edward, vi. 12, 63; xii. 66
Kelsey, John, i. 56, 118
Kelsey, Richard, iii. 7
Kelsey, William (c. 1354), i. 5
Kelsey, William (c. 1395), *see* Aslokby
Kempe, John, iv. 5, 38; v. 3; vi. 4, 113; vii. 2
Kempe (Kemp), Thomas, i. 66; v. 3, 12n; vi. 9n, 18, 26, 43(*bis*), 45, 63, 79; xii. 27
Kempe, William, v. 28, 45
Kempsey, John de, ii. 10, 18, 35
Kendal, William de (c. 1322–40), vi. 101
Kendal, William de (d. 1366), vi. 77
Kendale, Hugh de, v. 38
Kene, Nicholas, viii. 36
Kenleye, John de, vi. 88
Kenric, Elias ap, *see* Elias ap Kenric
Kent, Robert, ii. 9, 23; xii. 47
Kent, *see also* Kantia
Kentwood (Kentewode), Reginald, i. 78; ii. 14; iii. 50; v. 6, 8, 29, 63; vii. 18
Kepston, John de, vii. 8
Kerdeston (Gerdeston), Thomas de, iv. 28; xii. 59
Kernyk, John de, x. 7
Kernyk, *see also* Carnyka
Kersingham, Hugh de, v. 49
Kerver, Kervour, *see* Aleyne, John (d. 1516)
Kesteven, William de, ix. 28
Ketelbergh (Ketelbiri), Stephen de, iv. 17; vii. 10, 19; ix. 29; xi. 80
Keten, Robert, viii. 75
Ketene, John (c. 1365), iii. 59
Ketene, John de (d. 1316), iv. 13
Ketilton, William, x. 10 & n
Kette, John, v. 41
Ketterich, Ketterick, *see* Catryk
Kewys, Richard, vii. 16, 43
Kexby, John, vi. 9 & n; xii. 66
Kexby, William de, vi. 11, 20

Key (Kay), Thomas, i. 124

Keyes, Henry, see Kays

Keyes (Kyes, Kyesse), Roger, iii. 38, 74, 91; v. 36; ix. 8, 20, 51

Keynell, Robert, ii. 25; xii. 47

Keynes (Caynes), Thomas de, iii. 84; v. 64; vii. 19; ix. 10, 33

Keyr (Keir), Richard, xi. 65, 65n ('Robert')

Keyton, John, iii. 101

Kidwely, John, i. 52, 102; ii. 40; xii. 36

Kildesby, Robert de, vi. 24, 42; x. 67

Kildesby, William (de), see Kyldesby

Kilkenny, Andrew de, ix. 3, 21

Kilkenny, William de, ix. 23

Kilvington, Richard de, v. 5, 8; vi. 73

Kinebauton (Kinbolton, Kinebarton), Joceus de, iv. 60; v. 17; xii. 61

King (Kynge), Alexander, ii. 42; xi. 72

King, John, vii. 10, 38

King, Oliver, i. 14; ii. 5, 21; iii. 10; v. 60; vi. 38, 51; viii. 3, 17, 33; ix. 3 & n, 59; xii. 15, 44, 47, 69

King, Robert, i. 38, 57

King, William, viii. 32, 71

Kingscote (Kyngescote), John, iv. 61; vi. 98

Kingscote (Kyngoscot), William de, ii. 42, 44; viii. 49; ix. 4, 24

Kingsmill, see Basyng, William

Kingston (Kyngeston), Richard (de), ii. 6, 16, 20, 39; iii. 42; v. 13, 46; viii. 50; x. 38

Kingston, Robert, x. 58

Kingston, see also Kyngeston

Kington, John, i. 53; ii. 36; v. 35; xii. 23

Kington, Roger de, iii. 11

Kinnersley, see Kynardesley

Kirkby, John (c. 1332–3), see Kirkeby

Kirkby, John (c. 1351–68), i. 50, 101, 104; xii. 37(bis)

Kirkby, John (c. 1449–61), see Kirkeby

Kirkby, John de (d. 1352), vi. 97, 100

Kirkby, John de (d. 1423), vi. 102 & n

Kirkby, Stephen, i. 30

Kirkby, Thomas, see Kirkeby

Kirkby (Kirkeby, Kyrkeby), William (de) (c. 1344–51, ? W. de Kirkeby), i. 104; ii. 34

Kirkby, see also Kirkeby, Kyrkeby

Kirkeby (Kyrkeby), John (d. 1459), viii. 73, 78; ix. 54; xii. 83

Kirkeby (Kirkby), John (c. 1449–61), i. 99, 108; v. 48

Kirkeby, John (d. 1476), see Kirkeby, Thomas (d. 1476)

Kirkeby, John de (d. 1346), iii. 7, 69, 76; x. 7; xii. 52, 55, 56

Kirkeby, Richard de (c. 1336–51), ix. 6, 29

Kirkeby, Richard de (c. 1357–73), ix. 18n

Kirkeby, Thomas (d. 1459), viii. 71

Kirkeby (Kirkby), Thomas (d. 1476), iii. 60, 72, 79, 94, 98; vi. 28; ix. 11 & n ('John'), 54

Kirkeby, William (d. 1446), iii. 69

Kirkeby, William de (c. 1347–58, ? W. de Kirkby), vi. 52; x. 65

Kirkeby, see also Kirkby, Kyrkeby

Kirketon (de Kirton, Kyrketon), Alan, i. 69; v. 36; vi. 85; ix. 18; xii. 28

Kirketon, see also Kyrketon

Kirkham, Robert, i. 60, 121; iii. 16, 29; v. 22

Kirkland, Robert, vii. 42

Kirkstead, William, i. 80

Kirmington (Kirnington), Joceline, i. 3, 17, 21, 63; xii. 13, 16

Kirtlington, Robert de, x. 23

Kirton, see Kirketon

Kite (Kyte), John, iii. 90; vi. 99; vii. 49; xii. 72, 75

Knapton, John de, vi. 14n

Knapton, William de, ii. 26; iv. 26, 32

Knapton, see also Napton

Knesworth, see Strete

Knight, Thomas (d. 1417), xi. 14, 27

Knight, Thomas (d. 1525), i. 108

Knight, William, i. 10, 66; iii. 62; v. 30; vi. 27; viii. 3, 49; x. 14; xi. 16; xii. 27

Knight, see also Knyght

Knightley, Walter, v. 16, 19, 63

Knockyn, see Eyton, Thomas de

Knode, John, x. 17

Knolles, Ralph, i. 105; xii. 37

Knolles, Thomas, vi. 17, 30

Knollys, Christopher, x. 8

Knossyngton, Hugh de, iii. 21

Knovile, Nicholas (Gilbert) de, ii. 45 & n

Knovill, Ralph de, viii. 66

Knovyle, John de, ix. 23

Knyght, John, viii. 20, 33

Knyght, see also Knight

Kode, Walter, xii. 90

Kybow (Kebow), John, vii. 15

Kyes, Kyesse, see Keyes

Kyffin, see Cyffin; Hywel ap Madog ap Cyffin

Kylborn, John, i. 20

Kyldesby (Kildesby), William (de), i. 48, 113, 116; v. 47, 56 & n; vi. 13, 90, 92; vii. 44; viii. 77

Kymer, Gilbert, iii. 4, 20; viii. 38

Kynardesley (Kinnersley, Kynardeseye, Ky-
nardessey), John de, vi. 107; viii. 64;
x. 34, 37, 46; xii. 80
Kynchale, Nicholas, x. 28
Kynewellis, *see* Gynewell
Kynge, *see* King
Kyngescote, *see* Kingscote
Kyngeston, John de, vi. 112, 114
Kyngeston, Richard (de), *see* Kingston
Kyngman, John, viii. 28
Kyngoscot, *see* Kingscote, William de
Kynwalmerssh, *see* Kynwollmerssh
Kynwic, *see* Cynwrig
Kynwollmerssh (Kynwoldmerssh), William
(d. 1422), i. 117; v. 67; vi. 67
Kynwollmerssh (Kynwalmerssh, Kynwold-
mersh), William (d. 1469), ii. 49; vii. 45;
x. 43; xii. 51
Kyrkeby, John (d. 1459), *see* Kirkeby
Kyrkeby, John (c. 1478), xi. 31
Kyrkeby, William de, *see* Kirkby
Kyrkeby, *see also* Kirkby, Kirkeby
Kyrketon, Alan, *see* Kirketon
Kyrketon, Thomas, i. 74; viii. 65
Kyte, *see* Kite
Kyvelingwrth, Robert, i. 85

L—, J— de, ix. 27n
Laberd, Labere, *see* Delabere
Laches, William, ii. 7
Laci, William, xi. 81
Laci, *see also* Lacy, Lascy
Lacock, Thomas, viii. 22
Lacy, Edmund, i. 95; ii. 2, 27; ix. 2; xi. 57
Lacy (Lascy), John (de) (d. 1301, ? J. Lascy),
i. 120; vii. 8; viii. 68; xii. 74
Lacy, Peter de, vii. 58
Lacy, Robert (de), i. 21, 52, 83, 96, 106; vi.
66; xii. 37
Lacy, *see also* Laci, Lascy
Lagier, Bertrand, of Figeac, i. 95, 116; ii. 12
Laiburn, *see* Leyburn
Lakenham, Henry de, iv. 25
Lakenhyth (Lakingham), Adam de, iii. 98;
xii. 57
Lambard, John, *see* Lambert
Lambard, Walter, vi. 88
Lambert (Lambard), John, i. 126
Lambert, Nicholas, iii. 102; xii. 57
Lambert, William, v. 58
Lambeth (Lamhethe), William (c. 1361, ? W.
de L. c. 1349), ii. 30
Lambeth, William de (c. 1349, ? W.L. c.
1361), ix. 33

Lamborne, Simon, ix. 7
Lambrok, William, viii. 10, 18, 79
Lamhethe, *see* Lambeth
Lamport, *see* Langport
Lampton, William, ix. 54
Lampton, *see also* Langton
Lancaster, Robert of, xi. 38
Landreyn, John, xi. 32, 49
Landwath, *see* Langwath
Lane, John, viii. 75; x. 10; xii. 84
Lane, Thomas, viii. 68; x. 39; xii. 81
Lane, William, i. 45; vi. 51
Lang, Matthew, iii. 62
Langborough, William de, iii. 61; xi. 46
Langborough, *see also* Longebergh
Langdon, John, iv. 38
Langdon, *see also* Longedon
Langebergh, John de, iii. 55
Langebergh, *see also* Langborough
Langeton, John de, *see* Langton, John de
(d. 1337)
Langeton, Walter de, *see* Langton
Langham, Simon (de), i. 41; iv. 4(*bis*), 14 &
n; vi. 18, 93; viii. 13 & n; xii. 21
Langland, *see* Longland
Langley, John, vii. 11
Langley, Ralph (c. 1481, ? R. Longley), v. 37
Langley, Ralph de (c. 1363), xi. 82
Langley, Robert de, iv. 25
Langley (Longley), Thomas, i. 67; iii. 42 & n,
54; iv. 29; v. 2; vi. 4, 7, 72, 76, 108; viii.
80; xi. 45 & n
Langley, William, vii. 6, 53, 54
Langport (Lamport), Richard, i. 96; vi. 57;
viii. 17; xii. 35, 77
Langridge, Richard, vi. 21
Langrish, Robert, iii. 48, 83
Langstrother, Richard, v. 36
Langtoft, John, x. 70
Langtoft, Thomas, i. 85, 124
Langton, James, x. 56
Langton, John (c. 1389), viii. 28
Langton, John (d. 1447), i. 64; ii. 29, 36;
iii. 54; v. 51; vi. 49; x. 41; xi. 54, 78;
xii. 26, 70
Langton (Langeton), John (de) (d. 1337), i.
59; iii. 22; iv. 6, 13; vi. 50; vii. 1, 54;
viii. 10; x. 70;
Langton, Peter de, vi. 22n
Langton, Ralph, iii. 36, 54
Langton, Robert (d. 1524), i. 128; iii. 8, 43,
52; vi. 15, 89; xii. 43
Langton, Robert de (c. 1321), ix. 26
Langton, Roger de, vii. 56

Langton, Thomas, i. 99; iii. 2; iv. 5, 46; viii. 62; ix. 11; xi. 55 & n; xii. 36, 52, 80

Langton (Langeton), Walter de, v. 39; x. 1 & n

Langton, William (d. 1414), vii. 50; ix. 44, 45

Langton, William (d. 1496), i. 73; vi. 9, 12; xii. 29, 66

Langton, see also Lampton

Langvyle, see Longville

Langwath (Landwath), William, i. 17, 52; xii. 16

Lanton, William de, viii. 81

Lanwaryn, John, ii. 22

Lanwaryn, see also Lentwardyn

Lardo, William de, iii. 78; xii. 56

Larke (Lark), Thomas, i. 128; iii. 66; iv. 28, 32; vii. 5; xii. 43

Lascy, John (c. 1289–99, ? J. (de) Lacy), i. 94

Lascy, John (d. 1301), see Lacy

Lascy, John (d. 1493, ? J. Lassy), viii. 29, 76

Lascy, Robert, i. 120

Lassells, William, i. 9, 119; vi. 89

Lassy, John (c. 1463, ? J. Lascy), xi. 50

Latchebury, Simon, xi. 47

Latimer (Latomer), Hugh, iv. 58

Latimer, William, iii. 97

Launce, John, vii. 22, 44; xi. 72

Launceston, John de, ix. 25

Laurence, the Roman, v. 52

Lausanne, Albert de, i. 70; xii. 27

Lavagna, see Fieschi, Albert

Lavendre, Richard, i. 13, 56, 114

Lavenham, Firmin de, iv. 30; xii. 59

Lavenham (Moriel), Thomas, xi. 26 & n

Lavenza, Anthony de, viii. 79

Lavyngton, William de, viii. 11

Lawrence, see Laurence

Lax, John, iii. 40; vi. 65(bis) & n

Layburn, see Leyburn

Layot (Leyot, Leyott), John, i. 103; x. 50

Layot, Richard, see Leyot

Layton (Leighton), Edward, iii. 13

Layton, Richard, i. 16, 112; v. 28; vi. 9, 86; xii. 39, 63

Layton, see also Leghton

Lebdavy, see Lobdewe

Lech (Lechole), John (de), i. 74; ii. 30; iii. 92; v. 66; vii. 30, 39 & n, 46; ix. 27n, 33; xii. 29, 48

Leche, John, ii. 23

Leche, Thomas, ii. 38

Lechlade, Thomas de, ix. 4, 8, 22

Lechole, see Lech

Leck (Lek), Laurence de, iv. 25

Ledbury, Richard de, iv. 61; xii. 61

Ledbury, Stephen de, ii. 4, 15

Ledbury, Thomas, iv. 59

Lee, David, xi. 56; xii. 89

Lee, Edward, i. 122; iii. 18, 82; iv. 49; v. 14; vi. 5, 47; ix. 62, 64; xii. 41

Lee, George, x. 12, 22, 66

Lee, John, vii. 24

Lee, Philip, x. 17

Lee, Roland, vi. 91; viii. 17; ix. 17; x. 3 & n, 29

Lee, see also Legh(e)

Leeds, John de, vi. 39

Leek, Edmund, i. 35

Leek (Leke), John (d. 1462), i. 99, 101; xii. 35(bis)

Leek, John de (c. 1343–67), vii. 42

Leek, see also Leke

Legborne (Legbourne, Leybourne), John, i. 13, 74, 107; x. 54; xii. 29, 38

Legh (Leigh), Alexander, vi. 55; ix. 56

Legh, Walter de, iv. 57, 59

Legh, William, vii. 37

Leghe, William, ix. 41

Legh(e), see also Lee

Leghton, Walter de, xi. 81

Leghton, see also Layton

Legilden, see Gulden

Lehee, Hugh, x. 68

Le Hert, see Lyhart

Leicester, John de (d. 1289), v. 21

Leicester, Peter de, x. 20

Leicester, William de, x. 61

Leicester, see also Leycester

Leicestre, John de (d. 1340), x. 61

Leicestre, Ralph de, x. 55

Leicestre, see also Leycester

Leigh, see Legh

Leighton, see Layton

Leipyates, Philip, i. 5, 77, 100; vi. 41; xii. 14

Lek, see Leck

Leke, John, see Leek

Leke, Robert, i. 96, 117; xii. 35

le Mercer, see Rosse

Leminster, see Leominster

Lemosini, M—, ix. 31

Lemynistre, see Leominster

Lenia, Thomas de (c. 1399, ? T. Llyn), xi. 13 & n

Lenn(e), see Lynn

Lens, Baldwin de, viii. 28

Lentwardyn (Leyntwardyn), Richard, iii. 81; ix. 16; xi. 83

Lentwardyn, Thomas, v. 19

Lentwardyn, *see also* Lanwaryn
Leominster (Leminster, Lemynistre), Hugh de, ii. 17; xi. 17
le Penec, *see* Pennock
Lepton, Ralph, viii. 18
Lercedekne (Archedeakne, Lerchedekene), Martin, ix. 40, 42
Lercedekne (Archedeakne, Lerchedekene), Michael, ix. 11, 48
Lescheman, Roland, vi. 77
Lescrope, *see* Scrope
Leson, Gruffudd, *see* Leyshon
Leson, Thomas; William, *see* Leyson
Lestine (le Styne), Thomas, de Wissande, vii. 15
le Strange, *see* Strange
Levenaunt, Walter, ix. 39
Leversegge, Hugh de, xi. 44
Leverton, Alan, xi. 70
Leveson (Lewson), William, ii. 18; ix. 10, 64; xii. 83
Lewes, Dafydd, xi. 28
Lewes, Thomas de, vii. 58
Lewesham, Thomas, ii. 51; ix. 50
Lewis ap John, xi. 58, 67
Lewis ap Rhys (Price), xi. 57, 67
Lewis ap Tudur, xi. 16
Lewis, John, xi. 59
Lewis, Morgan, xi. 67, 79
Lewson, *see* Leveson
Lexham, Thomas de, ii. 50
Leybourne, *see* Legborne
Leyburn (Laiburn, Layburn), Roger, vi. 55, 99, 113
Leycester, Henry de, x. 1, 4 & n
Leycester (Leyset), Robert de, vii. 11
Leycester, *see also* Leicester, Leicestre
Leyntwardyn, *see* Lentwardyn
Leyot, John, *see* Layot
Leyot (Layot, Leyott, Wyott), Richard, i. 82; iii. 4, 58, 103; vi. 72; viii. 41; x. 36; xi. 41
Leyott, John, *see* Layot
Leyott, Richard, *see* Leyot
Leyset, *see* Leycester, Robert de
Leyshon (Leson), Gruffudd, xi. 31, 65
Leyson (Leson), Thomas, viii. 81; x. 43
Leyson (Leson), William, x. 43
Lichefeld, John, viii. 43
Lichefeld, Richard, *see* Lichfield
Lichfield, Edmund, i. 105; vii. 9, 52; xii. 37, 75
Lichfield (Teynterel), Nicholas de (c. 1322–1337), x. 23

Lichfield (Taverner), Nicholas de (d. 1375), x. 30
Lichfield (Lichefeld), Richard, i. 28; iii. 97; v. 12, 26, 52, 69; viii. 15, 59; xii. 19
Lichfield, William, v. 19, 30
Liddington, John, i. 97
Ligham, Peter, v. 70, 71; ix. 66
Likamstede, Richard de, viii. 72
Lilly, John, i. 100
Lillyford, John, i. 49, 53, 62; xii. 23(*bis*), 26
Lillylowe, Thomas, i. 120
Limbergh, Adam (de), i. 43, 59, 78, 107; v. 52
Linacre, Thomas, vi. 12, 72; viii. 47
Lincoln, John de (c. 1345), xi. 37
Lincoln, John (de) (of Grimsby) (d. 1415), i. 8, 26, 41(*ter*); iii. 27, 67, 79; iv. 31; vi. 53; viii. 19; x. 39, 42, 61; xi. 31, 68
Lineden, John, iii. 14
Lisieux, Thomas, v. 6, 60, 63; vii. 29
Lisle, John de; Peter de, *see* Insula
Lisle (Insula), Thomas de, iv. 13
Lisle, *see also* Ile
Litherland, Henry, i. 23, 57
Litlyngton, William, iii. 102
Littelton (Littleton, Lutleton), Wibert de, viii. 3, 13, 76; ix. 26, 28; xii. 76(*bis*), 81, 83
Littleton (Lutleton), William de, viii. 6, 8 & n, 27
Litton, Christopher, ii. 47
Lloyd, Owen, ix. 10n, 17n, 19, 20, 56
Llwyd (Lloyd), Dafydd (c. 1461), xi. 44n
Llwyd (Lolyd), Dafydd (c. 1534–5), xi. 16; xii. 88(*bis*)
Llwyd, Madog ap Dafydd, *see* Madog ap Dafydd Llwyd
Llwyd (Lloyd), Thomas, xi. 57 & n
Llyn, Thomas (c. 1400, ? T. de Lenia), xi. 13n, 14
Llywelyn ab Ynyr (Llywelyn de Bromfield), xi. 37
Llywelyn ap Hwfa, xi. 43
Llywelyn ap Madog (Lewis Rede) (d. 1462), viii. 30; xi. 62
Llywelyn ap Madog ab Elis (d. 1375), xi. 37, 40, 43
Llywelyn, Dafydd, xi. 33
Llywelyn, Philip ap, *see* Philip ap Lywelyn
Lobdewe (de Lebdavy), Bernard, vii. 39
Lobenham (Lubbenham), William de, iii. 5, 66
Lochard, William, ii. 9, 16
Lodelowe (Ludelawe, Ludelowe), Nicholas de, iii. 1, 87; vi. 59

Loggore, Loggoure, see Lugore
Logwardyn, John, viii. 65
Logwardyn, see also Lugwardyn
Lokyngton, Roger de, vii. 50
Lombard, William, vi. 73
Lombard, see also Lumbard
Lombe, William, x. 15, 16, 69
Lomelyne, James, iii. 62
Londethorpe (Lunderthorp), John de, x. 27
London, Edmund, i. 16
London, John (c. 1348), i. 123
London, John (d. 1513), ix. 61
London, John (d. 1544), i. 23, 29, 36, 94, 102
    (ter); iii. 85; vi. 34; vii. 38; xii. 17, 20
London, Thomas (de), i. 123; vi. 78; vii. 17
London, Walter (c. 1420), ii. 51
London, Walter (de) (d. 1348/9), i. 123; iii.
    59; iv. 7; v. 20, 21n; viii. 3; xii. 41
London, William de (? W. de Boudon), vi. 31
Long, Matthew, iv. 49
Long, Nicholas, ii. 24; xii. 47
Long, William, iii. 70
Longavilla, Nicholas Isambardi de, vi. 29
Longavilla, see also Longville
Longedon, John de, x. 32
Longedon, see also Langdon
Longespey, see Ragenhill
Longeville, see Longavilla, Longville
Longland, Edward, i. 106
Longland (Langland), John, i. 3, 100; iii. 5,
    23
Longley, Ralph (c. 1459, ? R. Langley), vi. 72
Longley, Thomas, see Langley
Longville (Langvyle, Longeville), John, i. 33;
    iii. 25, 52
Longville, see also Longavilla
Lopez, John de, v. 11
Loreng, Thomas de, vii. 58
Loring, John, i. 82
Loring (Loryng), William, i. 37; iii. 92; xi. 12
Lotrel, see Luttrell
Loughborough (Louthborough), Thomas, i.
    62, 119; xii. 26, 40
Loughburgh (Loughteburgh), William de, v.
    44; vii. 10, 13; viii. 4
Lound, John, iii. 69
Louth (Luda), Nicholas de, iii. 61; xi. 46
Louth, Ralph, i. 72
Louth, Thomas, i. 21, 76, 87, 106, 124
Louth, see also Luda
Louthborough, see Loughborough
Louthorp, George, iii. 20, 51, 75
Lovel, Fulk, v. 23 & n
Lovel, Gilbert, iii. 51, 53, 76

Lovel, Henry, vii. 5n
Lovel, John, i. 42
Lovel, Ralph, iii. 59, 100
Lovel, Roger, iv. 41n
Lovel, Thomas, viii. 12, 21, 79
Lovell, William, x. 44
Loveney, John, ii. 6, 7, 52
Lovibond, John, iii. 65
Lowe, Arthur, i. 47; xii. 22
Lowe, John (bp., d. 1467), iv. 39; xi. 38
Lowe, John (c. 1452–67), iv. 42
Lowys, Philip (c. 1424–5, ? P. ap Llywelyn),
    xi. 25 & n
Loxele, William, vii. 15
Lubbenham, see Lobenham
Luca, see Luco
Luceby, Henry de, vi. 109
Luco, Francis de, vi. 64
Luco, John de, v. 43 & n
Luco (Luca), Thomas de, iii. 73, 80
Luculo, see Spinula
Lucy, Geoffrey de, x. 71
Luda, Nicholas de, see Louth
Luda, William de, v. 49
Luda, see also Louth
Ludeford, William de, v. 53
Ludelawe, Ludelowe, see Lodelowe
Ludham, John (de), i. 63; iii. 86; v. 42;
    vii. 27
Ludham, Thomas, i. 87, 99, 107; xii. 38
Ludlowe, see Lodelowe; Walker, Geoffrey
Luffenham, Robert (de), iii. 11, 30; viii. 74;
    xii. 52, 81
Lugans, John, ix. 42
Luggore, Thomas (d. 1346), viii. 8; xii. 82
Lugore (Loggore, Loggoure), Thomas de
    (d. 1313), ii. 26; iii. 95; viii. 7; ix. 24;
    xii. 48
Lugwardyn, John, viii. 43, 67
Lugwardyn, see also Logwardyn
Luke (Lukk), John, iii. 46, 63, 86; v. 24; viii.
    37; ix. 46
Luke, Richard, v. 50
Lukk, see Luke, John
Lulimere, see Lynn
Lullyngton, William de, v. 19; vii. 4
Lumbard, John, viii. 45
Lumbard, see also Lombard
Lumley, John (c. 1467, ? J.L. d. 1484), i. 104
Lumley, John (d. 1484, ? J.L. c. 1467), i. 30
Lumley, Marmaduke, i. 2, 20; vi. 98, 115;
    vii. 15; xii. 13, 17
Luna, Peter de, viii. 15n
Lunderthorp, see Londethorpe

Luntley, John, xi. 63

Lupsett, Thomas, iii. 84

Lupton, Roger, i. 50, 52; iii. 85; xii. 23, 56

Luterel, Robert, iii. 97

Luterel, *see also* Luttrell

Lutiberugh, Henry de, v. 54

Lutleton, *see* Littelton, Littleton

Lutteleye, John de, ix. 38

Luttrell (Lotrel, Lutterell), John, iii. 24; vi. 59

Luttrell, *see also* Luterel

Luxemburg, Louis de, iv. 15

Lyde, Richard, xi. 48

Lyde, *see also* Lyth

Lydford, John, vii. 45; ix. 18, 39

Lye, Roger, x. 64

Lye, Thomas (d. 1464), x. 18; xii. 84

Lyes, Thomas (c. 1408–37), i. 105; xii. 37

Lyhart (Le Hert), Walter, iv. 24

Lynde, Richard de la, vii. 21

Lyndefeld (Clerc), John, vii. 5, 12, 43

Lyndrich, Walter de, vii. 13

Lyndwood (Lyndewode, Lynwod, Lynwood), William, i. 14n, 18; ii. 28; iii. 34, 83; viii. 65; ix. 48; xi. 54

Lyney, Nicholas, ii. 44

Lyng, Richard, iv. 27, 30, 32

Lynham, John de, xi. 84

Lynn (Lenn, Lenne, Lulimere, Lynne), William de, iv. 57; v. 2n; vii. 1, 4

Lyntesford, Richard, i. 118; xii. 40

Lynton, Thomas (de), v. 51; vii. 17; viii. 10, 79; xi. 12; xii. 88

Lynwod, Lynwood, *see* Lyndwood

Lyth, Richard de, vi. 101

Lyth, *see also* Lyde

Lywer, Robert, ix. 49

Mabott, Richard, i. 120

Macalpine, John, iii. 35

Macclesfield, John, vi. 28; viii. 34–5

Macclesfield, Thomas, x. 63

Macclesfield, *see also* Makelesfeld

Machell, Henry, vi. 70

Machyn, Richard, xi. 57

Mackworth (Macworth), John, i. 2, 4, 64, 96; iii. 8, 77; iv. 29; vi. 37; viii. 27, 80; xii. 13(*bis*), 26, 35, 52

Maddeis, *see* Mades

Maddynglee, Thomas, viii. 31, 51, 54

Madefrey (Madefray), Thomas, viii. 40, 82; ix. 37

Mades (Maddeis), Thomas, iii. 40; ix. 59; xii. 54

Madog ab Isaac, xi. 49

Madog ap Dafydd Llwyd, xi. 17

Madog ap Meurig, of Anglesey, xi. 9, 11

Madog, Dafydd ap, *see* Dafydd ap Madog

Madog, Gervase ap, *see* Gervase ap Madog

Madog, Hywel ap, *see* Hywel ap Madog

Madog, Iorwerth ap, *see* Iorwerth ap Madog

Madog, Ithel ap Bleddyn ap, *see* Ithel ap Bleddyn ap Madog

Madog, Robert, xi. 50

Magnus, Thomas, i. 55, 100; vi. 23

Magot, William, iii. 14

Maidstone, Walter (d. 1317), iv. 55

Maidstone, Walter (d. 1337), i. 5, 18n, 97

Maidstone, *see also* Maydeston

Maillesec, Guy de, vi. 18, 79

Maior, John (d. 1533), viii. 58

Maitel, John, viii. 81

Major, John (c. 1437), xi. 78

Makeblith, Thomas, ii. 37

Makelesfeld, John de, ii. 45; iii. 92

Makelesfeld, *see also* Macclesfield

Malabaila (Malebayle), Baldrac de, i. 113; xii. 39

Malabaila (Malabayla), John de, vi. 50

Malafortini (Malefurmity), Draco, iii. 81

Malaspina (Malapin'), Manfred son of Opizo, marquis, i. 83

Malberthorpe, William, i. 62

Malbet, *see* Malette

Maldesbertis, Giles de, of Cremona, vii. 39, 43n

Malebayle, *see* Malabaila

Malebys, William de, iv. 33

Malefurmity, *see* Malafortini

Maleon, *see* Malo Leone

Malet, Walter, v. 39

Malette (Malbet), Henry, i. 27

Malhom, William, v. 50

Mallet, James, i. 21, 28, 65, 73; xii. 19, 29

Malling, Ralph de, v. 11, 38

Mallon, Nicholas, ii. 18

Malmesbury, Richard de, ix. 31

Malocellus, Lazarinus, x. 39

Malocellus, Theodosius, x. 38

Malo Ingenio, Arnald de, viii. 32

Malo Leone, Stephen de (Stephen Maleon), of Flanders, iv. 50; vi. 58, 90

Malpas, Henry, *see* Maupas

Malpas (Maupas), William (c. 1383–9), iv. 63

Malpas, William (c. 1410–23), vii. 10, 27

Malstange (Malstang), Simon (de), ix. 38; x. 54

Malster, William, vi. 40, 49; xii. 69, 70
Malton, John, ii. 46
Malton, Thomas, see Corbridge
Malvern, John de (c. 1395), iv. 59
Malverne, John (d. 1422), v. 29, 37n
Malville, John, i. 34
Manchester, Richard, ix. 65
Manesford, see Maynesford
Manettis, John de, of Florence, see Portinariis
Manettis, Pigellus de, of Florence, i. 68
Manfeld, Robert (de), v. 22, 39, 60; vi. 20, 58, 93
Manfred, see Malaspina
Manneston, John, viii. 48
Manning (Mannynge), Thomas, i. 96; ii. 19, 25; iii. 20; v. 41; ix. 18; xii. 35, 46, 47
Mansel (Maunsel), John, i. 77; v. 41
Mansfield, Henry, i, 1, 3, 29, 100; xii. 36
Manso, John de, v. 23
Manton, William de, x. 6
Mantyll, Edward, vii. 30
Manupello, see Orsini, Thomas
Mapleton (Mapiltone), John, ii. 21
Mapurley, John, vi. 16
Mar, David de, vii. 57
Mar, Roger de, vi. 15n
Marbule, William, ii. 39
Marcell, John, x. 12n
Marchall, John, vi. 32, 89; viii. 68
Marchall, Thomas, vii. 27, 29, 51
Marcheford (Marchford, Mersshefeld), Simon, i. 110; iii. 21; vii. 36; xii. 38
Marcia, William de, viii. 1; xii. 76
Mardefield, Nicholas de, iii. 6
Mare, John de la, v. 27
Mare, Thomas de la, vi. 88
Mare, William de la, vi. 13, 71, 84, 92
Marescal, John, vi. 101
Marescal, see also Marshall
Mareschall, Roger le, x. 32
Mareschall, see also Marshall
Marewell (Yarewell), Gilbert de, iv. 30; xii. 59
Mari, William de, vii. 56
Marini (de Maronibus), Christopher, iii. 9, 49; v. 64; vi. 22, 58, 87; vii. 4; viii. 39; x. 64
Marisco (Marreys), Hugh de, x. 14–15, 16, 50
Marisco (Marreys), John de, x. 16, 19, 40, 46
Marisco, see also Merssh
Marke (Mark, Merke), Thomas, iv. 27, 29; vi. 72; ix. 17
Markeley, see Merkeley
Markenfield, John de, vi. 75, 86

Marlborough, Richard, iv. 48
Marmyon, Roger, vi. 61
Marnay, Amadeus FitzPeter de, see Fitz-Peter
Marnham, John, vi. 47
Maronibus, de, see Marini
Marreys, see Marisco
Marsden, Richard, vi. 39
Marsh, see Marisco, Merssh
Marshall, Cuthbert, vi. 25, 59
Marshall, John (d. 1387), vi. 20, 62
Marshall, John (d. 1446), i. 42, 87; xii. 21, 32
Marshall, John (d. 1496), i. 26; vi. 55, 63; ix. 55; xi. 23; xii. 18
Marshall, see also Marescal, Mareschall
Marston, William (c. 1402, ? Henry Merston), viii. 48
Martel, Philip, vii. 55
Martin, David (d. 1328), xi. 53
Martin, David, of Rosemarket (c. 1349–61), xi. 64, 81; xii. 90
Martin, John, xi. 6n; xii. 87
Martin, Philip, xi. 84
Martin, Richard, see Martyn
Martin, Stephen, of Hull, viii. 32; xii. 78
Martin, see also Martyn
Martival (Mortival), Roger (de), i. 3, 12, 48; iii. 1, 70; x. 36
Marton, Alexander de, vi. 77
Marton, Thomas, viii. 8, 16, 66
Martyn, Edmund, iii. 33; vii. 34
Martyn, Henry, ii. 8, 12, 25, 31, 39, 49, 51; xii. 44, 48
Martyn, John (c. 1382), xi. 6
Martyn, John (c. 1405–19), v. 53
Martyn, John (d. 1504), ii. 7, 14
Martyn, Richard (d. 1462/3), ii. 51; ix. 52
Martyn (Martin), Richard (d. 1483), ii. 6, 30, 35, 43, 47; iii. 10, 52, 81; v. 9, 34, 42; xi. 55 & n; xii. 44
Martyn, Roger, v. 55
Martyn, Thomas (c. 1390–9), iii. 65; xi. 14
Martyn, Thomas (d. 1524), iii. 31, 40, 97
Martyn, see also Martin
Marwin (Marvin, Merewin), Edmund, iv. 49
Mascall, Robert, ii. 2
Mason (Mayson), George, ii. 15, 18, 40
Mason, John, ii. 48; iii. 78, 88
Mason, Richard, vii. 15, 20, 22, 32, 46, 47
Mason, Robert (c. 1366), xi. 68n, 82
Mason, Robert (d. 1493), i. 21, 66, 99; vi. 115
Mason, William, i. 125, 128; xii. 42, 43
Massey (Masse), William, i. 88, 101, 112; xii. 33, 36, 39

Massingberd, Christopher, i. 21, 22, 24, 53, 65, 120; xii. 18, 24
Massingham, see Stalworth
Mather, William, xi. 34
Mathie, see Ricardi Mathie
Mattei, Luke, vii. 57
Matthew (Cour), Simon, v. 62
Matthew, Thomas, vii. 41
Maudeley, Richard (d. 1531), i. 13, 26, 28, 69, 110, 117; xii. 18, 19
Maudeleyn (Maudelyn), Richard (d. 1400), i. 7, 69; iii. 80; iv. 31; vi. 60; xii. 27, 59
Mauley, Stephen de, vi. 19, 39
Maunchell, Thomas, x. 52
Maundour, John, v. 15, 30; vi. 112; viii. 47
Maunham, Nicholas de, viii. 82
Maunsel, see Mansel
Maupas (Malpas), Henry, vi. 87; x. 42, 52
Maupas, William, see Malpas
Maureward, John, x. 9, 69; xii. 84, 86
Maurice ap David, iii. 88
Max, John, vi. 29
Maydenhyth (Maydenhith), John (de), iii. 21; vii. 4; viii. 82
Maydeston, Robert de, vii. 40
Maydeston, see also Maidstone
Mayew (Mayhew, Mayhewe, Mayow), Richard, i. 14; ii. 3; iii. 79; vi. 23; viii. 28; ix. 58
Mayhewe, Nicholas, i. 57
Mayhewe, Richard, see Mayew
Maynard, David, viii. 54
Maynelyn, see Tynmouth
Maynesford (Manesford), John, vii. 6
Maynwaring, John, v. 14
Maynwaryng, Nicholas, ix. 64
Mayo, —, xi. 31
Mayow, see Mayew
Mayson, see Mason
Medburn, Peter, i. 5
Medford, John, iii. 46, 59, 101
Medford (Medeford, Metford, Mitford), Richard (de), iii. 1, 42, 59; iv. 29; vi. 67; vii. 2, 24; viii. 2, 50; xi. 54n
Medford (Medeford, Mitford), Walter (de), iii. 8, 10, 12, 17, 29, 49, 52, 67, 74, 77, 100; v. 16, 26, 56; vii. 8; viii. 5, 19; x. 38
Medford, see also Metford, Mitford
Medici, Julius de, iv. 58
Medylton, see Middleton
Melborne (Melbourne), William de (c. 1330–1331), viii. 63 (line 8)
Melborne (Melbourne), William de (c. 1351–1371), iii. 71; viii. 63 (line 26); xii. 80

Melbourn, Thomas, i. 70
Melbourne (Mulleborn), John de, iii. 64; vi. 69, 80, 90; x. 35, 63
Melbourne, William de, see Melborne
Meledun, Philip de, xii. 27
Meleford, William de, v. 13, 47; xii. 62, 64
Meliorati, John de, iii. 42
Melreth, Philip, i. 88; v. 17
Melsonby, Stephen, vi. 39n
Melsonby, William, vi. 39
Melton, Ralph de, xi. 11; xii. 87
Melton, William (de) (d. 1340), i. 86; iii. 100, 102; vi. 3, 41, 44; ix. 19; xi. 11; xii. 87
Melton, William (de), (d. 1340), i. 86; iii. 100, 102; vi. 3, 41, 44; ix. 19; xi. 11
Melton, William de (d. 1528), vi. 10, 84
Melward, see Milward
Membury, Simon, iii. 48
Meneley, John, x. 48
Menethorpe, Hugh de, vi. 84
Menhir, John, viii. 39, 43
Menyman, John, viii. 43
Meopham (Mepham), Edmund de, vii. 32; xi. 30
Meopham (Mepham), Simon de, iv. 3; vii. 32
Mepham, William de, iii. 31, 68, 79, 86
Merbury, John, ii. 7, 52
Mercer, Thomas, vi. 63; vii. 26; xii. 71, 74
Mercer, William le, see Rosse
Merdon, Thomas, vii. 60
Mere, John, i. 67; viii. 7, 33; xi. 45
Mere, Richard de la, ii. 28
Mere, Thomas de, vii. 23
Merer, see Morer
Merewell, see Woodlock
Merewin, see Marwin
Mereworth, Lawrence, iv. 41
Merflete, Robert, xi. 67
Meriet, Walter, ix. 9, 27
Merke, Thomas (c. 1397–1400), vi. 98
Merke, Thomas (c. 1459–83), see Marke
Merkeley (Markeley), Nicholas, x. 32
Merlawe (Merlow), John, iv. 47
Mersowe, Edmund de, vii. 58
Merssh, Roger, i. 56
Merssh (Marsh), Thomas, viii. 50, 59, 73
Merssh, see also Marisco
Mersshefeld, see Marcheford
Merston, Henry (d. 1433, ? William Marston), v. 24, 53; vi. 85, 93; viii. 48, 64
Merston, Thomas de, vii. 58
Mertok, John, viii. 49
Merton, Walter de, v. 36
Mertoun, John de, x. 35

Meryng, Francis, iii. 31
Mesewers, Philip, vii. 32
Messager, John, vii. 23
Messenger, Roland, i. 40
Metcalfe, Nicholas, i. 108; iv. 42
Metford, John, iv. 18
Metford, Richard (de), see Medford
Metford, see also Medford, Mitford
Metham, John, i. 35
Methelwold, Thomas de, iv. 30
Metingham (Mettingham), John de, vi. 34, 88; viii. 81
Meurig, Einion ap, see Einion ap Meurig
Meurig, Madog ap, see Madog ap Meurig
Meux (Meuse), John, vi. 74
Mey (Meye), Roger, ii. 10
Mey (Meye), Walter, ii. 23, 49
Mey, William, xi. 84
Meysey, see Ycdvyn
Mezzavacca, Bartholomew, i. 25; iii. 20
Michel, John, ix. 43
Michel (Michaelis), Richard, v. 25
Michel, Thomas (d. by 1361), i. 40; x. 64
Michel, Thomas (d. 1533), ix. 62
Michel, see also Mitchell, Mychell
Micheldevere, see Mucheldevere
Middelham, see Middleham
Middelond (Middellond), Robert (de), vi. 69; viii. 82; ix. 10, 34; xi. 81
Middelton, see Middleton
Middilton, Robert, see Middleton
Middilton, William, vi. 47
Middilton, see also Middleton
Middleham (Middelham), William, ii. 9, 11, 16, 21
Middleton, Christopher, ix. 61 & n
Middleton, Gilbert (de), i. 10, 34, 57, 79, 116; ii. 26; iii. 61, 70; iv. 26n; v. 66, 68; vi. 107; vii. 43; viii. 49
Middleton, John de (c. 1324–8, ? J. de M. c. 1325–9), xi. 32
Middleton, John de (c. 1325–9, ? J. de M. c. 1324–8), v. 28, 40
Middleton, John de (c. 1337), viii. 8
Middleton, John de (c. 1361), xi. 25
Middleton, John de (c. 1379–99, ? J. de M. c. 1382), iv. 27, 29; vi. 44; xi. 68n, 75 & n; xii. 59(bis)
Middleton, John de (c. 1382, ? J. de M. c. 1379–99), viii. 23
Middleton, John de (d. 1394), ii. 4, 20; xii. 46
Middleton, Leonard, ix. 62
Middleton, Richard de, xi. 46
Middleton (Medylton, Middelton, Middilton), Robert, i. 98; vi. 47; viii. 80; x. 34
Middleton, Thomas (d. 1414), i. 82, 87
Middleton (Myddleton), Thomas de (d. 1396), v. 29; vii. 7; x. 25, 69
Middleton (Myddleton), William, x. 34
Middleton, see also Middilton
Midforde, see Mitford, John de
Mighell, see Mitchell
Milan, see Comite, Philip de
Mildenham, Thomas, iv. 60
Miles, Nicholas, vi. 84; xii. 71
Miles (Fitz Meles), Robert, i. 25; xii. 18
Militiis, see Riccardi
Milliaco, see Milly
Mills (Milly, Mylls), Thomas, x. 15, 31, 44, 66; xii. 84, 85, 86
Mills, see also Mylls
Milly (Milliaco), William de, vi. 31
Milton (Myddelton), William, i. 15; iii. 69, 94; vii. 5, 16, 28; xii. 16
Miltone, John de, xi. 32
Milton(e), see also Multon
Milward (Melward), John, viii. 32
Minutulis, Henry de, i. 114; iii. 54; vi. 76; viii. 4
Miramonte, Raterius de, iii. 39
Mirfield, William, i. 109
Misquinus, see Caraccioli
Mitchell (Mighell), William, iii. 92
Mitchell, see also Michel, Mychell
Mitford (Midforde), John de, vii. 24
Mitford, Richard (de); Walter (de), see Medford
Mitford, see also Metford
Mockyng (Mocking), Nicholas, ii. 36; v. 15; vi. 36; viii. 12; xi. 66 & n
Moclowe, Roger de, x. 61
Moel, John, xi. 43n
Moggys, William, x. 20 & n; xi. 10
Mogryche, John, ix. 63
Mohaut, see Montealto
Mohun, Baldwin de, iii. 93
Molashe, William, iv. 6
Molendino, William de, viii. 16
Moleners (Molineux), John, x. 51
Moleners, see also Molineux, Molyneux
Molens, see Moleyns
Molet, John, iv. 26
Moleyns (Molens), Adam, i. 30; iii. 4, 12, 34; v. 67; vi. 87; vii. 3, 15, 18; viii. 16, 70; x. 26; xi. 42; xii. 19
Mitford, see also Metford
Moleyns (Molens), Simon, vii. 6, 49

Molineux, Edward, iii. 35, 51, 70
Molineux, John, *see* Moleners
Molineux, *see also* Molyneux
Molton, James de, ix. 33
Molton, Roger de, ix. 23
Molyneux, Henry, ix. 57
Molyneux, *see also* Moleners, Molineux
Mome, *see* Monie
Mona, *see* Mone, Guy
Mondoule, Robert, x. 9
Mone (Mona, Moon, Moone), Guy (de), i.
    111; ii. 32; iii. 49, 56, 102; v. 15, 23;
    vii. 17–18, 41; viii. 4n, 25; xi. 54
Mone, Robert, *see* Monie
Mongeham, Stephen, iv. 6
Monie, Robert, i. 79 ('Mome *or* Mone'); x.
    54 ('Mome'); xii. 30, 85
Monkton, William, vi. 16, 40
Monlyshe (Moulissh), Martin, iii. 39
Monmouth, Alexander de, xi. 21, 23
Monmouth, John de, xi. 21 & n
Montacute (Montagu), Simon (de), i. 111;
    iii. 78; iv. 7, 13, 56; vi. 39; viii. 13;
    ix. 28; xii. 39
Montacute (Montagu), Thomas, iii. 4; xii. 52
Montealto (Mohaut), Benedict de (Benet ab
    Iorwerth), xi. 40 & n
Monte Florum, Dalmacius de, iii. 100
Monte Florum, Parvulus de, iii. 73
Monte Florum, Paul de, i. 20, 31, 48, 95; v.
    47; vi. 42; xii. 19
Monte Martini, Edward de (c. 1307, ? Odard
    de M.M.), ii. 34; xii. 49
Monte Martini, Imbert de, vii. 48
Monte Martini, Odard de (c. 1304–8, ? Ed-
    ward de M.M.), v. 62; vii. 48
Monte Martini, Perrin de, vii. 55
Monte Martini, Poinchard de, vi. 33, 64
Montenigro, Richard de, i. 45
Monte Peliologo, Anthony de, x. 16, 64
Monter, Robert, i. 97
Monterac, *see* Gorce
Monte S. Silvestri, Arnold de, iii. 15
Montfort, Almaric de, v. 34
Montfort, William de, v. 43
Montfort, *see also* Mountford
Montgomery, Robert, xi. 62, 78
Monyngton, Hugh de, *see* Monyton
Monyngton, Walter de, viii. 1, 60
Monyns, John, viii. 17
Monyton (Monyngton), Hugh de, viii. 33n;
    ix. 20, 34; xi. 12
Mooke, William, vi. 84
Moon(e), *see* Mone, Guy

Moore, John, i. 110
Moore, William (c. 1518–36), iv. 60 & n
Moore, William (d. 1541), i. 13, 115; vi. 54
Moore, *see also* More
Moot, Geoffrey, ii. 14
Moraunt (Morandi), Jordan (de), vii. 51;
    viii. 10
Morcester, Richard de, ix. 12, 19, 23
Mordon (Sottewell), Thomas, ii. 25; v. 16
More, Edward, vii. 14, 19, 20, 53
More, John, x. 38
More, Richard, ix. 12, 15 & n, 60
More, Robert de la, xi. 24
More, Thomas (de), i. 25, 78; ii. 29, 36; iii.
    85; v. 6, 13, 29, 51; vi. 67; xi. 70 & n
More, Walter, viii. 60
More, William (d. 1456), vi. 57
More, William (c. 1458), vii. 43
More, *see also* Moore
Morehay, John, viii. 69
Morel, John *dictus*, vi. 58, 64
Morel, Othoninus *dictus*, *see* Salinis
Moreland, William, iii. 31; v. 34
Morer (Merer), John, viii. 9, 23
Moresby (Morsby), Richard, i. 9, 67; v. 8,
    42; vi. 57; viii. 18
Moreton, John (d. 1440), *see* Morton
Moreton, John de (d. 1398), x. 32, 45
Moreton, *see also* Morton
Morewell, Ralph, ix. 52
Morewood, Henry, x. 33
Morgan ab Einion, xi. 61 & n, 85
Morgan, David, xi. 27n
Morgan, Henry, i. 79, 102; xi. 29
Morgan, Huw, xi. 6, 10n
Morgan (Young), John, v. 60; xi. 55, 65; xii.
    64
Morgan, Lawrence, xi. 28
Morgan, Philip (d. 1435), i. 37; iv. 14, 29, 57;
    vi. 4; xii. 66
Morgan, Philip (c. 1512–21), i. 44, 94
Morgan, Thomas, xi. 34
Morgan, William, i. 40
Moricotti, *see* Prignano
Moriel, *see* Lavenham
Morpath, Stephen, viii. 41, 58
Mors, William, viii. 24
Morsby, *see* Moresby
Mortemart, Peter (de), i. 10, 116; vi. 13, 75,
    92
Morteyn, Edmund de, ii. 32; vi. 82
Mortimer (de Mortuo Mari), Robert, viii. 3,
    13
Mortimer, Roger, ii. 17

Mortimer, William, ii. 19, 24

Mortival, *see* Martival

Morton (Moreton), John (d. 1440), iii. 98; vii. 9; xii. 57

Morton, John (c. 1454), vii. 12n

Morton (Bovy), John (d. 1459), ix. 49

Morton, John (d. 1463), viii. 38, 75

Morton, John (d. 1500), i. 5, 9, 13, 55; iii. 10, 52, 62; iv. 5, 15, 27(*bis*), 29, 51; v. 31, 45, vi. 72; viii. 43 & n, 62; ix. 56; x. 14 & n; xii. 14, 15, 24

Morton, Richard, ii. 37

Morton, Robert, i. 102, 119; iii. 62; iv. 51, 58, 61; v. 31, 32; vi. 61, 83; xii. 41

Morton, Thomas (d. 1449), ii. 27; iii. 21; vi. 70; vii. 41

Morton, Thomas (d. 1496), iv. 19; viii. 30, 64

Morton, Thomas (c. 1482–99, ? T.M. d. 1511), x. 22

Morton, Thomas (d. 1511, ? T.M. c. 1482–1499), ii. 6, 7, 27; xii. 44

Morton (Moreton), William, vi. 9, 36; ix. 55

Morton, *see also* Moreton

Mortuo Mari, *see* Mortimer

Morwyk, William, vi. 114

Mory, Henry, viii. 70

Mory, John, vii. 32

Moryn, Walter, viii. 51

Moryson, Richard, iii. 103

Mosslewyke (Sesselwyke), Richard de, xi. 56

Mossylwicke, Gilbert de, xi. 64n

Moston, Thomas de, vi. 76

Mota, John de, iii. 39

Motelet, Henry, xi. 29

Motini, Floreanus, iii. 45

Motoun, Henry, i. 18, 89

Motte, Gaillard de la, i. 14, 25, 91, 108; iii. 19; iv. 17; vii. 7; viii. 54; ix. 12n; xii. 33, 53

Mottrum (Mottrom), Adam, iii. 15, 63; iv. 8, 18; vi. 49; xii. 52, 55, 58(*bis*), 70

Moule, *see* Moylle

Moulissh, *see* Monlyshe

Mountford, Baldwin, x. 31

Mountford, *see also* Montfort

Mowbray, John, vi. 67, 86

Moylle (Moule, Mowle), Edward, v. 31

Mucheldevere (Micheldevere), Stephen de, iii. 61

Muchelney, Ralph de, viii. 52

Mugge, William (de), ix. 11, 20, 34; x. 67

Mulakyn, Zanobius, i. 10

Mulcastre, John, viii. 29

Mulleborn, *see* Melbourne, John de

Mulsho, William, i. 33

Multon, Robert, iv. 59

Multon, Simon de, vi. 35; xii. 69

Multon, Walter de, vii. 46

Multon, *see also* Milton(e)

Mundeham, Roger, i. 23

Murimuth, Adam (d. 1370), v. 38; ix. 26

Murimuth (Murymuth), Adam (de) (d. 1347), ii. 15; v. 35, 49; viii. 51; ix. 7, 25; xi. 11; xii. 87

Murimuth, Richard (de), i. 31; v. 52

Murimuth (Murymuth), Thomas de, viii. 51

Musard, Thomas, iv. 59

Muschamp, Elias, i. 52, 106; xii. 23

Muskham, Robert, ii. 50

Mychell, Sampson, vii. 23

Mychell, *see also* Michel, Mitchell

Myddelton, *see* Milton

Myddleton, *see* Middleton, Thomas de; William

Myle, Henry, ii. 9, 51

Myll, William, ii. 46

Mylls, John, x. 56

Mylls, Thomas, *see* Mills

Myllyng, Thomas, ii. 2

Myntryn, Thomas, iii. 101

Myrion, Richard, xi. 15

Nadale, William, iii. 102

Nahim, Henry, xi. 82

Nans, John, ii. 25, 47; viii. 12, 52 ('Hans'); ix. 60; xii. 76, 79

Nant, Dafydd, xi. 44

Nantolio, Peter de, viii. 19; xii. 77

Naples, cardinal of (? Nicholas Caraccioli *or* Misquinus), iii. 7 & n, 19

Naples, Piero Tomacelli of, *see* Tomacelli

Napton, Elias de, x. 16, 34

Napton, *see also* Knapton

Nardini, Stephen, iii. 4

Nase, John, vii. 51; viii. 62

Nash, Thomas, i. 126

Nassh, Roger, xi. 74

Nassington, Henry (de), i. 40; iii. 53; xii. 21

Nassington, John (de) (d. 1334), i. 18; vi. 34, 71, 92, 113

Nassington, John de (d. 1349), ix. 20, 27

Nassington, Robert de, vi. 10

Nassington, Roger (de), i. 94, 123; ii. 39; viii. 18; x. 9, 32; xii. 41

Nassington, Thomas de, vi. 71; ix. 13, 27

Nassington, William de, iii. 21; ix. 27

Navarre, *see* Porta

Navenby, *see* Eyvill

Navesby, Stephen de, xi. 27
Navesby, William (de), i. 43, 83, 123, 126; iv. 41; v. 25; vii. 24; x. 13; xii. 22, 31
Neapoleonis, Francis, *see* Orsini
Neel, John, vii. 6
Neel, Robert, vii. 9, 16, 28
Nele, William, xi. 67
Nerii, Philip, de Antilla, x. 71
Nerii, Thomas, of Florence, x. 58
Nesfield, John, i. 50
Nessingwick, William, iii. 6, 50, 77, 90
Netheravon, Richard de, iii. 86
Nettleton, Robert de, viii. 67
Neubald (Neubold), Peter, *see* Dalton
Neubald, Neubold, *see also* Newbald, Newbold
Neuby, Thomas, i. 41; xii. 21
Neucroft, Roger, i. 10, 46
Neuhagh, William de, x. 8, 13, 21, 26, 30
Neuport (Newport), John de, viii. 37, 63
Neuport, *see also* Newport, Nuporte
Neuton, William de, x. 37
Neuton, *see also* Neweton, Newton, Nyweton
Neuyn, Matthew de, xi. 17
Neville, Alexander de, vi. 4, 35, 112; ix. 15; xi. 38n
Neville, George, i. 11, 117; iii. 40; vi. 5, 67, 113; ix. 2 & n, 54; xii. 15, 40, 66
Neville, John, i. 122
Neville, Robert (d. 1457), i. 92; iii. 2; vi. 55, 65, 108; xii. 34
Neville, Robert (d. 1550), x. 41
Neville, Thomas (c. 1395–1415), iv. 46, 47
Neville, Thomas de (c. 1306), x. 11
Neville, Thomas (de) (c. 1319–22), i. 16; xi. 30; xii. 16
Neville, Thomas de (d. 1361), vi. 35 & n; xii. 69
Neville, Thomas (de) (d. 1363), i. 98; vi. 35n, 59(*bis*), 112; xii. 35, 70(*bis*), 73
Newark, Alan de, vi. 112; xii. 73
Newark, *see also* Newerk
Newbald, Robert, v. 31; viii. 59; xii. 63
Newbald, *see also* Neubald
Newbold, William, v. 20
Newbold, *see also* Neubold
Newburgh, Lewis, xi. 7, 16
Newcastle, David, xi. 31
Newcourt (Nywcourt), John, v. 57
Newenham, John (de), i. 84; viii. 20, 34; x. 21, 55, 66; xi. 26
Newenham, Thomas, xi. 31
Newerk, Henry de, v. 21n
Newerk, *see also* Newark

Neweton, John de, vi. 14, 46; xii. 67, 69
Neweton, *see also* Neuton, Newton, Nyweton
Newland, John, iv. 28
Newman, John, vi. 88
Newport, David, *see* Nuporte
Newport, Gregory, x. 18, 30, 38
Newport, John de (c. 1366–70), *see* Neuport
Newport, John de (d. by 1374), v. 53
Newport, John (de) (d. 1411), i. 20, 35; x. 60
Newport, Richard (d. 1436), xi. 67, 77
Newport, Richard (d. 1514), iii. 50, 68, 97
Newport, Richard de (d. 1318), v. 1, 5, 11, 13 & n, 43 & n; xii. 62
Newport, William de (d. 1366), vi. 85
Newport (Neuport), William (de) (d. 1436), ix. 50; x. 9, 17, 35, 44, 46; xi. 64 & n
Newport, *see also* Neuport, Nuporte
Newton (Nyweton), Henry, ii. 36, 44
Newton, Hugh, i. 31
Newton (Nyweton), John, iii. 38
Newton (Nyweton), Nicholas de, ii. 46; iii. 82; viii. 23; ix. 15, 35; xi. 29
Newton, Philip, iii. 67
Newton, William (c. 1397–1410), i. 27
Newton, William (d. 1547), iv. 30
Newton, *see also* Neuton, Neweton, Nyweton
Neylson, Thomas, x. 46
Nianser, John, i. 9n
Nicholas ab Elys (Elis), xi. 10n
Nicholas ap Philip, xi. 47
Nichole (Sudbury), John, ii. 29
Nicholls, Benedict (Nicholas Benet), xi. 4 & n, 54
Nicholls, Edmund, xi. 14, 60, 70, 76, 77n
Nicholls, Gilbert, xi. 74
Nicholls, William, xi. 64
Nigris, Lawrence de, i. 121
Nigro, Natavus de, of Genoa, i. 85
Nix (Nik, Nyk, Nykke, Nyx), Richard, iv. 25; vi. 52; viii. 14 & n, 80; ix. 14, 58
Nix (Nykke), William, viii. 14, 55
Noel, Robert, viii. 37
Noell, Thomas, ix. 6
Noel(l), *see also* Nowell
Noellet, William, iv. 33
Noion, William, i. 84; vi. 42, 46; vii. 16, 21
Nonnington (Noningtone), Richard de, ii. 14(*bis*)
Nook, John, xi. 56
Nooke, Robert, vi. 30
Norbury, Thomas, v. 36
Norbury, William, vii. 13, 17, 20, 40, 46
Normanby, Richard de, ix. 26

Normanton (Northmanton), Hugh, i. 31, 55, 79, 96, 111, 116; xii. 31, 39
Normanton, William, iii. 34, 44, 48, 50, 94, 98; vii. 12, 15
Normanville, Ralph de, x. 17
Norreys, Richard, vii. 57; ix. 32, 34
Norris, *see* Sugar
Northburgh (Northborough), Michael (de) (d. 1361), i. 31; ii. 17; iii. 64, 73; iv. 32; v. 2, 33, 46; vi. 46, 80; vii. 44, 48; x. 7, 13, 35, 45, 58, 68; xii. 19
Northburgh (Fre), Michael de (d. 1383), v. 13, 22; vii. 44
Northburgh, Peter de, x. 21, 37, 68
Northburgh, Roger (de) (d. 1358), i. 65, 108; ii. 39; iii. 37, 97; v. 5 & n, 51; vi. 25, 93; x. 1; xi. 80; xii. 26, 38, 49
Northburgh, Roger de (d. 1367), x. 27, 32, 42, 53
Northburgh, William de, x. 32
Northew, Simon, v. 12; vii. 60
Northflete, Thomas (de), i. 36; v. 28, 66; xii. 20, 63
Northmanton, *see* Normanton
Northorp, Richard, ii. 11
Northwell, Richard, v. 67
Northwell, Robert de, v. 32
Northwell, William de, x. 39
Northwode (Norwode), John (de) (d. 1349), i. 108; ix. 12, 17–18, 27, 28, 30(*bis*); xii. 38
Northwode, John de (c. 1366), iii. 77
Northwode, Otto de, vii. 16; ix. 10n, 13, 18n, 33
Northwode (Norwood), Richard, i. 17, 18
Northwode (Northwood), Simon de, ii. 17; xii. 46
Northwode (Norwood), Thomas (de) (d. 1354, ? Thomas, c. 1326/7), i. 5, 6, 18n, 22, 97, 124; vii. 15; xii. 16, 35
Norton, Gervase, vii. 35
Norton, John (d. 1402), iii. 17; vii. 31
Norton, John (d. 1462), iii. 10, 12, 32, 62
Norton, John (d. 1472), x. 62
Norton, Richard, i. 73; ix. 8, 21, 60; xii. 29
Norton, Roger, v. 59
Norton, William (c. 1400–15, ? W.N. c. 1402–4 or W. (de) N. c. 1385–6), vii. 15
Norton, William (c. 1402–4, ? W.N. c. 1400–15 or W. (de) N. c. 1385–6), i. 35
Norton, William (de) (c. 1385–6, ? W.N. c. 1400–15 or W.N. c. 1402–4), v. 23n; vi. 67; x. 30; xii. 85
Norwich, John, i. 5n

Norwich (Norwico), Richard de, iii. 27; iv. 27; v. 46
Norwich, William, i. 31
Norwich, *see also* Bateman
Norwico, *see* Norwich
Norwode, Norwood, *see* Northwode
Norwyco, *see* Bateman
Nottingham, John (c. 1340), i. 3n
Nottingham, John (de) (d. 1418), *see* Notyngham
Nottingham, Nicholas, i. 45
Nottingham, Richard, x. 4
Notyngham, Hugh de, vii. 56
Notyngham (Notingham, Nottingham, Nottyngham), John (de), ii. 12; v. 30; vi. 14, 24, 55, 63; vii. 18; viii. 29, 50: x. 40, 49, 69; xii. 45, 63, 67
Novodompno, Bernard de, vi. 73
Nowell, Edmund, viii. 33
Nowell, Richard, ii. 7
Nowell, *see also* Noel(l)
Nuporte (Newport), David, xi. 31
Nuporte, *see also* Neuport, Newport
Nyk, Nykke, *see* Nix
Nywcourt, *see* Newcourt
Nyweton, Henry (d. 1439), *see* Newton
Nyweton, Henry (c. 1322–3), ix. 9, 26
Nyweton, John; Nicholas de, *see* Newton
Nyweton, *see also* Neuton, Neweton, Newton
Nyx, *see* Nix

Obert, the Roman, v. 59
Obezis, *see* Opizis
Ock, William, i. 43
Ockham, William, i. 17(*bis*), 18, 32; xii. 16
Odecumbe, William de, viii. 29, 49, 59, 72
Odeland (Wodelond), John, ix. 51(*bis*)
Odyncells, Henry, i. 60
Offord (Dufford, Ufford), Andrew de, iii. 27, 73, 78; v. 11; vi. 15, 66, 71; viii. 34
Offord (Dufford, Ufford), John (de) (d. 1349), i. 4, 50, 79, 85; ii. 48; iii. 100; iv. 3, 17; v. 62; vi. 6, 66; viii. 33, 77; x. 12; xii. 51
Offord (Dufford, Ufford), John (de) (d. 1375), i. 72; iii. 66; iv. 33; xii. 28, 60
Offord (Dufford, Ufford), Thomas de, vi. 71
Ogle, Humphrey, ii. 8, 21, 35
Oglethorpe, Owen, i. 73
Okeborne, William de, iii. 33
Okle, Thomas, vii. 35, 42
Oldelond, *see* Odeland, Veteri Terra
Oldham, Bernard, ix. 12 & n, 17, 61 & n
Oldham, Hugh, i. 81; iii. 23, 74; v. 52; vi. 43; ix. 3, 14, 59; x. 26, 39; xii. 31

Oldham, William, iii. 95

Oldington (Aldyngton, Oldyngton), Thomas de, iii. 78; vi. 86

Oleari, Bartholomew, vi. 22

Olham, see Elham, John de (d. 1331)

Oliver, David, xi. 79

Oliver, John (c. 1349–50), iii. 80

Olneye, Ralph de, iii. 69

Olton, see Aulton, Elton

Olyver (Smythe), John (d. 1552), ii. 27, 39; iii. 91; xii. 48

Oo, see Ewe, Ho

Opizis (Obezis), John, vi. 34; viii. 23

Opizo, see Malaspina

Oppy, see Uppy

Oreby, John, iii. 62

Orell (Oryll), William, x. 56; xii. 85

Orewelle (Orwell), Thomas, xi. 24, 26, 33

Orford, Robert de, iv. 13, 16

Orgrave, Thomas de, vi. 28, 50; viii. 23; ix. 16, 38

Orleton, Adam de, ii. 1; iv. 45, 56; viii. 67

Orleton, John de, ii. 35, 37; iv. 62; viii. 67; xii. 49

Orleton, Thomas de, ii. 12

Orleyns, William de, xi. 58

Orsini (Ursinus), Angelus, ix. 25

Orsini, Francis Neapoleonis (d. 1311/12), iv. 62

Orsini (Ursini), Francis, son of Neapoleo (d. 1348), i. 65; vi. 13, 92; x. 7; xii. 26, 67, 72

Orsini (de Filiis Ursi, de Ursinis, FitzUrse, Ursinus), James, i. 12; iii. 4; vi. 112 & n; xii. 73

Orsini, John Gaetani de, see Gaetani

Orsini (de Ursinis, Ursinus), Marinus, iii. 14

Orsini, Neapoleo, i. 113; vi. 41

Orsini, Poncellus, i. 12, 13

Orsini (de Ursinis, Ursinus), Raynald, i. 12, 95; iii. 4; xii. 34

Orsini (de Ursinis, Ursinus), Thomas, de Manupello, iii. 4

Orsini, Ursus, de Urbe, i. 94; vi. 15, 68–9

Orton, Thomas, x. 57, 64

Orton, see also Horton

Orum, John, vi. 51; viii. 52; ix. 9, 16n, 20, 47

Orwell, see Orewelle

Oryll, see Orell

Osanne, Robert, i. 60; xii. 25

Osbern, John, viii. 33

Osbern, see also Osborn

Osberton, William de, xi. 65

Osborn, Walter, viii. 30, 64

Osborn, see also Osbern

Osger (Eseger), Adam, ii. 25

Osgodby (Osgodeby), Adam (de), iii. 37; vi. 84; viii. 81

Osgodby (Osgodeby), Richard de, iii. 37; vi. 84

Osgodby (Osgodeby), William, iii. 25, 32, 34, 45

Osmundeston, William (de), i. 103; iii. 39; xii. 36, 37

Oswestry, Richard de, xi. 49

Oteley, Thomas, vii. 14

Otery, Roger (d. 1387), ii. 28

Otery, Roger de (d. 1314), ix. 4, 8, 24

Otringham, Richard de, x. 50

Oudeby, John de, see Outheby

Oudeby, Walter, ii. 38; v. 39; ix. 57

Oudeby, see also Outheby

Ouseflet, see Usflet

Outheby (Awdeby, Oudeby), John de, ii. 50; x. 11, 16, 19, 21

Outheby, see also Oudeby

Outy, William, ii. 8

Overay, Thomas, viii. 7, 9, 41, 43n ('Overary'); xii. 76(bis), 79(bis)

Overtone, Thomas de, viii. 53

Ovingham, Richard, i. 107

Ovingham, see also Hovyngham

Owain, Dafydd (d. by 1558), xi. 46

Owain, Dafydd ab (d. 1513), see Dafydd ab Owain

Owain, Huw ab, see Huw ab Owain

Owain, Lewis, ab Owain (Bowen), xi. 63, 85

Owain, Richard, xi. 78

Owayn, Thomas, iii. 22

Owen, Richard, viii. 14n

Owren, Thomas, vi. 57

Oxenbrigge, John, vii. 26

Oxenden, Robert, iv. 6

Oxendon, see Oxyndon

Oxford, see Ho

Oxne, John, iv. 6

Oxonia, John de, vii. 58

Oxton, Robert de, vi. 83; x. 15

Oxton, Thomas, x. 33

Oxyndon (Oxendon), John de, ii. 20; iii. 63

Pace (Pacy), Richard, iii. 5, 8, 47; v. 7, 14, 38; ix. 5, 63; x. 12n

Packington, see Pakington

Pacy, see Pace

Padarn, Griffin, xi. 71

Page, Roger (d. 1393), viii. 29

Page, Roger (c. 1406), vii. 60

Pagliano, *see* Picalotti

Paine, *see* Payn(e)

Pakenham, Hugh, vi. 63

Pakenham, John, iv. 51; v. 71; vi. 14, 63, 81; viii. 36; xii. 60

Pakington (Packington, Pakyngton, Pakynton, Pekynton), William (de), i. 32, 80; iv. 8; v. 46; vi. 75; vii. 47; x. 6; xii. 20, 31

Palgrave, John, v. 57

Palmer, George, vi. 54

Palmer, Richard, viii. 65; ix. 46

Palmerna, *see* Polmorva

Palosius, Stephen, vii. 4

Pannell, Thomas, vii. 39

Pantry, Henry, xi. 78

Parfew, *see* Wharton

Parfit, Robert, ii. 24; viii. 38, 47

Parham (Perham), Thomas, i. 98; viii. 30

Paris, *see* Parys

Parke, John, i. 125; ix. 45

Parkehouse, William, ix. 64(*bis*)

Parkehurst (Parkhurst), Richard, ii. 39; vii. 44

Parker, John, iii. 67; vii. 33

Parker, Richard (c. 1518, ? R.P. d. 1534), iii. 66

Parker, Richard (d. 1534, ? R.P. c. 1518), i. 23, 102, 111

Parker, Robert, iii. 99

Parker, Thomas (d. 1423), i. 47; vi. 28; x. 26, 33

Parker, Thomas (d. 1538), ii. 9, 23, 30; iii. 18

Parkhurst, *see* Parkehurst

Parma, John de, i. 31, 32; xii. 19

Parry, John, *see* John ap Harry

Parry, *see also* Pavy

Parsons, *see* Persons

Partrich, Peter, i. 24, 45

Parys, Baldwin de, x. 59–60

Parys, Major, ix. 49; x. 23

Parys, Thomas, i. 33

Pascal, John, xi. 21

Pascow, John, ix. 56, 58

Paslew, Robert, iii. 38n

Paslewe, John, ii. 21; iii. 22, 34, 44, 69; xii. 47

Passelew, Thomas de, vi. 42n

Passemer (Passmer), Richard, ii. 51; xi. 29 & n

Passemere, William, v. 64, 70 & n

Passemere, *see also* Pesemere

Passhe, Thomas, iii. 70

Passmer, *see* Passemer

Paston, Benedict de, ix. 9n, 26

Paston, Thomas (c. 1540–2), iii. 38

Paston, Thomas de (c. 1342–3), ix. 31

Pate, *see* Pates

Paten, *see* Waynflete, John (d. 1479)

Patenson, William, v. 71

Paterici (Patricii), Bartholomew, vii. 30–1

Pates (Pate), Richard, i. 8, 52, 59, 102, 114; iv. 51; v. 25; vi. 41; viii. 46; xii. 23, 36

Pateshall, Walter, iv. 41n

Pateshull, Peter de, ix. 11n, 32

Patrica (Patrika), Robert de, iii. 76, 87; x. 18, 32, 42, 50

Patricii, *see* Paterici

Patrika, *see* Patrica

Patrington (Thursgate), Robert de, vi. 10

Patrington (Patryngton), Stephen, vii. 2; xi. 54

Patten, *see* Waynflete, John (d. 1479)

Pattesele, Thomas de, iv. 18

Pavy, Hugh (Huw) (d. 1496), iii. 14, 30, 58; viii. 46; xi. 55

Pavy, Huw (c. 1446), xi. 85

Pavy, John, ii. 20

Pavy, William, viii. 43

Paxton, John, v. 32; vii. 34

Paxton, Thomas (de), i. 58; iii. 9, 59; vii. 27; viii. 4

Payn, John, xi. 28 & n

Payn, Roger, viii. 27

Payne, John, iii. 31, 85; xii. 53

Payne, Richard (c. 1479, ? R.P. c. 1507), vii. 31

Payne, Richard (d. 1507, ? R.P. c. 1479), iii. 70; x. 41; xii. 55

Payne, Stephen, ix. 5, 46

Paynot, John, iii. 99

Pays, Thomas, iii. 7; xii. 52

Pearson (Pereson), Thomas, vi. 17; xii. 67

Pearson, *see also* Pirson, Peyrson

Pecham, Clement de, vii. 55

Pecham, Richard (c. 1460), iv. 40

Pecham, Richard de (c. 1363–6), *see* Beltryng

Pecock, Reginald, vii. 3; xi. 38

Pecorariis, Geoffrey de, iii. 91

Pede, Richard, ii. 5, 11, 27, 30, 35; x. 10, 44, 52

Pederton, *see* Petherton

Pedewell, John (c. 1418–52), iii. 6

Pedewell, John (c. 1464), viii. 72

Pedwell (Spedwell), William, i. 44

Peers, William, ix. 42

Peers, *see also* Percy, Peres, Pers, Piers(e)

Peese, John, iii. 58, 103; v. 24, 26

Peese, *see also* Pese
Pekynton, *see* Pakington
Pelegrini, Arnold, iii. 33
Pelegrini, Elias, iii. 73
Pelegrini, Hugh, i. 109; iii. 73; v. 27; x. 11; xii. 38
Pelegrini, Raymond (d. 1365), i. 54; iii. 33, 59; iv. 48; v. 23; viii. 49
Pelegrini, Raymond (c. 1378–86), i. 93
Pelleson, William, vi. 21, 83; xii. 67, 71
Pellican (Pellichon), Thomas, viii. 25; xi. 50
Pemberton, John, iii. 34; v. 24; viii. 64
Pembridge, Thomas de, ii. 10, 18
Pembroke, Walter de, ix. 19n
Pempel, Stephen de, viii. 4; ix. 13, 34, 37
Pencrich (Pencriz), William de (d. 1340), viii. 24; ix. 29; xii. 77
Pencriz, Hugh de, viii. 32
Pencriz, William de, *see* Pencrich
Pencryche (Pencrych), William (d. 1446), ix. 49; xi. 60
Penec, le, *see* Pennock
Penels, Richard, ix. 16, 47
Pennand (Pennaude), John, v. 25; viii. 33
Pennock (le Penec), Peter, i. 37, 100; v. 60
Penny, John, vi. 99; xi. 5
Pennybrooke, Walter, ix. 19n
Penreth, John de, vi. 100
Penwortham, Henry, viii. 28, 69; xii. 78
Penycoke, Lancelot, vii. 19
Penyfader, Richard, viii. 82
Perariis, Thomas de, i. 61; xii. 25
Percehay, William, of Spaldwick, i. 101
Percehay, *see also* Percy, Piers(e)
Perche, John, i. 47; viii. 26
Percy (Perse), Alan, vi. 47
Percy (Perse), George, viii. 26, 55
Percy, John, i. 5
Percy, Thomas, iv. 23; vii. 59
Percy (Perse), William, i. 69, 103; iii. 27; vi. 45, 76, 98; xii. 28, 37
Percy, *see also* Peers, Pers, Piers(e)
Peres, John, *see* Piers
Peres, Roger, iv. 61
Peres, *see also* Peers, Percehay, Pers, Piers(e)
Pereson, *see* Pearson
Perham, *see* Parham
Périgord, Archibald de, i. 6, 48
Périgord, Elias de, *see* Talleyrand
Périgueux, *see* Iterii
Periton (Piriton, Pyreton), Peter de, iii. 7, 26, 47, 100
Periton, *see also* Piriton
Perkinson, John, vi. 40n

Perle, Robert, xi. 28
Perott, John, v. 14, 22, 39; vi. 12
Pers, John, vii. 22, 27
Pers(e) *see also* Peers, Percehay, Percy, Peres, Piers(e)
Persons (Parsons), John, ii. 14, 24; xi. 8; xii. 87
Pert, *see* Spert
Pese, Walter, iii. 96
Pese, *see also* Peese
Pesemere, John, ix. 6
Pesemere, *see also* Passemere
Pestello, Guy de, i. 58; iii. 41; xii. 24
Petelyng, Thomas, i. 47
Peter (c. 1482), viii. 22
Peter, the precentor (13th cent.), v. 41
Peterborough, Henry of, iv. 17
Peterson, *see* Crowham
Petewynne, Walter, ii. 23, 51; vii. 21
Petham, Thomas, i. 107
Petham, *see also* Pettham
Petherton, John (d. 1458), viii. 57
Petherton (Pederton), John (d. 1460), viii. 65
Petherton (Pederton), Walter de, viii. 30; xi. 80
Petir, Richard, vii. 60; xi. 74, 76
Petre, William, i. 75
Petri, *see* Piers
Petteworth, Richard, i. 93, 110 ('Petteworth *or* Pettelborth'); vi. 94; vii. 36, 44; viii. 36; xii. 34, 38
Petteworth, William, vii. 22, 44
Pettham, William, iv. 6
Pettham, *see also* Petham
Peuesy, Robert (d. 1464), viii. 59, 73
Peuesy, *see also* Pevesay
Peverel (Peveral), Thomas, iv. 57; xi. 22 & n
Peverell, Robert, i. 45
Pevesay, Robert (d. 1498), v. 62
Pevesay, *see also* Peuesy
Peynthwyn, Hugh, iii. 26; iv. 9; xii. 58
Peyrson, John, iii. 72
Peyrson, *see also* Pearson, Pirson
Peyworden (Wotton), Matthew, xi. 11
Philip (c. 1319), xi. 59n
Philip ap Hywel (Powell), xi. 61
Philip ap Llywelyn (c. 1423, ? P. Lowys), xi. 25 & n
Philip ap Rees, v. 36
Philip, Hugh, xi. 34
Philip, Nicholas ap, *see* Nicholas ap Philip
Philippes, Rowland, ii. 9, 23; v. 50
Philippi, David, xi. 17
Phillips, Thomas, iii. 7, 99

Philpot, Richard, viii. 77
Phreas, *see* Free
Phylypp, Walter, iv. 41
Picalotti, Thomas, de Pagliano, vi. 88
Pickering, John, v. 33, 52
Pickering, Robert, i. 59; vi. 6, 56, 113
Pickering, William, vi. 6, 23, 52
Picton, Thomas, ii. 29; xi. 67
Pictoris, *see* Sarum
Piel, Henry, i. 11, 15
Piers, John (d. 1344), iii. 39; ix. 17–18, 30; xii. 54, 82
Piers, John (d. 1350), *see* Sarum
Piers, Walter, *see* Pierse
Piers (Pyers), William, viii. 7, 52
Pierse (Piers), Walter, x. 30 & n, 52 & n
Piers(e), *see also* Peers, Percehay, Percy, Peres, Pers
Pigge, Anthony, i. 77; vi. 54(*bis*)
Pigot (Pygot), John (d. 1433, ? J. Piquet), x. 63
Pigot, Thomas, xi. 5
Pigot, *see also* Pygott
Pikman, John, viii. 9, 15, 26, 55
Pilkington, Charles, vi. 80
Pilton, William (de), iii. 36, 57, 101; vi. 18, 45, 74; vii. 18; ix. 4, 14, 46; xi. 29
Pinchbeck, Robert de (c. 1344), xi. 49
Pinchbek (Pynchebek), Robert (de) (d. 1325), i. 96; vi. 71
Pinibus, Raymond de, i. 118
Pinnock, John, iii. 26, 41, 49; xii. 53, 54(*bis*)
Pinnock (Puinoli), Nicholas, ix. 35
Pipard, John (d. 1349), ix. 32
Pipe, John (de), i. 80; x. 15, 65; xii. 31
Pipe, Thomas, viii. 53; xii. 79
Pippard, John (c. 1305–9), x. 27
Piquet, John (c. 1426–32, ? J. Pigot), v. 35
Piriton, Peter de, *see* Periton
Piriton (Piryton), Richard de, v. 13, 32
Pirrye, William, xi. 65, 76
Pirrye, *see also* Pyrie
Pirson, Edward, xi. 79
Pirson, *see also* Pearson, Peyrson
Piryton, Peter de, *see* Periton
Piryton, Richard de, *see* Piriton
Pissiaco, *see* Poissy
Pistorio, Geoffrey de (c. 1328, ? Gualfred de Regalibus), ix. 27 & n
Pittes, John, ix. 53
Pittes, Richard, iii. 102; vi. 14, 20, 51, 55; viii. 39; xii. 57, 67(*bis*), 70(*bis*), 78
Planell, Raymond de, iii. 11
Plente, John, vii. 14, 25n, 38 & n; ix. 57

Plessis, Richard de, v. 13, 50; xii. 62
Ploufeld, John, ii. 36
Plumar (Plumer), Richard, x. 45
Plummer (Plummar), Christopher, i. 122; v. 25; vi. 36; vii. 43; xii. 41
Plumstock (Plumstok), Richard (de), i. 102; viii. 42; ix. 12
Plumstock, William de (c. 1341, ? W. de Borstan, W. de Worston), v. 17
Pobelowe, Robert, vii. 29
Poddesdon, John, ix. 6, 40
Podio Barzaco (Podio Barsiaco, Puy Barzac), John de, i. 79; iv. 50; xii. 31(*bis*)
Podio Barzaco, Pontius (Poncius) de, v. 8, 33; vi. 35
Poissy (Pissiaco), Maurice de, vi. 27
Pole, David, x. 18, 59
Pole (de la Pole), Edward, iii. 16, 64, 72; vi. 23, 26; xii. 55
Pole (Poole), Hugh, ii. 12, 25, 27, 33, 39
Pole (Poole), Humphrey de la, v. 69; xii. 65
Pole, John de la (d. 1304), ii. 26 ('John Pole'); xii. 47
Pole, John de la (d. 1416), vi. 93; xii. 72
Pole (Poole), Oliver, vii. 14
Pole (Poole), Owen (Owain), ii. 11, 46; xi. 46, 59; xii. 45
Pole, Ranulph, ii. 24
Pole, Reginald, iii. 84, 103; vi. 61; ix. 5, 64
Pole (de la Pole, Poole), Thomas, i. 55; v. 22, 31; vi. 49; x. 44; xii. 24
Polgrim, William, xi. 74
Pollard, John, iii. 14; ix. 65
Pollard (Poulard), Robert, ix. 32; xi. 17
Pollard, William, xi. 6
Pollesworth, William, x. 5
Polmorva (Palmerna), William de, v. 12; ix. 6
Polton, Philip, iv. 61
Polton, Thomas, i. 111; ii. 2; iii. 57; iv. 57; v. 3; vi. 7, 60, 81; vii. 2; viii. 16, 39; xii. 39, 44
Pomeray, William de la, ix. 35
Pomfreyt, John, vii. 42
Poninges, *see* Pownyngs
Ponte, John de, ii. 50
Ponteburgh (Boroughbridge), Gilbert de, vi. 77
Pontesbury, Nicholas de, viii. 11, 51
Pontissara (Pontoise), John de, iv. 45
Poole, *see* Pole
Pope, John (d. 1476), viii. 25, 50, 62, 74
Pope, John (d. 1558), i. 126; xii. 42
Porlessy, *see* Torkesey
Porta, Ardricinus de, of Navarre, i. 11

Porta, Stephen la, iii. 71; xii. 55

Portali, John, i. 34

Porter, John, xi. 74

Porter (Portare), William, i. 45, 57; ii. 9, 23; vii. 9, 31, 42, 45; xii. 45, 47

Portinariis, John de Manettis de, of Florence, i. 103

Portington, Thomas, i. 96; vi. 14, 30

Portyngale, see Gomecii

Possewyk, Richard, of Avignon, xi. 82

Postell, Richard, iii. 51

Poteman, William, i. 64; v. 61; vi. 21, 23, 32, 81, 89

Potesgrave, Richard de, iii. 5

Potyn, William, iii. 11

Pouget, Bertrand de, i. 58

Poulard, see Pollard

Poundestoke, William, ix. 41

Pouton, William, ix. 41

Powcher, William, iv. 16

Powell, Dafydd, see Dafydd ap Hywel

Powell, Edward, i. 47, 52, 115; iii. 28, 66; xii. 40

Powell, Henry, see Henry ap Hywel

Powell, John, see John ap Hywel

Powell, John, ap Brython, see John ap Hywel ap Brython

Powell, Philip, see Philip ap Hywel

Powell, Rhys, see Rhys ap Hywel

Powell, Thomas (c. 1487–1512), see Thomas ap Hywel

Powell, Thomas (d. 1551), vii. 51

Powell, see also Pole

Power, John, i. 56; viii. 15, 24, 44

Power, Walter, i. 50, 105; x. 23

Pownyngs (Poninges), Edward, iii. 92; vii. 21

Prat (Pratte), John (d. 1416), ii. 25; xii. 47

Prat (Pratte), John (d. 1513), ii. 48; v. 54; xii. 51

Prata, John, xi. 47, 82

Prata (Prés), Pileus de, i. 49; vi. 112; viii. 35; x. 9

Pratis, Peter de, see Prés

Prato, William de, vi. 71 (William 'de Prés'); xii. 71

Pratte, see Prat

Praty, Richard, iii. 18; vii. 3, 37

Prees, Robert (c. 1361, ? R. de P. c. 1374–1392), vii. 31

Prees (Prots), Robert de (c. 1374–92, ? R.P. c. 1361), iv. 28, 29

Pregeet (Excestre), William (c. 1389, ? W. Excestre, W. de Exeter), xi. 45 & n

Prene, John, i. 78

Prene, Walter, ii. 32

Prentys, Edward, iii. 16, 48, 54, 88; v. 10

Prentys, John, iii. 21, 72; v. 39; vi. 70; xi. 29

Prentys, Richard, iii. 54, 87; v. 10; vii. 38; xi. 13, 45

Prentys, William, iii. 92

Prés (Pratis), Peter de, iv. 41; vi. 17, 93

Prés, Pileus de, see Prata

Prés, William de, see Prato

Prestbury, Ralph, x. 20, 33

Preston, John, v. 29, 39

Preston, Thomas (c. 1404), vi. 35

Preston, Thomas (c. 1452–60), vi. 45

Preston, Walter, v. 62

Preston, William (d. 1488/9, ? John Pryston), viii. 36

Preston, William de (c. 1339–60), x. 17

Price, David, see Dafydd ap Rhys

Price, Gruffudd, see Gruffudd ap Rhys

Price, Iorwerth, see Iorwerth ap Rhys

Price, John, see John ap Rhys

Price, John, ap Roppert, see John ap Rhys ap Roppert

Price, Lewis, see Lewis ap Rhys

Price, Robert, see Robert ap Rhys

Prichard, see John ap Richard

Pricklove, John, vi. 40 & n

Prideaux, John, vii. 31, 34, 43

Prignano (Moricotti, Prignani), Francis, i. 25; iii. 19

Probert, Huw, see Huw ap Robert

Probert, Ithel, see Ithel ap Robert

Probert, John ap Rhys, see John ap Rhys ap Roppert

Proctor, Richard, ii. 13(bis)

Proctour, John, i. 127

Prophete, John (c. 1349), ii. 48

Prophete, John (d. 1416), i. 81, 93; ii. 4, 34, 40, 49; iii. 36, 74; vi. 7, 40, 62; vii. 42; viii. 27, 80; xi. 42

Prophete, Richard, ii. 48

Prots, see Prees

Provane, John, i. 85

Prowet, Alexander, i. 20; xii. 17

Prowett, Robert, i. 36

Pryce, David, see Dafydd ap Rhys

Pryce, Thomas, see Thomas ap Rhys

Pryde, Walter, ii. 22

Prynne, John, i. 6, 23, 71, 91; ii. 26; xii. 14, 28

Pryston, John (d. c. 1490, ? William Preston), viii. 36 & n

Pudsey, William, i. 65

Puinoli, see Pinnock, Nicholas

Puiz, see Puteo
Pulcis, see Sinabaldi
Puleston, Hugh, xi. 44
Puleston, Robert, xi. 44
Pulford, John, x. 23, 44
Pulham, Reginald, vii. 47
Pulle, John de, viii. 73
Pulteneye, John, viii. 65
Pulteneye, Thomas de, iii. 22; ix. 35
Pulter, Thomas, v. 53; x. 41, 48
Pultney, see Swain, Henry
Puntyngdon, William de, ix. 7, 17, 22
Purbior (Purveour), Thomas, v. 48; viii. 55,
    65 & n, 80 & n
Purcell, William, iv. 42
Purveour, see Purbior
Purviour, Robert, viii. 38
Puteo (Puiz), Imbert de, v. 20
Puteoli, John, iv. 37
Puy, Gerard de, vi. 79
Puy Barzac, see Podio Barzaco
Pycard de Carleton, see Carleton, John
    (d. 1405)
Pychard, Robert, vii. 5, 22
Pycott, see Pygott
Pye, John, xi. 15
Pyers, see Piers
Pygott (Pycott), Richard, viii. 38
Pygot(t), see also Pigot
Pyke, Henry de, ix. 6, 33
Pykeman, see Pikman
Pykenham (Pykman), William (d. 1497), i.
    81; iv. 33; v. 69; x. 41; xii. 60
Pykenham, William (d. 1535), iii. 55, 57, 83,
    99, 103; vii. 53
Pykman, see Pykenham, William (d. 1497)
Pykyng, John, ii. 25
Pyl, William le, ix. 38
Pylaton, Ralph, ix. 40
Pyldeston, Robert, xi. 15
Pynchebek, see Pinchbek
Pynge, John de, vii. 56
Pyreton, see Periton
Pyrie, John (de), i. 94; vi. 15
Pyrie, see also Pirrye
Pyville, John, iii. 94, 103

Quarre, John, iii. 95; xi. 25
Querendon, Ralph de, iii. 5, 6, 13, 66; xii. 55
Quixley, Robert, vi. 39

Radcliffe, John, x. 24
Radcliffe, Richard, x. 70
Radclyf, George, x. 12, 13

Radclyffe (Rowcliffe), Roger, iii. 12; v. 6, 34;
    vi. 68; ix. 55
Radclyffe (Radclyff, Rowcliffe), William, v.
    61; vi. 32; x. 12
Radeley (Rodeley), Humphrey, viii. 41; x. 47
Radener, see Redmere
Radewell (Reddeswell), Robert de, x. 12 & n
Radewell, see also Reddeswell, Redeswell
Radyng, see Ruding
Ragenhill, John (John Longespey de Regen-
    hill), i. 18
Ragenhull (Raynhill), Robert, iii. 7, 33, 67,
    94; xii. 52, 53, 55, 57
Raglan, William, xi. 34
Ragon, Miles, ii. 37, 45
Ragone, Hugh, ii. 25, 41, 52
Rainald, see Reynald
Ramberticuria, see Janini
Ramsbury (Remmesbury), Edmund de, iii.
    35
Ramsbury (Remmesbury), Stephen de, iii. 79
Ramsbury, Walter de, ii. 9, 50
Ranato, see Bernardi
Randolff, Thomas, i. 42, 61; iii. 35, 95; v. 60
Rands, see Holbeche
Rapistagno, Beraud (Richard) de (c. 1344,
    ? Jarrard de R.), vi. 40
Rapistagno, Jarrard de (c. 1343-58, ?
    Beraud or Richard de R.), vi. 40n
Rapistagno, Peter Raymond de, iii. 33
Rapistagno, William de, vi. 40
Rashall (Rushall), John, x. 48 & n
Rathur, see Rhaidr
Raulyn, Robert, xi. 67
Raulyn, see also Rawlings, Rawlyns
Raundes, Richard, vii. 19
Ravendale, Robert, x. 42
Ravensdale, Michael de, vi. 53
Ravenser, John (de), i. 49; iii. 75; vi. 56; xii.
    22, 56, 70
Ravenser, Richard (de), i. 4, 6, 49, 63, 123;
    ii. 50; iii. 77, 82; iv. 28; v. 42; vi. 60
Ravenser (del See), Stephen, i. 44, 52, 53; xii.
    22
Ravensworth, Henry de, vi. 76
Rawdon, Nicholas, i. 73; vi. 85
Rawlings, Richard (c. 1535), xi. 69 & n
Rawlings, Richard (d. 1536), see Rawlyns
Rawlings, see also Raulyn
Rawlyns, Henry, i. 61; iii. 13, 47(ter), 50, 55,
    64, 91, 99; viii. 38
Rawlyns (Rawlings, Rawlyngs), Richard,
    i. 10; v. 71; vi. 17, 21; viii. 66; xi. 56
Rawlyns, William, ii. 42

Rawlyns, see also Raulyn

Rawson, Richard, i. 75 ('John or Richard Rawston'); iii. 48; v. 11; vii. 52; viii. 51 & n; xii. 29, 54, 62, 75, 79

Rayader, see Rhaidr

Raymond (c. 1307), vi. 17n

Raymond, John, see Comminges

Raymond, Peter, see Rapistagno

Raymund (c. 1363), iii. 96

Raynald, see Reynald

Raynes (Rayne), John, i. 42, 117; iii. 55; xii. 21, 54

Raynes, see also Rayns, Reynes

Raynhill, see Ragenhull

Rayns, Thomas, viii. 42

Rayns, see also Raynes, Reynes

Reade (Rede), William, iii. 67; vii. 7, 9, 10, 12n, 26, 32

Reade, see also Rede, Reed

Reddeswell, Robert de (d. 1315), see Radewell

Reddeswell, Robert de (d. 1337), v. 11, 15, 43n, 44, 66

Reddeswell, see also Radewell, Redeswell

Rede, Lewis, see Llywelyn ap Madog

Rede, Robert, vi. 98; vii. 2

Rede, William (d. 1385), see Reed

Rede, William (d. 1411), see Reade

Redehill, Redehull, see Reedhill

Redeswell, John de, vii. 57; ix. 28

Redeswell, see also Radewell, Reddeswell

Redman, John (c. 1527–8, ? J.R. d. 1551), vii. 54

Redman (Reedman), John (d. 1551, ? J.R. c. 1527–8), x. 20

Redman, Richard, see Redmayn

Redman, Thomas, ix. 14, 44

Redmayn, John (d. 1558), viii. 17

Redmayn (Redman), Richard, iv. 15; ix. 3; xi. 39 & n

Redmere, Giles, i. 27 ('Radener'); xii. 18

Redyng, Robert de, vii. 58

Reed, John, i. 57; vii. 17, 33 & n

Reed (Rede), William, iv. 41 & n; vii. 1

Reed, see also Reade, Rede

Reedhill (Redehill, Redehull), John, iii. 56, 77; x. 49 & n, 62 & n

Reedman, see Redman

Rees, David ap, see Dafydd ap Rhys

Rees, John (d. 1353), ii. 27; xii. 48

Rees, John (c. 1368), see Rhys

Rees, Nicholas, vii. 7

Rees, Philip ap, see Philip ap Rees

Rees, Robert, see Rhys

Rees, Thomas ap, see Thomas ap Rhys

Regalibus, Gualfred de (c. 1327, ? Geoffrey de Pistorio), ix. 27 & n

Regenhill, see Ragenhill

Reigate, Nicholas de, ii. 10, 50

Reissaco, see Durfort

Remmesbury, see Ramsbury

Remston, Robert, of Corffe, viii. 74

Renzio, Francis, de Alifia, vi. 22, 48

Repham, John, vi. 114

Repingdon, see Repyngton

Repington, Philip, i. 2

Repington, see also Repynton

Repps (Rugg, Rugge, Rygge), William, iv. 25

Repton, John, x. 22

Repyngton (Repingdon, Repynton), Ralph (de), iii. 9, 96; v. 15; vii. 41, 48; x. 64; xi. 66

Repynton, John, xi. 44

Repynton, see also Repington

Resano, James de, vii. 54

Resteshale, Henry de, of Campeden (Henry de Campeden), ii. 32; v. 18, 61; xii. 49

Restwald, Ralph, iii. 30

Restwold, William de, vii. 58

Retford, Alan de, vii. 56

Retford, John, viii. 30

Retford, Richard de, ii. 32; vi. 66, 82

Retford, Thomas de, viii. 8, 30

Retford (Roteford), William (de), i. 53; iii. 56; v. 30; vi. 15

Revel, John (c. 1308, ? J. Rivet), vii. 6

Revell, see Ryvell

Rewys, Nicholas, xi. 6n

Reymund, William, see Banqueto

Reynald (Rainald, Raynald), John (d. 1506), vi. 21, 30, 80; xii. 68(bis), 71

Reynald, Thomas, see Reynold

Reynald, see also Reynold, Rynald

Reynes, Thomas, i. 124

Reynes, see also Raynes, Rayns

Reynham, John de (d. by 1349), vii. 48

Reynham, John de (d. by 1351), ix. 20, 32

Reynham, William de, v. 18, 52

Reynold, John (d. 1450), viii. 12, 26, 55

Reynold (Reynald), Thomas, x. 24, 28, 51, 62, 64, 66

Reynold, see also Reynald, Rynald

Reynolds, Thomas (d. 1559, ? T. Rynald), ix. 66

Reynolds, Walter, iv. 3, 55; v. 66; xi. 11

Reys, see Rhys

Rhaidr (Rathur, Rayader), Richard, v. 68; xi. 72

Rhiwlas (Ryulas), Maurice, xi. 59

Rhuddallt (Rudallt), Dafydd de, xi. 12

Rhydderch (Ruddock), Henry, xi. 56

Rhys ap Hywel (ap Howel, Powell), iii. 84; v. 37; xi. 80; xii. 90

Rhys, Dafydd ap, *see* Dafydd ap Rhys

Rhys, Gruffudd ap, *see* Gruffudd ap Rhys

Rhys, Iorwerth ap, *see* Iorwerth ap Rhys

Rhys (Rees, Reys, Rice), John, xi. 47(*bis*)

Rhys, John ap, *see* John ap Rhys

Rhys, Lewis ap, *see* Lewis ap Rhys

Rhys (Rees, Reys, Rice), Robert (c. 1361), xi. 58

Rhys, Robert ap (c. 1513–18), *see* Robert ap Rhys

Rhys, Thomas ap, *see* Thomas ap Rhys

Rhys, *see also* Rees, Ryse

Riby, Thomas, i. 53

Ricardi, Hugh, viii. 83

Ricardi Mathie, John, de Urbe, i. 92; xii. 34

Riccardi, Aldebrand, de Militiis, v. 9, 52

Riccardi, Richard, de Anibaldis, of Rome (Richard, son of Anibaldus Riccardi de Urbe) (d. 1329, ? Richard Riccardi de Militiis), 92; x. 14; xii. 34

Riccardi, Richard, de Militiis, of Rome (early 14th cent., ? Richard Riccardi de Anibaldis), v. 52;

Rice, *see* Rhys

Richard, John ap, *see* John ap Richard

Richardson, *see* Hochynson

Riche, *see* Roche, John

Richman, Richard, i. 60; iii. 69

Rider, *see* Ryder

Ridley, Robert, v. 45, 49, 55

Ringstede (Ryngstede), Ralph de, ix. 32; xi. 12

Ringstede, Roger de, vii. 57

Ringstede, Thomas (d. 1454), i. 42, 49; ii. 33; vii. 22; xii. 21

Ringstede, Thomas de (d. 1366), xi. 3

Ripariis, *see* Rivers

Ripon, Richard, i. 35

Ripon, Roger de, vi. 11, 20

Ripon, *see also* Rypon

Ripplingham, Robert de, vi. 9, 37 & n

Ripplingham, Thomas, i. 18

River, John (c. 1444–78), vii. 52; viii. 36

Rivers (de Ripariis), John (c. 1331–43), iii. 75; xii. 56

Rivet, John (c. 1306, ? J. Revel), vii. 6

Rivet, John (d. 1465), *see* Ryvet

Riviere, William de la, iii. 82

Rixton, *see* Ryssheton

Robelyn (Bokelyn, Rokelin), Adam (de), ii. 25; xi. 60

Robert (c. 1290), xi. 23

Robert ap Rhys, xi. 48

Robert the monk (13th cent.), v. 60

Robert, Aymer, vi. 22, 86

Robert, Huw ap, *see* Huw ap Robert

Robert, Ithel ap, *see* Ithel ap Robert

Robert, Thomas, xi. 34

Roberti, William (c. 1363), i. 95

Roberts, William (d. 1562), xi. 11

Robertson, Thomas, i. 68, 73, 122, 128; iii. 21

Robinson, John, iii. 7; xii. 52

Robinson, Richard, iv. 19

Robyns, John, xi. 7, 16

Roche, Androynus de la, iv. 18; vi. 35, 60; xii. 70

Roche, Aymar, iv. 7

Roche (Riche, Ryche), John, viii. 47, 65

Rochester (Roff'), Solomon de, v. 28 & n

Rochford, Richard de, ix. 36

Rocombe, William, iv. 63

Rodbourne, Rodburn, *see* Rudborne

Rodebourne, Robert, iv. 47

Rodebourne, *see also* Rudborne

Rodeley, *see* Radeley

Rodeneye, Richard de, viii. 41, 55, 78

Roderic, Peter, i. 91; iii. 95

Rodmarleye, *see* Rudmarley

Rodolphucci (Rodolfucii), Luke (Lucas), de Gentilibus, i. 41; x. 25

Roff', *see* Rochester

Roger (d. 1352), xi. 27

Roger (c. 1368), iv. 41

Roger, Peter, iv. 7

Rogers, Edward, viii. 79; xii. 81

Rogers, James, i. 28, 83; iii. 76; viii. 68

Roiston (Smith), Richard (? R. Smythe), i. 47, 51, 55, 59, 96; xii. 22, 23, 24, 25, 35

Roiston, *see also* Cruce Roys, Royston

Rokeby, William, iv. 49; viii. 46n

Rokelin, *see* Robelyn

Roland, John, viii. 18, 20, 25, 44, 72; xi. 29; xii. 77, 79

Rolfe, Hugh, vii. 11, 17, 32, 40

Roll, William, vii. 38

Rolleston, Robert, i. 45; iii. 85; v. 57; vi. 45, 90n, 113; ix. 49

Roman, *see* Laurence the Roman, Obert the Roman

Rome, John (d. 1415, ? J.R. d. by Jan. 1417), i. 126

Rome, John (d. by Jan. 1417, ? J.R. d. 1415), x. 39

Rome, Richard Riccardi de Anibaldis of, *see* Riccardi

Rome, Richard de Militiis of, *see* Riccardi

Romeseye, Thomas de, v. 66

Romeyn, Edward, i. 27n

Ronhale, Richard, vi. 45; xii. 69

Ronhand, John, de Thoren (John de Thoern) (d. 1389, ? J. de Thorne), vi. 18, 86, 94

Roos, I — de (c. 1312, ? John de Rosse), viii. 81

Roos, Peter, *see* Ros

Roos, *see also* Ros, Ross(e)

Rope, Thomas, i. 62; iii. 25, 45

Roppert, John ap Rhys ap, *see* John ap Rhys ap Roppert

Ros, Cynwrig ap, *see* Cynwrig ap Ros

Ros, Nicholas de, vi. 71, 92; xii. 71

Ros (Roos), Peter (de), i. 100; vi. 10, 31, 88; xii. 36

Ros, Philip, *see* Uske

Ros, William de, vi. 88

Rose, Thomas, xi. 84

Rose, William, xi. 77

Ros(e), *see also* Roos, Ross(e)

Rosedefe, William, viii. 50

Roselli, Nicholas, de Tarragona, iv. 18

Rosemarket, *see* Martin, David (c. 1349–61)

Ross, Robert de, v. 54; xii. 64

Rosse, John de (? I. de Roos), ii. 7, 34, 35; iii. 68; vi. 97

Rosse, William, son of Thomas le Mercer of, ii. 7; xii. 44

Ross(e), *see also* Roos, Ros(e)

Rossinhaco, Raymond de, i. 83

Roteford, *see* Retford

Roter, Richard, ii. 16; x. 11

Rothbury, Robert, v. 46

Rothbury, William, vi. 102

Rotherham, Richard, ii. 11, 13, 22, 30; ix. 9, 53(*bis*)

Rotherham, Roger, i. 13, 78, 112; iii. 99; iv. 42; x. 14n; xii. 15, 30, 39

Rotherham (Scot), Thomas, i. 3, 123; iii. 72; iv. 39; vi. 5, 113; ix. 55; xii. 13, 55, 58, 73, 83

Rothewell, William de (c. 1316), iii. 37

Rothwell, Richard, *see* Rowell

Rothwell (Rowell), Roger, i. 16, 124, 126; xii. 42(*bis*)

Rothwell, William (de) (d. 1361), i. 58; v. 10, 44; vii. 15, 20; xii. 24

Rothwell, *see also* Rowell

Rouceby, John, i. 33, 41, 46

Roucliffe, Guy de, iii. 61; vii. 50

Rouley, John, v. 23 & n

Rous, Anthony, x. 6

Rous, Thomas, ii. 18

Roussel, John, vii. 59

Roussel, *see also* Russel(l)

Roux, Raymond de, iv. 7

Rowcliffe, Rowclyff, *see* Radcliffe, Radclyf, Radclyffe, Roucliffe

Rowe, John, ix. 6, 52

Rowe, William, vii. 24

Rowell (Rothwell), Richard, i. 29

Rowell, Roger, *see* Rothwell

Rowell, *see also* Rothewell, Rothwell

Rowthall, Rowthull, *see* Ruthall

Royden, John, i. 125

Royston, John, v. 55

Royston, William de, *see* Cruce Roys

Royston, *see also* Roiston

Rudalbach, Dafydd de, xi. 16

Rudallt, *see* Rhuddallt

Rudborne (Rodbourne, Rodburn), Thomas, iii. 63; iv. 15, 31; xi. 54, 77

Rudborne, *see also* Rodebourne

Ruddock, *see* Rhydderch

Rudhale, Richard, ii. 6, 11, 16, 30

Ruding (Radyng), John, i. 7, 11, 17, 19n, 37, 55, 99, 114, 124

Rudmarley (Rodmarleye), Walter de, ii. 35

Ruffati, William, iii. 3, 53

Ruffo, Thomas, son of Peter count of Catansaro, i. 102 ('Catansano'); xii. 43

Rufini, Philip, i. 41; vi. 11

Rugge, John, vii. 36, 53

Rugge, William, *see* Repps

Rugge, *see also* Rygge

Ruggeley (Ruggele), Thomas, vii. 43; viii. 29; xi. 28

Rumworth (Circeter), Henry, i. 90, 114; iv. 8; xii. 33

Runcorn, Thomas, xi. 9 & n

Rushall, John, *see* Rashall

Rushall, William, x. 48n

Rushooke, Thomas, vii. 1; xi. 21, 43

Ruspis, Lewis, son of Lapus de, iii. 59

Russel, John (c. 1316), v. 26n

Russell, John (d. 1494), i. 3; iii. 10, 62, 99; iv. 39; v. 48; xii. 13

Russell, Simon, vii. 8, 12, 35

Russell, Thomas, i. 30

Russell, William, iii. 28, 97; v. 48

Russel(l), *see also* Roussel

Ruthall (Rowthall, Rowthull), Thomas, i. 81; iii. 5, 83; iv. 61; vi. 82, 109; viii. 67; ix. 61; xii. 31

Ruthyn, Eliseus, iii. 35
Ruthyn, Geoffrey, xi. 48
Ryall (Ruyhal), Edmund, ii. 44; xii. 50
Ryall, *see also* Ryell
Ryche, *see* Roche, John
Rydel, Robert, vii. 59
Ryder (Rider), John, i. 39; v. 44, 55, 67; xi. 27(*bis*)
Ryell, William, viii. 23
Ryell, *see also* Ryall
Rygge, Robert, viii. 44; ix. 9, 20, 43
Rygge, William, *see* Repps
Rygge, *see also* Rugge
Rykynghale, John, vi. 9, 51, 114(*bis*); vii. 2; xii. 66, 70, 73(*bis*)
Ryley, William, xi. 15, 60
Rynald, Thomas (c. 1540–5, ? T. Reynolds), vi. 70
Rynald, *see also* Reynald, Reynold
Ryngstede, *see* Ringstede
Rypon, John de, viii. 13
Rypon, *see also* Ripon
Ryse, John, ix. 8n, 12, 59
Ryse, *see also* Rees, Rhys
Rysham, Thomas, i. 107
Ryssheton, Nicholas (d. 1462/3), ix. 54
Ryssheton (Rixton, Ryshton), Nicholas (de) (d. 1413), i. 16; iii. 71
Rythre, Peter, i. 94
Ryulas, *see* Rhiwlas
Ryvell (Revell), William, iv. 34
Ryvet (Rivet), John, x. 63

S— (c. 1299), v. 14
Sabaudia, *see* Savoy
Sabello (Bokemar), James de, i. 108
Sabello (Sabellis, Savelli), Pandulph (Pandulf) de, i. 65; iii. 49; vi. 15, 68(*bis*)
Sabrano, Eliziarus de, iv. 33
Sacro Fonte, *see* Sancto Fonte
Sacrus, *see* Sayerus
Sadington (Sadyngton), John, i. 90; xi. 31
St Albans, *see* Sancto Albano
St Austolo, *see* Sancto Austolo
St Botulph, William de, vi. 111
St Fagans, Robert of, xi. 26
St Germain, John de, iv. 55
St Irieux, Elias de, vi. 80
St John, Edward, i. 57, 79, 104, 115
St John (Sancto Johanne), William de (c. 1297–1323), iii. 78
St John (Sancto Johanne), William de (d. 1316), ii. 23
St John, *see also* Sancto Johanne

St Just (Seyntjuste), Thomas, i. 84; ii. 44; iii. 16; v. 26; ix. 54; x. 13; xii. 32, 50
St Martial (Sancto Martiali), Hugh de, of Tulle, i. 93, 116; v. 12n; vi. 44; xii. 40
St Martial, Peter de (c. 1364–5, ? P. de St M. d. 1401), i. 91
St Martial, Peter de (d. 1401, ? P. de St M. c. 1364–5), i. 52; xii. 31
St Martial, William de, vi. 44
St Maur, Laurence de, ii. 27
St Maximo, *see* Sancto Maximo
St Melans, Lewis of, xi. 27
St Omer, Thomas de, ii. 20
St Paul, Saint-Pol, *see* Sancto Paulo
St Quintin, Anthony de, vi. 71; xii. 71
St Sauveur, *see* Garsie
Sais (Seis, Seys), Einion, xi. 3, 9
Sais (Seis, Seys), John, ix. 36; xi. 81
Sais (Seis, Seys), Richard, xi. 34
Salcote, *see* Capon, John
Salesbury, Nicholas, ii. 48
Salesbury, Thomas, *see* Salisbury
Salesbury, *see also* Salisbury, Sarum
Salinis (*dictus* Morel), Othoninus de, i. 36
Salisbury, Fouke, xi. 39, 41; xii. 88
Salisbury, John (c. 1397–1442), *see* Drewery
Salisbury (Tetforde), John (d. 1573), iv. 26; xi. 10
Salisbury (Salesbury), Thomas, i. 17, 34, 73; x. 18; xii. 16, 29
Salisbury, William (d. 1446), iv. 6
Salisbury, William de (c. 1376), iii. 37
Salisbury, *see also* Salesbury, Sarum
Salkeld, Launcelot, vi. 101
Sallowe, William de, vi. 64n; x. 14–15, 45
Salman, William, i. 86; xii. 32
Salmon, John, iv. 13, 23
Salop (Shrouesbury), John de, x. 71
Salop, *see also* Shrewsbury
Salopia (Shrewsbury, Shrouesbury), Ralph de, viii. 1, 83
Salopia, Walter de, xi. 80
Salopia, *see also* Shrewsbury
Salter, Richard, iii. 76; x. 8, 10, 44
Salter, Thomas, viii. 69
Salton (Selton), William de, iii. 45, 97; viii. 46, 68
Saluzzo (Saluciis), Boniface de, i. 15, 66; iii. 15; vi. 66; xii. 27, 52
Saluzzo (Saluciis), George de, i. 15; iii. 15, 41; vi. 6, 66; xii. 15
Salvago, John, v. 25
Salvago, *see also* Savage
Salyng, Geoffrey, xi. 73

Sambourne, Robert de, viii. 70, 71; xii. 81 (bis)

Sampson (c. 1487), xi. 79

Sampson, Hugh, vi. 66

Sampson, John, xi. 68n, 74, 75n

Sampson, Richard, i. 75; iii. 21; iv. 34; v. 7, 31; vi. 72; vii. 3; viii. 17; ix. 17; x. 7, 57; xii. 30, 60, 62, 63, 77

Sampson, Thomas, vi. 6, 19n, 56

Sancey (Sancy, Saucy), John (de), viii. 67; ix. 34n, 35

Sancii, Fernandus, vii. 39

Sancta Elena, William de, ix. 21

Sancto Albano, Elias de, iii. 17, 47

Sancto Albano, Reginald de, v. 7, 20, 59, 66 & n; xii. 64

Sancto Alberto, Francis de, iii. 76

Sancto Austolo (Cornewayleys), Philip de, iv. 50 ('St Austolo'); xii. 60

Sancto Cirico, Aymeric de, iii. 88

Sancto Claro, John de (c. 1298–1311), v. 7 & n, 11n, 66

Sancto Claro, John de (c. 1358–65), x. 55

Sancto Claro, Raymond de, x. 55

Sancto Edmundo, see Bury, Richard (de) (d. 1345)

Sancto Fonte (Sacro Fonte), Andrew de, viii. 56

Sancto Johanne, Amadeus de, vi. 88

Sancto Johanne, see also St John

Sancto Laurentio, Bartholomew de, ix. 4, 12, 19n, 22

Sancto Leofardo, Gilbert de, vii. 1

Sancto Leofardo, John de, vii. 4, 7

Sancto Martiali, see St Martial

Sancto Maximo, Francis de, i. 83 ('St Maximo'); iv. 32 ('St Maximo'); xii. 31, 59

Sancto Paulo (St Paul, Saint-Pol), John de, v. 33; vi. 46; viii. 34, 45, 67; ix. 15, 30; x. 52

Sancto Vito, John de, i. 83n

Sancy, see Sancey

Sandale, John (de), i. 57; iv. 45; v. 5, 51; vi. 25, 48, 52, 75; viii. 34, 40, 77; x. 11

Sandale, see also Sendall

Sandiforth, Roger, ix. 61

Sandwich, Hamo de, ii. 31, 45

Sandwich, Walter, i. 127; xii. 42

Sandwico, Adam de, see Chaumpeneys

Sandwyco, Henry de, viii. 14

Sangro, Gentilis de, vi. 44

Sante, see Saynte

Sapiti, Edward, of Florence, x. 58

Sapiti, Otto (de), vi. 93; vii. 43; xi. 30

Sapiti, Philip, iv. 50; xii. 60

Sapiti, Simon, of Florence, vii. 43; x. 58

Saracenis, Henry de (Henry Branke Saracenis de Urbe), v. 21

Sardene (Sarden, Sardinia), William (de), i. 14, 122; ii. 18; iii. 35; v. 34 & n, 43 & n; x. 59

Sarum, John de (John Pictoris), iii. 87 ('John Piers'); xii. 56

Sarum, see also Salesbury, Salisbury

Saucy, see Sancey

Saukevyll, John de, vii. 15

Saunders (Breakspear), Hugh, v. 21, 36

Saunders (Saundir), William (c. 1446–62, ? W.S. d. 1472), ii. 37; xi. 10, 15

Saunders, William (d. 1472, ? W.S. c. 1446–1462), v. 30; vi. 32

Saunders, see also Sawndyr

Saundir, see Saunders, Sawndyr

Saunford, John de, viii. 18

Savage, Ralph, vii. 55

Savage, Thomas (c. 1433–9), i. 69

Savage, Thomas (d. 1507), iv. 24, 39; v. 3; vi. 5

Savage, William, i. 105

Savage, see also Salvago

Savaric (d. 1205), viii. 22

Savelli, see Sabello

Savinhaco, William de, i. 83; vi. 56, 101; vii. 58

Savoy (Sabaudia), Amadeus (Aymo) of, i. 118; iii. 58; vi. 17, 80

Savoy (Sabaudia), Peter of (c. 1290, ? P. of S. d. 1312 or P. of S. d. 1332), ii. 17

Savoy (Sabaudia), Peter of (d. 1312, ? P. of S. c. 1290), iii. 28; iv. 55n; vi. 70n, 71, 92

Savoy (Sabaudia), Peter of (d. 1332, ? P. of S. c. 1290), i. 19, 20n, 76; iii. 3; vi. 70 & n

Savoy (Sabaudia), Thomas of (c. 1301–4), iii. 13

Savoy (Sabaudia), William of, iii. 58

Sawley, Miles, xi. 23

Sawndyr, — (c. 1535), xi. 34

Sawndyr, see also Saunders

Saxcy, William, v. 71

Saxeby, William de, viii. 59

Saxton, John (c. 1427–47), v. 57

Saxton, John de (d. 1382), ix. 7, 39; x. 54; xi. 65, 81

Say, Leonard, i. 45; iii. 99; vi. 30; xii. 57

Say, Philip de, ix. 22

Say, Simon, i. 28

Say, William, i. 11; iii. 28, 96; v. 6, 44 & n, 51, 69; vi. 63, 74; viii. 55
Sayerus (Sacrus) (c. 1298), iv. 32
Saynte (Sante), Thomas, xi. 61
Saynteloo, *see* Seylo
Scalampri, John, vi. 50
Scaldewelle, William, vii. 16
Scales, Henry de, viii. 17
Scampston, Robert de, vi. 86
Scapeya (Shepphey), John de, iv. 37, 40
Scapeya, *see also* Sheppey
Scardeburgh (Schardeburgh), John de, ii. 38
Scardeburgh, Robert de, v. 33
Scardeburgh, *see also* Shardeburgh
Scargill, Robert de, vi. 60
Scarle (Skarle), John (de), i. 7; iii. 51, 69; vi. 85, 89; x. 66
Scarle, Thomas de, vii. 57
Schalby, John, i. 32, 61, 120
Schardeburgh, *see* Scardeburgh, Shardeburgh
Schavington, Henry de, viii. 16
Schepton, Thomas de, viii. 65
Schepton, William de, viii. 53
Schepton, *see also* Schipton, Shipton
Scherter, *see* Sherer
Scheynton, *see* Sheynton
Schingham, John de, v. 60
Schipton, John, xi. 59, 77
Schipton, *see also* Schepton, Shipton
Schirebourne, *see* Sherborne
Schiryngton, *see* Sherrington
Schorne, *see* Shorne
Schute, John, ix. 14, 48
Scot, John (early 15th cent.), xi. 69n
Scot, John (d. 1545), x. 53
Scot, Thomas, *see* Rotherham
Scoter, *see* Askeby, William (dc)
Scotho, William de, v. 30
Scoville, Robert de, iii. 68
Scrivener, Richard, i. 36, 128 ('Skryven'); xii. 20, 43
Scrope, Geoffrey (le) (Geoffrey Lescrope) (d. 1383), i. 68; v. 56; vi. 29; xii. 27
Scrope, Geoffrey le (c. 1401–2), vi. 70
Scrope, Ralph, i. 26, 99; vi. 115 & n; xii. 18
Scrope, Richard (c. 1386), i. 91
Scrope, Richard (d. 1468), vi. 99
Scrope, Richard le (Richard Lescrope) (d. 1405), vi. 4; vii. 1, 4; x. 2
Scrope, Roger le (Roger Lescrope), v. 46
Scrope, Stephen (d. 1327), i. 124
Scrope, Stephen (d. 1418), vi. 26(*bis*), 45, 60(*bis*), 62; x. 26, 33, 47; xii. 84, 85

Scrope, William, i. 19, 30, 112; vi. 113
Sculthorpe, John de, vii. 11
Sebrond, John, ii. 46 & n; xii. 50
See, Stephen del, *see* Ravenser
See, William atte, vii. 22
Séez, Gervase de, vii. 11
Sefford, Richard de, vii. 51
Segden, John, iii. 60, 72; iv. 61; ix. 55
Segrave, Gilbert (de) (d. 1312), i. 14, 91; xii. 15, 33
Segrave, Gilbert (de) (d. 1316), i. 89; ii. 28; v. 1, 17, 56; xii. 48
Segrave, Stephen de, v. 9, 23; x. 5, 29
Segrave, Thomas de, v. 56; xii. 64
Segrave, Walter de, vii. 4, 10
Seguyn, Bydallus, i. 82
Seigar, John, vii. 32
Seis, *see* Sais
Selby, John (d. 1375), i. 101
Selby, John (d. 1417), *see* Sileby
Selby, Ralph (de), i. 15; iii. 23, 73; iv. 29; vi. 16, 44; xii. 15, 53, 55, 59, 67, 69
Selby, Richard, i. 125
Sellenger, Anthony, vi. 30
Sellowe (Sellow), John, ii. 41, 43; vi. 11, 37, 43
Sellyng, William, iv. 6
Selot, John, iv. 31; ix. 16
Selton, *see* Salton
Selvestone, John de, v. 33
Selveyn, George, vi. 73
Seman, William, xi. 13; xii. 88
Sendall (Sendale), John, v. 61; vi. 32, 89; xii. 68, 72
Sendall, *see also* Sandale
Sengle, William, vii. 25
Senhouse, *see* Senus; Sever, William
Senus (Senhouse), Simon, vi. 101
Sepham, Edward, v. 59
Sergeaux, Sergoys, *see* Cergeaux
Sesselwyke, *see* Mosslewyke
Seth, — (c. 1459), v. 71
Seton, Hugh de, ix. 31
Seton, Walter, i. 120; xii. 41
Sevenake, Roger de, ii. 10, 19; xii. 46
Sever, Henry, v. 19, 39; vii. 49
Sever (Senhouse), William, vi. 99, 109
Severley (Severle), John de, iv. 62; vii. 15
Sewell, John, vii. 18n
Sewell, Thomas, v. 42, 55
Seylo (Saynteloo), Edward, viii. 36
Seymour, John, i. 104, 127; iii. 103; viii. 47 & n; xii. 37
Seynkele, Robert, v. 32

Seyntjuste, *see* St Just
Seys, *see* Sais
Shaa, Ralph, iii. 56; v. 26
Shalston, Henry, xi. 66
Shankwyn, *see* Shenkwyn
Shapewyke (Horston), Thomas, v. 27
Shardeburgh, John de, vi. 79n
Shardeburgh, *see also* Scardeburgh
Shardelowe, Robert (d. 1383), *see* Derby
Shardelowe (Shardlowe), Robert de (c. 1359–1361, ? R. de Derby), vi. 54; xi. 17
Shareshull, John de, ix. 4, 7, 30(*bis*)
Sharnbroke, Edward, v. 70
Sharp, Henry, i. 17, 60, 93; iii. 92, 97; iv. 42; v. 24, 31, 32; viii. 45, 74n, 83 & n; x. 63
Sharpe, John, x. 34
Sharpuls, Robert, xi. 43
Sharsted, Bricius, i. 120
Shaxton, Nicholas, iii. 3, 21
Sheffield, Edward, x. 34
Sheffield, William, i. 19, 49n, 88; vi. 8, 14, 51, 84; xii. 33
Sheles, Thomas, i. 110
Shelford, Henry, ii. 5, 19
Shelford, John, viii. 19 & n
Shelford, Thomas (d. 1426), ii. 43; viii. 9, 44, 62, 69, 70
Shelford, Thomas de (c. 1294–1301), iv. 40
Shelley, Thomas, vii. 53
Shelton, Peter, vii. 10
Shelton, Richard, xi. 44
Shelton, William, de Defford, x. 58, 61
Shelwood, John, viii. 61
Shenkwyn (Shankwyn), Thomas, iv. 32; xii. 59
Shepard, Simon, vii. 47
Sheppey, John (de) (d. 1412), i. 4, 95; vi. 79; x. 9; xii. 13, 35
Sheppey, John de (c. 1380–1419), iv. 40
Sheppey, *see also* Scapeya
Shepphey, John de (d. 1360), *see* Scapeya
Shepton, *see* Schepton, Schipton, Shipton
Sherborne, Richard, x. 18, 41, 49
Sherborne (Schirebourne, Sherbourne, Sherburn), Robert, i. 9, 16, 77(*bis*), 93; ii. 11; iii. 95; v. 6, 7n, 38, 49, 68; vii. 3, 29; viii. 17, 75; xi. 55; xii. 30
Sherborne, *see also* Shirborn(e), Shirburne, Shyrebourn
Sherer (Scherter), John, vii. 60
Sheriff, Edmund, *see* Shireff
Sheriff, William, iii. 40, 68
Sheriff, *see also* Shireff

Sherrington (Schiryngton, Sheryngton, Shiryngton), Robert, iii. 85; vii. 26, 38; x. 58
Sherrington (Schiryngton, Sherington, Sheryngton, Shiryngton), Walter, i. 60; iii. 31, 69, 85; v. 48; vi. 53; vii. 41; viii. 25, 74, 82; x. 47, 59; xii. 25
Sherwood, Robert, x. 62
Sherwood, William, xi. 33
Sherwood, *see also* Shirwode
Sheryngton, *see* Sherrington
Sheynton (Scheynton), John de, ii. 40
Sheynton (Scheynton), William de, ii. 6, 19
Shifford, Thomas de, ii. 38
Shillingford, Baldwin de, ix. 39
Shillingford (Shillyngford), John (de), iii. 48; vii. 8; viii. 67; ix. 38, 45
Shipbrok, Roger de, iii. 24
Shipdeham, John de, vii. 51
Shipton, Henry de, ii. 7, 9, 10, 28, 47; vi. 75
Shipton, *see also* Schepton, Schipton
Shirborn, John (d. 1532), viii. 54
Shirborne, John (d. 1435), v. 10
Shirborn(e), *see also* Sherborne, Shirburne, Shyrebourn
Shirburne, John de (d. 1410), vi. 9
Shirburne, Nicholas de, x. 37
Shirburne, *see also* Sherborne, Shirborn(e), Shyrebourn
Shireff (Argentein, Sheriff), Edmund, i. 19, 42, 55
Shireff, *see also* Sheriff
Shirford, John, viii. 36
Shirford, Thomas de, iv. 33; xii. 60
Shirlagh, *see* Skirlaw
Shirley, Richard (c. 1504–26, ? R.S. c. 1538–46), vii. 51; xii. 75
Shirley, Richard (c. 1538–46, ? R.S. c. 1504–26), x. 34
Shirwode, John, vi. 26, 68, 109; ix. 10 & n, 54
Shirwode, *see also* Sherwood
Shiryngton, *see* Sherrington
Shorndene, William de, ix. 23
Shorne (Schorne), Henry de, ii. 5, 48; v. 35 & n; xii. 51
Shorton (Shorten), Robert, i. 87; vi. 47, 52; viii. 15, 45; xii. 76
Shotteswell, John, x. 4
Shrewsbury (Shrovesbury), Thomas de, iii. 78
Shrewsbury (Salopia, Shrouesbury, Shrovesbury), William de, v. 20; vi. 114; x. 17, 45

Shrewsbury, Shrouesbury, Shrovesbury, *see also* Salop, Salopia
Shuldham, Edward, i. 119
Shyrebourn, Thomas, iv. 48
Shyrebourn, *see also* Sherborne, Shirborn(e), Shirburne
Sidenham, *see* Sydenham
Sidey, Bartholomew, v. 12, 50, 64
Sidnor, *see* Sydnor
Sileby (Selby), John, v. 55
Silk, *see* Sylke
Silkested, Thomas, iv. 48
Silvaticus, Johanninus de, of Genoa, x. 39
Silvester, Robert, vi. 63, 94
Silvester, *see also* Sylvester
Silvestre, Gabriel, *see* Sylvester
Silvestre (Codeford), John, iii. 14; viii. 37
Silvestre, *see also* Sylvester
Simeon (Symeon), Geoffrey, i. 4, 24, 59, 78; v. 38; vi. 43; vii. 5, 43
Simons, John, xi. 62
Simons, *see also* Symonds
Sinabaldi, James, de Florentia (Pulcis), iv. 50
Sistre, Bernard, iv. 7; xii. 58
Skakelthorp, Adam, i. 124
Skarlawe, *see* Skirlaw
Skarle, *see* Scarle
Skellyngton, Richard, i. 66
Skelton, William (d. 1448), viii. 31, 35, 47
Skelton, William (d. 1501, ? W. Skylton), i. 22, 53, 62, 68, 124; xii. 27(*bis*), 42(*bis*)
Skelton, William de (d. 1342), x. 29
Skerning, Thomas de, iv. 26, 48; xii. 59, 60
Skevington, Thomas, xi. 5 & n
Skeyman, Thomas, i. 22, 62; xii. 17
Skidby, Richard de, v. 50
Skip (Skipp, Skypp, Skyppe), John, ii. 3; iii. 9; iv. 34
Skipton, *see* Skypton
Skirlaw (Shirlagh, Skarlawe), Walter (de), i. 11, 22, 91; vi. 4, 18n, 22, 48, 108; viii. 2; x. 2; xii. 15, 33
Skirlawe, John, vi. 28
Skirwyth, William, viii. 50
Skry, Richard, iii. 88
Skryven, *see* Scrivener
Skyby (Skybi), William, ii. 21
Skydemor, Thomas, xi. 32
Skyftelyng (Skyfteslyng), John, v. 29; viii. 29
Skylton, William (c. 1474), ? W. Skelton), vii. 14
Skynner, William, vii. 17, 20
Skypp(e), *see* Skip
Skypton, Richard, vii. 26

Skyret, John, of Buckingham, i. 15; xi. 84; xii. 15
Slake, Nicholas, v. 69; vi. 87; viii. 4, 14; x. 13
Slaughter, William, viii. 74
Slee, Christopher, vi. 100 & n
Sleford, John (de), ii. 15; iii. 56; viii. 80
Slimbridge, Robert, x. 8; xi. 48
Sloley, Simon, i. 29
Sloleye, John, xi. 10
Sloo, Robert atte, viii. 24, 72
Smale, Nicholas, i. 100
Smeton, John, i. 22, 119; xii. 17, 40
Smith, Charles, iii. 26
Smith, George, i. 63
Smith, Gilbert, i. 12, 68, 84
Smith, Humphrey, i. 89, 122
Smith, John (c. 1410–18), *see* Clere
Smith, John (c. 1458–73), xi. 60(*bis*)
Smith, John (d. 1478), xi. 23, 83
Smith, John (d. 1502), v. 24, 36, 57
Smith, John (d. 1509), i. 112
Smith (Smyth), John (d. 1539/40), v. 39; vi. 57; ix. 60
Smith, Matthew, i. 32, 37, 52
Smith, Nicholas, i. 111
Smith, Richard (d. 1525), *see* Roiston
Smith, Richard (c. 1540), *see* Smithe
Smith, Thomas (d. 1489), v. 19
Smith, Thomas (c. 1484–94), i. 30
Smith, William (c. 1486–92), iii. 101
Smith, William (d. Apr. 1505), i. 108; xii. 38
Smith, William (c. 1505, ? W.S. d. 1528), i. 53
Smith, William (d. 1507), i. 19, 71; xii. 28
Smith, William (c. 1508), vii. 30
Smith, William (d. Sept. 1508), i. 37; xii. 20
Smith, William (d. by Feb. 1509), x. 53
Smith (Smythe), William (d. 1514, ? W. Smythe c. 1487–93), i. 3; iv. 49n, 51; viii. 35n; x. 3; xii. 13
Smith, William (d. 1528, ? W.S. c. 1505), i. 8, 12, 87, 114
Smithe (Smith), Richard, xi. 69n
Smith(e), *see also* Smyth(e)
Smithson, William, *see* Bourbank, William (d. 1532)
Smithson, *see also* Smythson
Smyth, John (c. 1410–18), *see* Clere
Smyth, John (d. 1539/40), *see* Smith
Smyth, Nicholas, *see* Clerc
Smyth, Robert, viii. 29
Smythe, John, *see* Olyver

Smythe, Richard (c. 1510–16, ? R. Roiston), ii. 16, 31

Smythe, William (c. 1487–93, ? W. Smith d. 1514), viii. 35 & n, 47 & n

Smythe, William (c. 1490), viii. 33

Smythe, William (d. 1514), see Smith

Smyth(e), see also Smith(e)

Smythes, see Bedwardine

Smythson, Thomas, vi. 78

Smythson, William, see Bourbank, William (d. 1532)

Snaith, see Snayth

Snapp, John, viii. 68

Snayth (Snaith, Snayt), Henry (de), i. 67; ii. 8; v. 48; vi. 69; vii. 28; xi. 70

Snell, John, v. 8, 67

Snetisham, John, ix. 9, 51(bis)

Snetisham, Richard, ix. 9, 47

Snetisham, Roger de, iv. 26; xii. 59

Sneyd, Ralph, x. 24

Sobbury, John de (c. 1332, ? John Thebaud of Sudbury), viii. 31

Sobbury, see also Sudbury

Socton, Thomas de, iii. 77

Solario, George de, of Ivrea, i. 31; xii. 19

Solement, see Sulement

Somerby, John de, x. 50

Somerford, William (de), i. 38; ii. 17; xii. 21, 46

Somerhill, William, iii. 6

Somerset, Thomas, viii. 39

Somersete, Henry de, ix. 3, 8, 22

Somerton, John (c. 1386), x. 37

Somertone, John de (d. 1347), viii. 53

Sommastre, see Sumaster

Sompnour (Somner), Oliver, ii. 33; vii. 20

Sondey, William, v. 64

Soper, William, viii. 69

Soterworth (Suthworthe), William, x. 10, 27

Sottewell, see Mordon

Sotwell, Richard de, iii. 13

Soulby, John, vi. 58

Southam, John, i. 14, 29, 62, 98, 101, 121; iii. 9, 54; vi. 29; x. 63; xii. 15, 19, 26, 35, 36, 41, 54, 68

Southam, Thomas (de), i. 14, 84; iii. 10, 46; v. 27; xi. 24; xii. 15, 31

Southbroke, William, viii. 22

Southbury, see Suthbury

Southern, Thomas, ix. 12, 63

Southo, Alexander de, v. 64

Southwark (Southwerk, Suthewerk), Thomas de, v. 39; vii. 55

Southwode, John, viii. 44

Southworth, Thomas, i. 51

Sowi, Osmund de, viii. 56

Spaldwick, William (d. 1410), iii. 82

Spaldwick, William Percehay of (d. 1361), see Percehay

Spaldyngton, William, viii. 45, 75

Sparcheford (Sparchford), Richard, ii. 8, 41; v. 31; vi. 72

Spark, Thomas, i. 14, 63, 87, 122, 127; xii. 41

Spark, William, i. 13, 124, 127(bis)

Sparkeford, Thomas, viii. 16, 43, 45; xi. 31

Sparra (Sperra), Aquilinus (Ayquelinus) Guillelmi de, iv. 50; xii. 28

Sparrow (Herbard, Sparwe), Alexander, iii. 10, 12, 25, 52; v. 16; xi. 76, 77

Spechell, William, xi. 50

Spedwell, see Pedwell

Speke, John, ix. 58

Spekyngton, John, viii. 12, 25, 47, 52; xii. 76, 79

Spelderhurst, John de, iv. 40

Spencer, Adam, vi. 20

Spencer, Miles, iv. 32; vi. 76

Spencer, Robert, i. 77, 94, 119

Spendlove, John, v. 38, 45, 47; xi. 67

Sperkhauke, see Sperwhauke

Sperra, see Sparra

Spert (Pert), Thomas, iii. 82; viii. 8, 78

Sperwhauke, John, viii. 18 ('Sperkhauke'); xii. 77

Spicer (de Harleston), Henry, vii. 24

Spicer, Richard, viii. 45

Spineto, Hugh de, iii. 21, 68

Spinola, Manuel de, vii. 15

Spinula, Israel, son of James, of Luculo, x. 25

Spofford (Spofforth), Thomas, ii. 2; iv. 38

Sponne, William, iv. 29

Sprever, John (c. 1459, ? William S.), vii. 12

Sprever, William, i. 125; v. 32; vi. 16; vii. 12; viii. 15

Spridlington, Richard (de) (c. 1366–76), i. 35; iii. 102; xi. 40

Spridlington (Sprydlynton), Richard de (d. 1382), iii. 51, 100; x. 47

Spridlington, William (de), i. 35; xi. 37(bis), 40

Sprot, Thomas, xi. 69

Sprydlynton, see Spridlington

Spygurnell, William, v. 13

Spynke, William, iv. 26; xii. 59

Spyre, Thomas, vii. 54

Stacy, John, i. 15, 32, 80; vi. 67; vii. 19

Stafford, Arthur, ii. 8

Stafford, Edmund, i. 125, 126; vi. 7, 60; ix. 2 & n, 43; x. 64; xii. 42(*bis*)

Stafford, Fulk, ii. 9

Stafford, John (d. 1452), i. 93, 110; iii. 12, 18, 60; iv. 5; vii. 44; viii. 2, 5, 19; ix. 47; xii. 34, 38

Stafford, John (de) (c. 1362–80), i. 50, 105, 107; x. 23 & n

Stafford, Richard de, x. 69

Stafford, Roger, xi. 61

Stalworth (Massingham), Simon, i. 5, 28, 44, 57, 71, 79; ii. 11; iii. 16, 95; xii. 24, 30

Stambridge, John, i. 40

Stamford, Giles de, ii. 47; xii. 45, 50

Stamford, Henry de, vi. 107

Stamford, *see also* Stanford

Stanbridge, Giles, iii. 6

Stanbury, John, ii. 2; iv. 24; xi. 5; xii. 44

Stanbury, Robert, ii. 19

Standish, Henry, xi. 39

Standish, Richard, xi. 41

Standolf, John, v. 56; ix. 49

Stanewey, *see* Stanway

Stanford, Ralph de, iii. 66; v. 57

Stanford, *see also* Stamford

Stanhowe, Richard de, iv. 28; vii. 55; viii. 81

Stanley, Edward, x. 13

Stanley, James (d. 1485), v. 37; vi. 45; x. 14; xi. 38

Stanley, James (d. 1515), iii. 16, 31, 101(*bis*); iv. 15; vi. 27

Stanley, Richard, x. 13 & n, 38

Stanley, Thomas (c. 1528), i. 120

Stanley, Thomas (de) (c. 1393–1406), i. 74; iii. 42, 74; vi. 28, 67; viii. 4, 50; x. 35; xii. 29

Stannerton, *see* Stourton, John de

Stanton, Clement, vi. 20

Stanton, *see also* Staunton, Staynton

Stanway (Stanewey), John, ii. 5, 20; ix. 50; xii. 44, 83

Stanwey, Nicholas de, v. 53

Stapeldon, Robert de, ix. 24

Stapeldon (Stapleton), Thomas de, viii. 27, 82; ix. 25

Stapeldon, Walter de, ix. 1, 7, 23

Stapeldon, *see also* Stapleton, Stapulton

Staple, John, i. 29, 120

Stapleton, Gilbert de, iii. 9, 55

Stapleton, Thomas de, *see* Stapeldon

Stapleton, *see also* Stapeldon

Stapulton, John, x. 68

Stapulton, *see also* Stapeldon

Statherne, Hugh de, iv. 60; v. 10, 17

Staundon, Thomas, ii. 31; viii. 66; xi. 76

Staunton, Hervey de, vi. 58; viii. 40, 62; x. 36

Staunton, John (c. 1472), viii. 19

Staunton, John de (c. 1357–66), x. 64

Staunton, Thomas de (d. 1309), iii. 5

Staunton, Thomas de (d. 1349), ii. 34; iii. 15, 57; xii. 49, 52

Staunton, *see also* Stanton, Staynton

Stauren, Walter, i. 18, 22, 109; xii. 16

Staveley, John, xii. 89

Stayndrope, Thomas (de), ii. 38; ix. 42

Staynton, Simon, v. 50

Staynton, *see also* Stanton, Staunton

Stedman, David, xi. 83

Steele, William, ix. 18

Stephens, John (d. 1467), viii. 33

Stephens, John (c. 1488), viii. 59

Stephens, John (d. 1560), ix. 65

Stephens (Stephyn), Thomas (d. 1420), viii. 26, 55; ix. 47

Stephens, Thomas (d. 1520/1), viii. 52

Stephens, William (d. 1447), viii. 7, 37, 62

Stephens, *see also* Stevenys, Stevyns

Stephyn, *see* Stephens

Steur, Nicholas, viii. 72

Stevenys, John (d. 1461), ix. 47

Stevenys, *see also* Stephens, Stevyns

Stevyns, William (d. 1498), i. 51; xii. 23

Stevyns, *see also* Stephens, Stevenys

Steward (Stewart, Stuart), Edmund, iv. 34; x. 48 & n

Steward, Robert de, *see* Wells

Steward, *see also* Styward

Stewart, *see* Steward

Stillington, John, viii. 68

Stillington, Robert (c. 1473–86), viii. 55

Stillington, Robert (d. 1491), iii. 10, 40; v. 14; vi. 49, 91; vii. 34; viii. 2, 17, 45, 62, 75; xi. 71

Stillington, William (d. 1510), iii. 101; viii. 69

Stillington, William (d. 1528), iv. 28, 30, 32; v. 62; ix. 62, 64

Stock, *see* Hewet

Stockeslie, *see* Stokesley

Stocton, Nicholas de, ix. 15, 24

Stocton, William, i. 72

Stode, John, i. 88

Stoke, John (c. 1397), vii. 31n

Stoke, John de (d. 1376), v. 23n; vi. 40

Stoke, Nicholas, xi. 13

Stoke, Richard de, xi. 32

Stokeley, *see* Wenlock, Giles

Stokes, Alan (c. 1383–93), i. 69

Stokes, Alan de (c. 1376), xi. 40n
Stokes, John (c. 1410–41), iii. 65; v. 67; vi. 81; viii. 50, 75
Stokes, John (c. 1446–57, ? J.S. d. 1479), i. 51
Stokes (Stokys), John (d. 1466), i. 74; ii. 31; iii. 16, 46; iv. 18; vii. 10, 50
Stokes, John (d. 1479, ? J.S. c. 1446–57), viii. 58
Stokes, John de (c. 1369), vi. 112
Stokes, Ralph, i. 94; vi. 88
Stokes, Thomas, vi. 41
Stokesley (Stockeslie), John, iii. 8; iv. 49; v. 4
Stokesley, Nicholas, x. 22, 66
Stokys, see Stokes
Stone, Gilbert, ii. 21; v. 56; viii. 20, 70
Stone, John (d. 1419), i. 11; x. 58
Stone, John (d. 1449), i. 28; viii. 59; xii. 19(bis)
Stone, John (c. 1509–24), iii. 26, 41, 53, 95
Stone, Nicholas, vii. 13, 28, 39
Stonham, Robert, i. 39, 85; xii. 21
Stonore, Robert de, viii. 19, 26; xii. 77
Stopyndon (Stopyngton, Stopynton), John, iii. 8, 101; v. 14, 26; vi. 43; vii. 9; viii. 48
Stortford, William, v. 12, 25, 43n, 44
Storthwayte (Storthwayt), John, vii. 35; viii. 7, 9, 31, 47, 56; xii. 81
Storton, see Stourton
Story, Edward, vi. 99; vii. 3
Story, Robert, vii. 29
Stoure, John de, viii. 57
Stourton (Stannerton, Storton), John de, x. 40
Stourton, Ralph, iii. 25
Stourton, Richard, viii. 24
Stowe, G — de, v. 20
Stowe, Robert de, v. 56
Stowe, Thomas (d. 1405), i. 16, 101; iii. 42, 59; v. 6, 8, 46
Stowe, Thomas de (c. 1331), vii. 56
Stowe, William de, v. 13, 40, 56 & n; viii. 42
Stowford, Henry de, ix. 9n
Stradling, John, xi. 24
Stradling, William, xi. 58
Strange, Ebulo le, i. 126
Strange, Edward le, i. 61, 126; xii. 42
Strange, John, de Exon, ix. 22
Strange, see also Straunge, Stronge
Strangeways, Edward, x. 26 & n
Strangeways, George, x. 15 & n, 26n, 57 & n
Strangeways, William, vi. 57
Stratford, Andrew de, vi. 62

Stratford, John (de) (d. 1348), i. 6, 48; iii. 41; iv. 3, 45; x. 57; xii. 14, 22
Stratford, John de (c. 1366), ix. 37
Stratford, John Gerard de (c. 1336–66), see Gerard
Stratford, Ralph (de) (Ralph Hatton de Stratford), i. 31; iii. 19, 37; v. 2
Stratford (Stretford), Robert (de), i. 25; iii. 41; iv. 7; v. 47, 56; vii. 1 & n, 57; viii. 3, 80
Stratford, Simon de, v. 66
Stratford, Thomas de, iv. 61; xi. 32; xii. 61
Strathone, Gilbert de, v. 31
Strathone, see also Stretton, Strotton
Stratton, John, see Stretton
Stratton, Nicholas, viii. 53
Stratton, Robert, see Stretton
Stratton, see also Strathone, Stretton, Strotton
Straunge, John, x. 38
Straunge, see also Strange, Stronge
Straytbarell, James, iii. 23
Stretchay, Edmund, x. 51, 70
Strete, Edmund, vii. 46
Strete, Richard, x. 17, 18, 49
Strete, Thomas, de Knesworth, v. 15, 55; viii. 37, 63
Stretford, see Stratford
Stretley, John (de), i. 4, 31; iii. 78; v. 29; vii. 17; xii. 13, 19
Stretton (Stratton, Wode), John, iii. 28, 45, 46, 54, 99; vii. 10; x. 43
Stretton, Richard (c. 1311–31), i. 106, 118
Stretton, Richard (d. 1393), i. 89;
Stretton (Stratton), Robert (de) (d. 1382), i. 37, 95; vi. 67; x. 49, 50; xii. 13, 20, 35, 67
Stretton (Stratton), Robert (de) (d. 1385), i. 101; vii. 46; x. 1 & n; xi. 27, 42; xii. 84, 88
Stretton, Robert de (d. 1408), x. 15, 16, 63 & n
Stretton, Roger de, v. 51
Stretton, Thomas (de), i. 88; x. 6, 33
Stretton, see also Strathone, Stratton, Strotton
Streynsham, John, viii. 44
Strickland, Thomas, vi. 102
Strickland, William, vi. 98(bis); xii. 72
Stronge, William, viii. 28
Stronge, see also Strange, Straunge
Strotton, Robert, viii. 82
Strotton, see also Strathone, Stratton, Stretton

Strubby, Ralph, i. 89
Stuart, *see* Steward
Stubbes, John, *see* Stubbys
Stubbes, Lawrence, vi. 41
Stubbys (Stubbes), John, vii. 33; ix. 8, 11, 20, 56; x. 34
Stukeley (Stucle), Peter, viii. 11, 44, 62, 78; ix. 14, 50; x. 71; xii. 79
Stukeley, *see also* Styvecle
Sturdy, Henry, iv. 33
Sturgeon, Nicholas, v. 17, 28, 58; viii. 48, 50; ix. 49, 52
Sturmy, Hugh, iv. 31
Styne, *see* Lestine
Stynt, William, ix. 62, 63
Styvecle (Styuecle), William (de), v. 69; xi. 75
Styvecle, *see also* Stukeley
Styward, William, i. 40
Styward, *see also* Steward
Sudbury, Adam de (d. 1334), viii. 60
Sudbury, Adam Thebaud of (c. 1363–4), v. 12
Sudbury, Gerard de, viii. 77
Sudbury, John (c. 1423), *see* Nichole
Sudbury, John (d. 1444), v. 20
Sudbury, John (d. 1479), *see* Crall
Sudbury, John Thebaud of (c. 1361–71, ? John de Sobbury), v. 63; viii. 49
Sudbury, Nicholas de, x. 21
Sudbury, Simon of (de) (Simon Thebaud of Sudbury), i. 95; ii. 34; iii. 17; iv. 4; v. 2, 18n; viii. 49
Sudbury (Sobbury), Thomas of (de) (Thomas Thebaud of Sudbury), ii. 34; iii. 17n, 67; v. 18n; viii. 4, 49
Sugar (Norris), Hugh, viii. 11, 15, 29, 56, 71
Sulement (Solement), Thomas, ii. 35; vi. 61
Sulgrave, John de, x. 19, 21, 40, 45
Sulgrave, Roger de, x. 69
Sulthorn, John de, xi. 24, 27
Sumaster (Sommastre, Sumastre), William, ix. 6, 58; x. 28, 44; xii. 83(*bis*)
Sumpter, Robert, iii. 89; ix. 4, 36
Surland, Richard, i. 90; iii. 83
Surteis (Surtes), Stephen, ii. 31; xii. 48
Suthbury, Richard de, xi. 33
Suthewerk, *see* Southwark
Suthflete, Robert de, iv. 40
Suthworthe, *see* Soterworth
Sutton, Arthur, *see* Dudley
Sutton, George, vii. 53
Sutton, Griffin de, vii. 56
Sutton, Henry, i. 62; iii. 20, 45, 81; v. 32

Sutton, John (d. 1341), i. 44, 118
Sutton, John (d. 1397), x. 25
Sutton, John (d. 1416), ii. 19
Sutton, John (c. 1447), xi. 48
Sutton, John (d. 1460), i. 110
Sutton, John (c. 1451–62, ? J.S. d. 1480), ii. 40
Sutton, John (d. 1480, ? J.S. c. 1451–62), v. 60; vi. 38
Sutton, John de (c. 1306), vii. 55
Sutton, John de (c. 1341), viii. 25
Sutton, Lewis, xii. 89
Sutton, Oliver, i. 82
Sutton, Richard de, vi. 68
Sutton, Robert (c. 1389), v. 32; vii. 34
Sutton, Robert (d. 1438), i. 77
Sutton, Robert de (c. 1332), viii. 21
Sutton, Roger de (c. 1315), vii. 32 & n
Sutton, Roger de (d. 1378), ii. 20, 32; xii. 47, 49
Sutton, Thomas (d. 1316), i. 10, 115
Sutton, Thomas (d. 1531), viii. 58
Sutton, Thomas of (d. 1384), *see* Cotte
Swaby, Thomas (de), iii. 63; ix. 13, 38; x. 55
Swaffham, John, xi. 4
Swaffham, Walter de, xi. 6, 8, 9
Swain, Henry, de Pultney, x. 40
Swain, Thomas, i. 26, 55, 69, 110; xii. 39
Swain, *see also* Swayn, Sweyne
Swan, Richard, vii. 51; viii. 35, 73
Swan, William, vii. 23
Swayn, Henry, vi. 33
Swayn, *see also* Swain, Sweyne
Sweyne, Germanus, vii. 57
Sweyne, *see also* Swain, Swayn
Sweyveseye, John de, xi. 74 & n
Swift, *see* Swyft
Swindall, John, vii. 53 & n
Swinfield (Swinfelde), John de, ii. 8, 47; v. 49; xii. 44, 50, 64
Swinfield (Swinfelde), Richard de (d. 1311), ii. 14
Swinfield (Swinfelde), Richard de (d. 1317), ii. 1; v. 54
Swinfield (Swinfelde), Stephen de, ii. 30 & n
Swinnerton, Nicholas de, x. 40, 47
Swinnerton, Richard de, iii. 53; ix. 17, 18 & n
Swyft, John, viii. 26
Swyft, Thomas, iii. 25, 86; vii. 35; viii. 43
Swyft, William, iii. 76, 88
Swyndon, Thomas, iii. 23
Swyneshead (Swyneshevede), John (de), i. 76; ix. 38
Swynflet, William, iv. 27

Swynleigh (Swynlegh, Swynle), John (de), i. 8; v. 43n, 44(bis); xi. 82

Swynowe, Andrew, vii. 54; xii. 75

Sybeley, John, i. 56; xii. 24

Sydall, Henry, x. 57

Sydenhale, John de, viii. 46, 68

Sydenhale, Richard de, ii. 7, 10, 41

Sydenham, Christopher (d. 1524, ? George S.), viii. 36

Sydenham (Sidenham, Sydnam), George (d. 1524, ? Christopher S.), iii. 13, 53, 103; viii. 36; ix. 62

Sydenham, Simon, iii. 2, 4, 10, 12, 81, 103; vii. 2; xii. 52

Sydlesham, Richer de, vii. 55

Sydnam, see Sydenham

Sydnor (Sidnor), Richard, vi. 89; ix. 17n, 19, 60; x. 28

Sylke (Silk), William, viii. 31; ix. 8, 17, 57

Sylvester (Silvestre, Sylvestre), Gabriel, vii. 18; x. 65

Sylvester, see also Silvester, Silvestre

Symeon, see Simeon

Symond, Adam, vii. 6

Symondesburgh, John, iii. 14, 20, 89, 98; v. 16

Symonds, Simon, iii. 73; x. 45

Symonds, see also Simons

Symson, William, viii. 67

Synger, John, xi. 34

Tacham, see Thacham

Talami, Balsamus, of Florence, v. 59

Talbot, Baldwin, ii. 4

Talbot, Christopher, x. 14 & n, 31, 68

Talbot, John (c. 1327), ii. 50

Talbot, John (d. 1550), i. 6, 26, 53, 54, 96; xii. 14, 35

Talbot, Philip, ii. 6, 41

Talbot, Richard, ii. 9, 46; vi. 51; vii. 5; xii. 45, 50

Talbot, Robert, viii. 71

Talbot, Thomas, ii. 44

Talbot, William (c. 1407-15), i. 33, 60

Talbot, William (d. 1498), i. 62; iii. 45; v. 54; vi. 53; vii. 21; xii. 26, 74

Talley, John, xi. 58

Talleyrand, Elias (Elie), de Périgord, i. 116; iv. 32; v. 8, 45; vi. 6, 25, 64, 71, 80; xii. 40

Talleyrand de Grelino, see Grelino

Talour (Barnby), Thomas, i. 121

Talour, see also Taylor

Taminis, William de, i. 111

Tamworth, Christopher, i. 21, 91; xii. 17, 33

Taneto, see Thaneto

Tanfield, Richard de, x. 62

Tanfield, Thomas, vi. 76, 81, 83

Tanfield, William de, vi. 110

Tangmere, see Apelderham

Tanton, see Taunton

Tapton, Hugh, i. 24, 109

Tapton, John, i. 73, 86; v. 39; xi. 41

Tapton, Thomas, vi. 57

Tarenta, Nicholas de (c. 1337-45), i. 5

Tarente (Tarrant), Nicholas de (d. 1309), iv. 47

Tarragona, see Roselli

Tarrant, see Tarente

Tarry, Robert, ii. 29, 30; viii. 48

Tarvere, see Tawre

Tash, see Tesh

Tastario, Peter de, i. 81, 105; ix. 53, 55 & n

Tate, William, see Tayt

Taunton (Tanton), Robert (de), i. 48; iii. 28; v. 68; vi. 29, 111; viii. 34, 77; ix. 28

Taunton, Walter de, viii. 60

Taurer, see Tawre

Taverner, John, vii. 18(bis)

Taverner, Nicholas (d. 1375), see Lichfield

Taverner, Nicholas (c. 1497-1521), vii. 30, 35

Tawre (Tarvere, Taurer, Tawer, Tawere), Simon, ii. 13, 20, 49

Taylor (Taylour), John (d. 1492), iii. 64; viii. 30; ix. 10, 58

Taylor (Taylour), John (d. 1534), i. 16; viii. 72, 81; x. 17, 36

Taylor, John (d. 1554), i. 4, 36 ('Tayler'); xii. 13, 20

Taylor, see also Talour

Tayntrell, William, i. 64

Tayt (Tate), William, vi. 38; ix. 63

Tealby, see Coates

Tebbot (Tebber, Tebbet), Edmund, v. 48; x. 47

Tebrightone, Roger, viii. 51, 59

Tegwareth, Einion ap, see Einion ap Tegwareth

Tehy (They), Robert, ii. 15; xii. 46

Telesford, John, viii. 22

Tendring, John, v. 34

Teobaldeschi, Francis (de), i. 91; vi. 81; x. 6; xii. 33

Teramo, Simon de, i. 54; iii. 29; xii. 24, 53

Terier, Nicholas, ix. 31

Terry, John, vii. 44

Terry, Thomas, viii. 8, 20

Terynden, Richard, v. 36

Tesh (Tash), Thomas, vi. 74

Testa, Paul de, iii. 80

Testa, Peter de, iii. 29

Testa, Vitalis de, iii. 92; v. 5, 51; vii. 30

Testa, William (de), i. 19, 20n, 76; iv. 17; xi. 43n

Tetforde, see Salisbury, John (d. 1573)

Teynterel, see Lichfield, Nicholas de (c. 1322–37)

Teynton, Thomas, iii. 67; ix. 46

Thacham (Tacham), Robert, iii. 81

Thame, William, xi. 60, 66, 77

Thaneto (Taneto), Stephen de, ii. 4n, 26; xii. 48

Thebaud, see Sudbury

Thebolde (Tybollde), Thomas, iii. 49

Thefford, William de, vii. 9

Thelwall, Thomas, i. 118

Thewe, Thomas, i. 125

They, see Tehy

Thifayn, see Typhane

Thingull (Thinghull, Thynghull, Thyngull), William (de), i. 54; viii. 16; x. 63 & n; xi. 29; xii. 24, 77

Thirland, Humphrey de, vi. 102n

Thirlby, Thomas, iii. 101; iv. 19

Thirlow, William, viii. 44

Thirsford (Thyrsforde), William de, iv. 61; xii. 61

Thistleden, Richard de, viii. 6, 10, 45, 80

Thoern, see Ronhand

Tholite, Thomas, xi. 75

Thomas (c. 1326–7, ? T. Northwode), xii. 16, 33

Thomas (c. 1493), xi. 85

Thomas ap Hywel (Powell), xi. 63

Thomas ap Rhys (Rees, Reys, Rice) (Thomas Pryce), xi. 8

Thomas, John (d. 1412), i. 7, 29, 58, 61, 62, 71, 80; vii. 12 & n, 35 & n; xii. 43

Thomas, John (c. 1420), xi. 60

Thomas, Morgan, xi. 34

Thomas, Robert, xi. 25

Thomas, Rowland, xi. 9n

Thomas, William, x. 31

Thomas, William ap, see William ap Thomas

Thomasson, Ralph, i. 82

Thompson, William (d. 1511), viii. 19

Thompson, William (c. 1528–49), x. 29, 34, 66

Thomson, John, viii. 39

Thoren, John de (c. 1366), see Thorne

Thoren, John de (d. 1389), see Ronhand

Thoren, Richard de, see Thorne

Thoresby, John (de) (d. 1373), i. 118; iv. 56; v. 8, 33; vi. 3, 86; x. 6; xi. 53; xii. 40, 60

Thoresby, John (de) (d. 1381), vi. 54; x. 47

Thoresby, Richard de, x. 58; xi. 85

Thormerton (Thormeton, Tormerton, Tormeton), Richard (de), iii. 61; viii. 8, 10, 74; ix. 29

Thornbury (Thornborough), Philip, i. 49, 63; iii. 32

Thorne (Thoren), John de (c. 1366, ? John Ronhand de Thoren), vii. 50

Thorne (Thoren), Richard de, iii. 63; vi. 56; vii. 50; x. 50

Thornham, Thomas (d. 1544), ix. 65

Thornham, Thomas (d. 1548), v. 33

Thorntoft, William de, vii. 27

Thornton, John, i. 97

Thornton, Robert, i. 17

Thornton, William, i. 111; xii. 39

Thorp, John de (c. 1349), vi. 31

Thorp, John de (c. 1361–6), v. 70

Thorp, Robert de, xi. 84

Thorp (Thorpe), Walter (de), i. 38; v. 38; x. 29, 64; xii. 63

Thorp, William, i. 23

Thorpe, Adam de, vi. 69, 85

Thorpe, John (d. 1421), i. 54; iv. 33; xii. 24, 60

Thorpe, John (c. 1482–6), vii. 31

Thorpe, John (c. 1530–55), vii. 25

Thorpe, Walter (de), see Thorp

Thowe (Towe), Thomas, x. 8

Threkingham, Lambert, iii. 48; vii. 8, 12

Thresk (Tresk, Tresks), Robert (de), iii. 76; vii. 15; xi. 12; xii. 56, 74, 87

Thresk, see also Trysk

Thudden (Tudden), William, iv. 47

Thurban, Richard, ii. 46, 47, 48, 52 & n

Thurgarton, Robert (Robert Cooke de Thurgarton), i. 84

Thursgate, see Patrington

Thurstan, John (d. 1457, ? J. Thurston), x. 56

Thursteyn, John (d. 1361), iii. 89; vii. 4n, 45; viii. 83

Thurston, John (c. 1450, ? J. Thurstan), v. 14

Thwayts, John, i. 115(bis)

Thynghull, Thyngull, see Thingull

Thyrsforde, see Thirsford

Tibbay, John (de), i. 9, 53; vi. 37; xii. 14

Tibertis, Cassaleto de, iii. 37

Tideman (Tydeman), Robert, of Winchcombe, iv. 57; xi. 22

Tilheto, Gerald de, iii. 13, 26
Tilio, *see* Tylyo
Tilney, William de, xi. 57
Tilney, *see also* Tylney
Tirel, Bartholomew, viii. 41, 55
Tirel, *see also* Tyrell
Tiryngton, John, i. 62, 110
Tiryngton, William (de), i. 111; v. 61
Tischo (Tysho), Richard (de), ix. 11, 39; x. 61; xii. 83(*bis*), 86
Tissington, Richard, ii. 6
Toby, *see* Toly
Tocket, *see* Tucket
Todeworth, William, ix. 39
Tofte, Robert, i. 97
Toli, Thomas, vi. 83
Toli, William, *see* Toly
Tollet, Richard, ix. 6, 21, 62; x. 62
Toly (Toli), William, iii. 28; vi. 61; vii. 19; viii. 27 ('Toby'), 28; xii. 53, 74, 78(*bis*)
Tomacelli, Piero (Perinus), of Naples, i. 54, 113(*bis*); viii. 16; xii. 24, 40
Tomyow, Thomas, viii. 15, 32; ix. 58
Tone (Toyne), Richard, i. 72; vi. 23, 72, 83
Toneworth, Adam de, x. 39, 54n
Toneworth, *see also* Tonworth
Toneys (Toney), Robert, i. 53, 77, 124; iii. 25, 33; vi. 41; xii. 24, 53
Tonworth, Richard de, x. 25
Tonworth, *see also* Toneworth
Toppan, John, xi. 49
Toppeclyve, Richard de, x. 9, 19
Torkesey, John, vii. 59
Torkesey (Porlessy), William, ii. 46
Tormerton, Tormeton, *see* Thormerton
Tototh, John, i. 86
Totyngton, Alexander de, iv. 24, 25
Toueton, Thomas de, vi. 79
Toutlemonde, *see* Treçis, Nicholas de
Towe, *see* Thowe
Towne, William, i. 20, 62, 110; xii. 17
Townley, Nicholas, vi. 47
Townsend, Roger, iii. 18, 74
Toyne, *see* Tone
Toyt, *see* Cornubia
Tracy, Andrew, vii. 43
Tracy, William, vii. 31, 47
Trafford, Henry, vi. 10, 91
Traharn, John, xi. 33
Tratyngton, William de, x. 60
Travers, John, x. 53
Travesse, Adam, ix. 12, 15, 62
Trays, Robert, i. 33, 43; xii. 22

Treçis, Nicholas de (Nicholas Toutlemonde), ix. 31
Treçis, Theobald Rogerii de, vi. 27
Trefdyn, Walter de, xi. 58
Trefnant, Hywel (Hywel ap Dafydd), xi. 47
Trefnant, John (bp., d. 1404), i. 67; ii. 2; xi. 45
Trefnant, John (John ap Hoel, ap Howell, ap Hywel) (c. 1399–1404), ii. 47, 52; xi. 42; xii. 51(*bis*), 88
Trefnant, *see also* Trevenaunt
Trefor (Trefvawr, Trevaur), Dafydd, xi. 15
Trefor (Trefvawr, Trevaur), Edmund, xi. 12
Trefor (Trefvawr, Trevaur), Edward, xi. 44, 47
Trefor (Trefvawr, Trevaur), Griffin, xi. 37, 49
Trefor (Trefvawr, Trevaur), Gruffudd, xi. 13
Trefor (Trefvawr, Trevaur), John (d. 1357), xi. 12, 37, 49
Trefor (Trefvawr, Trevaur), John (d. 1410), ii. 31; viii. 6, 33; xi. 38(*bis*) & n, 45, 82
Trefor (Trefvawr, Trevaur), Lewis, xi. 50
Trefor (Trefvawr, Trevaur), Matthew, xi. 49
Tregar, Huw, xi. 17
Tregonwell, Robert, ix. 65
Tregrisiou, Ralph, ix. 4, 41
Treguran, John, v. 26
Treguran, *see also* Trygarn
Tregury, Michael, ix. 20, 53
Treisnorit, Griffin de, xi. 49
Tremayn, Thomas, ix. 48(*bis*)
Trengof, Walter, ix. 16
Tresgoet, Griffin, xi. 13
Tresham, William, i. 30; vii. 9, 37
Tresk, Tresks, *see* Thresk
Treton, Richard, iii. 69
Trevaur, *see* Trefor
Trevellys, William de, ix. 11, 37
Trevenaunt, John, viii. 35, 52, 71
Trevenaunt, *see also* Trefnant
Treverdow, William, vii. 43
Trevilian (Trevilion), George, vii. 29; ix. 63
Trevilian (Tryvilion), Henry, iii. 94; iv. 33; ix. 16, 53
Trewelove, Adam, viii. 29
Trillek, John de, ii. 1, 45, 50; x. 25
Trillek, Thomas de, ii. 4, 35; iii. 17; iv. 37 & n; v. 5; vii. 1; viii. 80
Trippe, Stephen, viii. 28
Trobelfyld, Richard, viii. 34
Trote, Walter, ii. 43 ('Grote'); ix. 44; xii. 50
Trotter, Hugh, vi. 12, 14, 47
Trove, Richard, iii. 22, 25, 34, 72

Trussel, Edmund, iii. 32; v. 11, 41
Trussel, Thomas, v. 11
Trussel, Warin, x. 30
Trusthope, *see* Graa
Trygarn, John, xi. 11n
Trygarn, *see also* Treguran
Trysk, Robert, ii. 49
Trysk, *see also* Thresk
Tryvilion, *see* Trevilian
Tubney, John, xi. 44
Tucket (Tocket), John, x. 45, 61
Tudden, *see* Thudden
Tudur ab Adda, xi. 10
Tudur ap Dafydd, xi. 10
Tudur, Lewis ap, *see* Lewis ap Tudur
Tuggel, Thomas (c. 1363–6), ix. 36, 37
Tughall, Thomas de (c. 1348), iii. 93
Tuit, Richard, ix. 5n
Tulle, *see* St Martial, Hugh de
Tully, Robert, xi. 55
Tunbridge (Tunebrigg), William, iv. 40
Tunstable, Thomas de, xi. 29
Tunstal (Tunstall), Cuthbert, i. 112; iii. 5,
    47; v. 4; vi. 38, 109; x. 14; xii. 39
Tunstal, John, v. 49, 71
Tunstall, Robert, xi. 66
Turberville, James, vii. 49
Turberville, *see also* Turvill(e)
Turbot, John, xi. 63
Turk, John, iii. 100; x. 47
Turner, William, iii. 68
Turre, Henry de, vi. 27
Turre de Adria, Robert de, iii. 41
Turvill (Turvil), Philip de, x. 24, 27; xi. 80
Turvill, Ralph, vi. 71; x. 62
Turville, Richard de, xi. 30, 80
Turvill(e), *see also* Turberville
Tutbury (Tuttebury), Thomas (de), i. 15,
    111; viii. 4, 13; xii. 15
Tuverton, John de, xi. 82
Twyer, Thomas, i. 86, 90
Twyneho (Twineley, Twynho, Twynhoe,
    Twynowe, Twynyho, Twynyoo), Chris-
    topher, i. 89; ii. 30, 33; iii. 11, 26, 40,
    60; viii. 23; ix. 61; xii. 33
Twynge, *see* Bonifant
Twynho, Twynowe, Twynyho, Twynyoo,
    see Twyneho
Twyselton, Adam de, vi. 62n
Tyake, John, ix. 6, 21, 61
Tybollde, *see* Thebolde
Tychenor, John, vii. 30
Tydeling, John, iii. 24, 31, 67, 89, 94, 98,
    103

Tydeman, *see* Tideman
Tyghe, John, x. 22n
Tylloy, Peter de, v. 31
Tylney, John, i. 90
Tylney, Philip, i. 39 ('John'); xii. 21
Tylney, *see also* Tilney
Tylton, John (*senior*, d. 1424), xi. 15
Tylton, John (*junior*, c. 1424), xi. 15
Tylyo (Tilio), Arnald de, of Béarn, vii. 56
Tymmore, Henry de, x. 30, 37
Tyndall, Martin, viii. 30
Tyngewick, Nicholas, iii. 28, 66; xii. 55
Tynmouth (Maynelyn), John, iii. 38
Typhane (Thifayn), John, ix. 18
Tyrell, William, xi. 42, 45
Tyrell, *see also* Tirel
Tysho, *see* Tischo
Tyssebury, John (de), iii. 81; viii. 58, 82
Tyttesbury, Richard, ix. 45

Udy, John, ix. 54 & n
Ufford, *see* Offord
Uguccioni, Francis, i. 84; vi. 18; x. 44
Ulf, William, x. 54
Ullerston, Richard, iii. 25
Umfray, Umfrey, *see* Humphrey
Underhill, John (d. 1537), i. 47; iii. 33, 90;
    v. 68; vii. 29 ('William'); xii. 22, 75
Underhill, *see also* Undrehull
Underwood, Edward (d. 1504), v. 50; vi. 30,
    34 & n
Underwood, Edward (c. 1503–18), v. 62
Undrehull, John de (c. 1370–81), x. 45
Undrehull, *see also* Underhill
Unert, *see* Haliday
Upcote, Robert, ii. 10; xii. 45
Uphaven, John de, ix. 6, 22
Uphull, John, ix. 33, 35
Uppy (Oppy), Robert, iii. 29
Upton, John (c. 1384, ? J. de U. d. 1397),
    ii. 46
Upton, John (de) (d. 1397, ? J.U. c. 1384),
    iii. 80; viii. 73
Upton, Nicholas, iii. 16, 68 ('Dounton'); v.
    67; viii. 43
Upton, Thomas, viii. 13
Urbe, Henry Branke Saracenis de, *see* Sara-
    cenis
Urbe, John de, *see* Gaetani, John; Ricardi
    Mathie
Urbe, Nicholas de, *see* Branche
Urbe, Richard de, *see* Riccardi
Urbe, Ursus de, *see* Orsini
Urbe, *see also* Rome

Urry, John (c. 1429–30, ? J.U. d. 1434), vii. 19

Urry, John (d. 1434, ? J.U. c. 1429–30), i. 26; viii. 69; xii. 18

Ursini, de Ursinis, Ursinus, Ursus, *see* Orsini

Urswick (Hursewik), Christopher, i. 9, 14, 92, 100; iii. 14, 30; iv. 24n, 30, 49n; v. 31; vi. 8, 27, 38, 52, 68, 84; viii. 47; ix. 10, 58

Usflet (Ouseflet), Robert de, iv. 28

Usk, Adam de, xi. 22n, 47, 64

Uske (Heske), John de, iv. 61; xii. 61

Uske (Heske, Ros), Philip, vi. 87

Vaggescombe, Robert, ix. 39

Vaghan, Hugh, ii. 26

Vaghan, John, ii. 25

Vaghan, *see also* Fychan

Vale, *see* Dale

Valenciis, Matthew de, viii. 11, 14, 25

Valognes, Valoines, *see* Waleyns

Vance, *see* Vauce

Vannes, Peter, ii. 20; iii. 5, 30, 55; iv. 63; vi. 36; viii. 41; xii. 47

Varesio, Pontius de, iii. 17, 53, 60

Varesio (Waresio), Tydo de, i. 48; iii. 9, 17, 55; x. 67; xii. 22, 86

Vassalli (Vassal), Fortanerius, i. 8; v. 8, 28

Vauce (Vance, Vaunce, Vaws), William, ii. 42 & n; iii. 36; iv. 63; x. 8

Vaughan, *see* Fychan, Vaghan

Vautort, John, xi. 6, 27

Vaws, *see* Vauce

Vele, Thomas (c. 1494, ? T. Wele), xi. 46; xii. 89

Veneys, *see* Devenesche

Vennor, William, xi. 66

Vercato, *see* Veyraco

Vereriis (Verreriis), Pontius (Poncius) de, v. 68; viii. 37

Vergil (Castellensis), Polydore, i. 104; ii. 38; v. 54; viii. 5n, 14

Vergne, *see* Vernhio

Verney, John, iv. 63; x. 6, 44

Vernham, John, iii. 54, 99

Vernhio (Everino, Vergne, Yvernio), Peter de, i. 25; ix. 13

Vernon, Bochard de, iii. 100(*bis*); vii. 32

Vernon, John, x. 62

Vernon (Vernoun), Peter de, iii. 45; vi. 88; vii. 34

Vernon (Vernoun), Richard de, ii. 30; x. 59

Verreriis, *see* Vereriis

Veteri Terra (Oldelond), Robert de, ix. 22

Veyraco (Vercato), William de, iii. 41

Veysey (Harmon, Voysey), John, iii. 23, 24; ix. 3, 5, 8, 21, 60; x. 14

Via, Arnold de, iii. 19

Via, James de, i. 57; iii. 19

Viall, John, ii. 40, 48; iii. 70

Vichio (Florence), Rayner de, x. 18

Vienna, John de, *see* Bateman

Vienne, Henry of, *see* Delphinus

Vigerous, *see* Vygerous

Villers, James, viii. 67 ('Villiers'); xii. 81

Villers, William (d. 1498), xi. 46 ('Villiers'); xii. 89

Villers, William (c. 1511–35), viii. 67 ('Villiers'); xii. 81

Viterbo, Mark de, vi. 80; vii. 7; viii. 10

Vowell, John, viii. 39

Voysey, *see* Veysey

Vuipenns, *see* Wippingen

Vygerous (Vigerous), William, v. 10; viii. 40

Vyncent, John, vii. 22

Vypaynes, *see* Wippingen

Vyse, John de, iii. 6; ix. 33; xii. 52

Wade, John (c. 1343–66), v. 38

Wade, John (d. 1424), i. 29, 99, 111; xii. 19

Wade, Richard, iii. 33

Wafer, John, iii. 35

Wager, *see* Cranborne, Henry de

Wagott, William, ix. 19, 56

Wakefield, Henry (de), i. 11; ii. 25; iii. 41, 63; iv. 7, 14, 57; v. 15, 54; vi. 79; xii. 14

Wakefield, William de, x. 71

Wakering, John, i. 117; iii. 29, 52; iv. 8, 24; v. 65; vii. 60; viii. 64, 82; xii. 40

Walbere, Thomas, v. 65

Walbrond, John, iii. 40

Walchan, *see* Fychan, Richard (c. 1344–52)

Walcote, William (de), i. 46; vi. 22; xii. 22

Waldby, Robert de, vi. 4; vii. 2

Waldebeff, John, xi. 62, 77

Walden, Roger (de), i. 49, 116; iii. 30, 33, 62; iv. 4, 50; v. 2 & n, 70; vi. 7, 60; ix. 2, 43; x. 49; xii. 22

Walesby, William, i. 82, 99; ii. 36(*bis*); iii. 52; vii. 12, 15

Waleton, Adam de, x. 7

Waleyns (Valognes, Valoines), Robert de, vi. 10, 86

Waleys, Walter, iii. 35

Waleys, *see also* Walles

Walgrave, William, i. 77

Walker, David, ii. 15, 33, 40

Walker (Ludlowe), Geoffrey, xi. 25
Walker, Richard, x. 22
Walkington (Walkyngton), Robert (de), i. 109; vi. 48; x. 61; xii. 38
Walkington, Thomas (d. 1410), vi. 20; ix. 4, 39, 40
Walkyngton, Thomas (c. 1388–1404), vii. 6
Walkyngton (Walkington), Thomas (d. 1470), i. 45; vii. 51
Wall (Walle), Roger, x. 15, 20, 36, 47
Wall, William, xi. 71
Waller, see Whalley
Walles (Walleys), John, i. 66, 72; v. 19; xii. 27, 28
Walles, see also Waleys
Walleworth, Thomas de, vi. 40, 62, 79
Walleworth, see also Walworth
Walley, see Whalley
Walleys, see Walles
Walmesford, Hugh, i. 43
Walpole, John, i. 78n
Walpole, Ralph de, iv. 13; xii. 58
Walpole, William, iv. 16
Walrond, John, iii. 87; viii. 63; xii. 80
Walsh, James, x. 35
Walsh, Thomas, vi. 59
Walsh, see also Walshe
Walsham, Robert (de), iii. 15, 80; xi. 24, 40
Walsham, William, iii. 65; vi. 28
Walshe, Edward, iii. 22
Walshe, see also Walsh
Walsingham, Alan de, iv. 13, 16
Walsingham, Edmund, iv. 16
Walter (c. 1311), ix. 15n
Walter, John, v. 50; vi. 23
Walter, Thomas, x. 43
Walter, William, xi. 57n, 62
Waltham, John (de) (d. 1384), i. 44; vi. 16, 71; x. 37; xii. 22
Waltham, John de (d. 1395), ii. 16; iii. 1, 44; vi. 26, 42; xii. 46
Waltham, Roger (c. 1322, ? R. de W. c. 1309–32), i. 15
Waltham, Roger de (c. 1309–32, ? R.W. c. 1322), v. 25
Waltham, William (de), i. 67, 84; iii. 91; v. 27, 64; vi. 22, 23, 43, 46; viii. 39; ix. 13; xii. 27, 31, 63, 68, 69(bis)
Walton, Henry (de), i. 78, 95; iii. 59, 100; vi. 25, 37; vii. 59; viii. 49; ix. 35
Walton, John, xi. 64
Walton, Robert de, vii. 8, 12n, 20, 33
Walton, Thomas (d. 1451), i. 26, 81, 119; ii. 34; xii. 18

Walton, Thomas de (c. 1382–93), x. 39
Walwayn, Elias de, viii. 83
Walwayne (Walwayn), John (d. 1326), iii. 49; vi. 107
Walwayne (Walwayn, Walwyn), John (d. 1330), ii. 15, 50; v. 66; xi. 80; xii. 51
Walwayne, John (c. 1412–15), see Walwyn
Walwen, Nicholas, ii. 12, 21, 37; xii. 45
Walwin, Richard, vi. 30, 41
Walworth, John de, vi. 77
Walworth, Robert of, see Bennington
Walworth, see also Walleworth
Walwyn, John (d. 1330), see Walwayne
Walwyn (Walwayne), John (c. 1412–15), ii. 28; xii. 48
Walwyn, see also Walwayne, Walwen, Walwin
Wamberg, John de, viii. 37
Wamberg, Robert de, viii. 13, 63, 76
Wandysford, George, v. 45
Wandysford, see also Wansford
Wanetyngg', Richard de, iii. 45
Wansford, John, viii. 12, 18, 65
Wansford, see also Wandysford
Ward, John, ix. 52
Ward, see also Warde
Wardall, John, i. 78; v. 65; ix. 55; xii. 30
Wardall, Thomas, vii. 18, 47
Warde, Nicholas, vii. 37
Warde, Thomas, i. 47, 119; v. 71; viii. 15
Warde, see also Ward
Wardeden (Wardedieu), Nicholas (c. 1316–1327, ? N. Wardian d. 1330), iii. 47; xii. 54
Wardeyn, John, iii. 65; xii. 55
Wardian, Nicholas (d. 1330, ? N. Wardeden c. 1316–27), i. 38
Wardieu, William, vii. 12
Wardrober (Wardroper, Wardropper), Thomas, i. 27, 33; vi. 29; x. 63; xii. 18
Wardroper (Waredroper), John, ii. 8, 11, 15; x. 20, 34, 46, 59; xii. 46
Ware, Henry, iii. 96; v. 60; vii. 2, 38; xi. 33; xii. 90
Ware, John (d. 1409), vii. 60
Ware, John de (c. 1366), viii. 32; xii. 78
Waredroper, see Wardroper
Warenne, John de (c. 1296–1330), vi. 82
Warenne, see also Wareyn, Warren, Waryn
Waresio, see Varesio
Wareyn, John (c. 1390), viii. 32
Wareyn, see also Warenne, Warren, Waryn
Warham, Edmund, vii. 39; xi. 64
Warham, Richard, vii. 42

Warham, William (d. 1532), i. 9; iv. 5; v. 4; viii. 7

Warham, William (d. 1557), iv. 9; v. 22, 52; ix. 62

Warini, John, de Wellesleigh, viii. 30, 46

Warknethby, Hugh de, vii. 10

Warley (Warle), Ingelard de, v. 27; vi. 64; viii. 39; xi. 80

Warman, John, vii. 29

Warmington, Christopher, i. 69

Warre, Thomas (de la), i. 71, 72, 82; vi. 55, 76; xii. 28(bis), 31, 71

Warren, Thomas, x. 57

Warren, see also Warenne, Wareyn, Waryn

Warsopp, John, i. 87; xii. 32

Warsopp, see also Worshop

Warthwyk, Adam de, vi. 99

Warton, see Wharton

Waryn, John, ix. 20, 48

Waryn, Nicholas, viii. 81

Waryn, see also Warenne, Wareyn, Warren

Washington, John de, vi. 110

Wassayle, Thomas, ii. 11

Wastnesse (Wasteneys), George, x. 61

Wasyn, Thomas, viii. 61

Watford, Robert de, vii. 58

Wavendon, Robert, v. 67

Waver (Wavere, Weaver), Nigel de, vii. 57; x. 65; xi. 80

Waver, see also Wever

Waynflete, John (d. 1421), i. 87

Waynflete (Paten, Patten), John (d. 1479), iii. 22; iv. 49; v. 28; vi. 74, 94; vii. 5

Waynflete, William, iv. 46

Wayte, Anthony, vii. 14; xii. 74

Weaver, see Waver, Wever

Webbe, David, xi. 79

Webbe (Wybbe), John, x. 5

Webbe, Thomas, see Wybbe

Webbe, William, ii. 6, 7, 25, 31, 35, 51; iii. 50

Webber, Henry, viii. 5n, 71; ix. 5, 8, 9n, 11, 51(bis)

Weborn, John, x. 18

Webster, William, i. 48

Wednesbury (Wednesburgh), John, iv. 60

Weffe, see Whasch

Weford, see Wyford

Welborne (Welbourne, Wellesbourne), John (c. 1379–1424), i. 39, 69; iii. 15, 63; iv. 18; vi. 49; vii. 41; viii. 38; xii. 21

Welborne (Welburne, Wellesbourne), John (de) (d. 1380), i. 22, 29; iii. 29; vi. 58; x. 55

Welborne, Thomas, i. 89

Welborne, William, i. 9, 64, 107; xii. 14, 26

Welburne, see Welborne, John (de) (d. 1380)

Welby, Adelard, i. 97

Weldon, William, i. 122

Wele, John, ix. 7, 12, 19, 25

Wele, Thomas (d. 1521, ? T. Vele), x. 51

Welewyk, Thomas de, iii. 15

Welewyk, see also Welwyk

Welhampton, Hugh de, xi. 84

Welles, John (d. 1417), viii. 26

Welles, John (d. 1440), xi. 22

Welles, John (d. 1475), vi. 77

Welles, Nicholas de, vi. 113; viii. 81

Welles (Wellis), Thomas (d. 1524, ?—Wellys) vii. 18, 48; viii. 55; ix. 60n

Welles, William, vii. 18; xii. 74

Welles, see also Wells, Wellys

Wellesbourne, see Welborne

Wellesleigh, see Warini

Wellewyk, see Welwyk

Wellington, John, viii. 57

Wellington, Robert, vi. 86; xii. 72

Wellis, see Welles, Thomas

Wellisford, Christopher (c. 1535, ? C. Welly-fed), xi. 43

Wells, Henry, i. 7

Wells, John, ii. 7

Wells, Robert de (Robert Steward), iv. 17

Wells, William (c. 1430), iv. 17

Wells, William (d. 1444), iv. 39

Wells, see also Welles, Wellys

Wellyfed, Christopher (d. 1538, ? C. Wellisford), vi. 50; x. 29

Wellyfed, William, i. 92; v. 47(bis); vi. 50, 68

Wellys, — (c. 1503, ? Thomas Welles), ix. 60 & n

Wellys, Ralph, xi. 41, 47

Wellys, see also Welles, Wells

Welshe, Edward, ii. 17

Welton, Gilbert (de), i. 104; vi. 73, 97

Welton, Nicholas (de) (Nicholas Hawe), i. 104; vi. 54; xii. 37, 70

Welwyk (Wellewyk), John de, iii. 102; v. 59; vi. 46, 56

Welwyk, see also Welewyk

Wemme, Thomas, vii. 36

Wendesley (Wensley), John, x. 20, 49 & n, 50, 62 & n

Wendlyngburgh, John de, v. 30; vii. 8n, 10

Wendlyngburgh, Robert de (Robert Hyne de Wendlyngburgh), vii. 8n, 25

Wendlyngburgh, William de, vii. 6, 8n

Wendover, John, vii. 13

Wengham, John (de), i. 27; v. 16, 41

Wengworth, Robert, i. 46
Wengworth, see also Wyngreworth
Wenllong, see Gwynllwg
Wenlock (Stokeley), Giles, iii. 61; vii. 50
Wenlock, William (d. 1392), v. 22; vii. 38
Wenlock, William Wynel of (c. 1363-4), see Wynel
Wenlocke, William (d. 1499), iv. 60
Wensley, John, see Wendesley
Wensley, Nicholas de, x. 23n
Went, see Gwent
Werkeman, William, i. 33; iii. 25, 39
Werkworth, John, i. 90; x. 54 & n; xii. 33, 85
Wermenstre, Andrew de, vii. 58
Wermington, Walter, i. 83, 106; xii. 31, 37
Wermyngton, Robert de, xi. 72
Werston, see Worston
Wesenham, Roger de, iv. 41
West, Nicholas, iv. 15; vii. 11; x. 17 & n
West, Reginald, i. 57; ii. 5, 43; viii. 12, 31, 52
West, Thomas (c. 1360, ? T.W. c. 1368-71), xi. 26
West, Thomas (c. 1368-71, ? T.W. c. 1360), x. 55
West, Thomas (c. 1414), xi. 14
Westacre (Westacra), William, iv. 27; xii. 59
Westbie, Thomas, i. 69; vi. 19; x. 36
Westbury, William, i. 75; iii. 85; v. 21
Westby, George, iii. 20, 24, 27, 52, 67, 75
Westcote, John, ix. 46, 47
Westerham, John de, iv. 40
Westgate, Richard, iv. 48
Westle, William de, vi. 112
Westminster, Roger, iv. 17
Weston, John (d. 1461), v. 61
Weston, John de (c. 1327-35), iii. 53
Weston, Lawrence, viii. 45
Weston, Nicholas, ix. 7; xii. 83
Weston, Philip (de), i. 46, 111; v. 30; vi. 6, 62; vii. 50; x. 58
Weston, Robert, ix. 7, 62
Weston, Thomas (de), i. 72; v. 64; vi. 55, 90, 112; viii. 46
Weston, Walter de, vii. 28
Weston, William (de) (d. 1330), i. 79; x. 29; xii. 31
Weston, William de (d. 1357), vi. 19; viii. 38; ix. 26; xii. 78
Westons, John, i. 108
Westwode, Roger, i. 33, 74, 103, 107; x. 54; xii. 29
Westwood, John, x. 57

Wetewang, Walter de, vi. 44, 90
Wetewang, William de, vi. 15
Wetewang, see also Wetwang
Wetheryngesete, Richard, iv. 18
Wetheryngsete, Robert, i. 49n
Wetton, Peter (de), see Wotton
Wetton, Richard, i. 51; iii. 99; xii. 23
Wetwang, Richard, v. 61, 69
Wetwang, see also Wetewang
Wever, Thomas, iii. 95
Wever, see also Waver
Whalley (Waller, Walley), Edward, i. 75; xii. 30
Wharton, Geoffrey, i. 113; v. 9, 45
Wharton (Parfew, Warton), Robert, xi. 39
Whasch (Weffe), Augustine, x. 24
Whelpdale, John, i. 51; x. 46, 61
Whelpdale, Roger, vi. 98
Whelpington, Roger de, vi. 77
Wheteleye, Elias, i. 85
Whetley, William, v. 55
Which, Lewis, xi. 34
Which, see also Wiche, Wyche
Whiston, Thomas, i. 99, 125; xii. 42
Whitbergh (Witeberg), Robert (de), iii. 84; xi. 81
Whitby, Richard (d. 1494), iii. 20, 29, 44, 86
Whitby, Richard de (c. 1292), vi. 101
Whitby (Whitteby), Robert, i. 61, 65, 71; v. 67
Whitchurch, John de, iii. 13, 24, 63
Whitchurch (Whitechurch), Nicholas, i. 120, 126; xii. 41, 42
White, Henry, i. 91
White, Roger le (Roger Wyte), iii. 86; viii. 70; xii. 81
White, see also Whyte, Wyte
Whitechurch, see Whitchurch
Whitefeld, Henry, ix. 20, 39
Whitefeld, see also Whitfeld
Whitegreve, Thomas, x. 26
Whitehead, John, x. 10
Whitehead, Ralph, x. 10, 51, 65
Whitehead, Thomas, v. 22
Whitehead, see also Whithead
Whitelee, Richard, x. 63
Whitfeld, Thomas, i. 64; xii. 26
Whitfeld, see also Whitefeld
Whithead, Hugh, vi. 111
Whithead, see also Whitehead
Whitmay (Whitmaye, Witney), Andrew, xi. 61 & n
Whitney (Whyteneye), Baldwin de, ii. 43; x. 21, 65

Whitney, Robert de, xi. 68

Whitstons, James, i. 32, 68, 124; xii. 27(*bis*), 42(*bis*)

Whitteby, *see* Whitby

Whittemer, John, iii. 88

Whittington, Guy, x. 46, 54

Whittlesey, *see* Wittlesey

Whitwell, Richard, i. 63

Whytclyf, John, vii. 27

Whyte, William, viii. 12

Whyte, *see also* White, Wyte

Whyteneye, *see* Whitney, Baldwin de

Whyting, Henry, vi. 48, 75

Whyting, Richard, viii. 61

Wiat, *see* Wyat

Wiche (Wyche), Thomas, x. 28

Wiche, *see also* Which, Wyche

Wideslade, Richard de, ix. 10, 19, 26

Widevyle, *see* Woodville

Widewe, Robert, viii. 12, 24, 52

Wiggenhall, John, iv. 31; xii. 59

Wigmour, John, xi. 67

Wigmour, *see also* Wyggemore

Wikeford (Wykford), Robert (de), i. 103; iv. 50; vi. 69; vii. 58; ix. 36; xii. 36

Wikes, *see* Wykes

Wilcock, William, xi. 68, 69, 72n

Wilcocks, Henry, i. 13, 59, 63, 86, 108, 127; iii. 93; xii. 15, 25

Wilcox, Thomas, vi. 39

Wilde, *see* Wylde

Wilford, Edmund, *see* Wylsford

Wilford, Gervase de, iii. 24

Wilford, Thomas de, vii. 26

Willelmi, Thomas, de Honyngg, vii. 59

Willen, Miles, iii. 97

William (c. 1317–18), vii. 11n

William (c. 1328), xi. 8

William (c. 1376), viii. 13n

William (c. 1408), xi. 14; xii. 88

William ap John, xi. 33

William ap Thomas, xi. 62

William, John, xi. 63 & n, 85

Williams, Dafydd, xi. 60 & n, 78 & n

Williams, Henry, i. 87; iii. 28; vi. 52, 74; x. 7, 31

Williams, John, ix. 65

Williams, Thomas, *see* Baghe

Willisford, *see* Wylsford

Willoughby, Brian, i. 126; xii. 42

Willoughby (Willughby), Edward, iii. 57; viii. 78; ix. 5, 59; x. 20, 36

Willoughby (Wyllughby), Hugh de, vi. 31, 94

Willoughby (Willughby, Wyleby, Wyllughby), Philip (de), i. 3, 96; v. 20; vi. 33; x. 22, 51

Wilson, Christopher, vi. 32

Wilson, James, vii. 6

Wilson, Nicholas, i. 14

Wilson, Robert, viii. 9, 67

Wilton, John de, iii. 17, 87

Wilton, Stephen, i. 18, 64, 97; iii. 12, 34, 40; iv. 51; v. 12, 34; vi. 21, 43, 81, 83; xii. 35

Wilton, Thomas de, v. 18, 59; viii. 18; xii. 62

Wilton, William, iii. 18, 58

Wimundeswold, Wimundewold, *see* Wymundeswold

Winchcombe (Winchecombe), John (de), i. 88; v. 17; vii. 23

Winchcombe, Richard (d. 1303), i. 38

Winchcombe, Richard (d. 1404), ii. 32; iv. 61; xii. 49, 61

Winchcombe, Robert de (d. 1335), iii. 75, 85

Winchcombe, Robert of (d. 1401), *see* Tideman

Winchelsea (Winchelse, Winchelsey, Wynchelse), John (de), i. 120; ii. 32; iii. 35, 66; viii. 19; xii. 41

Winchelsey, Robert, iv. 3

Winchester, Thomas de, ii. 8; iv. 30; xii. 45, 59

Winckley (Wynkeleye), John de, iii. 35

Windelzore (Wyndesore), Ralph de, viii. 72

Windelzore, *see also* Wyndesore

Windsor, *see* Broun, William

Winsford, John, viii. 76

Winter, John, *see* Wynter

Winter (Wynter), Maurice (c. 1454, ? M. Wynter), xi. 63n

Winter (Wynter), Thomas, i. 92; iii. 18, 30; iv. 30, 34; vi. 19, 27, 52, 82, 113; viii. 6, 56; ix. 17; xii. 34, 73, 76, 79

Winter (Wynter), Walter, xi. 64

Winter, *see also* Wynter

Winterborne (Winterbourne, Wynterbourne), Thomas, iii. 48; iv. 8; v. 6, 48, 63; viii. 38; xii. 58

Winterton, Henry de, iii. 27, 96; v. 10

Winterton, William de, ii. 44; xii. 50

Winton, Thomas de, viii. 21

Winton, *see also* Wynton

Wintringham, Robert, i. 85; xii. 32

Wiot, *see* Wyat

Wippingen (Vuipenns, Vypaynes), Gerard von, vi. 25, 80

Wisbech, Thomas, iii. 75, 87; v. 70

Wissande, see Lestine
Witeberg, see Whitbergh
Witham, William, i. 13, 19, 32, 47, 55, 71, 90, 109; v. 29; viii. 5, 55; xii. 24
Withers, John, iii. 72; v. 47; vi. 43(bis), 61
Withers, see also Wyther
Witherton, Henry, xi. 49
Withington, Roger de, ii. 22
Withornwick, John de (c. 1367, ? J. de Wythornwyk), iii. 77
Withrington, see Griffin, Thomas
Witney, see Whitmay, Whitney
Wittlesey, William (c. 1510–15), iv. 17
Wittlesey (Whittlesey), William (de) (d. 1374), i. 8, 32; iv. 4, 37, 56; vii. 31; ix. 33; x. 55; xii. 14, 20 60(bis), 75, 83
Witton, Simon de, xi. 85
Witton, see also Wytton
Wittour, William, i. 96
Wod, William, iv. 40
Wodde (Wode), John, v. 12, 47, 67
Wodderoff, see Wodrofe
Wode, John (d. 1475, D.C.L.), see Stretton
Wode, John (d. 1475, D.Th.), see Wodde
Wode, Patrick atte, xi. 30
Wode, Roger, i. 34, 119
Wode, William atte, vi. 28
Wodechurche, Henry, v. 13
Wodeford, see Woodford
Wodehale (Wodehele, Woodhall), Roger, iv. 31; xii. 82
Wodeham, John, i. 97
Wodehele, see Wodehale, Wodhull
Wodehous, John de (d. 1395), x. 66
Wodehouse, John de (d. 1355), vi. 37; xii. 69
Wodehouse, Robert (de), i. 70; ii. 23; vi. 25, 59 ('Robert or Thomas'); x. 25 & n; xii. 28
Wodehouse, Walter de, vi. 33, 56, 82 ('William'); xii. 68, 70, 71
Wodele, Roger, xi. 6
Wodelond, see Odelond
Woderoue, William (c. 1355, ? W.W. c. 1360–87), i. 65
Woderoue, William (c. 1360–87, ? W.W. c. 1355), vi. 31, 84
Woderoue, see also Woodrowe
Wodeville, see Woodville
Wodeward, William, i. 72
Wodham, John, vi. 23, 24, 49, 79
Wodhorne, William de, vi. 77
Wodhull, Robert de, ii. 48
Wodhull, see also Wodehale
Wodnesbergh, John, iv. 6

Wodrofe (Wodderoff, Wodrove, Wooderoff), John (d. 1533, ? J. Woodroff), ii. 23, 30, 33
Wodroff, see Woodroff
Wodville, see Woodville
Wodyngton, Thomas, vii. 11
Wogan, Dafydd, xi. 79
Wogan, Richard, xi. 58, 76
Wolcy, see Wolsey
Wolde, John, xi. 9
Woleman, see Wolman
Wolfet, George, iii. 36
Wollaston, Thomas, xi. 56
Wollore, David (de), i. 41; v. 33; vi. 50; vii. 50
Wolman (Woleman, Wuleman, Wulman), Richard, i. 59; iv. 32; v. 38; viii. 6; xii. 59
Wolsey (Wolcy, Wulcie, Wulcy), Thomas, i. 3, 4, 112, 124; ii. 5, 44; iv. 47; v. 18; vi. 5, 8, 41, 109; viii. 3, 41; xii. 13
Wolstone, Reginald, ii. 27, 38; xii. 48
Wolveden, Robert, iv. 27; vi. 14, 60, 72, 83, 90; x. 6, 8
Wolveleye, John (c. 1361), iv. 50
Wolvesley, John de (c. 1348–52), iii. 71
Wombwell, Richard de, vi. 39
Wood, see Wode
Woodcock, Laurence, vii. 53, 54
Woodcock, William, i. 28; v. 65; xii. 19, 64
Wooderoff, see Wodrofe
Woodford (Wodeford), John de, iii. 57; v. 52
Woodford (Belton, Wodeford), Thomas, i. 39, 64; ii. 27; v. 24, 63
Woodhall, see Wodehale
Woodlock, Henry, de Merewell, iv. 45, 47; xii. 60(bis)
Woodroff (Wodroff), John (c. 1508–17, ? J. Wodrofe), iii. 26, 31, 83
Woodrowe, John, iv. 14
Woodrowe, see also Woderoue
Woodville (Wodeville, Wydeville), Edmund, vi. 51
Woodville, Edward, i. 81
Woodville (Widevyle, Wodville, Wydeville), Lionel, i. 14, 81, 96, 117; iii. 2, 43, 46; iv. 49; v. 49; ix. 5, 57; xii. 15
Woolton, Matthew, iii. 57
Wooton, see Wotton, Nicholas
Worcester (Wygorn'), Robert de (c. 1337–1349, ? R. de Wygornia), iv. 62
Worcester, see also Wygornia
Wormebrugge, Richard, xi. 25
Wormenhale, Thomas de, vii. 15; xii. 74

Wormonhale, John, iii. 1, 92
Worshop (Chesterfield, Chestrefeld, Wursop), Thomas, ii. 35; x. 18, 60
Worshop, see also Warsopp
Worsley, Edmund, vi. 41, 53
Worsley, Thomas, x. 59
Worsley, William, v. 6, 71; vi. 24, 43; viii. 17; x. 59; xii. 65, 85
Worsted, William, iv. 25
Worston (Werston, Wrofton, Wroghton), Thomas, iii. 57; xii. 55
Worston, William de (c. 1333–44, ? W. de Borstan, W. de Plumstock), v. 17
Worth, Robert de, iii. 5, 21, 44, 47
Worthe, Simon, i. 109
Worthiall, John, vii. 9, 13, 19, 23, 25, 33, 40(bis)
Worthington, Richard, viii. 35, 78
Worton, see Wotton, Peter (de)
Wotton, John (d. 1409), xi. 14
Wotton, John (d. 1418), vii. 47
Wotton, John de (c. 1335), iii. 5
Wotton, Matthew, see Peyworden
Wotton (Wooton), Nicholas, iv. 62; ix. 66; xii. 61
Wotton (Wetton, Worton), Peter (de), i. 31; ii. 46; iii. 30; v. 21; xii. 88
Wotton (Wutton), Walter, i. 8, 42, 68; xii. 14, 21
Wouldham, Thomas de, iv. 37
Wraby, John, vii. 37
Wrangill, Richard, x. 54
Wraxall (Bele), Richard, viii. 57
Wrenne, Geoffrey, vi. 43, 61; x. 28, 29; xii. 70, 84
Wright, John, ix. 56
Wrighte, William, i. 57
Wrixham, William, ii. 37; x. 53
Wrofton, Wroghton, see Worston
Wroth, William, ii. 15; xi. 58
Wulcie, Wulcy, see Wolsey
Wuleman, Wulman, see Wolman
Wursop, see Worshop
Wutton, see Wotton
Wy, William de, ix. 27
Wyat (Wiat, Wiot, Wyatt, Wyott), Richard (d. 1522), vi. 12; viii. 47; x. 22, 53
Wyatt, Richard (d. 1569), vii. 16
Wybbe, John see Webbe
Wybbe (Webbe), Thomas, ii. 38; viii. 25
Wych, see Wyche
Wychampton, Thomas, iii. 11
Wyche (Wych), Richard, iii. 79; x. 40
Wyche, Thomas, see Wiche

Wyche, see also Which
Wychecote, Robert, i. 55
Wycheford, Robert de, ii. 29; iii. 32
Wychtringes, Richer de, vii. 54
Wydeville, see Woodville
Wyford (Weford), Thomas, x. 5
Wygeton, William de, xi. 32
Wygetoune, Gilbert de, xi. 32
Wyggemore, Adam, vii. 35
Wyggemore, see also Wigmour
Wyggeworth, John, i. 39
Wygorn', see Worcester
Wygornia, Robert de (c. 1343, ? R. de Worcester), vii. 44
Wygrome (Wygrym), John, i. 60 ('Wygryne'); viii. 23; xii. 25, 77
Wyk (Wyke), Samuel de, xi. 10 & n, 73(bis) & n
Wyke, John (d. 1428), v. 17, 58, 71; vii. 19; x. 42
Wyke, John de (d. 1317), iv. 59
Wyke, Nicholas de, iii. 6
Wyke, Samuel de, see Wyk
Wyke, William (d. 1504), viii. 53
Wyke, William de (c. 1311–60), ii. 22, 44
Wykeham, John de, vii. 60; ix. 42
Wykeham, Nicholas (de), iii. 14, 29; iv. 50
Wykeham, William of (de), i. 6, 10, 113; ii. 17; iii. 27, 51, 100; iv. 46; v. 53, 63(bis); vi. 61, 64; viii. 69; x. 37; xi. 30, 81; xii. 14, 39
Wykersley, Thomas, i. 97
Wykes (Wikes), Gilbert, i. 61; v. 70
Wykes, William, viii. 24
Wykford, see Wikeford
Wykley, John, vii. 30
Wykyngeston, William de, v. 58
Wylberfosse, Peter, v. 71
Wylde (Wilde), Edmund, viii. 77
Wylde, William, v. 16, 17, 21, 54
Wyle, Henry de la, iii. 17, 47, 51, 68; ix. 8
Wyle, Nicholas de la, iii. 15, 95
Wyleby, see Willoughby
Wyliet, see Wylyot
Wylle, John, i. 20
Wyllughby, see Willoughby
Wylsford (Wilford, Willisford), Edmund, vii. 52 ('Edward'); x. 70; xii. 75, 86
Wylyot (Wyliet), John (de), v. 60; ix. 9, 32
Wymbysh, Robert (c. 1458), vi. 65n
Wymbyssh, Nicholas, i. 71, 127; vi. 24, 36; vii. 47; xi. 69
Wymbyssh, Robert (d. 1478), i. 5, 36, 47, 51, 103; xii. 14, 20, 22, 23, 37

Wymondeswold, Hugh de, iii. 46, 78; vi.
    10n, 11, 52, 86; x. 65; xii. 86
Wymondham, see Wyndham
Wymundeswold (Wimundeswold, Wimun-
    dewold), Richard de, ii. 12; x. 29
Wyncaulton, Walter, viii. 69
Wynchelse, see Winchelsea
Wyndesore, Ralph de, see Windelzore
Wyndesore, Walter, ix. 6, 55
Wyndesore, William, vii. 17–18
Wyndham (Wymondham), George, iv. 28;
    v. 18
Wyne, John, vii. 7
Wynel, William, of Wenlock, iv. 41 ('Wy-
    vel'); v. 48
Wyneyarde, William, viii. 71
Wynferthyng, Robert de, ii. 12
Wyngreworth, Giles de, vii. 23, 42
Wyngreworth, Robert, i. 46
Wyngreworth, see also Wengworth
Wynkeleye, see Winckley
Wynter (Winter), John, xi. 31
Wynter, Maurice (c. 1438–43, ? M. Winter),
    ii. 34
Wynter, Maurice (c. 1454), see Winter
Wynter, see also Winter
Wynterbourne, see Winterborne
Wynton (Winton), Adam de, iv. 45
Wynton, Richard de, iii. 35, 100
Wynton, see also Winton
Wynwyk, John (c. 1395), iii. 9
Wynwyk (Winwick), John (de) (d. 1360), i.
    27n, 40; iii. 102; vi. 13, 20 (line 3), 69;
    vii. 23; viii. 78; x. 35, 63; xii. 18, 21
Wynwyk, Richard (de), i. 27, 74, 98; vi. 55,
    69, 90; xii. 35, 70
Wynwyk, William, i. 67
Wyot (Wyott), Robert, i. 64; v. 12, 20
Wyott, Richard (d. 1449), see Leyott
Wyott, Richard (d. 1522), see Wyat
Wyott, Robert, see Wyot
Wyppyll, John, v. 36
Wrye, Simon de, iv. 59
Wyse, Thomas, ix. 63
Wyte, Roger, see White
Wyte, Walter le, viii. 73n
Wyte, see also White, Whyte
Wytehurst, Roger de, viii. 73
Wyther, John, iii. 6
Wyther, see also Withers
Wythornwyk, John de (c. 1394, ? J. de With-
    ornwick), xi. 28
Wytton, Robert, v. 65; viii. 38; xii. 64, 78
Wytton, see also Witton

Wyvel, see Wynel
Wyville, John, iii. 47
Wyville (Wyvile), Robert (de), i. 66; iii. 1, 69;
Wyville, Walter, iii. 19, 41, 69; xii. 55

Yale, David, xi. 6 & n, 15
Yale, Richard, xi. 6n
Yardburgh, see Yerdeburgh
Yarewell, Gilbert de, see Marewell
Yarewell, Walter de, vi. 31
Yarnemothe, see Yernemouth
Yatton, see Forde, William de la
Yedvyn (Meysey), Henry, ii. 49
Yeen, see Yone
Yerdeburgh (Yardburgh, Ʒerburgh), John
    (de), iii. 56; v. 32; vi. 71
Yernemouth (Yarnemothe, Yernemuth, Ʒer-
    nemowthe), John, vii. 9, 26; viii. 37
Ycsham (Isham), Robert, i. 92; ii. 45; xii. 34
Yesham (Isham), Thomas, ii. 45
Ynge (Inge), Hugh, viii. 42, 46 & n
Ynge, William, see Inge
Ynge, see also Inge, Yonge
Ynyr, Llywelyn ab, see Llywelyn ab Ynyr
Yokflete (Ʒokflete), Thomas, i. 111; iii. 9; xii.
    39
Yone (Yeen), Thomas, ii. 7, 13, 43
Yonge, Andrew, vii. 36
Yonge, Griffin le, xi. 4 & n, 11, 14, 43n, 54n,
    84
Yonge, Hugh le, xi. 42, 74
Yonge, Richard, see Young
Yonge, Thomas (d. 1436), xi. 76, 77
Yonge, Thomas (d. 1487), i. 122
Yonge, see also Young
York, Adam of (Adam de Eboraco), vi. 11
York, Ralph of (Ralph de Eboraco), iii. 16
Yorke, John, see Gorle
Yotton, John, vi. 61; x. 6, 38
Young, John (d. 1504), see Morgan
Young, John (d. 1516), v. 41, 52; vi. 8, 30, 41;
    vii. 5; ix. 5, 21; xii. 64, 66, 69
Young, John (d. 1526), v. 9; vii. 49
Young (Yonge), Richard, i. 78; iv. 38; xi.
    4; xii. 30
Young, Robert, viii. 31
Young, Thomas (d. 1377, ? T.Y. d. by
    1382), v. 18; viii. 27; xii. 62
Young, Thomas (d. by 1382, ? T.Y. d.
    1377), vii. 59
Young, see also Yonge
Yoxall, William de, x. 21
Ypres, see Berenger
Yrford, see Irford

Ysarni (Isarmy), Roger, v. 27
Yve (Ives), Robert, ii. 22
Yve, William, *see* Ive
Yvernio, *see* Vernhio

Zarabella, Francis, i. 114; vi. 18; x. 44
Zouche, Edmund de la, v. 20
Zouche, Eudo (de) la, i. 9, 64, 76(*bis*), 95, 107, 116; iv. 31; vi. 62; viii. 36; xii. 14, 26, 30, 59, 71

Zouche, Henry de la, iv. 30; vi. 27, 42; xii. 59, 68, 69
Zouche, John de la (c. 1349), x. 59
Zouche, John la (d. 1423), xi. 22
Zouche, Roger la, vii. 56
Zouche, William (de) la (c. 1328–48), vi. 64 & n; ix. 13, 20, 27, 29
Zouche, William de la (d. 1352), vi. 3, 6, 64; x. 61

INDEX OF PLACES

Abergwili, Carm., colleg. ch., prebs. in: Boughrood (Radnor.), v. 19; xi. 71; Llanarthney (Carm.), ix. 43(*bis*); Llanddarog (Carm.) *or* Llanganten (Breck.), v. 57; Llandogy (Llandygwydd, Card.), ii. 32; Llangamarch (Llangammarch, Breck.), i. 25; Trallwng (Trallong, Breck.), ii. 46; ix. 15; unnamed, iii. 89; vii. 45

Abingdon, Berks., xi. 54

Achonry, co. Sligo, Ireland, bp., xi. 5

Achurch, Northants., x. 26

Agen, Lot-et-Garonne, France, iii. 51

Albano, Italy, bp., i. 54, 113; iv. 13, 32, 55

Albi, Tarn, France, bp., i. 6

Aldenham, Herts., vii. 11

Aldington, Kent, xi. 24, 27

All Saints in Hungate, preb., *see* Lincoln

Allington, Lincs., *see* Ellington

Allington, nr. Amesbury, Wilts., iv. 62

Alrewas, Staffs.:
  ch., xi. 41
  preb., *see* Lichfield

Althorpe, Lincs., vi. 22

Alton Australis, preb., *see* Salisbury

Alton Borealis, preb., *see* Salisbury

Amiens, Somme, France, cath., preb. in, vi. 13

Ampleforth, preb., *see* York

Amport, Hants, vii. 6

Anglesey (Môn), Caern., archdcnry, xi. 9–10

Antivari, Italy, bp., iv. 24

Apesthorpe, preb., *see* York

Aquila, Italy, iv. 3

Aragon, Spain, viii. 15n

Aran, Spain, archdcnry, xi. 43n

Ardingly, Suss., vii. 25

Armagh, Ireland, abp., v. 23; vi. 99; x. 5, 6

Arras, Pas-de-Calais, France, cath., canonry in, v. 27

Asgarby, preb., *see* Lincoln

Ashill, preb., *see* Wells

Asti, Italy, bp., i. 113

Astley, portion, *see* Bromyard

Aston Clinton, Bucks., viii. 64

Athelhampton, Dors., iii. 48

Athelney, Som., abbey, viii. 56

Auckland St Andrew, co. Dur., colleg. ch. of Auckland, vi. 114; prebs. in: West Merrington (Merrington, co. Dur.), v. 59; vi. 78; Witton (Witton-le-Wear, co. Dur.), xii. 37; unnamed, i. 105, 106

Autun, Saône-et-Loire, France, bp., i. 67

Auxerre, Yonne, France, bp., vi. 25

Avara, Lebanon, vii. 49, 53

Avignon, Vaucluse, France, i. 82, 91; iv. 3, 14, 23(*bis*), 37, 38, 45, 55(*bis*), 62; vi. 3, 97(*ter*); x. 1; xi. 3(*ter*)

Axbridge, Som., viii. 42

Axford, preb., *see* Salisbury

Aylesbury, preb., *see* Lincoln

Bainton, Yorks., v. 12

Banbury, preb., *see* Lincoln

Bangor, Caern.:
  archdcnry, xi. 8–9
  bp., i. 39, 78; ii. 2(*bis*); iii. 3, 4; iv. 38; vi. 98, 99; ix. 49; xi. 3–5, 47, 48, 54, 59
  cath., prebs. in, 11–16: Llanfair (Llanfair Dyffryn Clwyd, Denbighs.), xi. 11; Penmynydd (Anglesey, Caern.), xi. 11

Banham, Norf., iii. 98; viii. 41

Bargham, preb., *see* Chichester

Barking, Suff., i. 121

Barlinch, formerly in Brompton Regis parish, Som., priory, ix. 10, 24

Barnby, preb., *see* Howden and York

Barnstaple, Devon, archdcnry, viii. 33 & n; ix. 19–21

Barnwell, Cambs., iv. 14

Barnwell All Saints, Northants., x. 24 & n

Barnwell St Andrews, Northants., x. 24 & n

Barrowby, Lincs., v. 13

Barton-in-the-Clay, Beds., vi. 56

Barton St David, preb., *see* Wells

Bartonsham, preb., *see* Hereford

Barwell, Leics., x. 32

Barwick in Elmet, Yorks., iii. 34

Bath, Som.:
    archdcnry, viii. 14–15
    ch. of St Mary, viii. 21
    priory, viii. 21
Bath and Wells, Som., bp., i. 7, 10, 16, 66,
    81, 94, 110; ii. 3; iii. 1, 2, 9, 10, 29, 37,
    47, 52, 60, 62; iv. 4, 5, 8, 14, 56, 62;
    v. 14(bis), 30(bis), 40; vi. 4, 7, 27, 60, 66,
    79, 91, 108, 109; vii. 29, 34, 44; viii. 1–3,
    5, 44, 49, 50, 78, 83; ix. 3(bis), 47; x. 2,
    14, 46, 67 & n; xi. 16, 47, 55, 56, 71, 80;
    xii. 33. See also Wells
Bawtry, Yorks., ii. 48; vii. 50; x. 37
Beaulieu, Hants, abbey, xi. 5 & n
Beauvais, Oise, France, iv. 55; cath., preb. of
    Gerberoy (Oise), vi. 27
Bec, Eure, France, abbey, iii. 76; viii. 22
Beckingham, preb., see Southwell
Beddingham, Suss., vii. 25n
Bedford, archdcnry, i. 16–17
Bedford Major, preb., see Lincoln
Bedford Minor, preb., see Lincoln
Bedminster and Redclyffe, preb., see Salis-
    bury
Bedwyn, preb., see Salisbury
Beechamwell, Norf., xi. 25
Belford, Northumb., vi. 16
Beminster Prima, preb., see Salisbury
Beminster Secunda, preb., see Salisbury
Bentworth, Hants, iii. 6
Berkshire, archdcnry, i. 14; iii. 9–11; vi. 87
Berkswell, Warwicks., ii. 4
Berwick St John, Wilts., iii. 14; vii. 35
Besançon, Doubs, France, abp., v. 11; viii. 14
Bethlehem, Israel, bp., xi. 21
Beverley, Yorks., colleg. ch., v. 22, 60; vi. 20;
    prebs. in: St Katharine's altar, iii. 90;
    St Martin's altar, iii. 91; St Mary's altar,
    viii. 50; St Stephen's altar, x. 50; un-
    named, i. 123
Beverleyhall, preb., see Gnosall
Biddenham, Beds., xi. 26n
Bideford, Devon, ix. 16
Biggleswade, preb., see Lincoln
Bilton, preb., see York
Binbrook, Lincs., xi. 26n
Bingham, Notts., i. 105; ix. 23
Binham, Norf., ix. 39
Birdbrook, Essex, ii. 6
Birtley, preb., see Chester-le-Street
Bishop Wearmouth, co. Dur., i. 41; xii. 21
Bishop's Cleeve, Glos., vi. 10; vii. 52
Bishops Itchington, preb., see Lichfield
Bishopshull, preb., see Lichfield

Bishopshurst, preb., see Chichester
Bishopstone, preb., see Salisbury
Bitton, preb., see Salisbury
Bladon, Oxon., viii. 24
Blaenporth, preb., see Llanddewi Brefi
Blaston, Leics., x. 32
Blaye, Gironde, France, i. 31
Bleadon, Som., viii. 8
Bletchley, Bucks., xii. 37
Blewbury, preb., see Salisbury
Blofield, Norf., vi. 114
Bloxworth, Dors., v. 16
Blyborough, Lincs., i. 18
Bobenhull, preb., see Lichfield
Bockingfold, see Goudhurst
Bole, preb., see York
Bolney, Suss., vii. 32n, 33
Bologna, Italy, i. 7
Bolton, preb., see Lichfield
Bolton Percy, Yorks., i. 47
Bonehill, preb., see Tamworth
Bordeaux, Gironde, France, abp., xi. 3
Bosham, Suss., colleg. ch., sacristanship, ix.
    29, 34; prebs. in: Funtington (Suss.), ii.
    14; viii. 23; Westbrooke (a tithing in
    Bosham, Suss.), i. 38; ix. 18
Bossall with Buttercrambe, Yorks., vi. 20
Botevant, preb., see York
Bottesford, Leics., i. 79
Boughrood (Bochrwyd), preb., see Abergwili
Bracklesham, preb., see Chichester
Bradenstoke, Wilts., priory, vi. 59
Bradford-on-Avon, Wilts., iii. 5
Bradninch, Devon, vii. 13
Bramham, preb., see York
Brampton, preb., see Lincoln
Bramshott, Hants, iv. 49
Brantingham, Yorks., x. 62
Brawdy (Breudeth), preb., see St Davids
Brecon (Aberhonddu), archdcnry, xi. 61–2
Bredon, Worcs., iv. 61, 63
Brewood, preb., see Lichfield
Brickhill, Great, Bucks., xi. 8
Bridgnorth, Salop, colleg. ch., i. 123
Brightwell, Berks., viii. 39
Bringhurst, Leics., v. 8
Brington, Hunts., ix. 15
Bristol, Glos.:
    bp., iii. 35; iv. 60n
    ch. of St Nicholas, iii. 82
    see, iii. 9
Brixworth, Northants.:
    ch., iii. 16
    preb., see Salisbury

Brompton, nr. Scarborough, Yorks., iii. 82; vi. 11

Bromyard, Herefs., ch., portions in: Astley (Salop), iii. 81; unnamed, vii. 29; x. 27

Brooke, Norf., i. 123

Broomesbury, preb., *see* London, St Paul's

Broseley, Salop, viii. 65

Broughton Gifford, Wilts., xii. 74

Brownswood, preb., *see* London, St Paul's

Bubwith, Yorks., vi. 20

Buckby, Long, Northants., x. 27

Buckden, preb., *see* Lincoln

Buckingham, archdenry, i. 15–16; iii. 15; vi. 16; ix. 15

Buckland, Berks., iii. 66

Buckland Dinham, preb., *see* Wells

Bugthorpe, preb., *see* York

Bullinghope, preb., *see* Hereford

Bulverhythe, preb., *see* Hastings

Burley, Rut., xi. 12, 13

Burmarsh, Kent, vi. 115

Bursal, preb., *see* Chichester

Burton, Ches., x. 47; Denwall hospital, x. 47

Burwell, Cambs., xi. 69, 74n

Bury, preb., *see* Chichester

Buxted, Suss., iv. 62

Caddington Major, preb., *see* London, St Paul's

Caddington Minor, preb., *see* London, St Paul's

Caerau, preb., *see* Llandaff

Caerfai, preb., *see* St Davids

Caerfarchell, preb., *see* St Davids

Caergybi, *see* Holyhead

Caistor, preb., *see* Lincoln

Callipoli, Thrace, bp., v. 9; vii. 49

Calne, preb., *see* Salisbury

Cambrai, Nord, France, x. 1

Cambridge, vi. 4; xi. 55:
   Sturbridge hospital, i. 67

Canterbury, Kent, i. 63; ii. 16; iv. 13(*bis*), 23, 24, 25, 38(*bis*), 39, 45(*ter*), 47, 55(*ter*) 56(*bis*); vii. 1; viii. 1 & n; xi. 3(*ter*), 21, 37, 53(*bis*) & n, 54, 55n
   abbey of St Augustine, viii. 22
   abp., i. 4, 49, 70, 85, 121; iii. 2, 3, 62, 100; iv. 3–5, 14, 15(*bis*), 45(*bis*), 47, 55(*bis*), 56(*bis*); v. 2(*bis*), 4, 18, 25, 48, 62, 70; vi. 4(*bis*), 7, 33, 60, 66(*bis*); vii. 32; viii. 2, 17, 54, 77; ix. 1, 4(*bis*), 14, 26; x. 49, 53, 60; xi. 37, 38 & n, 41, 54; xii. 21
   archdenry, ii. 4; iv. 6–9, 56; viii. 4; ix. 3

ct., iii. 17, 37, 38, 42, 43, 71; ix. 4, 27
   priory of Christ Church, i. 2; v. 1; ix. 1; x. 2; xi. 37, 53(*bis*)

Cantlers, preb., *see* London, St Paul's

Cardigan (Aberteifi), archdenry, xi. 62–3

Carhampton, preb., *see* Wells

Carlisle, Cumb., vi. 99; xi. 3:
   archdenry, vi. 101–3
   bp., i. 2, 61, 69, 73, 105; ii. 34; iii. 27, 68; iv. 61; v. 14(*bis*); vi. 45, 55, 73, 97–9, 102, 109, 111, 113; vii. 2, 3, 15; viii. 73; x. 2; xi. 4, 5

Carlton-cum-Dalby, preb., *see* Lincoln, Carlton Kyme

Carlton-cum-Thurlby, preb., *see* Lincoln, Carlton Paynell

Carlton Kyme, preb., *see* Lincoln

Carlton Paynell, preb., *see* Lincoln

Carmarthen (Caerfyrddin):
   archdenry, x. 18; xi. 64–5
   priory, xi. 85

Caron, preb., *see* Llanddewi Brefi

Carpentras, Vaucluse, France, bp., iv. 7; v. 27; vi. 75

Carperby cum Thoresby, Yorks., x. 32

'Castrikuby', *see* Holyhead

Cawood, Yorks., vi. 98

Centum Solidorum, preb., *see* Lincoln

Chagford, Devon, vii. 42

Chalfont St Giles, Bucks., i. 35

Chalke, preb., *see* Wilton

Chamberlainwood, preb., *see* London, St Paul's

Chardstock, preb., *see* Salisbury

Charing, Kent, i. 97; vii. 42

Charminster and Bere, preb., *see* Salisbury

Chartham, Kent, iv. 37; viii. 16; x. 27

Checkendon, Oxon., xi. 28

Chelmsford, Essex, free chap. of St Margaret, i. 27–38; vii. 8, 47; viii. 23, 69

Chelsea, Mdx., xi. 75(*bis*)

Chertsey, Surr., vi. 108

Chester, xi. 40:
   archdenry, x. 12–14
   bp., xi. 5
   ch. of St Mary's upon the Hill, iii. 23
   colleg. ch. of St John, x. 19, 47; prebs. in, i. 119; viii. 20; x. 42(*bis*), 47, 50, 55; xi. 67

Chester-le-Street, co. Dur., colleg. ch., prebs. in: Birtley (co. Dur.), xii. 37; Lamesley (co. Dur.), v. 44

Chichester, Suss.:
   archdenry, vii. 11–13

Chichester, Suss.—*contd.*
 bp., i. 25, 59, 75, 103; ii. 2, 19, 36; iii. 1, 4(*bis*), 18, 21, 22, 25, 41, 42, 96; iv. 6, 7, 29, 34, 38, 39, 57(*bis*); v. 2n, 3, 4, 7, 46, 47, 56, 60; vi. 4, 9, 26, 50, 87, 98, 99(*bis*); vii. 1–4; viii. 10, 16, 17; ix. 52; x. 7, 33, 70; xi. 21, 33, 38, 54 & n, 55; xii. 19, 77
 cath., prebs. in: Bargham (Barpham, in Angmering, Suss.); vii. 53; Bishops-hurst (in Albourne, Suss.), vii. 14–16; Bracklesham (in East Wittering, Suss.), vii. 16–17, Dursal, vii. 53, Dury (Suss.), vii. 17; Colworth (in Oving, Suss.), v. 30; vii. 17–19; ix. 14; Eartham (Suss.), vii. 19–20; x. 42; Exceit (Exceat, E. Suss.), vii. 53–4; Ferring (Suss.), ii. 51; vii. 20–1; Firle (West Firle, Suss.), ii. 33; vii. 21–3; Fittleworth (Suss.), i. 88; vii. 23–4; Gates (Westergate, Suss.), vii. 24–5; Hampstead (Hempstead in Ar-lington, Suss.), vii. 25–6; Heathfield (Suss.), vii. 27; x. 27; Henfield (Suss.), vi. 46, 69; vii. 28–9; xi. 70; Highleigh (Suss.), vii. 29–30; Hova Ecclesia (Hove, Suss.), iii. 92; vii. 30–2; Hova Villa (Hove, Suss.), vii. 32–3; Ipthorne (in Rumboldswyke, Chichester, Suss.), v. 32; vii. 33–4; Mardon (East Marden, Suss.), vii. 34–6; Middleton (in Arling-ton, Suss.), vii. 36–7; xii. 38; Oving (Suss.), vii. 7, 37; Seaford (Suss.), vii. 37–9; Selsey (Suss.), vii. 39–40; Sidles-ham (Suss.), viii. 40–2; Somerley (in East Wittering, Suss.), vii. 42–3; Sutton (by Seaford, Suss.), vii. 43–4; Thorney (in East Wittering, Suss.), iii. 89; vii. 45–6; Waltham (Upwaltham, Suss.), vii. 46–7; viii. 63; Westgate (in Chichester city, Suss.), vii. 4, 48; Wiccamical prebends, vii. 53–4; Wightring (West Wittering, Suss.), vii. 48–9; Wilmington (Suss.), vii. 49; Windham (Wyndham in Sher-manbury, Suss.), vii. 54; Wisborough (Wisborough Green, Suss.), iii. 62; v. 31; vii. 50–1; Woodhorn (in Oving, Suss.), vii. 51–2
Chinnor, Oxon., i. 126
Chipping Campden, Glos., viii. 25
Chisenbury and Chute, preb., *see* Salisbury
Chiswick, preb., *see* London, St Paul's
Chrishall, preb., *see* London, St Martin's-le-Grand
Christian Malford, Wilts., viii. 70
Chrysopolis, Turkey, bp., xi. 61

Church Withington, preb., *see* Hereford
Claverham (in Yatton), Som., vii. 38
Cleeve, Som.:
 abbey, viii. 22
 preb., *see* Wells
Cleveland, Yorks., archdcnry, v. 9; vi. 19–21
Clifford-by-Shefford, *see* Clifton
Clifton, Beds., i. 16; xii. 16
Clifton, preb., *see* Lincoln
Clonmethan, preb., *see* Dublin
Cloyne, co. Cork, Ireland, bp., xi. 4, 55
Clydey (Clydau), preb., *see* St Davids
Cobham, Kent, college, preb. of Cobham-bury (in Cobham), vi. 54
Colchester, Essex:
 archdcnry, v. 13–14
 bp., i. 13; vi. 54
 ch. of St Mary, xi. 6
Cold Ashton, Glos., viii. 31, 32
Cold Overton, Leics., x. 19
Colwall, preb., *see* Hereford
Colwich, preb., *see* Lichfield
Colworth, preb., *see* Chichester
Combe, prebs. I–XV, *see* Wells
Compton, Suss., vii. 31
Compton Bishop, preb., *see* Wells
Compton Dundon, preb., *see* Wells
Connor, co. Antrim, Ireland, bp., xi. 21
Consumpta-per-Mare, preb., *see* London, St Paul's
Cookham, Berks., x. 38
Coombe and Harnham, preb., *see* Salis-bury
Corhampton, Hants, viii. 75
Cornwall, archdcnry, vi. 50; viii. 23; ix. 15–17
Corringham, preb., *see* Lincoln
Coton, preb., *see* Stafford
Cottenham, Cambs., ii. 34; iv. 18(*bis*)
Cottingham, Yorks., iii. 43; vi. 11, 91; x. 41; xii. 45
Coutances, Manche, France, cath., preb. in, vi. 40
Coventry, Warwicks., viii. 64
Coventry and Lichfield, bp., i. 2, 3, 91, 101, 108; ii. 2, 20; iii. 13, 33, 90, 97; iv. 5, 27, 29, 51, 61; v. 29, 39, 41, 62; vi. 4(*bis*), 8, 22, 48, 82, 93, 98(*bis*); vii. 4 (*bis*), 46; viii. 2, 17, 35n, 36; ix. 2, 3, 5(*bis*), 17, 51, 57; x. 1–3; xi. 22, 54, 80; xii. 15, 88. *See also* Lichfield
Cowpes, preb., *see* London, St Martin's-le-Grand
Crackpole St Mary, preb., *see* Lincoln

Cranfield, Beds., i. 41; v. 53

Crantock, Cornw., colleg. ch. of St Crantock, prebs. in, i. 57; iii. 98; v. 35; vii. 19; viii. 71; ix. 25(*bis*), 29(*quater*), 44, 47; xi. 72

Crawley, North, Bucks., ix. 18

Credenhill, Herefs., ii. 10

Credie, preb., *see* Crediton

Crediton, Devon, colleg. ch., prebs. in: Credie (in Crediton, Devon), viii. 66; Pruscombe (Priestcombe in Crediton, Devon), ix. 33, 38; West Sandford (Devon), iii. 10, 12; unnamed, iii. 32; viii. 23, 51; ix. 24(*bis*); x. 55

Cremona, Italy, bp., xii. 19

Cressingham, Great, Norf., iv. 33

Creswell, Staffs., x. 21

Crewkerne, Som., iii. 15, 63; iv. 18; vi. 49; ix. 11

Crick, Northants., v. 39

Cropredy, preb., *see* Lincoln

Crowhurst, preb., *see* Hastings

Croydon, Surr., iv. 16; x. 3; xi. 5, 38

Cublington, preb., *see* Hereford

Cudworth, preb., *see* Wells

Curborough, preb., *see* Lichfield

Curry Mallet, Som., i. 30

Cusop, Herefs., ii. 48

Cutton, preb., *see* Exeter castle

Daria, Dalmatia, bp., vi. 56n

Daria, Mesopotamia, bp., vi. 56n

Darlington, co. Dur., colleg. ch., prebs. in, v. 64; vi. 37, 44

Dasset Parva, preb., *see* Lichfield

Decem Librarum, preb., *see* Lincoln

Deeping St James, Lincs., x. 24

Denham, Bucks., vii. 50

Denwall, *see* Burton

Derby:

archdcnry, x. 16–17

colleg. ch. of All Saints, prebs. in: Little Chester (Derbys.), vi. 71; unnamed, i. 122; x. 53

Dereham, East, Norf., i. 67

Dernford, preb., *see* Lichfield

Dinder, preb., *see* Wells

Doddington, Cambs., viii. 64

Doddington, Great, Northants., ix. 18

Dorset, archdcnry, iii. 7–9

Driffield, preb., *see* York

Dromore, co. Down, Ireland, bp., xi. 62

Dublin, Ireland:

abp., i. 42; iv. 49; v. 33, 59; vi. 46, 51, 61,

69; vii. 2, 5; viii. 34, 46 & n, 67; ix. 15, 20, 30, 36, 53, 64; xii. 19

cath., prebs. in: Clonmethan (co. Dublin), vi. 19; xii. 67; Hoath (Howth, co. Dublin), vi. 79; Lusk (co. Dublin), x. 54; xii. 29, 38; Swords (co. Dublin), vi. 59

Dultingcote, preb., *see* Wells

Dunham, preb., *see* Southwell

Dunham and Newport, preb., *see* Lincoln

Dunnington, preb., *see* York

Durham:

archdcnry, vi. 111–13

bp., i. 70, 81, 109; iii. 2, 5, 19, 32, 41, 42, 54, 61, 103; iv. 8, 14, 29, 47, 61; v. 4, 6, 12, 52, 62, 63, 68; vi. 4, 5(*bis*), 7, 8, 26(*bis*), 29, 42, 50, 68, 69, 72, 80, 82, 91, 97, 99, 107–9; vii. 14, 21; viii. 2, 3(*ter*), 4, 45, 78, 80; ix. 28, 61; x. 29, 60; xi. 45, 70; xii. 20

Durnford, preb., *see* Salisbury

Dymmerghion, *see* Tremeirchion

Dyserth (Diserth), Flints., xi. 43 & n, 44n

Ealdland, preb., *see* London, St Paul's

Ealdstreet, preb., *see* London, St Paul's

Earley White Knights, in Earley, Berks., vii. 41

Eartham, preb., *see* Chichester

East Grinstead, Suss., viii. 49

East Riding, Yorks., archdcnry, vi. 22–3

Eastbourne, Suss., vii. 6

Eastharptree, preb., *see* Wells

Eastington, nr. Stroud, Glos., ii. 7

Eastleach Martin (formerly Leach), Glos., ii. 10;

Easton, *see* Easton-on-the-Hill

Easton in Gordano, preb., *see* Wells

Easton-on-the-Hill, Northants., i. 18; v. 32; xii. 16

Eastwood, Essex, vii. 42

Ecchinswell (formerly in Kingsclere), Hants, Nuthanger portion in, ii. 46; viii. 56

Eccleshall, preb., *see* Lichfield

Eccleston, Ches., ii. 21

Ecton, Northants., xi. 26

Edgmond, Salop, x. 17

Edington, Wilts.:

ch., xi. 24, 60

preb., *see* Romsey

Eigne, preb., *see* Hereford

Ellington, Hunts., xi. 12(*bis*); xii. 88(*bis*)

Elphin, co. Roscommon, Ireland, bp., vi. 29

Eltisley, Cambs., iii. 24; ix. 41(*bis*); xi. 30

Ely, Cambs.:
  archdcnry., iii. 15, 63; iv. 17–19; vi. 49
  bp., i. 11, 13, 117; iii. 10, 16, 31, 62, 96;
    iv. 4, 5(bis), 13–16, 29, 51, 56(bis), 57(bis),
    58(bis); v. 3, 31, 49; vi. 4, 26, 27, 32, 78,
    108; vii. 11, 59; viii. 1, 16, 21n, 62; ix.
    3, 56; x. 14 & n, 17, 46
Embrun, Hautes-Alpes, France, abp., iv. 3
Empingham, preb., see Lincoln
English Bicknor, Glos., xi. 73, 74
Episcopi, preb., see Hereford
Epping, Essex, i. 63; viii. 63; xii. 80
Ermington, Devon, ix. 14
Esh, preb., see Lanchester
Essex, archdcnry, v. 9–11; vi. 65
Eton College, Berks., iv. 46, 58
Ewell, Surr., viii. 6
Ewithington, preb., see Hereford
Exceit, preb., see Chichester
Exeter, Devon:
  archdcnry, vi. 7; vii. 18; ix. 12–15
  bp., i. 8, 14, 43, 81, 108, 117, 125; ii. 2, 24,
    38, 42; iii. 10, 14, 24, 40, 43, 56, 74, 90;
    iv. 15, 46; v. 22, 46, 49, 52, 60; vi. 5, 7,
    23, 26, 36, 43, 60, 67, 99, 113; vii. 46, 49;
    viii. 3(bis), 10, 17, 33, 34, 68, 74; ix. 1–3;
    x. 2, 3 & n, 14, 39, 58, 64; xi. 39; xii. 15, 38
  castle, preb. of Cutton (in Poltimore,
    Devon) in chap. of, ix. 36, 39
  cath., prebs. in, i. 27; ii. 51; iii. 67; v. 17;
    viii. 48; ix. 21–66; x. 23, 54; xi. 30(bis)

Faenol, preb., see St Asaph
Fairwater (Tyllgoed), preb., see Llandaff
Fairwell, preb., see Llandaff
Fareham, Hants, Whipstrode St James chap.,
    viii. 61; xii. 80
Faringdon, preb., see Salisbury
Farndon-cum-Balderton, preb., see Lincoln
Fawkeners, preb., see London, St Martin's-
    le-Grand
Fenton, preb., see York
Ferns, co. Wexford, Ireland, cath., preb. in,
    i. 43
Ferriby, North, Yorks., vi. 13
Ferring, preb., see Chichester
Finsbury, preb., see London, St Paul's
Firle, preb., see Chichester
Firsby, Lincs., i. 127
Fittleworth, preb., see Chichester
Flamstead, Herts., ii. 7
Flixton, preb., see Lichfield
Florence, Italy, v. 59
Fontmell, preb., see Shaftesbury

Fordingbridge, Hants, iv. 18
Fordington and Writhlington, preb., see
    Salisbury
Freeford, preb., see Lichfield
Fréjus, Var, France, bp., vii. 43
Fridaythorpe, preb., see York
Frinstead, Kent, i. 74
Frobury, Hants, i. 101
Fugglestone, St Peter, Wilts., iii. 14
Fulham, Mdx., iv. 5; v. 28
Funtington, preb., see Bosham

Gaia Major, preb., see Lichfield
Gaia Minor, preb., see Lichfield
Gates, preb., see Chichester
Gavrus, Calvados, France, v. 35
Genoa, Italy, x. 2
Gerberoy, preb., see Beauvais
Gilling East, Yorks., vi. 11
Gillingham, Dors.:
  ch., iv. 31; xii. 59
  preb., see Salisbury; Shaftesbury

Girton, Cambs., i. 27
Givendale, preb., see York
Glasney, formerly by Penryn, Cornw., colleg.
  ch., ix. 56(bis); prebs. in, viii. 46; ix.
  25(bis), 35(bis), 37
Glastonbury, Som., abbey, viii. 60
Glatton, Hunts., v. 18, 61
Gloucester, iv. 57:
  abbey of St Peter, iv. 24(bis)
  archdcnry, iv. 60–2; v. 17
Gnosall, Staffs., colleg. ch., prebs. in: Bever-
    leyhall (Beverley Hall in Gnosall), x. 50,
    69; unnamed, i. 76, 103; x. 46
Godalming, Surr., iii. 38
Good Easter, preb. in, see London, St Mar-
    tin's-le-Grand
Goodworth, preb., see Wherwell
Gorwell and Overbury, preb., see Hereford
Gosberton, Lincs., vi. 62
Goudhurst, Kent, Bockingfold chap. in, i. 74;
    ix. 33, 35; xi. 58
Grado, Italy, abp., i. 93; v. 8, 28
Grantham Australis, preb., see Salisbury
Grantham Borealis, preb., see Salisbury
Greatford, Lincs., i. 33
Greencroft, preb., see Lanchester
Grestain, Eure, France, abbey, vii. 49
Gretton, preb., see Lincoln
Greystoke, Cumb., vi. 102n
Grimston, preb., see Salisbury
Grindale, preb., see York

Gurk, Carinthia, Austria, bp., iii. 62

Hadleigh, Suff., vi. 26
Halesowen, Worcs., x. 1
Halley, preb., *see* Westbury-on-Trym
Halling, Kent, v. 48
Halsall, Lancs., x. 13, 30
Ham, High, Som., x. 67
Hambleden, Bucks., vi. 115n; xii. 18
Hampstead, preb., *see* Chichester
Hampton, preb., *see* Hereford
Hampton Lucy, formerly Hampton Episcopi, Warwicks., vii. 28
Hanbury, Staffs., x. 18
Hanney, West, Berks., iii. 91; v. 5, 51
Hansacre, preb., *see* Lichfield
Hanslope, Bucks., v. 13
Hardres, Upper, Kent, xi. 27
Hardwick, Norf., ix. 16
Harleston, preb., *see* London, St Paul's
Harmston, Lincs., v. 23
Harrimere Drain, *see* Stretham
Harting, Suss., i. 90
Haselbere, preb., *see* Wells
Haseley, Great, Oxon., i. 93; v. 15; ix. 35(*bis*)
Hastings, Suss.:
  ch. of All Saints, vii. 9
  colleg. ch., i. 90; ii. 21; vii. 18; viii. 29; prebs. in: Bulverhythe (Bulverhithe, Suss.), v. 20; ix. 41(*bis*); Crowhurst (Suss.), ii. 17; viii. 69; xi. 81, 82; Stone (location doubtful), v. 23n; Wartling, Ninfield and Hooe (Suss.), xi. 66; unnamed, i. 74, 106; x. 57
Hatfield, Herts., iv. 57
Haughton-le-Skerne, co. Dur., v. 49
Havant, Hants, iii. 87; vii. 14
Haydour-cum-Walton, preb., *see* Lincoln
Headley, Hants, ix. 6
Heathfield, preb., *see* Chichester
Heigham, Norf., iii. 102
Hemingford Abbots, Hunts., xi. 15(*bis*), 60
Henbury, preb., *see* Westbury-on-Trym
Hendon, Mdx., v. 54
Henfield, preb., *see* Chichester
Henry III, preb., *see* Llandaff, St Nicholas
Henry Morgan, preb., *see* Llandaff, St Cross
Henstridge, preb., *see* Wells
Hereford:
  archdcnry, ii. 5–6
  bp., i. 13, 14, 16, 66, 67, 95; ii. 1–3; iii. 2, 3, 8, 9, 68, 79; iv. 33, 34, 38, 39, 56; v. 2, 3, 4, 31, 34, 43, 54, 59; vi. 7, 23, 27, 74, 78, 81, 98, 113; vii. 2; viii. 3, 28, 40, 67;

ix. 2, 27n, 37; x. 3, 12; xi. 4, 5, 23, 39, 45(*bis*), 54, 57
  cath., prebs. in: Bartonsham (Herefs.), ii. 14–15; Bullinghope (Herefs.), ii. 15–17; vi. 42; Church Withington (Withington, Herefs.), ii. 17–18; iii. 64; Colwall (Herefs.), ii. 18–19; Cublington (in Madley, Herefs.), ii. 19–20; Eigne (Eign St., etc., Hereford), ii. 20–2; viii. 70; Episcopi, ii. 22–3; Ewithington (Withington, Herefs.), 23–4; Gorwell and Overbury (Gorwall in Woolhope parish, Herefs.; Overbury nr. Hereford), ii. 24–5; Hampton (Hampton Bishop, Herefs.), ii. 26; Hinton (Herefs.), ii. 26–7; Hunderton (Herefs.), ii. 28–9; Huntington (Herefs.), ii. 29–30; Inkberrow (Worcs.), ii. 30–1; viii. 66; Moreton and Whaddon (Moreton Valence, Glos.; Whaddon, Glos.), ii. 31–3; iii. 92; vi. 82; vii. 22; Moreton Magna (Moreton-on-Lugg, Herefs.), ii. 34–5; Moreton Parva (Moreton-on-Lugg, Herefs.) ii. 35–7; Nonnington (Nunnington in Withington parish, Herefs.), ii. 37–8; Norton (Norton Canon, Herefs.), ii. 38–9; Piona Parva (Canon Pyon, Herefs.), ii. 39–41; iii. 97; v. 65; Pratum Majus (in Withington parish, Herefs.), ii. 41–2; Pratum Minus (in Withington parish, Herefs.), ii. 42–4; Preston (Preston-on-Wye, Herefs.), ii. 44–5; Putson Major (in Hereford), ii. 45–7; Putson Minor (in Hereford), ii. 47–8; Warham (Herefs.), ii. 48–9; Wellington (Herefs.), ii. 50–1; vii. 21; ix. 50, 52; Withington Parva (Withington, Herefs.), ii. 51–2; xi. 42; Woolhope (formerly preb., Herefs.), ii. 32, 45
Herne, Kent, i. 69
Hexham, Northumb., priory, vi. 76–8, 78n
Heytesbury, Wilts.:
  colleg. ch., prebs. in: Swallowcliffe (Wilts.), ii. 17; vii. 31; Tytherington and Horningsham (Wilts.), v. 70
  preb., *see* Salisbury
High Wycombe, Bucks., i. 31
Highleigh, preb., *see* Chichester
Highworth, Wilts.:
  ch., iii. 26, 49
  preb., *see* Salisbury
Hilton, preb., *see* Wolverhampton
Hinton, preb., *see* Hereford
Hinton, Little, Wilts., vii. 15

Hippo, North Africa, bp., ix. 61, 65; xi. 14

Hoath, preb., *see* Dublin

Holbourn, preb., *see* London, St Paul's

Holcombe, preb., *see* Wells

Holdgate, Salop, colleg. ch., preb. in, vii. 44

Hollingbourne, Kent., iii. 86

Holme, preb., *see* York

Holyhead (Caergybi, 'Castrikuby'), Anglesey, colleg. ch., preb. in, x. 56 & n

Holywell, preb., *see* London, St Paul's, Finsbury

Horningsham, preb., *see* Heytesbury

Horsley, East, Surr., ix. 3

Horton, nr. Eton, Bucks., i. 110; vii. 36

Horton, preb., *see* Salisbury

Hotot-en-Auge, Calvados, France, ix. 18

Hova Ecclesia, preb., *see* Chichester

Hova Villa, preb., *see* Chichester

Howden, Yorks., colleg. ch., i. 53, 112; prebs. in: Barnby (Yorks.), i. 49; ii. 50; vi. 53; vii. 41; Saltmarshe (Yorks.), i. 44; vi. 84

Hoxton, preb., *see* London, St Paul's

Huish and Brent, preb., *see* Wells

Hunderton, preb., *see* Hereford

Huntingdon, archdcnry, i. 8–10

Huntington, preb., *see* Hereford

Hurstbourne and Burbage, preb., *see* Salisbury

Hurstmonceaux, Suss., vii. 25

Hurworth, co. Dur., vii. 50

Husbands Bosworth, Leics., i. 43

Husthwaite, preb., *see* York

Ickham, Kent., x. 27

Ilfracombe, Devon:
  ch., x. 16
  preb., *see* Salisbury

Ilminster, preb., *see* Wells

Ilton, preb., *see* Wells

Imber, Wilts.:
  ch., ii. 21; iii. 71; v. 66
  preb., *see* Romsey

Imbers, preb., *see* London, St Martin's-le-Grand

Ingleby, Lincs., i. 35

Inkberrow, preb., *see* Hereford

Ipplepen, Devon, viii. 69; ix. 44(*bis*)

Ipthorne, preb., *see* Chichester

Ireland, vii. 1

Islington, preb., *see* London, St Paul's

Ivychurch, Wilts., priory, iii. 93

Jobia (Laupjubeo), ch. of St Leger, St Genis, Hautes-Alpes, France, viii. 77

Kedington, Suff.(?), ii. 7, 52

Kentish Town, preb., *see* London, St Paul's. Cantlers

Keton, preb., *see* London, St Martin's-le-Grand

Ketton, preb., *see* Lincoln

Kilmanagh, preb., *see* Ossory

Kilmore, co. Cavan, Ireland, bp., vii. 2

Kilsby, preb., *see* Lincoln

Kings Ripton, Hunts., xi. 60

Kingsclere, Hants, *see* Ecchinswell

Kingsley, Staffs., x. 19

Kingsthorpe, Northants., x. 44

Kinvaston, preb., *see* Wolverhampton

Kippax, Yorks., vi. 20

Kirby (Kirkby) in Cleveland, Yorks., i. 33

Kirtling, Cambs., xi. 46; xii. 89

Knaresborough, preb., *see* York

Lafford, preb., *see* Lincoln

Lambeth, Surr., iv. 4, 15(*bis*), 39(*ter*); xi. 5, 39(*bis*), 56(*bis*)

Lamesley, preb., *see* Chester-le-Street

Lampeter-pont-Stephen (Llanbedr Pont Steffan), preb., *see* St Davids

Lamport, Northants., i. 15; x. 21, 40

Lanchester, co. Dur., colleg. ch., i. 24, 106; xi. 32, 33; prebs. in: Esh (co. Dur.), iv. 27; Greencroft (co. Dur.), i. 69; ix. 56, 58

Langford, preb., *see* York, Masham

Langford Ecclesia, preb., *see* Lincoln

Langford Manor, preb., *see* Lincoln

Langley Burrell, Wilts., viii. 11

Langtoft, preb., *see* York

Langton, Leics. (St Peter de Langton), ii. 36; xii. 49

Laughton, preb., *see* York

Laupjubeo, *see* Jobia

Lausanne, Switzerland, i. 54; bp., 25, 80

Lavant, Suss., x. 42

Leach, dioc. Worc., *see* Eastleach Martin

Ledbury, Herefs., colleg. ch., preb. of Netherhall, ix. 33, 38

Leek, Staffs., x. 23

Leicester, iv. 57;
  abbey, ix. 36; xi. 5
  archdcnry, i. 12–13
  colleg. ch. of St Mary's-by-the-castle, prebs. in: E, 1. 50, 70; v. 44, 54; H, v.

44; ix. 38(*bis*); unnamed, i. 89; vi. 62, 69; viii. 49; x. 23

New College of the Annunciation, i. 124

Leicester St Margaret, preb., *see* Lincoln

Leighlin, co. Carlow, Ireland, bp., xi. 22

Leighton Buzzard, preb., *see* Lincoln

Leighton Ecclesia, preb., *see* Lincoln

Leighton Manor, preb., *see* Lincoln

Lerida, Spain, cath., canonry in, x. 5

Leverton, Lincs., i. 27

Lewes, Suss.:
  archdcnry, vii. 13–14
  priory, v. 21; vii. 11, 17

Lichfield, Staffs.:
  cath., prebs. in: Alrewas (Staffs.), x. 9–10; Bishopshull (in Lichfield), x. 20–2; Bishops Itchington (Warwicks.), x. 7–8; Bobenhull (Bubbenhall, Warwicks.), i. 107, 119; ix. 49(*bis*); x. 22–4; Bolton (Lancs.), x. 12–14; Brewood (Staffs.), x. 5–7; Colwich (Staffs.), x. 24–7; Curborough (Curborough and Elmhurst, Staffs.), vii. 27; x. 27–9; Dasset Parva (Avon Dasset, Warwicks.), x. 29–31; Dernford (in Lichfield), x. 31–4; Eccleshall (Staffs.), iii. 64; x. 34–6; Flixton (Lancs.), vi. 58; x. 36–8; Freeford (Staffs.), x. 38–40; Gaia Major (in Lichfield), x. 40–1; xii. 45; Gaia Minor (in Lichfield), vii. 19; x. 42–3; Hansacre (Handsacre, Staffs.), x. 43–5; Longdon (Staffs.), x. 45–6; Offley (Bishops Offley, Staffs.), iii. 100; v. 48, 53; viii. 41; x. 46–8; Pipa Minor *or* Prees (Prees, Salop), x. 48–9; Pipa Parva (Little Pipe, in Pipe Hill, parish of St Chad, Lichfield), x. 49–51; Ryton (Warwicks.), vi. 46; viii. 34; x. 51–3; Sandiacre (Derbys.), i. 107; ix. 38, 39; x. 53–4; xi. 65; xii. 29, 33; Sawley (Sawley and Wilsthorpe, Derbys.), x. 11–12; Stotfold (in St Michael's parish, Lichfield), vi. 35; x. 55–7; Tachbrook (Bishops Tachbrook, Warwicks.), x. 57–9; Tervin (Tarvin, Ches.), iii. 80; x. 59–61; Ufton Cantoris (Ufton, Warwicks.), x. 61–2; Ufton Decani (Ufton, Warwicks.), vi. 29; x. 62–4; Weeford (Staffs.), x. 64–5; Wellington (Salop), vi. 52; x. 65–6; Whittington and Berkswick (Whittington, Staffs.; Milford and Walton Baswich, Staffs.), x. 66–8; Wolvey (Warwicks.), v. 8; x. 68–70
  colleg. ch. of St Chad, ii. 43

  See also Coventry and Lichfield

Liddington, preb., *see* Lincoln

Liège, Belgium:
  bp., i. 31; vi. 12
  ch. of St John, preb. in, i. 96

Limerick, Ireland, cath., preb. in, i. 43

Limington, Som., iii. 6

Limoges, Haute-Vienne, France, bp., vi. 25

Lincoln, xi. 38:
  archdcn., i. 6–8
  bp., i. 1–3; iii. 5(*bis*), 14, 16, 18, 29, 53(*bis*), 55, 57, 62, 64, 84(*ter*), 89; iv. 5, 14, 24, 39(*bis*), 46, 56; v. 3, 18, 46; vi. 4, 5(*ter*), 8, 41, 52, 75, 76, 98; viii. 3, 4, 41; x. 2, 3, 6; xi. 69, 70
  cath., prebs. in: All Saints in Hungate, i. 27–9; ix. 40(*bis*); Asgarby (nr. Horncastle, Lincs.), i. 29–30; Aylesbury (Bucks.), i. 24–7, 120–1; Banbury (Oxon.), i. 31–2; Bedford Major (Bedford), i. 32–4; iii. 25; v. 20; Bedford Minor (Bedford), i. 34–6; Biggleswade (Beds.), i. 36–8; Brampton (Hunts.), i. 40–2; Buckden (Hunts.), i. 42–4; Caistor (Lincs.), i. 48–50; Carlton Kyme *or* Carlton-cum-Dalby (Carlton, North, Lincs.; Dalby, Lincs.), i. 44–5; Carlton Paynell *or* Carlton-cum-Thirlby (Carlton, South, Lincs.; Thurlby by Newark, Lincs.), i. 45–8; viii. 26; Centum Solidorum *or* De Prepositis, i. 50–2; v. 62; viii. 42; Clifton (Notts.), i. 52–4; xi. 71, 76; Corringham (Lincs.), i. 54–5; Crackpole St Mary (in Lincoln), i. 55–7; vi. 36; Cropredy (Oxon.), i. 57–9; iv. 51; iv. 51; Decem Librarum, i. 59–61; iii. 69; Dunham and Newport (Dunholme, Lincs.; Newport, in Winterton, Lincs.), i. 61–3; iii. 24; xi. 30(*bis*), Empingham (Rut.), i. 63–5; v. 42; Farndon-cum-Balderton (Farndon, Notts.; Balderton, Notts.), i. 65–6; iii. 68n; x. 7; Gretton (Northants.), i. 66–8; Haydour-cum-Walton (Haydor, Lincs.; Walton, in Aylesbury, Bucks.), i. 68–9; vi. 49; Ketton (Rut.), i. 70–1; Kilsby (Northants.), i. 71–2; Lafford *or* Sleaford (Lincs.), i. 72–3; Langford Ecclesia (Langford, Oxon.), i. 73–6; viii. 65; x. 54; Langford Manor (Langford, Oxon.), i. 76–7; iv. 17; Leicester St Margaret, i. 77–9; v. 29; Leighton Buzzard (Beds.), i. 79–81; Leighton Ecclesia (Leighton, Hunts.), i. 82–3; Leighton Manor

Lincoln—*contd.*
(Leighton, Hunts.), i. 83–4; v. 27; vi. 43, 46; Liddington (Rut.), i. 85–6; Louth (Lincs.), i. 86–7; Marston St Lawrence (Northants)., i. 87–9; v. 17; vii. 23; Milton Ecclesia (Milton, Oxon.), i. 24, 25, 91–2; v. 40; Milton Manor (Milton, Oxon.), i. 92–4; vi. 24; xii. 68; Nassington (Northants.), i. 94–6; North Kelsey (Lincs.), i. 98–100; Norton Episcopi (Bishop Norton, Lincs.), i. 96–8; v. 34; St Botolph, i. 38–40; St Martin's in Dernestall, i. 89–91; x. 54n; xii. 85; Sanctae Crucis *or* Spaldwick (Hunts.), i. 100–2; v. 32; ix. 18; Scamblesby *or* Melton Ross-cum-Scamblesby (Melton Ross, Lincs.; Scamblesby, Lincs.), i. 102–4; iii. 39; Sexaginta Solidorum, i. 106–8; x. 23, 54; South Scarle (Notts.), i. 104–6; vii. 9; Stoke (Stoke, East, Notts.), i. 108–9; Stow Longa (Stow, Hunts.), i. 111–13; Stow St Mary *or* Stow-in-Lindsey (Stow by Gainsborough, Lincs.), i. 109–11; vii. 36; Sutton-cum-Buckingham (Kings Sutton, Northants.; Buckingham), i. 113–114; Sutton-in-Marisco *or* Sutton-by-Markby (Sutton-le-Marsh, Lincs.), i. 23, 114–15; Thame (Oxon.), i. 115–17; Thorngate (in Lincoln), i. 118–20; x. 23; Welton Beckhall (Welton, by Lincoln), i. 120–2; vi. 83; Welton Brinkhall, i. 122–4; Welton Paynshall, i. 124–6; Welton Ryval, i. 126–8; Welton Westhall, i. 128
Lingfield, Surr., v. 40
Lismore, *see* Waterford, and Lismore
Little Chester, preb., *see* Derby
Litton, preb., *see* Wells
Llanarth (Llannarth), Card., xi. 82, 83
Llanarthney, preb., *see* Abergwili
Llandaff (Llandaf), Glam.:
    archdcnry, xi. 23–5
    bp., i. 26; iv. 38, 57(*bis*); v. 40; vi. 63; vii. 1; ix. 55; x. 2; xi. 21–3, 43, 83
    cath., prebs. in: Caerau (Caerau, nr. Cardiff, Glam., and Llandogo, Mon.), xi. 27; Fairwater *or* Thomas Jones (Fairwater, Glam.), xi. 28; Fairwell (in Llandaff), xi. 28; Llangwm (Llangwm Uchaf (Llan-gwm Uchaf), Mon.), xi. 28; St Andrew *or* Thomas Basschurch (in Llandaff), xi. 28; St Cross *or* Henry Morgan (Ely (Trelai), Glam.), xi. 28–9;

St Dubritius (Caerleon (Caerllion), Mon.), xi. 29; St Nicholas *or* Master Mayo *or* Henry III (St Nicholas, Glam.), xi. 29; Warthacwm (Llangwm Isaf (Llan-gwm Isaf), Mon.; Llandevaud, Mon.), xi. 29–30; unnamed, i. 61; ix. 41(*bis*)
Llanddarog, preb., *see* Abergwili
Llanddewi Aberarth (Llanddewi Aber-arth), preb., *see* St Davids
Llanddewi Brefi (Llanddewibrefi), Card., colleg. ch., prebs. in: Blaenporth (Card.), ix. 38, 40; Caron (Caron-is-Clawydd, Card.), xi. 58
Llandinam, Montgom., xi. 6n
Llandogy, preb., *see* Abergwili
Llandyfriog, preb., *see* St Davids
Llandyssilio-gogo (Llandysiliogogo), preb., *see* St Davids
Llandyssul (Llandysul), Card., xi. 63n
Llanfair, preb., *see* Bangor
Llanfair, first comportion, preb., *see* St Asaph
Llanfair, second comportion, preb., *see* St Asaph
Llangammarch, preb., *see* Abergwili
Llangan (Llan-gan), preb., *see* St Davids
Llanganten, preb., *see* Abergwili
Llangwm (Llan-gwm), preb., *see* Llandaff
Llannefydd (Llanefydd), preb., *see* St Asaph
Llanrhian, preb., *see* St Davids
Llanvaes (Llan-faes), preb., *see* St Davids
Llawhaden (Llanhuadain), Pemb., xi. 57n; preb., *see* St Davids
Lockington, Yorks., vi. 114
Loders, preb., *see* Salisbury
London, vi. 99:
    archdcnry, v. 7–9; x. 68
    bp., i. 2, 9, 11, 26, 89, 114, 116; ii. 2, 4, 17, 28, 34; iii. 2(*bis*), 4, 5, 8(*bis*), 17, 19, 29, 33, 42; iv. 4(*ter*), 5(*bis*), 15, 24, 39, 49, 57; v. 1–4; vi. 4, 5, 7, 8, 26, 38, 43, 45, 74, 80, 85 & n, 99, 109; vii. 1, 2, 3, 44; viii. 7, 49, 63; ix. 44; x. 2, 14, 25(*bis*), 68; xi. 72; xii. 27
    Blackfriars conv., iv. 58
    cath. ch. of St Paul, iv. 4, 14, 24, 46, 56, 57; vi. 108; x. 2; xi. 5, 23:
    chap. of St Radegund, ii. 14, 46; iii. 32, 81; v. 29; vi. 52, 78; viii. 27, 43; x. 41, 47
    Northburgh chantry, ii. 24
    prebs. in: Broomesbury (Brondesbury, Mdx.), i. 33; v. 20–1; Brownswood (in Willesden, Mdx.), v. 21–2; Caddington Major (Caddington, Beds.), iii. 34; v.

23–5; Caddington Minor (Caddington, Beds.), v. 25–6; Cantlers (Kentish Town, Mdx.), i. 84; v. 26–8; Chamberlainwood (in Willesden, Mdx.), i. 78; v. 28–30; Chiswick (Mdx.), v. 30–1; vii. 18, 50; Consumpta-per-Mare (in Walton-on-the-Naze, Essex), v. 31–3; vi. 71; vii. 34; Ealdland (in Tillingham, Essex), i. 97; v. 33–4; Ealdstreet (in Shoreditch, Mdx.), v. 34–6; Finsbury (Mdx.), v. 36–8; Harleston (Harlesden, Mdx.), v. 38–9; Holbourn (Holborn, Mdx.), i. 92; v. 39–41; Hoxton (Mdx.), i. 63; v. 41–2; Islington (Mdx.), v. 43–5; Mapesbury (Mdx.), v. 45–7; Mora (in St Giles without Cripplegate, London), v. 47–9; x. 47; Nesden (Neasden, Mdx.), v. 49–50; Newington (Stoke Newington, Mdx.), iii. 91; v. 51–2; Oxgate (in Willesden, Mdx.), v. 52–4; x. 48; Pancratius (St Pancras, Mdx.), v. 54–5; vii. 52n; Portpool (in Holborn, Mdx.), v. 56–7; Reculversland (in Tillingham, Essex), v. 57–9; viii. 48; Rugmere (in St Pancras, Mdx.), v. 59–60; vi. 46; Sneating (in Kirby-le-Soken, Essex), v. 60–2; vi. 32; Totenhall (Tottenham Court, in St Pancras, Mdx.), i. 50; v. 62–4; Twiford (East Twyford, in Willesden, Mdx.), ii. 40; v. 64–5; viii. 39, 64; Weldland (in Tillingham, Essex), v. 66–8; Wenlocksbarn (in Shoreditch, Mdx.), v. 68–70; Wilsden (Willesden, Mdx.), v. 70–1
chap. of St Mary in the bp's palace, iii. 59; v. 29, 33; viii. 49; x. 55
ch's:
  All Hallows the Great, viii. 9
  St Alphage, London Wall (St Alphege within Cripplegate), xi. 45
  St Botolph, Billingsgate, ii. 25
  St Bride, Fleet Street, iii. 15
  St Clement Danes, ii. 13
  St Dunstan in the East, vii. 4
  St James, Garlickhithe, x. 28
  St John the Baptist, Walbrook, iii. 69
  St Mary Abchurch, viii. 14
  St Mary-le-Bow, i. 19
  St Michael, Cornhill, vii. 51
  St Michael, Crooked Lane, iv. 61; xi. 42
  St Vedast, Foster Lane, viii. 28
colleg. ch. of St Martin-le-Grand, i. 74; x. 35; prebs. in: Chrishall (Essex), vi. 31; Cowpes (probably in Maldon, Essex), ii. 46; viii. 32; Fawkeners (in Good Easter,

Essex), vi. 29, 35; viii. 43; x. 56; Good Easter (Essex), preb. in, vi. 79; Imbers (in Good Easter, Essex), iii. 44; v. 58; Keton (in Maldon, Essex), v. 15; Tolleshunt (Tolleshunt Knights, Essex), v. 18, 59; vi. 37; unnamed, i. 22; iii. 80; vii. 4; Wykhambrok's chantry, v. 64
See also Westminster
Long Sutton, preb., see Wells
Longdon, preb., see Lichfield
Lopham, North, Norf., v. 10
Loughborough, Leics., iii. 54
Louth, preb., see Lincoln
Lowther Castle, Westmld., vi. 100n
Ludlow, Salop, ch. of St Lawrence, ii. 9
Lusk, preb., see Dublin
Lydd, Kent, xi. 58
Lydda, Palestine, bp., v. 42
Lydeard St Lawrence, Som., x. 67
Lyme and Halstock, preb., see Salisbury
Lyminge, Kent, iii. 11; vii. 41
Lymington, Hants, viii. 28
Lympsham, Som., viii. 51
Lyons, Rhône, France, abp., i. 19, 76; iii. 3; vi. 70 & n

Maidstone, Kent, i. 111; xi. 54
Maioren, Israel, bp., viii. 66
Major pars altaris, preb., see Salisbury
Maldon, Essex, vi. 69
Malling, South, Suss., colleg. ch., vii. 42; treasurer's preb., iii. 81
Malpas, Ches., i. 46
Manchester, colleg. ch., v. 37
Mapesbury, preb., see London, St Paul's
Mapledurham, Hants, ii. 30
Mardon, preb., see Chichester
Market Lavington, Wilts., viii. 13, 76
Marlborough, Wilts., i. 68; vii. 50
Marlow, Great, Bucks., vii. 11
Marnhull, Dors., xi. 57
Marseilles, Bouches-du-Rhône, France, bp., x. 6
Marston St Lawrence, preb., see Lincoln
Martley, Worcs., ix. 35(bis)
Masham, preb., see York
Massingham, Great, Norf., vi. 72
Master Mayo, preb., see Llandaff, St Nicholas
Mathry (Mathri), preb., see St Davids
Mawgan in Meneage, Cornw., ii. 14
Mayfield, Suss., vii. 12; xi. 21
Meath, Ireland:
  archdenry, v. 12n; xi. 69
  bp., viii. 46n; ix. 16

Meifod, Montgom.:
  ch., viii. 6, 33; xi. 45 *passim* & n, 46
  preb., *see* St Asaph
Meliden (Allt Melyd), preb., *see* St Asaph
Mells, Som., vii. 46
Melton Ross-cum-Scamblesby, preb., *see* Lincoln, Scamblesby
Membury, Devon, xi. 76, 77
Meonstoke, Hants, iv. 62
Merioneth (Meirionnydd), archdcnry, xi. 10–11
Mersham, Kent, xi. 63
Michelmersh, Hants, ii. 46; x. 10
Middlesex, archdcnry, v. 11–13
Middleton, preb., *see* Chichester
Middleton Cheney, Northants., i. 30
Milan, Italy, abp., iii. 4
Milston, Wilts., iii. 6
Milton Ecclesia, preb., *see* Lincoln
Milton Manor, preb., *see* Lincoln
Milverton Prima, preb., *see* Wells
Milverton Secunda, preb., *see* Wells
Minor pars altaris, preb., *see* Salisbury
Mold (Yr Wyddgrug), Flints., viii. 63; xi. 40n
Molton, South, Devon, ii. 37
Monkton, preb., *see* Ripon
Mora, preb., *see* London, St Paul's
Moreton and Whaddon, preb., *see* Hereford
Moreton Magna, preb., *see* Hereford
Moreton Parva, preb., *see* Hereford
Mortlake, Surr., iv. 15, 45
Mottisfont, Hants, iii. 6
Moulton, Suff., iii. 99
Muchelney, Som., abbey, viii. 52
Myddle, Salop, x. 17
Mydrim (Meidrim), preb., *see* St Davids

Naples, Italy, iii. 7, 19
Naseby, Northants., xi. 26
Nassington, preb., *see* Lincoln
Nazareth, Israel, abp., viii. 66n
Negroponte, Greece, bp., vi. 25, 53, 86
Nesden, preb., *see* London, St Paul's
Netheravon, preb., *see* Salisbury
Netherbury in Ecclesia, preb., *see* Salisbury
Netherbury in Terra, preb., *see* Salisbury
Netherhall, preb., *see* Ledbury
Newchurch, Kent, xi. 6
Newington, Oxon., ii. 32
Newington, preb., *see* London, St Paul's
Newland, nr. Monmouth, Glos., xi. 25

Newstead, in Staplehurst, Kent, ix. 33, 35
Newthorpe, preb., *see* York
Newton, in Kesteven, Lincs., xii. 88(*bis*)
Nonnington, preb., *see* Hereford
Norfolk, archdcnry, iv. 28–30
Normanby-le-Wold, Lincs., xi. 13(*bis*)
North Curry, preb., *see* Wells
North Kelsey, preb., *see* Lincoln
North Leverton, preb., *see* Southwell
North Newbald, preb., *see* York
Northallerton, Yorks., v. 23n
Northampton:
  archdcnry, i. 10–12
  ch. of St Peter, x. 44
Northfleet, Kent, iii. 51
Northill, Beds., x. 32
Northumberland, archdcnry, vi. 113–15
Norton, co. Dur., colleg. ch., prebs. in, v. 33; viii. 42; x. 35
Norton, preb., *see* Hereford
Norton Episcopi, preb., *see* Lincoln
Norton-juxta-Twycross, Leics., iii. 5, 66
Norwich, Norf.:
  archdcnry, iv. 26–8; xi. 12
  bp., i. 3, 4, 11, 93, 98, 108, 117; ii. 50; iii. 4, 12, 52, 53; iv. 4, 8, 13(*bis*), 23–5, 39; v. 10, 11, 22, 45, 52, 61, 65, 67; vi. 5(*bis*), 50, 52, 60, 70; vii. 21, 25, 59(*bis*); viii. 5, 14 & n, 32, 36; ix. 14, 44; x. 65; xi. 30
Nostell, Yorks., priory, vi. 38–9, 39n
Notley, Bucks., abbey, i. 30
Nottingham, archdcnry, i. 92; vi. 23–5
Nunwick, preb., *see* Ripon
Nuthanger, portion, *see* Ecchinswell

Offley, preb., *see* Lichfield
Ogbourne, preb., *see* Salisbury
Olveston, Glos., viii. 8
Orcheston St Mary, Wilts., i. 60
Orpington, Kent, v. 24
Osbaldwick, preb., *see* York
Osney and Thame, Oxon., bp., i. 38
Ossory, Ireland, cath., preb. of Kilmanagh (co. Kilkenny), v. 59
Ostia, Italy, bp., i. 25; ii. 12; iii. 37; iv. 37, 45; v. 30; vi. 67, 80; viii. 78; ix. 14; xi. 37, 53
Otford, Kent, iv. 14, 37, 46; viii. 25; xi. 39, 53
Outre-Vienne, France, archdcnry, i. 15 ('Transuigenen'); xii. 15, 16
Oving, preb., *see* Chichester
Owston, Lincs., i. 18

Oxford, vi. 91:
  archdcnry, i. 14, 23, 26; iii. 10; ix. 12n
  Merton College, vii. 49
Oxgate, preb., *see* London, St Paul's
Oxton and Cropwell Prima, preb., *see* Southwell
Oxton and Cropwell Secunda, preb., *see* Southwell

Pagham, Suss., i. 70
Palestrina, Italy, bp., i. 25; iii. 19; iv. 3; vi. 18, 93
Pancratius, preb., *see* London, St Paul's
Paneas, in Thrace, Greece, bp., x. 51 & n
Paris, France, royal chap., ix. 18
Patrick Brompton, Yorks., ii. 18
Peasemore, Berks., x. 18
Peckham, East, Kent, x. 42
Pembridge, Herefs., ii. 22
Pendeford, preb., *see* Tettenhall
Penffoes, preb., *see* St Davids
Penkridge, Staffs., colleg. ch. of St Michael, prebs. in: Stretton (Staffs.), iii. 87; unnamed, ix. 30; x. 30, 69
Penmynydd, preb., *see* Bangor
Penrith, Cumb., bp., xi. 5
Peterborough, Northants.:
  bp., x. 18, 59
  dioc., i. 12
Petersfield, Hants, ii. 30
Petworth, Suss., vi. 114
Pilton, preb., *see* Wells
Piona Parva, preb., *see* Hereford
Pipa Minor, preb., *see* Lichfield
Pipa Parva, preb., *see* Lichfield
Pisa, Italy, abp., iii. 19, 20
Plasnes, Eure, France, ix. 18
Plemonstall, Ches., x. 27
Plymouth, *see* Sutton by Plymouth
Polebrook, Northants., i. 60
Pontesbury, Salop, colleg. ch., portion or preb. in, ii. 22, 40
Porto, Italy, bp., i. 10, 117; iv. 37; vi. 18, 25, 81; xi. 21
Portpool, preb., *see* London, St Paul's
Potterne, preb., *see* Salisbury
Potterspury, Northants., vii. 20
Pratum Majus, preb., *see* Hereford
Pratum Minus, preb., *see* Hereford
Prees, preb., *see* Lichfield, Pipa Minor
Prescot, Lancs., iii. 40
Preston, preb., *see* Hereford and Salisbury
Probus, Cornw., St Probus colleg. ch., prebs. in, i. 35; iii. 15, 63; iv. 18; vi. 49; viii. 27

Pruscombe, preb., *see* Crediton
Pulborough, Suss., viii. 24
Pulham, St Mary the Virgin, Norf., vi. 16
Putson Major, preb., *see* Hereford
Putson Minor, preb., *see* Hereford

Ramsbury, preb., *see* Salisbury
Rasen, West, Lincs., x. 63
Ratfyn, preb., *see* Salisbury
Reculversland, preb., *see* London, St Paul's
Reynalton, Pemb., ii. 38, 52
Rheims, Marne, France:
  cath., preb. in, x. 14
  dioc., xi. 38
Rheon, Greece, bp., i. 38, 57
Riccall, preb., *see* York
Richmond, Yorks., archdcnry, iv. 18; v. 8; vi. 25-7
Rieti, Italy, bp., iii. 20
Rieux, Haute-Garonne, France, xii. 31
Ripley, Hants, *see* Ripple
Ripon, Yorks.:
  colleg. ch. of SS Peter and Wilfrid, prebs. in: Monkton (Yorks.), iii. 32, 102; xii. 77; Nunwick (Nunwick with Howgrave, Yorks.), x. 47; Sharow (Yorks.), iii. 82; Studley (Studley Magna, now Studley Royal, Yorks.), vi. 60; unnamed, viii. 19
  hospital of St John the Baptist, i. 97
  hospital of St Mary Magdalene, viii. 50
Ripple, Worcs., iii. 75; xii. 75
Rochester, Kent, i. 105:
  archdcnry, iv. 41-2; x. 14 & n
  bp., i. 3, 8, 32, 41, 66, 76, 123; ii. 2, 3, 19; iii. 4, 10, 23, 62, 72; iv. 3, 5(*bis*), 15, 37-40, 42, 56, 58, 60 & n; v. 3, 5, 10, 16, 22, 36, 48(*bis*), 51, 57; vi. 23, 53, 74, 113; vii. 2, 3, 31; viii. 42, 66, 80; ix. 55; x. 1; xi. 4, 21, 22n, 38; xii. 58
Rome, Italy, ii. 4, 16; iii. 61; iv. 13, 23, 24, 45, 55, 58(*bis*); v. 1, 3, 40, 45, 52; vi. 3, 109; xi. 4, 22, 23, 37, 38, 53(*bis*)
  ct., iii. 37, 41, 55, 61; ix. 1, 12, 41
Romsey, Hants, conventual ch., portions or prebs. in: Edington (Wilts.), vi. 46; x. 52; Imber (Wilts.), iii. 51
Ropsley, Lincs., x. 32
Ross, Ross and Cromarty, Scotland, bp., xi. 4, 14
Ross-on-Wye, Herefs., iii. 50
Rouen, Seine-et-Marne, France, iv. 38, 57:
  abp., iv. 15
  cath., preb. in, vii. 32; ix. 18
Rougham, Norf., v. 12

Rue in Ponthieu (Rue, Somme), France, iv. 3
Rugmere, preb., *see* London, St Paul's
Ruscombe Southbury, preb., *see* Salisbury
Ryton, preb., *see* Lichfield

Sabina, Italy, bp., i. 8, 12, 95; iv. 3, 33; x. 13
Sacristy, preb., *see* Southwell
St Albans, Herts., Abbey, iv. 26, 45
St Andrew, preb., *see* Llandaff
St Andrew's, Fife, Scotland, abp., iv. 4; vi. 4; xi. 38 & n
St Asaph (Llanelwy), Flints.:
archdcnry, xi. 43–4
bp., ii. 31; iv. 39; vii. 3; ix. 3; xi. 12, 37–9, 82
cath., prebs. in: Faenol (in Bodelwyddan, Flints.), xi. 42 & n; Llanfair, first comportion (Llanfairtalhaiarn (Llanfair Talhearn), Denbighs.), xi. 44; Llanfair, second comportion (Llanfairtalhaiarn (Llanfair Talhearn), Denbighs.), xi. 44; Llannefydd (Denbighs.), xi. 41; Meifod (Montgom.), xi. 45–6; Meliden (Flints.), ii. 52; xi. 42–3; unnamed, iii. 61
St Avit Sénieur, Dordogne, France, v. 23
St Bertrand-de-Comminges, Hte-Garonne, France, cath., xi. 43n
St Botolph, preb., *see* Lincoln
St Crantock's colleg. ch., *see* Crantock
St Cross, preb., *see* Llandaff
St Davids (Tyddewi), Pemb.:
archdcnry, xi. 14, 23n, 59–61
bp., i. 10, 16, 18, 43, 58, 77, 79, 111, 118; ii. 2, 6, 11, 28, 35; iii. 2, 10, 14, 17, 30, 49, 52, 54, 63(*bis*), 73, 80; iv. 5, 49(*bis*), 56; v. 6, 8, 9, 15, 16, 21, 23, 33, 42, 49, 51, 60, 71; vi. 32, 66, 74; vii. 2, 3, 14, 41; viii. 5, 13, 17, 25, 46, 62, 70; ix. 11, 32, 49, 51; x. 2, 6, 66; xi. 4, 39, 53–6; xii. 26, 36
cath., prebs. in: Brawdy (Pemb.), xi. 65; Caerfai (in St Davids), x. 54; xi. 65–6; Caerfarchell (in St Davids), xi. 66–7; Clydey (Pemb.), xi. 67; cursal, xi. 73–79; Lampeter-pont-Stephen (Lampeter, Card.), xi. 56–7; Llanddewi Aberarth (Card.), xi. 68; Llandyfriog (Card.), xi. 62–3; Llandyssilio-gogo (Carm.), xi. 58–9; Llangan (Carm.), xi. 68–9; Llanrhian (Pemb.), xi. 64–5; Llanvaes (Breck.), xi. 61–2; Llawhaden (Pemb.), xi. 57–8; Mathry (Pemb.), vi. 69; vii. 28; viii 45; xi. 70–1; Mydrim (Carm.), xi. 59–61; St Nicholas Penffoes (St Nicholas (Sain Nicolas), Pemb.), v. 19; viii. 29; xi. 71–2; Trefloden (Treflodan, in Whitchurch (Eglwys Wen), Pemb.), xi. 72–3
St Decumans, preb., *see* Wells
St Dubritius, preb., *see* Llandaff
St Germain des Prés, Paris, France, iv. 23
St Jean de Maurienne, Savoie, France, bp., ii. 4
St Katherine's altar, preb., *see* Beverley
St Martin's altar, preb., *see* Beverley
St Martin's in Dernestall, preb., *see* Lincoln
St Martin's-le-Grand, *see* London
St Mary's altar, preb., *see* Beverley
St Mawgan in Meneage, *see* Mawgan in Meneage
St Nicholas (Sain Nicolas), Glam., xi. 29 & n; preb., *see* Llandaff
St Nicholas Penffoes, preb., *see* St Davids
St Pancras, preb., *see* London, St Paul's, Pancratius
St Paul's cath., *see* London
St Peter de Langton, dioc. Lincoln, *see* Langton
St Probus, colleg. ch., *see* Probus
St Radegund's chap., *see* London, St Paul's
St Stephen's altar, preb., *see* Beverley
St Wandrille, Seine-et-Marne, France, abbey, iii. 93
Ste Marie Montebourg, Manche, France, iii. 64
Salisbury, Wilts.:
archdcnry, iii. 11–13
bp., i. 3, 9, 14, 48, 66, 93, 114; ii. 2, 3; iii. 1–3; iv. 5, 8n, 46, 49, 58; v. 3; vi. 26(*bis*), 42, 65, 68, 108; vii. 2, 49; viii. 2(*bis*); ix. 5, 57; x. 24, 36; xi. 5(*bis*), 55
cath., prebs. in: Alton Australis (Alton Pancras, Dors.), iii. 21–2; vi. 70; Alton Borealis (Alton Pancras, Dors.), iii. 22–4; vii. 16; Axford (Wilts.), i. 33; iii. 24–6; xi. 30; xii. 25; Bedminster and Redclyffe (Bedminster, Som.; Redcliffe, Som.), iii. 26–8; Bedwyn (Wilts.), iii. 28–30; Beminster Prima (Beaminster, Dors.), iii. 30–1; vii. 52n; Beminster Secunda (Beaminster, Dors.), iii. 31–3; Bishopstone (nr. Swindon, Wilts.), iii. 33–5; v. 24; Bitton (Glos.), iii. 35–6; Blewbury (Berks.), iii. 36–8; Brixworth (Northants.), iii. 38; Calne (Wilts.), iii. 38; Chardstock (Devon, formerly Dors.), i. 103n; iii. 39–41; xii. 36; Charminster and Bere (Charminster, Dors.; Bere

Regis, Dors.), iii. 41–4; vi. 91; ix. 14; Chisenbury and Chute (Wilts.), iii. 44–5; Coombe and Harnham (Coombe Bissett, Wilts.; Harnham, nr. Salisbury, Wilts.), iii. 45–7; vii. 10; Durnford (Wilts.), iii. 47–9; vii. 8; Faringdon (Berks.), iii. 49–51; v. 15; Fordington and Writhlington (Fordington, Dors.; Writhlington, Som.), iii. 51–3; Gillingham Major (Gillingham, Dors.), iii. 79; Gillingham Minor (Gillingham, Dors.), iii. 26; Grantham Australis (Grantham, Lincs.), iii. 53–5; Grantham Borealis (Grantham, Lincs.), iii. 55–7; Grimston (Grimstone, Dors.), iii. 57–8; Heytesbury (Wilts.), iii. 58; Highworth (Wilts.) iii. 58–60; Horton (Glos.), iii. 60–2; xi. 46(*bis*); Hurstbourne and Burbage (Hurstbourne Tarrant, Hants; Burbage, Wilts.), iii. 62–4; iv. 18; vi. 49; vii. 50; Ilfracombe (Devon), iii. 44; Loders (Dors.), iii. 64; Lyme and Halstock (Lyme Regis, Dors.; Halstock, Dors.), ii. 17; iii. 64–6; x. 35; Major Pars Altaris (in Salisbury cath.), iii. 66–8; ix. 46(*bis*); Minor Pars Altaris (in Salisbury cath.), i. 60; iii. 68–70; Netheravon (Wilts.), iii. 70–3; Netherbury in Ecclesia (Netherbury, Dors.), iii. 73–4; Netherbury in Terra (Netherbury, Dors.), iii. 75–6; ix. 14; Ogbourne (Ogbourne St Andrew and Ogbourne St George, Wilts.), iii. 76; Potterne (Wilts.) iii. 76; Preston (Dors.), iii. 76–8; Ramsbury (Wilts.), iii. 78–9; vi. 86; Ratfyn (Wilts.), iii. 79–82; iv. 31; x. 60; Ruscombe Southbury (Ruscombe, Berks.), iii. 82–4; viii. 23; Sherborne (Dors.), iii. 84; Shipton (Shipton-under-Wychwood, Oxon.), iii. 84–5; vi. 90n; Slape (in Netherbury, Dors., cf. Slape Manor), iii. 85–7; Stratford (Stratford sub Castle, Wilts.), iii. 87–8; Stratton (Dors.), iii. 88–90; vii. 45; Teinton Regis (Kingsteignton, Devon), iii. 90–1; Torleton (Tarlton, Glos.), ii. 33; iii. 91–3; v. 5, 51; vii. 30; Upavon (Wilts.), iii. 93; Warminster (Wilts.), iii. 93–5; Wilsford and Woodford (Wilts.), iii. 95–7; Yatesbury (Wilts.), ii. 39; iii. 97–9; Yetminster Prima (Yetminster, Dors.), iii. 100–1; x. 47; Yetminster Secunda (Yetminster, Dors.), iii. 102–3

    ch. of St Thomas the Martyr, iii. 17

Salkeld, Great, Cumb., vi. 102 & n, 103 & n; xii. 72
Salop, archdcnry, x. 17–18; xi. 64. *See also* Shropshire
Saltmarshe, preb., *see* Howden
Salton, preb., *see* York
Saltwood, Kent, ii. 32
Sampford Courtenay, Devon, ix. 18n
Sanctae Crucis, preb., *see* Lincoln
Sandiacre, preb., *see* Lichfield
Sandon, in Esher, Surr., i. 22
Sawbridgeworth, Herts., vi. 88; viii. 10
Sawley, preb., *see* Lichfield
Saxthorpe, Norf., x. 60
Scamblesby, preb., *see* Lincoln
Scotter, Lincs., i. 27
Seaford, preb., *see* Chichester
Sedgefield, co. Dur., i. 13; iii. 13
Selsey, preb., *see* Chichester
Sexaginta Solidorum, preb., *see* Lincoln
Shaftesbury, Dors., conventual ch., prebs. in:
    Fontmell (Fontmell Magna, Dors.), i. 41; v. 37; Gillingham (Dors.), iii. 80
Shalfleet, Isle of Wight, Hants, iii. 35; xi. 65
Shalford, preb., *see* Wells
Shap, Westmld., abbey, xi. 39 & n
Sharow, preb., *see* Ripon
Sheering, Essex, iii. 71
Shenley, Bucks., vii. 50
Shepton Mallet, Som., viii. 31
Sherborne, Dors.:
    abbey, iii. 84
    preb., *see* Salisbury
Sherburn-in-Elmet, Yorks., vi. 109
Sherston, Wilts., iii. 81
Shimpling, Norf., viii. 37
Shipton, preb., *see* Salisbury
Shoeburyness, Essex, viii. 29
Shoreham, Kent, v. 17; viii. 25
Shrewsbury, Salop:
    abbey, xi. 38
    colleg. ch. of St Chad, xi. 66; xii. 64; prebs. in, iii. 56; vi. 52; x. 18, 21, 30, 32, 45(*bis*), 55, 65
    colleg. ch. of St Mary, v. 35
Shropham, Norf., ii. 8
Shropshire, archdcnry, ii. 6–8. *See also* Salop
Sible Hedingham, Essex, v. 10
Sibson, Leics., i. 48; x. 37 & n
Sidlesham, preb., *see* Chichester
Sidon, now Saida, Syria, bp., xii. 53, 54
Siena, Italy, iii. 2; xi. 54
Sirescote, preb., *see* Tamworth
Skirpenbeck, Yorks., iii. 90

Slape, preb., *see* Salisbury

Sleaford, Lincs., iv. 37; preb., *see* Lincoln, Lafford

Slimbridge, Glos., iv. 61

Smithfield, *see* London

Sneating, preb., *see* London, St Paul's

Solihull, Warwicks., x. 8

Somerley, preb., *see* Chichester

Somerton, Oxon., xi. 71

South Cave, preb., *see* York

South Hill, Cornw., x. 52

South Newbald, preb., *see* York

South Newton, preb., *see* Wilton

South Scarle, preb., *see* Lincoln

Southampton, Hants, St Mary's ch., iii. 92

Southfleet, Kent, i. 99

Southwark, Kent, iv. 46; ch. of St Mary, iv. 37

Southwell, Notts.:
  colleg. ch., i. 123; prebs. in: Beckingham (Notts.), v. 53; Dunham (Notts.), x. 37; North Leverton (Notts.), iii. 98; v. 29; viii. 51; Oxton and Cropwell Prima (Oxton, Notts.; Cropwell Bishop, Notts.), v. 66; Oxton and Cropwell Secunda (Oxton, Notts.; Cropwell Bishop, Notts.), i. 72; v. 64; vi. 55, 76; Sacrists' preb., i. 56; v. 67; unnamed, ix. 29
  hospital of St Mary Magdalen, x. 50

Spaldwick, preb., *see* Lincoln, Sanctae Crucis

Spofforth with Stockeld, Yorks., vi. 84

Stafford:
  archdcnry, x. 18–20
  castle, St Mary's chap., x. 30
  colleg. ch. of St Mary, prebs. in: Coton (in Stafford), vi. 40; Whitgreave Parva (Whitgreave, Staffs.), iii. 77; unnamed, x. 33

Stanford-le-Hope, Essex, v. 37

Stanhope, co. Dur., i. 127

Stanton St Bernard, Wilts.:
  ch., viii. 46
  preb., *see* Wilton

Staunton-on-Wye, Herefs., ii. 10, 41

Stepney, Mdx., i. 20

Sticklepath, Devon, x. 52

Stillington, preb., *see* York

Stoke, preb., *see* Lincoln

Stoke-upon-Trent, Staffs., i. 109; xii. 38

Stone, Kent, viii. 15

Stone, preb., *see* Hastings

Stotfold, preb., *see* Lichfield

Stow, Lincs., archdcnry, i. 17–19

Stow-in-Lindsey, preb., *see* Lincoln, Stow St Mary

Stow Longa, preb., *see* Lincoln

Stow St. Mary, preb., *see* Lincoln

Stratford, Essex, Stratford Langthorn abbey, viii. 39

Stratford, preb., *see* Salisbury

Stratford-on-Avon, Warwicks., i. 6; vi. 88

Stratford sub Castle, Wilts.:
  chap., xi. 82(*bis*)
  preb., *see* Salisbury, Stratford

Strathfieldsaye, Hants, ii. 48; iii. 87

Stratton, preb., *see* Salisbury

Strensall, preb., *see* York

Stretham, Cambs., x. 56;

Stretton, preb., *see* Penkridge

Strood, Kent, vii. 9

Studley, preb., *see* Ripon

Sturbridge hospital, *see* Cambridge

Sturton-le-Steeple, Notts., i. 18; vi. 16; viii. 29

Sudbourne, Suff., ii. 19

Sudbury, Suff., archdcnry, ii. 8; iii. 80; iv. 30–2

Suffolk, archdcnry, iv. 32–4; vi. 80; viii. 66

Surrey, archdcnry, iv. 48–9; viii. 46n

Sutton, Surr., iv. 5

Sutton, preb., *see* Chichester

Sutton-by-Markby, preb., *see* Lincoln, Sutton-in-Marisco

Sutton by Plymouth (now Plymouth), Devon ii. 18

Sutton Courtenay, Berks., vii. 8; viii. 34; ix. 18; x. 52

Sutton-cum-Buckingham, preb., *see* Lincoln

Sutton-in-Marisco, preb., *see* Lincoln

Sutton-le-Marsh, Lincs.:
  ch., iv. 33; viii. 66
  preb., *see* Lincoln, Sutton-in-Marisco

Sutton, Long, Lincs., vii. 12, 35

Swaffham, Norf., vi. 16

Swallowcliffe, preb., *see* Heytesbury

Swanscombe, Kent, viii. 29

Swansea (Abertawe), Glam., xi. 74n

Swavesey, Cambs., xi. 74n

Swindon, Glos., ii. 26

Swords, preb., *see* Dublin

Symondsbury, Dors., ii. 24; viii. 8

Tachbrook, preb., *see* Lichfield

Talley (Tallyllychau), Carm., abbey, xi. 79

Tamworth, Staffs., colleg. ch., iv. 31; vi. 29; ix. 50, 51; prebs. in: Bonehill (Staffs.), iii. 21; vi. 70; xii. 87, 88; Sirescote

(Syerscote, Staffs.), x. 27; Wigginton (Staffs.), ix. 43(*bis*); Wilmcote (Warwicks.), ii. 21; viii. 68, 70

Taplow, Bucks., ix. 6

Tarporley, Ches., chap. of SS Mary and Leonard of the Rood by, iii. 71

Tarring, West, Suss., vi. 50

Tarsus, Syria, abp., viii. 7n

Taunton, Som.:
  archdcnry, viii. 16–17
  preb., *see* Wells

Tawton, North, Devon, xi. 24

Tealby, Lincs., i. 119

Teinton Regis, preb., *see* Salisbury

Terrington, St Clement, Norf., vii. 41

Tervin, preb., *see* Lichfield

Tettenhall, Staffs., colleg. ch., prebs. in:
  Pendeford (nr. Wolverhampton, Staffs.), vi. 52; Wrottesley (Staffs.), iii. 91; x. 70

Tettenhall Wood, Staffs., xi. 24

Thame, Oxon., iv. 56:
  abbey, i. 38
  preb., *see* Lincoln
  See also Osney and Thame

Thebes, Greece, abp., vi. 99

Thetford, Norf., bp., iv. 26; xi. 10

Thockrington, preb., *see* York

Thomas Basschurch, preb., *see* Llandaff, St Andrew

Thomas Jones, preb., *see* Llandaff, Fairwater

Thomas the priest, canonry of, xi. 42n

Thoresby, *see* Carperby cum Thoresby

Thorney, preb., *see* Chichester

Thorngate, preb., *see* Lincoln

Thurcaston, Leics., ii. 13

Tickhill, Yorks., iii. 77

Tidenham, Glos., vii. 42

Tilbury, West, Essex, vii. 35

Timberscombe, preb., *see* Wells

Tine, bp., viii. 7, 9, 41, 42

Tolleshunt, preb., *see* London, St Martin's-le-Grand

Torleton, preb., *see* Salisbury

Totenhall, preb., *see* London, St Paul's

Tothill, *see* Westminster

Totnes, Devon, archdcnry, i. 101; ix. 17–19

Tours, Indre-et-Loire, France, cath., preb. in, i. 15

Trallwng, preb., *see* Abergwili

'Transuigenen', archdcnry, *see* Outre-Vienne

Tredington, Glos., iii. 8; xii. 52

Trefloden, preb., *see* St Davids

Tremeirchion (Dymmerghion), Flints., xi. 42n

Treviso, Italy, bp., vi. 50

Trowse, Norf., xi. 29

Tusculum, Italy, bp., i. 15, 54; iii. 54; vi. 13, 90, 97; viii. 13, 35; ix. 15; x. 7; xi. 53

Twiford, preb., *see* London, St Paul's

Tydd St Giles, Cambs., iii. 15

Tydd St Mary, Lincs., viii. 10

Tytherington and Horningsham, preb., *see* Heytesbury

Uffculme, Devon, viii. 6, 8

Ufford, Northants., v. 39

Ufton Cantoris, preb., *see* Lichfield

Ufton Decani, preb., *see* Lichfield

Ulleskelf, preb., *see* York

Upavon, Wilts.:
  preb., *see* Salisbury
  priory, iii. 93

Uppingham, Rut., xi. 27

Upton, nr. Northampton, x. 44

Upway, Dors., viii. 51

Urchfont, preb., *see* Winchester, conventual ch. of St Mary

Vaison, Vaucluse, France, bp., iii. 39

Velletri, Italy, bp., iv. 45

Vercelli, Italy, bp., iii. 71, 90; vi. 27; xii. 34

Vernon, Eure, France, Ste Marie colleg. ch., v. 35

Vienne, Isère, France, abp., iv. 23

Waddesdon, Bucks., ix. 38, 39, 41(*bis*)

Wakerley, Northants., v. 32

Wallop, Nether, Hants, v. 18

Wallop, Over, Hants, x. 67

Walsoken, Norf., v. 37

Waltham, preb., *see* Chichester

Walton-upon-Trent, Derbys., x. 27

Wanborough, Wilts., xi. 28

Wanstrow, preb., *see* Wells

Wappenbury, Warwicks., ii. 38

Warham, preb., *see* Hereford

Warminster, preb., *see* Salisbury

Warminster al. Luxville, preb., *see* Wells

Warthacwm, preb., *see* Llandaff

Warthill, preb., *see* York

Wartling, Ninfield and Hooe, preb., *see* Hastings

Warwick:
  ch. of St James, x. 42
  colleg. ch., preb. in, viii. 72

Waterford and Lismore, co. Waterford, Ireland, bp., vi. 98; viii. 16; xi. 21, 31
Watton, Yorks., priory, xi. 23 & n
Watton at Stone, Herts., xi. 69
Waverley, Surr., abbey, iv. 23
Wearmouth, co. Dur., *see* Bishop Wearmouth
Wedmore, prebs. I–V, *see* Wells
Weeford, preb., *see* Lichfield
Weighton, preb., *see* York
Welbeck, Notts., abbey, vi. 29
Weldland, preb., *see* London, St Paul's
Wellington, preb., *see* Hereford and Lichfield
Wells, Som.:
    archdcnry, viii. 12–14
    cath., prebs. in: Ashill (Som.), viii. 17–18; Barton St David (Som.), viii. 19–20; Buckland Dinham (Buckland Denham, Som.), viii. 20–1; Carhampton (Som.), viii. 21–2; Cleeve (Old Cleeve, Som.), viii. 22; Combe Prima (Combe St Nicholas, Som.), iii. 82; vi. 50; viii. 23–4; ix. 16; Combe Secunda, viii. 24; Combe Tercia, viii. 24–6; Combe Quarta, i. 47; viii. 26–7; Combe Quinta, viii. 27–8; Combe Sexta, viii. 28; Combe Septima, viii. 29–30; xi. 72; Combe Octava, viii. 30; Combe Nona, viii. 31; Combe Decima, viii. 31–3; Combe Undecima, viii. 33–4; ix. 20; xi. 45; Combe Duodecima, viii. 34–5; x. 52; Combe Terciadecima, viii. 35–7; Combe Quartadecima, viii. 37–8; Combe Quintadecima, viii. 38–9; Compton Bishop (Som.), v. 64; viii. 39–40; Compton Dundon (Som.), viii. 40–1; Cudworth (Som.), viii. 41–2; x. 47; Dinder (Som.), i. 50; viii. 42–4; Dultingcote (Doulting, Som.), viii. 44–5; Eastharptree (East Harptree, Som.), viii. 45–6; xi. 71; Easton in Gordano (Som.), viii. 46–7; Haselbere (Haselbury Plucknett, Som.), v. 58; viii. 48–9; ix. 37, 38; Henstridge (Som.), viii. 49–51; Holcombe (Holcombe Burnell, Devon), viii. 51–2; Huish and Brent (Huish Episcopi, Som.; South Brent, Devon), viii. 52; Ilminster (Som.), viii. 52–4; Ilton (Som.), viii. 54–5; Litton (Som.), viii. 55–6; Long Sutton (Som.), viii. 56–8; Milverton Prima (Milverton, Som.), viii. 58; Milverton Secunda (Milverton, Som.), viii. 58; North Curry (Som.), viii. 59–60; Pilton (Som.), viii. 60–1; St Decumans (Som.), vi. 49; viii. 61–2; Shalford (Essex), v. 65; vii. 46; viii. 62–4; Taunton (Som.), i. 74; viii. 64–6; Timberscombe (Som.), ii. 31; iv. 33; viii. 66–7; Wanstrow (Som.), viii. 67–8; Warminster al. Luxville (Warminster, Wilts.), viii. 68–70; Wedmore Prima (Wedmore, Som.), viii. 70; Wedmore Secunda, ii. 21; viii. 70–1; Wedmore Tercia, viii. 71–2; Wedmore Quarta, viii. 72–3; Wedmore Quinta, viii. 73–4; Whitchurch (Whitchurch, in Binegar, Som.), viii. 74–5; Whitelackington (White Lackington, Som.), viii. 76–7; Wiveliscombe (Som.), viii. 77–8; Wormenstre (Worminster, Som.), viii. 78–9; Yatton (Som.), viii. 79–81; unnamed, viii. 81–3, ix. 37
    See also Bath and Wells
Welton Beckhall, preb., *see* Lincoln
Welton Brinkhall, preb., *see* Lincoln
Welton Paynshall, preb., *see* Lincoln
Welton Ryval, preb., *see* Lincoln
Welton Westhall, preb., *see* Lincoln
Wenlocksbarn, preb., *see* London, St Paul's
West Dean, Wilts., iii. 6
West Merrington, preb., *see* Auckland
West Riding, archdcnry, *see* York, archdcnry
West Sandford, preb., *see* Crediton
Westbourne, Suss., iii. 30
Westbrooke, preb., *see* Bosham
Westbury, Salop, colleg. ch., portion in, ii. 47
Westbury-on-Trym, Glos., colleg. ch., prebs. in: Halley (? in Henbury, Glos.), v. 25, 67; Henbury (Glos.), i. 65; viii. 66; Weston (Lawrence Weston, Glos.), i. 38; unnamed, v. 44; viii. 25, 51; ix. 26(*bis*)
Westgate, preb., *see* Chichester
Westminster, Mdx., iv. 39, 58; vi. 4, 5, 98, 107, 109:
    abbey, iii. 73
    bp., iii. 101; iv. 19
    colleg. ch. of St Stephen, iv. 4, 5; prebs. in, i. 20, 45, 53, 74, 99, 107, 123; ii. 8, 37; iii. 22, 31, 40; iv. 33; v. 20, 24, 34, 48, 63; vi. 114; vii. 37, 44; viii. 50(*bis*); x. 54, 55
    Durham House, iv. 39
    London House, iv. 40
    Tothill chap., vii. 32; xi. 72
Weston, Hunts. (? Hail Weston or Old Weston), i. 41
Weston, Suff., viii. 65

Weston, preb., *see* Westbury-on-Trym

Weston Longville, Norf., ix. 20

Westwell, Kent, v. 8; x. 68

Wetwang, preb., *see* York

Whatton, Long, Leics., x. 23

Wherwell, Hants, conventual ch., prebs. in: Goodworth (Hants), i. 67; unnamed, iii. 86

Whipstrode St James, *see* Fareham

Whitchurch, preb., *see* Wells

Whitchurch (Eglwys Wen), by Haverfordwest, Pemb., xi. 73

Whitelackington, preb., *see* Wells

Whitgreave Parva, preb., *see* Stafford

Whittington, Glos., ii. 8, 10

Whittington and Berkswick, preb., *see* Lichfield

Wigginton, preb., *see* Tamworth

Wighton, Norf., iii. 89

Wightring, preb., *see* Chichester

Wigston Magna, Leics., x. 9

Willey, Salop, vi. 54

Wilmcote, preb., *see* Tamworth

Wilmington, preb., *see* Chichester

Wilsden, preb., *see* London, St Paul's

Wilsford and Woodford, preb., *see* Salisbury

Wilton, Wilts., conventual ch., iii. 75; prebs. in: Chalke (Broad Chalk, Wilts.), iii. 44, 47; v. 33; vi. 26; viii. 39; South Newton (Wilts.), iii. 16; Stanton St Bernard (Wilts.), i. 48

Wilton, preb., *see* York

Wiltshire, archdcnry, iii. 13–14

Wimborne Minster, Dors., colleg. ch., iii. 10; x. 11; preb. in, x. 63

Wimpole, Cambs., x. 63

Winchester, Hants, iv. 39:
archdcnry, i. 59; iv. 50–1; v. 25
bp., i. 2, 6, 13, 48, 57, 83; ii. 45; iii. 2, 28, 41, 51, 71, 91; iv. 3, 4(*ter*), 5(*ter*), 14, 23, 30, 37, 40, 45–7, 56(*bis*), 58, 60, 63; v. 5, 35, 51, 63; vi. 64, 75, 107, 108, 109; viii. 17; ix. 3; x. 11, 57, 58
conventual ch. of St Mary, preb. of Urchfont (Wilts.), iii. 37

Windham, preb., *see* Chichester

Windsor, Berks., iv. 24(*bis*); St George's chap., prebs. in, ii. 9, 13; v. 22; vii. 16, 19; ix. 37, 58(*bis*); x. 41; xi. 78(*bis*); xii. 45

Winfrith Newburgh, Dors., v. 10

Wisborough, preb., *see* Chichester

Wistow, preb., *see* York

Witherley, Leics., x. 9, 17, 35

Withern, Lincs., i. 107; xii. 14, 26

Withington, Herefs.:
ch., ii. 10
preb. of Withington Parva, *see* Hereford

Witney, Oxon., x. 39

Witton, preb., *see* Auckland

Wiveliscombe, preb., *see* Wells

Wobaston, preb., *see* Wolverhampton

Wolsingham, co. Dur., x. 56

Wolverhampton, Staffs., colleg. ch., prebs. in: Hilton (Staffs.), x. 15; Kinvaston (Staffs.), viii. 63; Wobaston (in Bushbury, Staffs.), i. 43; unnamed, i. 119

Wolvey, preb., *see* Lichfield

Wonston, Hants, ix. 18

Woodhorn, preb., *see* Chichester

Woolaston, Glos., xi. 6, 13(*bis*); xii. 87

Woolhope, preb., *see* Hereford

Wootton Courtney, Som., viii. 27

Worcester:
archdcnry, iv. 62–3; vii. 52n
bp., i. 30, 37, 55, 111; ii. 1, 25, 30, 32, 39; iii. 41, 45, 53, 62, 78, 85, 93; iv. 3(*bis*), 4, 7(*bis*), 13, 14(*bis*), 15(*ter*), 29, 37, 39, 40, 45, 51, 55–8, 59, 60, 61(*bis*), 62; v. 3, 8, 15, 28, 31, 34, 49, 59, 66; vi. 3, 5, 7, 10, 34 & n, 39, 48, 61, 76, 79, 94; vii. 1, 2; viii. 1, 2, 36, 38, 50, 70; ix. 28, 29; x. 1, 26; xi. 11, 22(*bis*), 53(*bis*)

Wormenstre, preb., *see* Wells

Worth Matravers, Dors., i. 60; xii. 25

Wraysbury, Bucks., ix. 7

Wrotham, Kent, i. 33

Wrottesley, preb., *see* Tettenhall

Wroughton, Wilts., iii. 64, 79

Yarlington, Som., viii. 24

Yatesbury, preb., *see* Salisbury

Yatton, preb., *see* Wells

Yaxley, Hunts., vi. 64n; ix. 13; x. 62

Yelvertoft, Northants., vii. 7

Yeovil, Som., x. 13

Yeovilton, Som., viii. 11

Yetminster Prima, preb., *see* Salisbury

Yetminster Secunda, preb., *see* Salisbury

York, i. 15, 47, 72, 97; vi. 5(*bis*), 6, 107:
abbey of St Mary, vi. 108
abp., i. 2, 3, 122; iii. 2, 18, 36, 62, 100; iv. 4, 5, 8 & n, 14, 49, 56, 58; v. 3(*bis*), 14, 21n, 39; vi. 3–5, 98, 109(*bis*), 112; vii. 2, 4; viii. 2, 22, 58, 61; ix. 2, 16, 45, 64; x. 2(*bis*), 61; xi. 23, 38n, 40
archdcnry, vi. 17–19
hospital of St Leonard, xi. 43

York—*contd.*

minster, canonry in, viii. 80; prebs. in: Ampleforth (Yorks.), vi. 27–9; Apesthorpe (Habblesthorpe, Notts.), vi. 29–30; x. 63; Barnby (Barmby on the Moor, Yorks.), v. 61; vi. 31–2; Bilton (Bilton *or* Bilton Ainsty, Yorks.), vi. 33–4; Bole (Notts.), i. 56; vi. 34–6; x. 56; Botevant, vi. 37–8; Bramham (Bramham-cum-Oglethorpe, Yorks.), vi. 38–9; Bugthorpe (Yorks.), vi. 39–41; Driffield (Great and Little Driffield, Yorks.), vi. 44–5; Dunnington (nr. York), vi. 46–8; vii. 28; x. 52; Fenton (Church Fenton, Yorks.), iii. 15, 63; vi. 48–50; viii. 62; xii. 21, 27; Fridaythorpe (Yorks.), vi. 50–2; viii. 23; ix. 16; Givendale (Little Givendale, Yorks.), vi. 52–4; x. 66; Grindale (Yorks.), vi. 54–6; Holme (Holme Archiepiscopi, now lost, nr. Fridaythorpe, Yorks.), vi. 56–7; Husthwaite (Yorks.), vi. 58–9; x. 36; Knaresborough (Yorks.), vi. 59–61; Langtoft (Yorks.), vi. 61–3; Laughton (Laughton-en-le-Morthen, Yorks.), v. 10; vi. 64–5; Masham (Kirkby Malzeard, Yorks.; Langford, Notts.; Masham, Yorks.), vi. 66–8; Newthorpe (Yorks.), vi. 73; North Newbald (Yorks.), iii. 21; vi. 68–70; vii. 28; xi. 70; Osbaldwick (Yorks.), vi. 73–5; Riccall (Yorks.), vi. 75–6; Salton (Yorks.), vi. 76–8; South Cave (Yorks.), i. 84; ii. 16; vi. 41–4; South Newbald (Yorks.), v. 32; vi. 70–3; Stillington (Yorks.), vi. 78–80; Strensall (Yorks.), iv. 32; vi. 80–2; Throckington (Northumb.), i. 121; ii. 32; vi. 82–4; Ulleskelf (Yorks.), vi. 84–6; Warthill (Yorks.), iii. 9, 78; vi. 86–8; Weighton (Market Weighton, Yorks.), vi. 88–9; Wetwang (Yorks.), iii. 43, 85; vi. 90–1; Wilton (Bishop Wilton-with-Belthorpe, Yorks.), vi. 92; Wistow (Yorks.), vi. 92–4; chap. of St Mary and Holy Angels, prebs. in, vi. 79n; vii. 35; x. 70; xi. 70